The Open Corporation
Effective Self-regulation and Democracy

The Open Corporation sets out an innovative and realistic blueprint for effective corporate self-regulation, offering practical strategies for managers, stakeholders and regulators to build successful self-regulation management systems. Christine Parker examines the conditions under which corporate self-regulation of social and legal responsibilities are likely to be effective, covering a wide range of areas – from consumer protection to sexual harassment to environmental compliance. Focusing on the features that make self-regulation or compliance management systems effective, Parker argues that law and regulators need to focus much more on 'meta-regulating' corporate self-regulation if democratic control over corporate action is to be established.

Christine Parker is Senior Lecturer in Law at the University of Melbourne. She is the author of *Just Lawyers* (1999) and a contributor to *The Survival Guide for Compliance Professionals* (2001).

To Joyce Ethel Parker (1941–2000)

The Open Corporation

Effective Self-regulation and Democracy

CHRISTINE PARKER

University of Melbourne

CAMBRIDGE
UNIVERSITY PRESS

PUBLISHED BY THE PRESS SYNDICATE OF THE UNIVERSITY OF CAMBRIDGE
The Pitt Building, Trumpington Street, Cambridge, United Kingdom

CAMBRIDGE UNIVERSITY PRESS
The Edinburgh Building, Cambridge CB2 2RU, UK
40 West 20th Street, New York, NY 10011–4211, USA
477 Williamstown Road, Port Melbourne, VIC 3207, Australia
Ruiz de Alarcón 13, 28014 Madrid, Spain
Dock House, The Waterfront, Cape Town 8001, South Africa

http://www.cambridge.org

First published 2002

Printed in China by Everbest Printing

Typeface Palatino (*Adobe*) 10/12 pt.   *System* QuarkXPress®   [PK]

A catalogue record for this book is available from the British Library

National Library of Australia Cataloguing in Publication data
Parker, Christine.
The open corporation: effective self-regulation and democracy.
Bibliography.
Includes index.
ISBN 0 521 81890 7.
1. Corporations law. 2. Industrial management. I. Title.
346.066

ISBN 0 521 81890 7 hardback

15836

Contents

Tables and figures

Preface

Acting on a tip-off, Japanese Ministry of Transport officials conducted a raid at Mitsubishi Motors in mid-2000.[1] They found thousands of reports of customer complaints about potentially serious vehicle defects hidden in an employee locker room. They should have been reported to the Ministry of Transport which is responsible for coordinating and supervising recalls and free repairs. A few weeks later, Mitsubishi announced that its internal investigation showed that the practice of not reporting serious customer complaints to the Ministry of Transport had been occurring since 1969 and senior Mitsubishi executives had been aware of it, but done nothing to stop it. Apparently, Mitsubishi staff wanted to avoid the embarrassment and cost of recalls.

Mitsubishi's legal responsibility was clear. So was their social responsibility. Faults and serious complaints about their vehicles from individual consumers should have been reported to the Ministry of Transport. They should then have been stored in the company's quality guarantee section, where Ministry of Transport officials could annually inspect the complaints register. Instead, according to newspaper reports, Mitsubishi repair workshops would make covert repairs for individual complainants, before there was a chance to conduct an investigation as to whether there should be a recall. The complaints were then hidden or 'misplaced' in codenamed files, so that Ministry of Transport inspections of Mitsubishi's complaints handling procedures would not find them. By the end of August, Mitsubishi had had to recall more than a million vehicles that should have been recalled earlier.

No regulator or motorist advocacy group could have discovered the paperwork hidden away in employee lockers and codenamed files. It seems that employees did not question what was a standard company practice for thirty years. The regulators and Mitsubishi's customers had to rely on Mitsubishi's internal complaints and fault handling systems to collect, categorize and determine how to treat different faults. It would be preposterous to expect the regulator to be able to keep track of every fault and complaint itself. But once the story came out, the results were dramatic. Sales fell by almost 20 per cent in Japan. All executives took pay cuts of between 20 and 35 per cent in order to demonstrate their responsibility for the cover-up. The president and the general manager of quality both resigned. The recall itself cost many millions of dollars. Most seriously, Mitsubishi's controlling shareholder, Daimler Chrysler (which acquired a stake in Mitsubishi only shortly before the scandal) was able to secure a 10 per cent price cut on its shareholding. Daimler Chrysler also changed its 'hands off' policy in the wake of the scandal and was able to install one of its own executives as chief operating officer for Mitsubishi.

The Mitsubishi case illustrates some of the problems and potential for corporate social and legal responsibility in contemporary democracies. On the one hand, both legal responsibilities and motorist concerns for vehicle safety and reliability failed to improve the internal handling of complaints and faults for thirty years. The capacity of law to regulate corporations is limited by the opacity and complexity of corporate structures, the desire to avoid over-regulation, and the fact that corporate management has such a great capacity to control employee workplace behaviour. On the other hand, once the cover-up was eventually exposed, it was not merely state regulatory agencies that sought to enforce responsibility on the company. A combination of an internal whistleblower (who tipped off the Ministry of Transport), government inspections, media scrutiny, customer reaction, stockholder action, and internal feelings of shame and responsibility motivated Mitsubishi management to conduct an internal investigation that brought out the full story (the Ministry of Transport inspection had only discovered part of the story), to redress the problems identified (through recalls) and to make internal changes that might improve Mitsubishi's handling of complaints and potential recalls for the future.

As this chain of events illustrates, the possibilities for democratic influence over corporate behaviour are not restricted to the capacity of state agencies to regulate them. Democracy, ideally, requires corporate permeability to a range of external values and voices. At the same time, responsible corporations must self-regulate themselves to prevent, detect and/or correct irresponsibility. Neither corporate legal obligations nor corporate social responsibility will have any impact if corporate decision-makers fail to take them on board as a part of everyday management. Corporate responsibility requires corporate responsibility management. This book examines how the open corporation – the company that democratically self-regulates – can be made a reality.

The empirical findings in this book are based largely on my own qualitative fieldwork (interviews and participant observation) with corporate 'compliance' or self-regulation practitioners in Australia, Europe and the USA. (The Appendix sets out the methodology used.) The purpose is to examine the regulatory and social conditions in which self-regulation systems have been adopted by large companies with some modest successes. In particular, I focus on the way that best practice self-regulation practitioners understand the methodology and challenges of accomplishing corporate self-regulation. Mine is a 'pragmatic' approach (Selznick 1992: 23). I use *empirical* evidence on the nature and success of regulatory innovations and implementation of corporate self-regulation systems to build a conception of how corporate responsibility management *ought* to be understood.

The 'open corporation' is a marriage between management and democracy and law. Figure 2.3 diagrammatically represents the relationship: formal government regulation, democratic and stakeholder action, and internal corporate self-regulation all inter-relate through a dynamic of three phases of corporate management of social and legal responsibility:

1   the commitment to respond via self-regulation;
2   the acquisition of specialized skills and knowledge for self-regulation; and
3   the institutionalization of purpose in self-regulation.

Corporate management responds to issues that external regulators and stakeholders manage to put on the table; and regulators and stakeholders can only put matters on the table to the extent that corporate management comes out to invite them in (through appropriate management systems and approaches). Each of the three phases of self-regulation management represents a decision point at which external influences can transform corporate practice and decision-making; but continuing interaction with external stakeholders and regulators at the next decision point must help to ensure the management response is appropriate. Ultimately, external stakeholders and regulators must prompt self-critique and continuous improvement through accountability and meta-evaluation, which keep the cycle of engagement moving forwards.

Corporate self-regulation professionals are key agents of the active engagement between management and stakeholders in the open corporation. They will both bear and exert pressures at all the phases of self-regulation management. Indeed, in the marriage of democracy and management, self-regulation professionals play match-maker and crisis counsellor. However, their ability to institutionalize responsibility through both the harmonizing and conflict-handling aspects of their role is only robust when: (a) the broader democracy reaches in to make management democratically responsible for how the company governs itself; and (b) corporate management opens out, by affording the self-regulation function respect and integrity by making legal and social responsibility an integral part of management.

Effective corporate self-regulation therefore means putting 'stakeholders' in a position where they can influence corporate management. It also means that law and regulatory enforcement should be designed to move companies through each of the three phases of self-regulation management. Thus, regulation aimed at companies who have not yet reached Phase One should attempt to create crises of conscience in those who can do something to change corporate culture and self-governance. It prompts commitment to respond to responsibility issues via self-regulation. Regulation aimed at Phase Two fosters and harnesses industry dynamics of innovation and modelling in self-regulation skills and knowledge. Regulation aimed at Phase Three ensures that companies report on the standard of self-regulation process they have introduced, its outcomes and effects. This means that stakeholders and regulators can check that self-regulation is robustly institutionalized. This is done through reporting and verification, using regulatory requirements (such as licence conditions, liability, and so on) as an opportunity for meta-evaluation of corporate self-evaluation.

Meta-evaluation in Phase Three enables meta-learning: corporations that learn to improve their self-regulation and regulators that learn to improve their regulatory strategies to reinforce leaders and move along laggards. The ultimate test of corporate management's self-regulation is the extent to which they evaluate and learn from their own self-regulation performance and failures (double-loop learning). The ultimate test of regulatory success is the extent to which regulators and law test companies' self-evaluations, and learn from them how to improve law and regulatory practice – a 'triple loop' of regulation, self-regulation and meta-regulation (see Figure 9.2).

Acknowledgements

The research for this book was largely completed while I was enjoying a Vice-Chancellor's Postdoctoral Fellowship in the Law Faculty, University of New South Wales, and was also supported by two small research grants from the Australian Research Council. The hospitality of the Law Faculty, London School of Economics and Political Science, enabled me to finish the research.

I would like to thank all the practitioners who were interviewed for this project (who must mostly remain anonymous) for making their time and experiences available. Without their input this book would not be possible, and any practical insight I have gained was certainly stolen from them. I am particularly grateful to Sandra Birkensleigh, Les D'Alton, Bill Dee, Neill Buck, Cal Duffy, Randal Dennings, John Howell and Joe Murphy for keeping me in touch with reality, and believing in the significance of academic research on this topic. I am also thankful to all the students in the Corporate Self-Regulation and Compliance course over the last four years who have allowed me to refine my ideas by experimenting on them, and inspired me to discover things I would never have found out about otherwise. I would also like to thank the staff of the Regulatory Reform Unit, Public Management Service, at the OECD in Paris – Cesar Cordova-Novion, Rex Deighton-Smith, Scott Jacobs, But Klaassen and Kirsi Kuuttiniemi – who gave me an opportunity to research the regulators' perspective on compliance in more depth and improved my ideas by their engagement with my work.

My research assistants, Simson Chu, Olivia Conolly and Liz Mifsud, each contributed diligently and with enthusiasm to this project. Sue Bazzana and Rosemary Wright deserve special gratitude for offering me superior and repeated hospitality on research trips to Melbourne and London, respectively. This research has also benefited from discussions, comments on drafts and friendly support from colleagues at the University of New South Wales, the London School of Economics and elsewhere, including Stephen Bottomley, Steven Freeland, Arthur Glass, Martin Krygier, Matt Rimmer, Colin Scott, Robert Shelly, Leon Wolff and Sarah Worthington. Julia Black provided detailed and enormously helpful comments on an early draft of the whole manuscript, and continued to comment on new drafts, even on her maternity leave. John Braithwaite has been mentor and intellectual inspiration throughout the project; he provided comments on every draft with diligence, grace and enthusiasm. It is a privilege to learn from such a wise scholar and loyal colleague. Angus Corbett, whom I dragooned into helping me set up a new postgraduate course on corporate self-regulation and compliance, modelled the linkage between practical engagement and scholarly understanding in his teaching and thinking in a way I hope to emulate. Angus has also spent more time reading, discussing, debating and teaching the ideas in numerous draft chapters than it is reasonable to expect of any colleague. Any useful idea or concept in this book was probably stolen or derived from discussions with my friends and colleagues. I maintain sole responsibility for all the half-baked thoughts.

I thank Greg Restall for giving my heart and mind a home, a secure foundation from which to think and write. I also thank baby Zachary for being himself and for sleeping well enough to allow me to make the final revisions to this manuscript. This book is dedicated to my mother, who passed away while I was writing but who first made sure she told me how proud she was of this project and the vocation that drives it.

1 | Introduction: Corporate self-regulation in the new regulatory state

In his book on *Management and Machiavelli*, Anthony Jay draws a parallel between the relationship of employees to today's large corporations and of medieval or Renaissance citizens to the city-state (say, Florence or York):

> For most of the employees of big corporations, the power of the government to make them happy or miserable is very small: a rise in bank rate may slightly affect the costs of a mortgage; over a long period the establishment of a health service, the abolition of military service, the building of roads, the preservation of the countryside, and so on may raise the general quality of their lives ... The power of the corporation over their lives is far greater. They can be told to go and live in another part of the country, or another part of the world ... they can be publicly exalted in the eyes of all their colleagues ... or publicly humiliated, passed over in favour of a subordinate; and these are not things that happen to all alike but specifically and personally to them. Of course they are free to resign, just as the Neapolitan could go and live in Venice; but he might arrive with a record and a reputation ... The government is like Christendom, an overriding system of law which only very marginally affects the actual physical conditions of their lives, but gives them an illusion of equality in that their vote weighs as heavy in the ballot box as the Chairman's or the Managing Director's. In the important part of their lives, their forty years of work, they have none of the freedoms that matter: no political freedom ... no freedom to publish ... no freedom of speech ... no right of trial and no judiciary which is independent of the executive ... and they have no sort of representation in the councils which decide how the firm shall be run, no say in its government, however much the decisions may affect their lives. The twentieth-century junior in Shell or ICI lives in a state of voteless dependence on the favour of the great just like the sixteenth-century Italian. (Jay 1987: 27–8)

Jay analysed only the position of employees. Many more are affected by exercises of corporate power: Consider the Ogoni in Nigeria whose interests and rights were ignored and sold in a contract between Shell and the Nigerian government (see Chapter 6), the people of the American town who lost seven children to leukaemia caused by corporate giants' use of the local water supply as a chemical dump (Harr 1997), the millions of consumers whose choices are both enlivened and constrained by corporate production runs and marketing schemes, and the governments, councils and public bodies that depend upon affordable corporate tenders to provide schools, roads and sewerage systems. We should not trivialize the suffering of those who have been victims of nation-states' special capacity to imprison, execute, torture or otherwise destroy life indiscriminately (e.g. Cambodia's killing fields, Britain's miscarriages of justice in relation to supposed Irish terrorists, and Australia's systematic policies of taking Aboriginal children away from parents). However, Jay is correct to point to the fact that large corporations frequently exercise similar powers (and benefits) as medieval city-states.

In 1982 James S. Coleman described *The Asymmetric Society* as one that had emerged over the last hundred years in which corporate actors play an increasing role and natural actors, a decreasing one.[1] It is now only a small exaggeration to say that corporations 'have emerged as the dominant governance institutions on the planet, with the largest among them reaching into virtually every country of the world and exceeding most governments in size and power' (Korten 1995: 54; see also Derber 1998). There is a disjuncture between our concern with constitutionalizing, delimiting and democratizing state powers (a concern with its modern origins in Renaissance city-states, like Florence, whose thinkers were rediscovering Classical democratic theory: Cronin 1992), while framing and directing the proper exercise of corporate powers in a much more piecemeal fashion.

This book addresses the relation of corporate decision-making and action to legal responsibility and democracy. In order to match the power and consequences of corporate action on social and political relations, management decision-making should be open to democratic influences. For the empirical reasons reviewed in the second part of this chapter, governments and business have lost confidence in the ability of traditional regulation via 'command and control' to adequately control corporate conduct – to make corporations responsible citizens. This book examines the emerging technologies that the 'new regulatory state' uses to enforce corporate self-regulation, and the growth in voluntary use of corporate compliance management systems.[2] The aim is to determine whether internal self-regulation systems show a potential for a more satisfactory solution to the problem of democratic control and accountability of corporate power than 'command and control'.

CORPORATE SOCIAL RESPONSIBILITY

Ways of understanding the place of corporations in society can be roughly divided into two categories: those that see the corporation primarily as a set of *property* or *contractual* relations; and those that see the company as an *entity* in its own right (Allen 1992).

Theorists of companies as sets of property or contractual relations aim to reduce the analysis of the company to individuals ('methodological individualism': Fort and Noone 1999: 171–4). The legal and economic form of the corporation is a response to market failure: individuals choose to use the company as a convenient way to hold and exploit property while avoiding market failures, especially agency costs (e.g. Fama 1980; Friedman 1972; Hayek 1948; Hessen 1979). The focus is on the extent to which it is economically rational to organize production within a corporation and to what extent it is rational to contract out. The company is seen as either the *property* of the shareholders or as a *'nexus'* *of private contracts* (that substitute governance contracts for market contracts) between shareholders, managers and certain others. Issues of social responsibility, and of obligation to stakeholders other than shareholders, are purely externalities, issues to be resolved by the market or by regulation. Theorists of companies as property relations or contracts frequently make a normative jump to the conclusion that corporations should only be governed in the interests of the property owners or the contracting parties. At its most radical this implies that short-term shareholder wealth maximization is the only proper purpose of corporate management (Friedman 1972). Or that the company is regulated by a series of private contracts and there is little or no role for regulatory law (Hayek 1948). This approach to understanding the company tends to lead to resistance to the idea of *public* accountability of internal governance processes, because the assumption is that corporate governance can be reduced to property and contractual relations between *private* individuals.

Those who argue in favour of corporate social responsibility often justify their view via a 'concession' theory of the corporation that sees the legal qualities of limited liability and/or separate legal personality as a privilege granted from the state and therefore inherently justifying state intervention (Dahl 1972; Parkinson 1993: 30).[3] Proponents of concession theory see corporations as *entities* that exercise substantial power in fact, regardless of any contractual or ownership relations that might also be used to describe them. The fact that they exercise power in itself justifies the constraint of that power by the state. This is a political theory. It contends that private power 'may be legitimately held only for the purpose of furthering the public good' (Parkinson 1993: 30–1). Even if a company can be described in contractual or property terms, this does not mean that normatively it should necessarily be managed purely in the interests of shareholder wealth maximization.

The concession theorists correctly recognize that companies are social and political entities that govern themselves to a certain extent, and can also exercise power over others. Sometimes that power is exercised over people who did not choose to enter into a contractual (or property) relationship with the company, or had little bargaining power in doing so. Stakeholders who are not shareholders or managers, and who have no fundamental contractual or property relations with the shareholders, may still be within the corporation's sphere of influence and control to a greater or lesser extent: employees, customers, consumers, local residents, and many others. The corporate entity is much more than the formal incidents of legal personality and limited liability, or even a sum of individual contractual or property relations. It exercises power and purposes that extend far beyond agency relations between shareholders, corporate officers and managers, and has the potential to develop its own integrity of action and purpose, whatever its origins.

To say that the company is a social and political entity that governs itself to some extent and exercises power over others is not to preclude economic accounts of its nature. However, it does mean that we cannot reduce the company purely to private property or even a nexus of private contracts (even in principle). For example, Blair and Stout's (1999) version of team production theory is an economic theory of the corporation that modifies the nexus of contracts theory, yet also sees the company as an entity in its own right. They argue that corporations are formed, and then managed by a board of directors 'not to protect shareholders per se, but to protect the enterprise-specific investments of all the members of the corporate "team," including shareholders, managers, rank and file employees, and possibly other groups, such as creditors' (they even include local communities in one place). Indeed, the governance mechanisms of the corporation are purposefully created to insulate the directors (and other decision-makers) from the direct 'command and control' of any of the particular groups that comprise the corporate team, including its shareholders (Blair and Stout 1999: 755–6). On this view the company is more open. A variety of different stakeholders with different goals and values can have a legitimate, but not controlling, impact on the corporate entity's decision-making processes.[4]

This makes the economic and political contexts in which corporations operate all important, since these contexts determine the bargaining power of different stakeholders. Law and regulation can strengthen various stakeholders' positions through mandatory disclosure, facilitating suits, and markets for control. Donaldson and Davis' (1991) 'stewardship theory' can help us flesh out what this means for management structure. 'Stewardship theory' (Donaldson 1990; Donaldson and Davis 1991) contends that senior managers can respond to non-financial motivators when they self-identify with the corporation. This is because they must balance conflicting stakeholder interests (including interests that are not strictly economically rational) within the organization in order to be effective 'stewards' of corporate property. In this context, the management and governance structure of the company should empower the executive to formulate and implement strategic plans for high corporate performance which take into account various stakeholder interests (Donaldson and Davis 1991: 51–2). A tranche of management research supports this by finding that business cultures that highly value *all* of a variety of stakeholders (customers, employees and others as well as shareholders) outperform their competitors in the longer term (Deal and Kennedy 1999: 28–31).

The implication of team production and stewardship theories for corporate social responsibility is that management systems should be (a) easily permeable to stakeholder concerns and interests[5] (i.e. information about the corporation's handling of social responsibility goes out to stakeholders, and management is in turn based on relevant and reliable inward-coming information about its social and normative environment as well as its economic one); and (b) roles, responsibilities and decision-making powers in relation to social and legal responsibility are well defined and accepted.

Entity theories of the company recognize the complexity of the corporation as a social, political and economic entity, and nudge us towards seeing issues of social responsibility as an organizational problem, not just a market or externality problem. It is certainly legitimate to wish to protect the integrity of goal-oriented corporate activity in the sphere of productive and economic wealth-creation. But the inevitable interaction of any organization with its environment (human, social, physical and political) also makes it legitimate to ask how the corporation can be made responsible for those interactions in the sphere of human, social, environmental and political justice (see Selznick 1992: 291). The entity theory – whether the company is an economic, social, or political entity, or all three – implies that shareholder profit maximization cannot be the only legitimate potential purpose of the company. This is for two very simple and obvious reasons.

Firstly, a variety of people join any corporate organization to accomplish a variety of positive objectives, not just to exploit investments in property. Even as people join together in corporations for primarily economic purposes, the entities they create take on broader social and political functions that mean that short-term profit is no longer the only objective. Indeed, many of the largest, most successful and most enduring companies have made their success in pursuing broader visions and eschewing narrow concerns with shareholder wealth maximization (see, for example, the research reported by Collins and Porras 1998 in *Built To Last*).

Secondly, no matter what the intentions of the founders of any company, it will have a variety of impacts on a variety of people, including many who were not included in the original formation process and may not ever be formally recognized in a contractual or property relationship with other members of the company. At the very least most medium to large-sized corporations, once established, tend to see social legitimacy as necessary for their survival, if not their flourishing. It is an essential aspect of corporate strategy to address stakeholder concerns in order to ensure business sustainability through brand loyalty and social legitimacy (see, for example, Centre for Corporate Public Affairs 2000: 55–73). For example, in Australia, even a company with a reputation for rapacious profit-making activity, mining giant Rio Tinto (see ICEM 1997, 1998), now does a variety of things to foster good relations with local Aboriginal people in the areas it mines (Centre for Corporate Public Affairs 2000: 68–70).

Improving the way in which the decision-making of large corporations with tens of thousands of employees, and the capacity to influence millions of lives, connects with social values and concerns ought to be as much the concern of democratic theory as is framing the power of the state (see Selznick 1992: 300). The empirical reality of corporate influence on the one hand, and the general contemporary normative aspiration towards democratic integrity on the other, force us to ask how democratic responsibility can be institutionalized within and around corporate organizations. The corporation should be seen as both a participant in and a receptor for democratic deliberation. It is a 'citizen' subject to democracy, and constituted by its own citizens, who influence its decision-making, and over whom it exercises influence. The concession theory, however, easily leads us into the trap of assuming that the company is a black box and that it is unproblematic to impose democratic requirements on it. The self-management capacity, indeed essence, of large organizations (and various factors that shape this self-management, including economic, productive and financial ones) must be recognized. Concession theory does not give us a fine-grained analysis of economic and other forces that affect corporate decision-making and action. Neo-institutionalism in organizational and economic theory (including team production theory) can help correct this (Black 1997; W. Scott 1995; see also Chapter 3).

The institutionalization of democratic responsibility in an age of complex governmental activity is difficult (see Habermas 1996: 436). It is the problem of insufficient institutionalization of democracy within and around corporations, not just the state, that this book addresses. Indeed, feeble democratization of corporate action makes the whole democracy frail. We are unnecessarily constrained by the belief that the representative institutions and legal system of the state should be the exclusive, or even primary, home of political deliberation. It is not that democratic principles are irrelevant to business organizations – it is simply that institutional imagination has failed so far to make them real to corporations. The focus of democratic theory on the state ties us 'to a needlessly thin conception of democracy, growing ever thinner in light of the constraints that the capitalist market economy imposes' (Dryzek 2000: 3).

Chapter 2 sets out a deliberative democratic model of permeability of the corporation to responsibility to external values and stakeholders. But first we need to consider the inadequacies of the dominant twentieth century means of 'democratizing' corporate government. This was (and is) the 'command and control' model of imposing certain regulatory requirements on companies via legislative action and administrative enforcement by regulatory agencies.

CRITICISMS OF COMMAND AND CONTROL

The orthodox form of social regulation of corporations is 'command and control', defined by Ogus (1994: 5) as regulation 'in which standards, backed by criminal sanctions are imposed on suppliers'. It is the substitution of decisions by democratically elected legislatures and administrative agencies for the decisions of corporate management in certain circumstances defined by law. Since the early 1980s, command-and-control regulation has met criticism by scholars and policy analysts from two main perspectives: (1) an economic analysis that sees the costs of assessing, understanding and complying with such regulation as unacceptably high; and (2) a socio-political analysis of the ineffectiveness of much of this regulation to produce compliance with regulatory objectives. Both converge on a list of inherent weaknesses of command-and-control regulation that includes:

- a tendency towards unnecessarily complex rules that are too difficult or costly for business to access, understand and comply with;
- over-regulation, legalism, inflexibility and unreasonableness in design and implementation that tend to break down the natural willingness to comply with reasonable, substantive objectives;
- evasion and 'creative' compliance by taking advantage of technical and detailed rules, rather than compliance with the substance and goals of regulation;
- 'capture' of regulatory agencies by regulated entities;
- dependence on strong monitoring and enforcement where sufficient resources, expertise and strategy are not necessarily available.

Complexity

The most recurrent criticism of command-and-control regulation is of its propensity towards greater and greater complexity, the 'regulatory ratchet effect' (Bardach and Kagan 1982: 184). In regulatory design and rule-making there is a constant tendency towards making new rules and increasing the complexity of existing rules to cover loopholes. This leads to a loss of simplicity and therefore loss of ability to understand what compliance with rules involves. Even where an effort is made to reform regulation to make it more easily understood and to include the private sector in drafting rules, regulation tends to become more technical and unworkable as details are added and loopholes are closed.

For example, Robens-style reforms to occupational health and safety regulation initiated in England and modelled in many other countries were supposed to be accessible and comprehensible. The aim was to facilitate employer self-regulation of occupational health and safety on an individualized site-by-site basis. However, over time many technical and detailed 'codes of practice' have been developed under the general provisions of the occupational safety and health regulation to address specific hazards and make the law more certain for employers. The proliferation of these codes of practice, which have the effect of law, means that many businesses in Britain now find them too complex and voluminous to be easily comprehensible (e.g. Genn 1993: 227; Quinlan and Bohle 1991: 212).

Costs of compliance

For those concerned with economic analysis and competitiveness, the biggest concern is that complexity and strict uniform application of command-and-control rules entail compliance costs to business that unjustifiably decrease competitiveness (see OECD 1997a: 21ff, 199–201, 236–9; OECD 1997c). A worldwide movement for regulatory impact assessment has attempted to assess the costs and benefits of compliance with proposed and existing regulation in order to improve the effectiveness and efficiency of governments and the competitiveness and performance of their economies (see OECD 1997b).

Overly legalistic regulation

In socio-political analyses of command and control, the insight is that overly legalistic regulation can be ineffective because its very legalism dissipates voluntary responsibility – the will to comply with reasonable regulatory objectives. In their 1982 work, *Going by the Book*, Bardach and Kagan argued that in the USA many regulators were being too legalistic in their approach to drafting and enforcing regulation via:

- 'regulatory unreasonableness': the imposition of uniform, detailed and stringent rules in situations where they do not make sense; or
- 'regulatory unresponsiveness': failure to consider arguments by regulated enterprises that exceptions should be made.

Bardach and Kagan found in their fieldwork that legalistic regulation can give basically compliant enterprises a positive disposition to resist or to scale down efforts to comply with the intent of the law and instead aim for only the minimal level of compliance the rules required.

Since then a series of studies by John Braithwaite and collaborators of the effects of different inspection styles used by regulators in coal mine safety, nursing home regulation and environmental regulation have shown that when regulators use strict, coercive strategies to achieve compliance they often break down the goodwill and motivation of those actors who were already willing to be socially responsible (Ayres and Braithwaite 1992; Braithwaite 1985; Makkai and Braithwaite 1994).

Creative compliance

For businesses that have little voluntary willingness to be responsible to start with, legalistic command-and-control regulation invites evasion through loopholes and 'creative compliance'. Overly technical rules can also increase non-compliance by encouraging evasion and creative adaptation. As the technicality of rules increases, so does the possibility for less scrupulous players to find loopholes. This is a problem in tax compliance where professional advisers can act as avoidance entrepreneurs who do the work of creating legal techniques, definitions and devices that render the law irrelevant (McBarnet 1994: 74, 83). Indeed, the mere proliferation of law in and of itself advantages powerful organizations because they have a greater ability to hire lawyers to bend its technicalities to their own purposes.

Regulatory capture

Because orthodox command and control assumes an essentially adversarial and antagonistic relationship between regulators and regulatees, it is also said to be susceptible to the possibility of 'capture'. Capture is loosely identified as a pathology of regulation in which regulatory staff may be subverted by pressure, influence or bribery to protect the interest of regulatees or at least not to pursue them strictly (Ogus 1994: 57–8, 94–5). This might occur indirectly through the formation of friendships and social networks, or because regulatory staff expect to work in industry after an initial stint with a regulator. Or it might occur directly through political influence or bribery. In practice, 'capture' is multiplex and it is hard to empirically pin down a strong structural capture effect. Rather, Makkai and Braithwaite (1995) find it weak and situational. In his review of the theory and research on regulation, Ogus (1994: 94–5) notes that there is little empirical evidence of capture actually affecting regulators' public interest orientation. Indeed, not all formation of social bonds between regulator and regulatees is undesirable. For example, it may be desirable for regulators to show some understanding of regulatees' genuine difficulties in complying, or their principled objections to compliance, and to exercise flexibility; or, as we shall see, it may be desirable for industry to be able to hire ex-regulatory staff to act as compliance officers, bringing values, commitments and skills with them from the regulator into the company. The 'capture' problem is one of orthodox command and control sometimes positing an unachievable, and probably undesirable, social disjunction between regulator and regulatee.

Failures of monitoring and enforcement

Command-and-control regulation is dependent on effective monitoring and enforcement. Its effectiveness is therefore susceptible to the intentional or unintentional abuse of democracy because laws and regulations are put on the books to pacify public concerns, without being effectively enforced. This may occur through lack of availability of adequate resources, or lack of wisdom and leadership to monitor and enforce strategically. Regulation that is on the books but never monitored is unlikely to elicit compliance. Furthermore, monitoring that is not targeted at high-risk areas will be less effective. For example, analyses of the effectiveness of occupational safety and health regulatory inspections in the USA and Canada found that superficial inspections that checked only the firm's injury records were ineffective in decreasing injuries by the next inspection, but that frequent inspections were much more important than the level of the penalties imposed in improving business safety performance (Gray and Scholz 1991; see also Tucker 1995; Weil 1996). Governments' fiscal consolidation can also lead to more pressure to deal with an issue by promulgating regulations rather than spending money on solving it, making the situation doubly worse by multiplying law on the books without devoting sufficient resources to effective implementation. Because so many kinds of business law-breaking have high rewards and low probabilities of detection or low penalties, regulators often confront a 'deterrence trap' in which threatened application of sanctions may fail to deter non-compliance (Coffee 1981).

As the last point illustrates, the mere proliferation of regulation will not necessarily increase compliance with the goals of regulation. Indeed, greater regulatory rule-making and activity may decrease compliance through increased failure of knowledge or understanding of regulation, increased costs of regulatory compliance, or increased complexity facing regulatory agencies which therefore cannot implement strategic enforcement activities. It is these problems that have led some scholars and policy makers to seek alternatives to command-and-control regulation. Others argue for an ever heavier emphasis on command and control to overcome these stumbling blocks. While the rhetoric of the contemporary state has emphasized deregulation, in practice contemporary states have simultaneously increased command-and-control regulation and also deregulated and looked for alternatives to command and control. The result has been regulatory reform, not deregulation. Regulatory regimes now incorporate complex layers of activity. Responsibility for control and self-reporting is being pushed down to corporate managements, first instance monitoring may be done by third party gatekeepers such as auditors, while final responsibility for oversight, inspections and sanctioning remains with regulators (see Power 1997: 57). Can such regulatory reform push democratic control and accountability of corporate conduct to the level of corporate management?

THE NEW REGULATORY STATE

New regulatory techniques

Critiques of command-and-control regulation have met a receptive audience in the prevailing political climate of globalizing competition and neo-liberalism. Yet state regulation continues to be used more than ever before. This produces a particular style of business regulation in contemporary western nation-states which began in the late 1980s and 1990s – the 'new regulatory state'.

The 'new regulatory state' is, in part, an unforeseen consequence of Thatcher's and Reagan's approaches to economic regulation in which public ownership and monopoly holding of utilities and other services were broken down in favour of competition, an approach that was globalized in the 1990s (see Braithwaite and Drahos 2000). Thatcher's and Reagan's ideologies of small government and competition led to the corporatization and privatization of public sector operations, paradoxically leading to regulatory growth rather than the abandonment of state regulation. The newly privatized entities were frequently heavily re-regulated or forced to self-regulate under certain conditions to ensure they met adequate competitive and public service standards (Hood et al. 1999; Ogus 1994: 10; Power 1997; Rhodes 1997: 91–3) – regulatory reform, not deregulation.

In their *Regulation inside Government*, Hood and others (1999: 187ff) argue that, on the whole, the rise of regulation within government is a compensatory 'mirror image' development to the rise of 'new public management' that introduces competition into government service provision together with generalized oversight of the new forms of provision of the service. Instead of a state providing telecommunications or job placement for the unemployed, it now specifies the outcomes it wants from either private or public providers of those services and then regulates to secure those outcomes through audit, inspection, grievance-handling and judicial review. Over all of government, policy functions are being separated from operational functions, mirroring the move in private corporations to less inhouse production of goods and services and greater outsourcing, a move which requires more arms-length controls, but a less complex internal management structure (Power 1997: 43–52; Rhodes 1996: 655–6).

At the same time that public ownership was questioned as a mechanism for the control of the provision of services such as electricity, gas and prisons, governments also began to change their approach to private sector business regulation. In response to domestic criticisms of command and control and international economic agreements such as NAFTA (North America Free Trade Agreement) and GATT (General Agreement on Tariffs and Trade), governments engaged in comprehensive attempts to deregulate business. Many set up 'deregulation' or 'regulatory reform units' within central government departments (OECD 1997a: 210).

A variety of studies have shown that while governments have professed a greater commitment to business deregulation, the actual quantum of legislation or regulations affecting business has not actually decreased in most developed countries. Indeed, it has probably increased. Data on regulatory reform in OECD countries have shown that 'the volume and complexity of new regulations from all levels of government reached unprecedented levels in the 1980s, and that the total volume of regulation is continuously increasing' (OECD 1997a: 197). For democratic legitimacy reasons, national governments have been unable to demolish much social and economic regulation of business. The global deregulatory movement has therefore matured in some countries into a regulatory reform movement which first required cost–benefit analysis and regulatory impact assessment (see OECD 1997a: 191–248; Ogus 1994: 162–5) and now seeks principles for 'better regulation' (e.g. Better Regulation Taskforce n.d.; OECD 1997a). Central regulatory reform units now regulate the regulators, requiring regulatory impact assessment, review of regulation for compliance with competition policy and flexibility reform where possible.

While command-and-control measures are still the most heavily used form of regulatory instrument, the character of regulation in the new regulatory state is changing. Techniques for controlling privatized public entities have flowed over into private sector regulation, where regulatory compliance and market incentives are used to steer corporate conduct towards public goals without appearing to interfere directly with corporate autonomy. In the USA, for example, the 're-inventing regulation' program (Geltman and Skroback 1998; Nesterczuk 1996) aims to control 'regulatory inflation' by ensuring that the design of regulation and regulatory enforcement strategy meets its goals in an effective and efficient way that maximizes voluntary compliance by business from the beginning. In countries like the Netherlands, Canada and Britain (Ogus 1994: 210), central government units have produced guides for agencies responsible for developing and implementing regulations to encourage them to only produce regulation that is necessary and likely to be effective, to consider alternatives to regulation, and to produce the least coercive form of regulation necessary to do the job.

The later work of Foucault and, after his death, other scholars (Burchell et al. 1991) identifies a special ability of the 'neo-liberal' state to govern by 'the devising of forms of regulation which permit and facilitate natural regulation'. Thus, neo-liberal 'governmentality' utilizes a 'dual-tier structure of public order and private order' (Gordon 1991: 19, 27). Neo-liberal technique is 'to promote prosperity and happiness … indirectly, working with the grain of things, relying upon the interests and actions of others to bring about its ends' (Garland 1997: 178). Neo-liberal governance, according to this perspective, involves two overlapping tendencies: the subordination of governmental functions to market regulated structures and institutions; and 'an effort to endow existing economic structures (those of the enterprise as well as those of the market) with certain of the functions of a governmental infrastructure' (Gordon 1991: 26). The 'paradox of the new economy' is that at the same time that state regulation is being reined in by reference to the need for deregulation and increased competitiveness, the rule of law is requiring more of civil society and private organizations than ever before (Arthurs and Kreklewich 1996: 29; see also Shearing and Stenning 1987).

Writers such as Power (1997: 52) and Day and Klein (1987) see the 'new public management' and its approach to governance as heralding a fundamental shift from welfare state to regulatory state. According to Hood and co-authors' (1999) analysis, the new public management involves a loosening of managerial controls, but an increase in arms-length regulatory style controls – the regulation of government by government. Majone (1994, 1996: 47–60) characterizes the rise of the new public management in Europe as the rise of a 'new' regulatory state to mark the fact that it follows on, but is conceptually distinct, from the earlier regulatory state inaugurated by the US New Deal. I use the term 'new regulatory state' to describe a pan-continental convergence in public management and regulatory style in which the state is attempting to withdraw as direct agent of command and control and public management, in favour of being an indirect regulator of internal control systems in both public (or formerly public) and private agencies (Parker 2000a; see also Braithwaite 2000). Osborne and Gaebler (1992: 25) capture this shift well in their metaphor of a state that 'steers' rather than 'rows'. Indeed, 'meta-regulation' – regulating the regulators, whether they be public agencies, private corporate self-regulators or third party gatekeepers – is the characteristic strategy of the new regulatory state.[6] This layered approach to regulatory activity is evident in the popularity of internal corporate compliance systems as a managerial attempt to incorporate legal considerations into organizational cultures and decision-making, even as state agencies claim to regulate corporations with a lighter touch. This occurs at the level of the nation-state, but partially as a response to globalizing pressures for competition and regulatory harmonization.

Compliance-oriented regulation

Empirical studies have shown that in practice certain individual tax, environmental, financial and occupational health and safety officials have often relied on education, persuasion and cooperation rather than deterrence to persuade businesses to preventively comply with regulatory goals in certain circumstances (e.g. Braithwaite 1985; Grabosky and Braithwaite 1986; Hawkins 1984; Hutter 1997). But now legislators and regulatory agencies are experimenting with formal programs that provide incentives for voluntary implementation of sophisticated compliance systems by business, and sanctions for lack of a program (Baldwin 1997; Grabosky 1994, 1995; Manning 1987).

Environmental regulation already requires corporations to take responsibility for the effects of their activities on the environment by preparing environmental impact statements about the consequences of proposed developments (Fischer and Schot 1993: 5). There is a trend towards expecting corporations to environmentally 'audit' all their activities, not just new developments (e.g. International Auditing Practices Committee 1995). In Britain, Europe and Australia enforced compliance programs are common in occupational health and safety (Smith et al. 1993). 'Regulatory crime' laws, such as trading standard and consumer protection statutes, frequently encourage self-regulation by providing businesses with a defence to offences if they can show they exercised 'due diligence' by having in place management and quality assurance systems aimed at ensuring compliance with the standards (Ogus 1994: 197; Parker and Connolly forthcoming; C. Scott 1995). Equal employment opportunity (EEO) and affirmative action (AA) regimes require companies, government departments, and universities to consider whether women (and sometimes other minorities) are discriminated against within their organizations and in their employment practices, and to develop corporate plans for improving their position (V. Braithwaite 1993).

These changes in control of corporate conduct reflect a broader change in governance styles in which it is recognized that the state is not the only source of regulation (Grabosky 1995). Indirect governance is also the characteristic strategy of international agencies that do not have the coercive powers available to nation-states. At a global level, there is a proliferation of voluntary codes of practice and standards, promulgated by international bodies with varying degrees of enforcement and success, to facilitate and encourage corporate self-regulation systems. To date, the promulgation of voluntary international standards has been most successful in the environmental and safety areas, with the ISO 14000 series (Gunningham and Sinclair 1999), the European Community's EMAS accreditation system, and a number of national and industry standards such as the Canadian Standards Association's Sustainable Forestry Management Standards initiative, the British standard for occupational health and safety management (BS8800–1996) and the International Council of Chemical Associations' Responsible Care Scheme (which runs on a national basis in forty countries; see International Council of Chemical Associations 1998).

But a range of other voluntary codes and standards is shaping the way in which international companies define and manage social responsibility issues: from specific initiatives, such as the World Health Organization's International Code of Marketing of Breast Milk Substitutes, the US Department of Labor's Apparel Industry Partnership and the UK Fair Trade Initiative (aimed at eliminating exploitation of child and other workers in non-western countries), to general attempts to define corporate responsibility, such as the OECD's (1997d) guidelines for multinational enterprises, the Tripartite Declaration of Principles Concerning Multinational Enterprises and Social Policy (adopted by the International Labour Organisation), and the United Nations' 1999 Global Compact.[7]

Non-government organizations (NGOs) are also using this strategy in attempts to improve corporate conduct. The Council for Economic Priorities has developed Social Accountability 8000 (SA 8000), a system defining auditable standards and independent auditing processes for the protection of workers' rights based on the conventions of the International Labour Organisation and other human rights documents (Fabian 1998). Consumers International have developed the Consumer Charter for Global Business, which transnational corporations are being asked to sign if they can demonstrate that their operations comply with its standards of ethics, competition, marketing practices, product standards and consumer information (ACT Consumer Affairs Bureau 1996).

CORPORATE COMPLIANCE PROGRAMS

Emergence of compliance programs

One of the most significant trends in regulatory compliance is the great increase in utilization of formal corporate compliance systems by regulated companies and organizations over the last ten to fifteen years. According to one definition, corporate compliance systems are management systems that 'aim to prevent, and where necessary, identify and respond to, breaches of laws, regulations, codes or organisational standards occurring in the organisation; promote a culture of compliance within the organisation; and assist the organisation in remaining or becoming a good corporate citizen' (AS3806–Compliance Programmes, Standards Australia 1998 para. 1.2). As I will argue below, however, it is the concept of 'self-regulation' rather than 'compliance' that is important in understanding what makes these programs effective.

A compliance system can be as simple as the appointment of an officer with responsibility for ensuring that the paperwork required for regulatory compliance purposes is filled out and sent in, or as complex as the setting up of a compliance department with educational programs, advice and auditing functions and a computer system to keep track of legal requirements and whether they have been fulfilled.

In 1988 Sigler and Murphy reported that, in America it was 'commonplace' for larger corporations to have substantial legal departments whose activities included active compliance and compliance education (1988: 55; see also Bardach and Kagan 1982: 95–9). The history of implementation of corporate compliance programs is one of compliance systems becoming popular in a few areas in the USA where regulatory enforcement was particularly strict; then moving to other US regulatory arenas as scandals or problems arose; moving beyond risk-specific programs with the US Sentencing Commission's Sentencing Guidelines for Organizations (see below); and finally being modelled by companies and regulators in countries other than the USA. Overall the evidence points to corporate compliance programs receiving either a new prominence or being introduced for the first time in the USA in the late 1980s, and in the early 1990s in Canada, Britain and Australia.[8]

Particular regulatory arenas

In the USA, legal compliance systems appear to have become popular first in two areas: in antitrust and in the regulation of financial institutions. At the same time environmental, health and safety management systems were also being adopted. In 1988 Sigler and Murphy (1988: 57) reported that US compliance strategies were most advanced in relation to antitrust, which they saw as directly related to the severity of antitrust laws and the government's practice in enforcing them. Indeed, there is evidence that antitrust compliance programs have been reasonably common in the USA since at least the late 1970s (Beckenstein and Gabel 1983). In Australia, antitrust compliance programs have existed since the early 1980s, but were strengthened and increased in popularity during the 1990s (Parker 1999a). They have only recently become significant in Britain.[9]

Financial services compliance programs have been popular in the USA since at least the 1960s (McCaffrey and Hart 1998). Friedrichs (1996: 298) traces the emergence of compliance officers in major financial firms to the 1950s when a prominent stock brokerage firm was suspended by the Securities and Exchange Commission for thirty days for failing to adequately supervise brokers who defrauded clients. The status of the compliance function, although originally modest, was raised in response to a series of scandals and banking house collapses in the late 1980s and early 1990s. Again in this area Britain lagged behind the USA. Financial services compliance programs became popular in the early 1990s when financial services regulation was substantially restructured, and continued to grow in significance in response to a number of spectacular regulatory scandals throughout the 1990s. Those firms with links to the USA already had compliance staff but the Financial Services Act 1986, and the rules of the new Self-Regulatory Organizations (SROs) created by it, prompted the rest to do so. They became popular and compliance officers gained higher status after the banking house scandals and collapses of the early 1990s (Weait 1994: 381).

In the USA, health care compliance systems have become very popular in recent years due to stricter enforcement practices and government concern to crack down on fraud. According to Freyer (1996: 226), the generic drug scandals of the late 1980s led to a noticeable increase in criminal prosecutions against pharmaceutical companies, with courts imposing compliance programs as part of the relief in these cases. More recently, the Food and Drug Administration (FDA) has targeted resources at identifying and rectifying poor compliance cultures in companies (Freyer 1996: 228) and evaluation of regulatory compliance programs has been tied to eligibility for medicaid payments. The Department of Health and Human Services Office of Inspector General (HHS/OIG) has also introduced a major program to detect and prevent health care fraud by encouraging health care providers to discover and disclose fraud within their entities in return for a negotiated settlement, rather than a full scale investigation and full fines, and an agreement to implement an approved 'integrity compliance' program (Morris 1998).

One regulatory arena that put compliance systems most insistently into corporate executive consciousness beyond the financial services sector in the USA was the control of bribery and other misconduct in defence contracting in the wake of the Lockheed Martin and other scandals. The Defense Industry Initiative on Business Ethics and Conduct was a response to the Blue Ribbon Commission on Defense Management (chaired by David Packard) into scams and mischarging in defence contracting (Yuspeh 1998). This program required companies to implement codes of ethics, ethics training, internal reporting of misconduct, self-governance of compliance, attendance at Best Practice forums and public accountability, and attracted thirty-five signatories (Yuspeh 1998: para. 16.02). It was this program that created the context for the USA's most successful mechanism for encouraging the proliferation and strengthening of corporate compliance programs to be born and supported by business. This was the Federal Sentencing Guidelines for organizations which came into effect on 1 November 1991 (Fiorelli 1993: 403; Gruner 1994: 444, 817–94). When the Federal Sentencing Guidelines were being drafted in the late 1980s, business leaders had already seen how self-regulation through the Defense Industry Initiative was a useful tool for warding off public criticism and strict government regulation and enforcement. Business therefore supported the Sentencing Commission's idea of rewarding companies for having general compliance programs in effect.[10]

This scheme uses decreased fines to encourage corporations to voluntarily put in place compliance programs to help them avoid committing offences. A base fine is adjusted according to a corporation's 'culpability score' in relation to a particular violation. An effective compliance program is one of the major mitigating factors for decreasing the culpability score, and convicted organizations with fifty or more employees that do not have an effective compliance program are placed on probation until they implement such a program. A survey of 300 US businesses found that almost 45 per cent self-reported that they added vigour to their compliance programs because of the guidelines, and another 20 per cent added compliance programs for the first time because of the Guidelines (Harvard Law Review 1996: 1787). Another survey of 262 US companies in 1996 found that 14 per cent modified their pre-existent compliance system or introduced a compliance program for the first time as a response to the Guidelines, and 48 per cent implemented a compliance policy for the first time partially because of the Guidelines (Price Waterhouse 1997). Despite the fact that the Sentencing Guidelines fines provisions are only applied to criminal convictions under federal laws (excluding environmental, FDA and export offences), they have put compliance programs on management agendas generally and have also influenced regulatory enforcement policies in a variety of state and federal arenas.

The evidence is strong that management systems in the areas of environment and occupational safety and health have simultaneously become popular throughout developed western nations since about the mid-1980s. (These management systems incorporate compliance as well as quality management considerations.) Fischer and Schot's (1993: 5) international research on industrial firms suggests that 'somewhere in the mid-1980s firms changed from fighting or resistantly adapting to external pressures to embracing them and incorporating environmental considerations into their policies in a more rigorous way'. Voluntary environmental management systems are now globally popular (e.g. Parry 2000; Power 1997: 60–6). In 1974 a survey found that top managers in a majority of US companies viewed environmental management as a threat. By 1991 the same survey found that 77 per cent of US companies had a formal system in place for proactively identifying major environmental issues. Also by 1991 forty-nine Fortune 100 companies had environmental vice-presidents and thirty-one of the Fortune 50 had them (Hoffman 1997: 3–4, 23, 80–1, 123). (Sheikh's survey of British companies showed that well over half had already begun to regularly audit more than one area of social activity by 1996 (Sheikh 1996: 194).)

Occupational health and safety are now frequently included with environmental management in one environmental, health and safety system (EHS) in large international companies.[11] However, in fact, safety management systems have a longer history of implementation than environmental management systems. Interviewees in the chemical and pharmaceutical industries in Europe reported that safety engineers were already being employed in operational units as early as the beginning of the 1960s. In the USA, systematic approaches to corporate safety management systems became widespread in the 1970s after the US Occupational Safety and Health Administration (OSHA) was set up and the threat of enforcement and high sanctions increased (Bardach and Kagan 1982: 95). For example, OSHA's voluntary protection program which helps companies voluntarily implement occupational safety and health management systems has attracted higher and higher numbers of voluntary participants every year since it was launched in 1982.[12]

Summary

Table 1.1 summarizes the (limited) quantitative evidence available on the implementation of corporate compliance programs.[13] This evidence and other studies suggest that globally compliance management programs are strongest in the areas of environmental, OHS and financial services regulation (see, for example, Aalders and Wilthagen 1997: 421; Andersen 1996; Genn 1993). EEO and AA compliance policies are also widely implemented, but to a lesser extent. An emerging popular area, especially in the USA, is anti-bribery and corruption programs, partly in response to the US Foreign Corrupt Practices Act and the OECD Anti-Bribery Convention (Berenbeim 2000).

The evidence also shows that the USA is an influential centre for the proliferation of compliance programs. KPMG's 1998 survey of Canadian companies found that those with a US parent were much more likely to have a larger number of elements of a compliance program in place (US-owned companies averaged 6.6 out of 9 elements of a compliance program while Canadian-owned companies averaged only 3.5 out of 9) (KPMG 1998: 16). The evidence also shows that corporate compliance systems are much more likely to be implemented by large enterprises than small and medium-sized enterprises (SMEs).

The fact that formal compliance management systems have become popular shows that the presumption of the new regulatory state that regulation can be pushed down into private domains of corporation and market has some plausibility. Nevertheless, we need to define and understand corporate compliance systems in order to evaluate their effectiveness as a tool of democratic social control of corporate power.

Corporate responsibility and corporate compliance

The compliance management systems that are increasingly popular with large companies take many forms and have many purposes. Their adoption can be a response to any one of a number of issues, including attempts to manage the complex legal requirements of apparently ever increasing command-and-control regulation; responses to more flexible regulatory strategy and rewards for 'voluntary' compliance; and trying to appear to be a good corporate citizen in response to accidents, scandals or regulatory crises, and community concern about unbridled corporate power. It is therefore difficult to define what is precisely meant by a corporate 'compliance program'. It is apparent, however, that there is a broad continuum of relevant corporate practices ranging on the one hand from formal legalistic compliance management systems to vague ethics or codes of conduct and from legally-oriented to quality-oriented management systems on the other hand.

Regulatory compliance always means compliance with something. It can most easily be defined as obedience by a target population to a regulatory rule – 'rule compliance'. A corporate compliance system is therefore a management system aimed at ensuring that the rules applicable to

TABLE 1.1 *Summary of studies on extent of implementation of corporate compliance programs*

Author/year	Weinberger 1990	V. Braithwaite 1993	Andersen 1996
Country	USA	Australia	Norway
Sample	Surveyed 27 Missouri-based top 1000 companies; 74% response.	Reports of all companies reporting to Affirmative Action Agency.	Surveyed 100 top corporate managers.
Findings	70% had implemented formal compliance policy re insider trading.	86% issued affirmative action policy to all staff; 70% set objectives for affirmative action progress for year ending 1990.	31% strongly engaged in environmental, health and safety (EHS) work; 37% medium to strongly engaged in EHS work; 32% not interested in implementing EHS actions; 29% companies with sales up to 10m kroner had no knowledge of requirement for EHS system; 6% companies with sales over 100m kroner had no knowledge of requirement.

TABLE 1.1 (cont.) *Summary of studies on extent of implementation of corporate compliance programs*

Author/year	Laufer (USSC) 1995	Ethics Resource Center (USSC) 1995	Ward/Price Waterhouse 1997
Country	USA	USA	USA
Sample	212 small businesses with 50–500 employees.	Surveyed 4035 business employees; 53% response rate.	5000 companies; 262 usable responses.
Findings	75% had standards of conduct (written or unwritten) overseen by high-level personnel; 71% thought their compliance programs were effective; nearly 50% had a designated compliance person who was a high-level employee who reported directly to the owner, CEO or president; 33% each considered compliance in performance appraisals and in promotion decisions.	33% reported their company had some sort of ethics office to which they could report violations or from which they could seek advice.	86% had a formal compliance policy; 9% were developing a policy; 5% had no policy. The top eight areas covered by compliance programs were: Ethics, conflicts of interest and gifts (86%); Employment/ labour law (75%); Antitrust, trade regulation and procurement (68%); Environment, health and safety (65%); Lobbying, government relations and political contributions (60%); Securities law (55%); Intellectual property (52%); International business practices (46%).

TABLE 1.1 (cont.) *Summary of studies on extent of implementation of corporate compliance programs*

Author/year	Still 1997	Schwartz 1998	Weaver et al. 1999a
Country	Australia	Canada	USA
Sample	Top 75 financial institutions reporting to Affirmative Action Agency.	Not stated.	An ethics-knowledgeable officer (identified by name) of 990 of the Fortune 1000; 254 returns (i.e. response rate of 26%).
Findings	87% management actively promoted workplace free of sexual harassment; 81% had formal procedures in place to deal with complaints of sexual harassment.	65% had explicit compliance standards and procedures; 63% had publications that communicated the standards and procedures to staff; 58% had assigned responsibility to oversee compliance to high-level staff; 54% periodically reviewed or audited compliance program; 47% monitored systems to detect misconduct; 44% used compliance training programs; 41% had mechanisms to enforce compliance procedures; 38% had systems for employees to report misconduct.	78% had a separate code of ethics; 45% required employees to acknowledge compliance with code at least annually; 30% had a separate ethics or compliance office. (63% were created in the 1990s); 51% had telephone systems for ethics/compliance complaints and queries.

the corporation (whether they be laws, regulations, codes of practice or self-regulatory standards) are met. Historically, this is exactly where the earliest compliance programs were aimed. For example, in US pharmaceutical and financial services industries in the early 1970s, low-status employees worked in compliance as an essentially paperwork job ensuring that licences were applied for and kept up to date, and that required information was printed on labels or provided to customers.[14]

A corporate sector that uniformly and successfully implemented legalistic compliance systems would be a major accomplishment. It would certainly be an improvement on the status quo where many are unaware of the law, unable to ensure all their employees meet its requirements, or simply uninterested in complying. However, focusing on rule compliance as a way of defining the function of corporate compliance systems is conceptually inadequate as a basis for evaluating what such systems contribute to the democratic opening out of corporations. This is because rule compliance potentially perpetuates all the same problems as command-and-control regulation, but one level further down. Business complains that legalistic compliance systems are disproportionately costly to implement (e.g. Roberts et al. 1995: 37–8; see, generally, the US journal *Regulation*). More significantly, formal compliance systems do not guarantee achievement of the objectives that regulation sets out to achieve (see Chapter 6). Internal compliance officers may perpetuate within the company the evils of unreasonably legalistic external regulatory inspectors, made all the worse for them being agents of corporate domination of employees. Compliance systems can be formal systems for diffusing or obfuscating the real blame and laying it on a scapegoat. Formal programs can also mean a system that ensures apparent compliance with the letter of the law through creative compliance, but not engagement with its substance. Surely the new regulatory state is aiming for something more than pushing command-and-control rules (with all their weaknesses) down to the managerial level?

This does not mean that instead of looking for a legal compliance system in a company we should be looking for an 'ethics' program. Companies with an ethics program that consists of a code of conduct or statement of principles and values, perhaps with a training program, are not superior to companies with a legalistic compliance program. The evidence suggests that these codes of conduct are generally purely window dressing and have very little effect on what people actually do (e.g. Cleek and Leonard 1998; see also Bureau of International Labor Affairs 1996; Office of Fair Trading 1998). Similarly systems aimed at quality management in some areas that intersects with regulation such as ISO 14000, OHS management systems or consumer complaint-handling standards are not necessarily a substitute for compliance with legal requirements. While EHS and risk management systems that build on the total quality management approach have some value, they mostly focus on systems and procedures of internal controls to the exclusion of outcomes and substantive principles or values (see Chapter 6).

Legalistic or rule compliance on its own is an inadequate criterion for assessing corporate compliance systems because it connotes a reactive conception of the corporation as a recipient of rules, rather than an actively responsible citizen. The term 'compliance' is too passive to indicate a company that is engaged with its legal, social, environmental and ethical responsibilities. Indeed, some leading compliance consultants prefer the term 'integrity program', because 'compliance' connotes a simplistic obedience to rules rather than engagement with ethical and social responsibilities. As Shearing (1993: 75) writes, 'policy makers should be very wary of an approach that regards compliance with rules whether achieved through cooperation or coercion as hallmarks of sound regulatory practices. Regulatory policy should be goal rather than rule oriented.' In this sense the business critique of the trend towards implementation of compliance systems as costly, slavish obedience indicates a fundamental problem with the idea of corporate regulatory compliance systems. While we may be (rightly) uncomfortable with this as a justification for lack of compliance commitment to democratically created regulation, business critics are correct in thinking that systems which attempt only to ensure non-participatory obedience to technical rules set by the state are not ideal.

Goal-oriented regulatory policy focuses on achieving substantive objectives such as a more healthy environment, a safer workplace, better informed consumers, more competition, equity in the workplace, and so on. Compliance through the achievement of substantive regulatory objectives is 'substantive compliance' as opposed to mere 'rule compliance'. Effective or best practice corporate compliance systems must be about the internalization of responsibility for socially (and economically) desirable outcomes, not just of rules. This requires a thorough internalized commitment to showing responsibility in changing circumstances, not just ticking off a set of boxes. Substantive compliance ought to be more acceptable than rule compliance to regulators, genuinely committed regulatees, and the public alike (see LeClair et al. 1998; Paine 1994).

Compliance practice in this conception is not the infiltration of command-and-control rules into stable corporate regimes, but corporate citizenship that requires the active engagement of corporate management with regulatory norms and of regulatory norms with corporate concerns (see Silverstein 1987). In his classic, *Law, Society and Industrial Justice* (1969: 249–50), Philip Selznick argued that citizenship has been disentangled from private law in modern times so that citizenship is conceived as a status and set of responsibilities that applies to individuals, but not to corporations.

From Stone to Selznick, a predominant scholar's solution to the problem of ensuring that legal and social values permeate the internal workings of the corporation, rather than bouncing off the corporate veil, is to require large institutions to regulate themselves in a way that is responsive to social and community concerns (Bardach and Kagan 1982; Chayes 1960; Selznick 1992: 336ff; Sigler and Murphy 1988; Stone 1975). The 'moral institution' is one that enhances its integrity by governing itself within general standards established by the legislature and courts. Responsible institutions like responsible individuals must have 'an *inner* commitment to moral restraint and aspiration' (Selznick 1992: 345, emphasis in original). Aspirations such as 'fairness in industrial discipline; affirmative action to overcome discrimination and its effects; environmental protection; quality control; occupational safety ... cannot be achieved through rhetoric or through grudging conformity to external rules. They usually require specialized units [within the organization] capable of determining policy, monitoring practices, and establishing appropriate procedures' (Selznick 1992: 352).

Similarly, John Braithwaite's policy-oriented criminology (1989; Ayres and Braithwaite 1992; Fisse and Braithwaite 1993) proposes that responses to offences (whether individual or corporate, suite or street) should communicate the wrongfulness and shame of an offence and maximize the moral educative functions of punishment, allowing individuals and institutions to internalize the shame and be reintegrated into the moral community by demonstrating their internal commitment to abiding by the laws of the community. In the case of individuals this might occur through expressions of remorse and an agreement to make restoration in a restorative justice conference. For organizations it will mean punishment targeted at mobilizing those who can change corporate cultures to do so, and then giving self-regulation a chance. The theory of 'responsive regulation' (Ayres and Braithwaite 1992) is designed to maximize self-regulatory possibilities by the strategic use of legal sanctions.

This approach to corporate compliance and regulation draws attention to the 'regulatory space' (Hancher and Moran 1989; C. Scott 2001; Shearing 1993) inside corporations and away from the usual primary focus of scholars of regulation on public policy. It means recognizing that organizations already have significant internal systems, or at least capacities, for regulating employee conduct, supplier relations, management of environmental and health and safety risk and other issues, regardless of external regulatory intervention. Pre-existent regulatory orderings within organizations will interact with external attempts to regulate business conduct so that the outcome of public regulation will be conditioned by a variety of endogenous factors, including regulatees' capacity to comply, managerial and cultural orderings within organizations, self-regulatory capacities of industry associations, and gatekeeper roles played by third parties including professionals, insurance companies, rating agencies, and so on. This approach to compliance and regulation fits well with the 'entity' theory of the corporation set out above, since it recognizes that the corporation is both an appropriate object of democratic responsibilities, and an appropriate subject for responsive self-regulation.

CONCLUSION

Regulation within the new regulatory state is aimed as much at reinventing regulation within private 'regulatory space', such as corporations, as at reforming external regulatory agencies. The experience of command and control shows that it is not reasonable, practical or efficient for external legislatures and regulators to be solely responsible for determining how organizations should manage social issues. The design and enforcement of regulation to govern every potential social dilemma facing business is simply not achievable. And even if it were, it would not make businesses better citizens, since citizenship implies an internal capacity to respond with integrity to external values. The new regulatory state uses enforced self-regulation and incentives for voluntary compliance in its attempts to steer corporate conduct towards public goals without interfering too greatly with corporate autonomy and profit. Since many large companies in the USA, Canada, Britain and Australia have already voluntarily implemented compliance management systems, the internal corporate compliance program is now one of the main frontiers of engagement between external regulatory messages and internal corporate orderings of management, control and culture. Do these compliance systems simply push command and control down the line into management chains? Are they merely symbolic – a ploy to ensure that the real work of deregulation can go ahead with apparent legitimacy?

The issue for judgment is whether and when these 'compliance' programs and the like (e.g. environmental management systems, ethical codes) might succeed in accomplishing a measure of democratic responsibility in corporate decision-making and action. And if so, in what conditions – regulatory, legal, political, social and political – they might be most effective and robust. Ultimately these questions are resolved on a practical and daily level by those individuals most intimately involved: compliance managers, lawyers, environmental managers and other designated 'compliance professionals'. Empirically and normatively it is most illuminating to begin with them. To that end, this book combines empirical inquiry (interviews and participant observation with self-regulation professionals) with normative critique and goal-setting (corporate citizenship and regulatory theory). The empirical focus is on 'best practice' compliance practices, since we are searching for the potential, not the extent of current achievements (see the Appendix for the empirical methodology used). Chapter 2 sets out a hypothesis of the external conditions and internal corporate dynamics by which corporate citizenship might be effectively institutionalized in an open corporation, which will form the basis for the discussion in the rest of the book.

2 | The potential for self-regulation

What are the factors that make corporate responsiveness to democratic social control inherently difficult? The first part of this chapter reviews the organizational factors that business ethics researchers have shown often fragment and destroy possibilities for organizational integrity. This is the problem of disconnection between corporate life and individual integrity and external values. In the remainder of this chapter I set out a normative ideal of how corporations should be democratically responsive; and a hypothesis as to how this might be institutionalized in fact. Democracy would, ideally, require corporate permeability to external values – the 'open corporation'. In order to accomplish this in fact, corporate management must move through *each* of three phases of response to social and legal responsibility issues:

1   the commitment to respond;
2   the acquisition of specialized skills and knowledge; and
3   the institutionalization of purpose.

Each of these phases represents a decision point at which external influences can transform corporate practice and decision-making. But continuing interaction with external stakeholders and regulators at the next decision point must help to ensure that the management response is appropriate (see Figure 2.3). As I will show, the existence of internal constituencies (Sigler and Murphy 1988: 103–4) with the responsibility for implementing self-regulation systems or ensuring the company addresses integrity issues is a linchpin for ensuring appropriate managerial responses at each decision point.

DIFFICULTIES OF INSTITUTIONALIZING RESPONSIBILITY

The methods of the new regulatory state require us to look inside corporations in order to evaluate their potential for institutionalizing responsibility. However, one of the major themes of empirical research on business ethics is that organizational life makes it hard for individuals to maintain their own integrity by acting according to their own sense of ethics and social responsibility. Organizations often tend to destroy individuals' integrity by tearing apart their constituent 'selves' – their commitment to the business goals of the organization on the one hand, and, on the other, their personal ethical commitments (e.g. to family) and sense of social responsibilities (e.g. environmentalism). This literature implies that even organizations full of perfectly 'ethical', well-intentioned managers and employees with decent values are unlikely to corporately act with social responsibility all the time.

Organizational influences towards irresponsible behaviour are most obvious when employees feel constrained directly or indirectly by management considerations to do unethical things in order to balance work and family, or to meet work expectations. For example, in a 1997 survey of a cross-section of US workers, the Ethics Officer Association found that 56 per cent of respondents reported feeling some pressure to act illegally or unethically on the job. Forty-eight per cent of them reported that they had engaged in one or more of twenty-five listed unethical or illegal actions in the last year because of workplace pressure. The most common source of such pressure was balancing work and family lives (mentioned by 52 per cent of respondents) (Petry et al. 1998). Survival in the face of organizational expectations can require unethical or illegal conduct. Jackall's qualitative research on top managers' ethics, *Moral Mazes* (1988, especially p. 94), is famous for its description of how organizational realities encourage top managers to take a short-term view in their decision-making in order to survive for the short time they are in the job, rather than to contribute to the long-term interests and public image of responsibility of their corporation. Jennifer Hill (1998) diagnoses chief executive officers (CEOs) as suffering from the 'supermodel effect'. Their short lifespan as a CEO means that they must maximize their gains during that short term, and militates against them seriously considering the future including ethical and long-term legal responsibility issues. Other commentators have described how formal and informal organizational hierarchies have been intentionally used by superiors to undermine individuals' sense of the ethically right thing to do (see Boisjoly et al. 1989; Vandivier 1972).

People who on the whole believe in obeying the law and doing the right thing in their personal and civic lives can also be subtly seduced into doing unethical or illegal things within organizational structures. A persuasive literature in business ethics suggests that corporate decisions are often immoral, illegal or just bad, because although many individuals are involved in making them, none feels personal responsibility for the ultimate outcome (Bovens 1998). Psychologists and management theorists have noted phenomena such as 'risky shift', 'groupthink' and the 'Abilene paradox' in which, respectively, people take greater risks on behalf of their organizations than they would on their own account, act in accord with organizational norms even when they clash with their own principles, or go along with group decisions against their better judgment in order to avoid conflict (Metzger 1987; Sims 1994).

Slovak (1981) attributes this to a problem of role morality which arises from the difference between corporate actors and individual persons. When they act on their own behalf, individuals have many interests that they pursue in each of their many social roles. Their multiple interests often provide alternative standards against which to judge conduct which in turn generates role conflict or strain that acts as a form of social control (Slovak 1981: 777). Individual actors in corporations, by contrast, are subsumed and socialized by organizational bureaucracies. They are disposable actors hired to play one role and to use organizational resources to pursue one corporate interest by whatever means necessary (Slovak 1981; cf. May 1996). People tend to see it as illegitimate to use alternative extra-organizational standards to critique and test the value and consequences of the behaviour they are hired to perform in their organizational role. Therefore social control becomes more difficult, unless the corporation itself institutionalizes some internal control. The reality is therefore often the exact opposite of the corporate responsibility ideal advocated by Selznick, Ayres and Braithwaite, and Stone (discussed in the previous chapter). There it was argued that companies ought to become more like individuals in terms of internalizing moral restraints. Here the business ethics research suggests that when organizational ethical failures occur, it is because bureaucratic ways of thinking have colonized individuals' consciences.

Bird (1996) describes the way that ethical silence surrounds organizational decision-making. His research suggested that ethical issues are generally not discussed and people assume they are alone in their concerns and therefore say and do nothing. He (Bird 1996: 25) points to the famous Milgram experiments and other psychological research to argue that people are measurably more likely to act on their convictions when they have opportunities to speak with others about the misgivings they feel. The ethical conversation brings their multiple selves back into the conversation and frees them from one-dimensional role morality. Similarly Gioia (1992) describes how organizational scripts (intentionally or unintentionally) encode ways of doing things that insulate against discovering and identifying new ethical problems. Gioia uses this theory to explain why he, a socially aware recall officer at Ford in the 1970s, did not see the need to recall the Pinto despite emerging evidence that the car was liable to explode into flames when hit from behind, even at low speeds. Vital information which would have helped him to assess the situation was not passed on to him as recall officer, including the original tests in which the problem had been discovered before the car was on the market and not rectified: 'Although the outcomes of the case carry retrospectively obvious ethical overtones, the schemas driving my perceptions and actions precluded consideration of the issues in ethical terms because the scripts did not include ethical dimensions' (Gioia 1992: 151).

The reality of fragmented decision-making within organizational bureaucracies also undermines attempts at integrity, even in organizations that ostensibly have ethics or compliance policies. Organizational theorists have shown that while it is tempting to see intra-organizational processes as rational and goal-determined, they are frequently chaotic or ad hoc 'because of the limits of human intellective capacities in comparison with the complexities of the problems that individuals and organizations face' (March and Simon 1958: 169). As Heimer (1996: 44) explains it, 'Which decisions get made depends on what participants happen to be there at the time, what is identified as a problem needing a solution, what solutions are available in the organization, and consensus that a choice point has arrived and it is time to make a decision'. This is attributed to 'bounded rationality': the limited capacity of people to process information and therefore their inability to consider many alternatives in decision-making (March and Simon 1958: 169).

Heimer (1997) takes this analysis one step further in her detailed empirical analysis of how legal norms interact with other norms in neonatal intensive care units. She coins the term 'bounded imagination' to describe how people fail to be able to fully imagine and consider alternatives to the status quo. The scripted knowledge that is formed out of the existing practices of an organization preclude imaginative alternatives:

... people also have rather limited capacities to imagine alternatives to the one that exists or that they have chosen, and not much capacity to imagine the perspective of others. In short, people are only boundedly imaginative ... While organization theorists are pointing to the limited number of alternatives we can compare, I am pointing to our inability to make anything but shallow comparisons when any alternative to the status quo or the selection option is abstract or undeveloped. Our limited capacity to envision alternative plans or alternative social arrangements is an important impediment to responsibility. (Heimer 1997: 25)

Ulrich Beck (1992) gives a more dramatic and global view of this phenomenon in his analysis of *The Risk Society*. His argument is that late modernity is increasingly characterized by concern with, and the production of knowledge about, the catastrophic risks that have been produced by modernization itself, including environmental disaster, technological breakdown and nuclear radiation. These risks are produced as a result of techno-economic development, the sphere largely of private corporations and private decisions rather than decisions made in the public political, democratic sphere. Although stated at a more macro level, Beck's insights are very similar to the empirical researchers of business ethics mentioned above:

Lacking a place to appear, the decisions that change society become tongue-tied and anonymous. In business they are tied into investment decisions which shunt their potential for social change off into the 'unseen side effect'. The empirical and analytical sciences that plan the innovations remain cut off by their self understanding and institutional ties from the social consequences of their innovation and the consequences of those consequences. (Beck 1992: 187)

One of Beck's main policy recommendations about this situation is that science ought to be more self-critical, and in particular so should those private organizations that make important decisions in contemporary society about the development and deployment of new technology. This means protecting the ability of individuals within an organization to criticize, and nurturing possibilities for 'sub-politics' to exert influence on organizations:

[T]hings that until now have only been able to make their way with great difficulty against the dominance of professions or operational management must be institutionally protected: alternative evaluations, alternative professional practice, discussions within organizations and professions of the consequences of their own developments, and repressed skepticism ... Enabling self-criticism in all its forms is

> not some sort of danger, but probably the only way that the mistakes that would sooner or later destroy our world can be detected in advance ... Much would be gained, however, if the regulations that make people the opinion slaves of those they work for were reduced. (Beck 1992: 234)

Organizations of all types, however, show a great aptitude and capacity for discouraging dissent and challenge, and for demanding a loyalty that quashes integrity. This is particularly true of the experience of potential whistle-blowers who might otherwise be a valuable check and balance (see, generally, Bovens 1998: 190–214; King 1999). Consider the troubling case of Stanley Adams (1984), an executive with Swiss pharmaceutical giant, Hoffman La-Roche. He blew the whistle on the company's price-fixing and market-sharing with competitors, and its aggressive dominance of the world vitamin market, to the European Economic Community (EEC) competition authorities, and then left the company to set up his own business in Italy. During their investigation EEC officials gave Roche's lawyers documents that enabled them to identify Adams as the whistle-blower. When Adams next crossed the border into Switzerland, to visit his family for Christmas, he was arrested for economic espionage for leaking Roche's confidential documents to the European competition authorities. He spent three months on remand in jail, during which time his wife committed suicide. After he had escaped back to Italy, Adams was found guilty in Switzerland in his absence and sentenced to twelve months prison.

This unconscionable use of state power to back up economic power to punish and deter employee responsibility is often repeated (in less dramatic circumstances). There are many cases in which EEO officers, compliance officers, inhouse lawyers and others have been sacked for whistle-blowing or dissenting from corporate decisions on ethical grounds, and then denied any legal remedy by the courts (especially in the USA), because of their 'disloyalty' to their corporate employer (see Chambliss 1996; Giesel 1992).

Even when on the whole people want to do the right thing, organizational structures lack ethical intelligence, and when an organization as a whole lacks ethical intelligence, this leaves plenty of space for the unscrupulous, greedy or evil to break the law or have their way. For example, Gioia's lack of access as recall officer to all the relevant paperwork on the Pinto left the way clear for those who had made the calculated decision to sacrifice lives for economy in the Pinto's design to direct events without challenge (until publicity and litigation challenged the corporation's external legitimacy). Thus, a series of inherent organizational factors can easily lead to failures of responsibility for corporations. The implication is that it is not enough for corporate management to refrain from deliberately promoting irresponsible action. Organizational managers must proactively and systematically do something to overcome corporate irresponsibility. Accidental failures are much more likely than accidental successes in organizational mazes. It is for this reason that compliance or self-regulatory systems may be useful.

MOVING TOWARDS CORPORATE CITIZENSHIP

Corporate compliance or self-regulation systems are worth study because they might provide a means of constituting organizations' social responsibility in relation to their members, stakeholders and the rest of the world. From a public policy perspective, encouraging internal corporate self-regulation systems not only recognizes the need for democratic responsibility of corporate action, but also recognizes that companies have the capacity to govern themselves and their relationships with others. From the corporate perspective, a compliance program is a system for managing the risk of irresponsible, unethical or illegal action. Before we can assess potential institutions for corporate responsibility, however, we need to move up one level of abstraction to a theory of democracy. Making corporations democratically accountable is not simply about copying public institutions of representative democracy within the corporate microcosm (see Chapter 8). Rather, the challenge is to understand the norms of democracy and then to create new institutions for applying them to the unique world of corporate enterprise.

A deliberative version of democratic theory is a helpful way to approach this task. This is because deliberative democracy, at its best, is about responsiveness and reflexiveness, not about particular institutions of democracy (see Pettit 1997). The creation of a deliberative democracy – a polity where decisions are made on the basis of dialogue and public justification accessible to all citizens – is central to a variety of recent political theories, including Habermas' discourse theory of law and democracy (1996), Dryzek's discursive democracy (1990), and Young's communicative democracy (1990, 1993). It is a traditional concern of republican theory (Pettit 1997: 188–9), particularly of US republicanism (Sunstein 1988, 1993), and of a whole literature on active participatory citizenship inspired by the ancient Greek ideal of citizenship (Boucher and Vincent 1993: 89) and the Classical civic republican tradition (Barber 1984; Oldfield 1990).

The basic idea is that in order to secure citizens' freedom, not only should government be constrained by checks and balances, such as the rule of law and the separation of powers, but also citizens should have the opportunity to make their presence felt in public decision-making that offends against their interests by ensuring that:

> at every site of decision-making, legislative, administrative and judicial, there are procedures in place which identify the considerations relevant to the decision, thereby enabling citizens to raise the question as to whether they are the appropriate considerations to play that role. And ... that there are procedures in place which enable citizens to make a judgment on whether the relevant considerations actually determined the outcome. (Pettit 1997: 188)

This does not necessarily require the unrealistic ideal that all public decisions originate in collective consent and universally satisfactory resolution of differences. Pettit puts forward the more practically feasible ideal of *contestatory* democracy as an instantiation of deliberative democracy. Here decisions are legitimate if they are open to contestation in forums and through procedures that are acceptable to all concerned *after* they are made (Pettit 1997: 183–200). This tends to encourage decisions to be made on the basis of publicly acceptable reasons and with enough consultation and participation to ensure that all the relevant arguments and considerations are on the table. It also requires a 'republic of reasons' in which decisions that have been made are open to debate and justification, and in which citizens have access to means of contestation, and forums that adjudicate contestations fairly.

In this conception, deliberative democracy is fundamentally about *permeability* of governance to people's reasons, values and stories. While most political theorists focus on decision-making by public (government) bodies, I have argued in Chapter 1 that any entity that exercises power must be subject to some level of democratic responsibility, and that this includes corporations. Marxist and feminist critics of traditional political theory have often pointed out how little it deals with unjust and undemocratic practices in the private spheres of market and family (e.g. Phillips 1991). The argument here is similar: democratic theory should pay as much attention to the justice of corporate exercises of power as to the exercise of power by nation-states. The catchphrase that democracy is where 'people obey just those laws that they give themselves' (Habermas 1996: 445–6) indicates that the central point is for every social actor to be both the subject and object of democratic governance, including corporate entities. In a deliberative version of democracy, it means that every social actor has the privilege and responsibility of 'citizenship', that is the ability to participate in or at least contest decisions that affect them, and the obligation to make their own decisions and actions subject to just that same input and/or contest. Classical civic republican conceptions of deliberative democracy made the scope of citizenship very narrow: at first, propertied males, later all males, and later still all those males and females who were not defined out of citizenship by reason of ethnicity, country of origin, criminal offences, and so on (Lister 1995). The implication of my conception is to make citizenship very broad – all those who are affected by, or who exercise, power in fact – including corporations (cf. Fraser's 1998 defence of republican elitism in corporate governance).

'Permeability' is not command and control in this conception (although command and control may be appropriate at certain points). Deliberative democracy is a very open, yet also demanding concept of democracy. It is *open* because the pivotal concern of deliberative democracy is simply to make sure deliberation occurs, whether it is by requiring disclosure of information (to spark debate or make informed action possible in the marketplace), process regulation (to require a corporation to go through a process of self-regulation without specifying the outcomes) or command and control. Deliberative democracy does not impose a particular conception of democratic institutions on any decision-making. Indeed, in most cases it will prefer to work indirectly or as cooperatively and persuasively as possible (the 'principle of parsimony' – Braithwaite and Pettit 1990: 79–80, 87; Parker 1999b: 48–55; Pettit 1997: 212–29) by putting stakeholders directly in a position to bargain with management decision-makers. Imposition closes off deliberation. A deliberative approach to democracy is free to recognize the integrity of self-governance processes, but it will ask them to justify themselves.

This makes deliberative democracy a *demanding* approach to democratic accountability. The ideal is that every decision is open to deliberation and/or contest at some level – whether it be through dialogue and respect between two lovers, constitutional review of government legislation in a supreme judicial body, administrative review of bureaucratic decision-making, or discussion and attempts to reach consensus decisions by the local parents and citizens association. In the case of corporations this may include anything from tax incentives (to encourage companies to have an internal deliberation about whether to take advantage of those incentives), to mandatory post hoc reporting of decisions (disclosure to allow external contestation of corporate decisions), to enforced introduction of a consumer complaints-handling function (to allow individual consumers to contest corporate actions), to command and control (imposition on the company of a decision that has been deliberated upon by the democratically elected legislature). Decisions about how to best promote deliberation will be contextually specific. (Chapters 8 and 9 consider the best techniques for improving the democratic accountability of corporations.)

This ideal is sympathetic with Habermas' (1996: 186–93, 430–46) ideal of deliberative democracy in the regulatory administrative functions of the state, in *Between Facts and Norms*. In a state burdened with a growing set of regulatory and administrative tasks, especially where government agencies (including regulators) must of necessity have 'neocorporatist' relations with large, powerful private organizations, 'the only thing that serves as a "palladium of liberty" against the growth of independent, illegitimate power is a suspicious, mobile, alert, and informed public sphere' (Habermas 1996: 441–2).

The model I propose gives the state a role in *facilitating* the permeability of private organizational systems and social power directly to civil society and the public sphere. Indeed, following and developing Habermas, I will argue that it is only in facilitating and coordinating this type of participation and permeability that the new regulatory state will find democratic legitimacy: Habermas sees the permeability of the 'political centre' (i.e. the parliamentary complex) to civil society and the public sphere as the only guarantors of legitimate law and regulation (Habermas 1996: 442). I propose that this must be extended. It is not only the political power of state law-making that must be permeable to deliberative democracy, but also corporate political power.

In practice, however, business organizations frequently build walls around themselves that isolate them from external social values and protect the pursuit of short-term profit from challenge. Figure 2.1 illustrates how business values can dominate in interactions with the outside world, through non-dialogic communication with stakeholders, through manipulating legal techniques in litigation, through attempting to capture regulators and buying influence with political elites (see Chapter 6). In this picture the business of short-term profit, standard practices and operating procedures, and/or the management priorities of the organization dominate the personal values of individual mem-

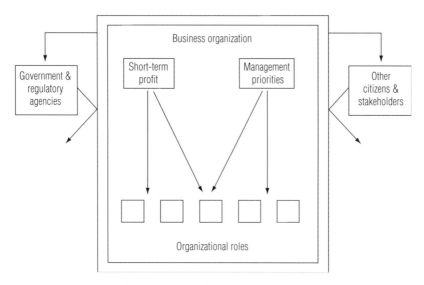

FIGURE 2.1 The dominating business organization

bers of the organization, and also dominate in interactions with external agencies of government and stakeholders that seek to influence business with external values. To use Habermas' (1987) terminology, the business 'system' dominates the 'lifeworld' of individual employees and managers. It defines their concerns and normative judgments as irrelevant.

This is a picture of organizations that cannot be made democratically responsible. They refuse to allow values deliberated upon in external democratic processes to infiltrate the corporate shell, nor do they allow individuals within the organization to debate the organization's values and how they are pursued. Looking at the same problem from the other angle, in Teubner's terms (e.g. Teubner 1987; see also Black 2000, 2001), the normative systems of law, or of other stakeholders, fail to permeate and democratize business systems. Rather, those external values have an effect, but an indirect and unpredictable one. The reverberations felt within the organization are mere echoes of what might have been if corporate management had reached out to truly engage with external concerns.

An alternative is illustrated in Figure 2.2. In this picture the business organization is permeable to external values from regulators and other external stakeholders. Individual members of the organization are encouraged to bring to bear values that come from social bonds other

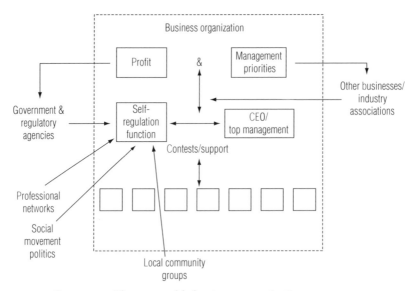

FIGURE 2.2 The permeable business organization

than their organizational role on their organizational conduct. Here the business is permeable to all the debate and deliberation over conflicting values envisaged by the ideal of democracy. There is a two-way flow of information and action: corporate management is drawn out of its bunker and employees' and stakeholders' values and concerns are invited in. This picture does not ignore the likelihood of conflict between business values and practices and other values, or between the values expressed by different regulators and/or social movements or communities (cf. Figure 5.1 in Chapter 5, which sets out the naive hope of some compliance professionals that they can easily harmonize and accommodate compliance and business). There need be no assumption here that there are some 'community values' with which everyone agrees. Rather, there is a plurality of values which different nations and different corporations will balance in different ways. The important thing is to democratize the corporation through permeability to the values debate, not to make all companies uniform.

The compliance system, as an internal management mechanism, can be central in pushing down the barriers to allow both shared and contested values to be embraced through engagement with social movements, media, regulators, courts and law. A compliance or self-regulation function can facilitate this by monitoring and identifying where corporate values and practices conflict with other values. It then notifies and activates the business unit, top management, regulators and broader democratic communities to decide how to resolve that conflict in each circumstance.

In order to propose institutions for realizing this integrative ideal of corporate citizenship, we must consider the empirical possibilities. This book is based on the hypothesis that corporations do have an inherent capacity to manage their own social responsibility. Furthermore the impulse to democracy will inevitably concern itself with corporate power (see, for example, Klein 2000). Therefore there must be incipient, at least partial, examples of the corporate institutionalization of social responsibility to be discovered from which we can learn. The next section considers empirical studies of corporate self-regulation that show just such an incipient possibility for corporate social responsiveness. This is a basis for moving forward.

WHEN DO COMPANIES BEST INSTITUTIONALIZE RESPONSIBILITY?

What are the empirical conditions in which companies are most likely to institutionalize integrity? There are a relatively small number of scholarly studies that identify factors both external *and internal* to organizations that are related to the success of self-regulatory and compliance initiatives at the level of the individual organization.[1]

Table 2.1 is a summary of these studies and the factors identified in each as important. This summary of results should be treated with some caution: the studies evaluate compliance and self-regulation programs according to varying and sometimes subjective criteria. (Indeed, one of the arguments of Chapter 9 will be about the need for the 'meta'-evaluation of different evaluation criteria and mechanisms.) There are also many methodological difficulties in this area, including the difficulty of gaining access inside organizations, a lack of measures for evaluating quality, and an over-abundance of self-assessment rather than independent measures of performance. In effect most studies take best practice as a starting-point for evaluating success because it is still relatively rare to find companies with thorough compliance practices, let alone an objectively excellent level of compliance. The studies summarized in Table 2.1 use a variety of different methodologies (including surveys, before/after case studies, qualitative interviews, site visits and secondary data) and different evaluative criteria in a variety of areas, yet still converge on a few key factors.

TABLE 2.1 *Summary of empirical studies of self-regulatory/compliance initiatives and factors identified as leading to success*

Study	Sample and methodology	Factors identified
J. Braithwaite 1984 Crime in the Pharmaceutical Industry	In-depth interviews with 131 senior executives in pharmaceutical companies in the USA, Australia, UK, Mexico and Guatemala as well as with public interest activists, regulators and ex-regulators.	1. CEO actively involved in setting compliance and social responsibility goals for the organisation. 2. Standard operating procedures establish controls which make violation of the law difficult. 3. Compliance group with organisational muscle. 4. History of effectively sanctioning employees who violate standard operating procedures designed to prevent crime. (page 362)
Taylor 1984 Environmental Impact Statements in Public Bureaucracies	In-depth interviews with environmental impact assessment officers and others.	1. A group inside the organisation committed to the value. 2. Goals clear enough to provide guidance for action [from regulators]. 3. Autonomy and power for this group so they can protect the value. 4. Outside support for the inside group's goals [public interest groups, litigation, environmental agencies]. (page 252)
J. Braithwaite 1985 Coal Mine Safety	The 5 mines with the best safety records in USA. In-depth interviews and site visits.	1. Give a lot of informal clout and top management backing to their safety inspectors. 2. Make sure that clearly defined accountability for safety performance is imposed on line managers. 3. Have mostly formal (though sometimes informal) programs for ensuring safety training and supervision (by foremen in particular) is never neglected, safety problems are quickly communicated to those who can act on them, and that a plan of attack exists for dealing with all identified hazards. (page 65)

DiMento 1986 Environmental Regulation of Business	Case studies/60 interviews with executives and small businesspeople about firm's reactions to a charge of non-compliance or enforcement action, and interviews with government lawyers. Case studies of 30 other cases of non-compliance using secondary data. Survey of 44 enforcement officials.	1. Enforcement: especially how potential sanctions affect firm's cost–benefit calculations. 2. Communicating the law: regulation must be understood by business. 3. The actors: (a) traits of public agencies – strong/weak reputation, tenure, professionalism of officers, agency structure and organisation; (b) business – size and complexity, corporate culture; (c) environmental interest groups – inform business and regulators of citizen concerns.
Rees 1988 Occupational Safety and Health Cooperative Compliance Experiment	Case study of 2 construction companies before and after joining California OSHA cooperative compliance experiment, and of all 4 companies in program after joining.	1. Safety personnel who were already part of safety management movement, who were strongly committed to safety goals, whose authority and autonomy within organization had grown and developed over time, whose base of social support had expanded (via new reporting systems, accountability mechanisms and avenues of participation). 2. Involvement of labour in site safety programs through labour-management committees.

(page 231)

TABLE 2.1 (cont.) *Summary of empirical studies of self-regulatory/compliance initiatives and factors identified as leading to success*

Study	Sample and methodology	Factors identified
J. Braithwaite 1993 Equal Employment Opportunity Programs	Assessment of procedural (development of policy as required by legislation) and substantive (actual implementation of practices accommodating to women in the workforce) compliance with Australian affirmative action legislation which requires companies to develop, implement and report on implementation of EEO policies. Analysis of reports, survey/interviews with EEO officers and corporate executives, and survey of management/ industrial relations practices.	Procedural and substantive compliance were highly correlated, but: 1. Procedural compliance was more likely: (a) in business units in which unions were active on EEO matters; (b) in business units which see the requirements of the legislation as reasonable and the basic eight steps required as desirable and practicable; (c) in companies which viewed their relationship with government as a 'social bargain'. 2. Factors that were strongly associated with substantive compliance in some cases were: (a) a strong informational basis for business to comply; (b) ideological commitment to EEO on the part of management; (c) a 'top-down' social network between EEO officers as change agents and the Affirmative Action Agency; and (d) a 'bottom-up' social network of female workers who were interested in EEO and EEO officers who devoted time and effort to their needs, with EEO officers also networking with other EEO personnel outside their own companies.
Rees 1994 Nuclear Safety Self-Regulation	In-depth interviews with industry and regulatory informants.	1. Community of shared fate forged out of Three Mile Island accident and recognition of shared interdependence of operators in nuclear energy industry. 2. Peer review program combined regulatory staff with commitment to safety and staff from civilian nuclear industry. 3. CEO personal attention to safety or public shame. 4. Self-regulatory body (INPO) backed by government regulator (NRC). 5. Nuclear professionalism within industry.

Study	Method	Findings
Pastin and Brecto 1995 Ethics-Compliance Environment Assessment	Survey by Council of Ethical Organizations of 750 000 employees in 203 large US companies over five years; 660 000 usable surveys.	Factors correlated with a poor ethics-compliance environment: 1. Performance measurement/reward systems that attach financial incentives to behaviour inconsistent with ethical conduct and voluntary disclosure of compliance concerns. 2. Fear of retribution or reprisal by supervisors or higher-level managers for reporting apparently unethical or illegal conduct.
Haines 1997 Management Responses to Worker Deaths	Case studies and in-depth interviews re corporate responses to all 15 deaths at multiple-employer worksites in 1987 in Victoria, Australia.	1. (a) Virtuous responses emanated from harmonising cultures (where safety and business success seen as compatible and safety integral part of success; input of unions, regulators and safety committees welcomed); (b) non-virtuous responses from blinkered cultures (dichotomised choices between safety and profit; safety initiatives perceived as threats; wary of regulators and unions). 2. Size bore strong relationship to culture and behaviour, with large organisations more likely to act in a virtuous manner. 3. Concerns about legal liability had potential to trigger considerable change within organisation, but not necessarily desirable change. 4. Increased competition was threat to virtue in long term, but virtuous organisations sought to use safety and quality assurance to harmonise conflicting imperatives. (pages 215–18)

TABLE 2.1 (cont.) *Summary of empirical studies of self-regulatory/compliance initiatives and factors identified as leading to success*

Study	Sample and methodology	Factors identified
Eyring and Stead 1998 Best Practice EEO Policies	1000 companies with over 200 employees in Houston (US area surveyed); 69 usable returns. Each company scored on their EEO performance according to 34 practices and also asked to describe their programs. Eleven companies identified as 'distinguished' and visited.	Five programs most commonly identified by distinguished companies: 1. Training/education programs for women. 2. Hiring/affirmative action programs. 3. Succession planning/identification of high-potential women. 4. Task forces/special committees. 5. Mentoring and networking programs. Ten practices most likely to be used by distinguished companies: 1. Taskforce re women's issues. 2. Clearly communicate goals for movement of women to managers in organisation. 3. Women represented on special taskforces. 4. Including women of colour in women's programs. 5. Including issues important to women on regular employee surveys. 6. Minority networks to provide support for women of colour. 7. Hold managers accountable for development of women through performance appraisal. 8. Systems in place for identifying high-potential women. 9. Facilitate movement of women into line positions. 10. Diversity awareness training for managers.

McCaffrey and Hart 1998	Analysis of New York Stock Exchange disciplinary actions 1990–96 and in-depth interviews with 34 compliance managers and legal advisers in 14 New York firms, and with 22 regulators.	1. External regulatory pressures and private litigation.
Compliance Systems in Broker-Dealer Firms		2. Priorities of top management.
		3. Technical and political skills of legal and compliance personnel.
		(page 173)

Note: Page numbers refer to direct or abridged quotes from the particular study cited in first column.

Table 2.2 summarizes the studies in terms of the five most frequently identified factors:

- management commitment
- external regulatory pressures
- internal compliance/self-regulation constituencies
- integration into operational procedures, appraisals
- interest group involvement/community opinion.

Management commitment

The studies summarized in Table 2.1 predominantly point to the importance of top-management commitment as the first factor for internal corporate compliance systems to be successful at self-regulation. For example, McCaffrey and Hart (1998: 174) find that 'the differences among firms reflect, more than any other factor, how strongly top management communicates that complying with the rules is one of the firm's core critical tasks'. From his research on coal mine safety, John Braithwaite (1985: 61) repeats the lesson he learnt from one safety manager, 'you can't cookbook safety'; there is no magic formula for implementing an effective compliance system. Yet each of the companies, in different ways, exhibited 'a corporate message that top management perceives cutting corners on safety to achieve production goals as not in the interests of the corporation' (J. Braithwaite 1985: 61).

The studies also make it clear that this does not mean that senior executives merely mouth support for compliance, but that they are actively involved in setting compliance goals and reviewing performance (see J. Braithwaite 1984; cf. Clinard 1983). One vivid example of a program initiative that aimed at and secured top-management commitment was Rees' (1994) study of the self-regulatory US Institute of Nuclear Power Operators (INPO) nuclear safety regime. He found that one of the key factors leading to its success was the fact that senior executives would be held accountable in front of their peers for the safety inspection ratings their facilities received. This occurred in a private meeting in which all the executives from all facilities saw what rating each received, and in which one or two senior executives would have to confess to a mistake that had been made in the past and what they had learnt from that.

TABLE 2.2 *Factors most commonly identified in studies as leading to success of compliance/self-regulatory programs*

Studies	Management commitment	External regulatory pressures	Internal compliance constituencies	Integration into operating procedures, appraisals	Interest group involvement/ community opinion	Other factors
J. Braithwaite 1984	Yes (1)	Separate detailed discussion	Yes (3)	Yes (2, 4)	–	
Taylor 1984	–	Yes (2, 4)	Yes (1, 3)	–	Yes (4)	
J. Braithwaite 1985	–	Separate detailed discussion	Yes (1)	Yes (2, 3)	–	Size and complexity; culture
DiMento 1986		Yes (1, 2, 3a)			Yes (3c)	
Rees 1988	–	–	Yes (1)	–	Yes (2)	–
V. Braithwaite 1993	Yes (1b, 2b)		Yes (1c)	–	Yes (1a, 2d)	Information; social bargain
Rees 1994	Yes (3)	Yes (4)	Yes (5)	–	Yes (1)	Peer review program
Pastin and Brecto 1995	–	–	–	Yes (1, 2)	–	–

TABLE 2.2 (cont.) *Factors most commonly identified in studies as leading to success of compliance/self-regulatory programs*

Studies	Management commitment	External regulatory pressures	Internal compliance constituencies	Integration into operating procedures, appraisals	Interest group involvement/ community opinion	Other factors
Haines 1997	?? (1)	Yes (3)	–	?? (1)	–	Harmonizing vs dichotomizing management philosophy; size; competition
Eyring and Stead 1998	–	–	–	Yes (all factors)	–	–
McCaffrey and Hart 1998	Yes (2)	Yes (1)	Yes (3)	–	–	–

Note: Numbers in brackets refer to the factors identified in Table 2.1.

External regulatory pressures

The second factor that is mentioned in almost every study is the existence and character of external regulatory pressures, including not only the existence of law on the books but also changes in regulatory enforcement and inspections policy, and sometimes also private litigation. For example, McCaffrey and Hart (1998: 173) found that 'all the major broker-dealer firms attend more to legal and compliance matters now than they did five years ago because of greater regulatory scrutiny, private lawsuits and arbitration'. Taylor (1984) points to the need for external regulatory pressures to back up internal compliance constituencies. Rees (1988, 1994) and Taylor (1984) identify the background threat of stricter government regulation, if self-regulatory or internal compliance schemes fail, as critical to success. Similarly Haines (1997) saw the threat of liability as capable of prompting considerable change but cautions that it is not necessarily helpful change.

In a series of studies mentioned in Chapter 1 (and further discussed in Chapters 8 and 9), the particular styles and character of regulatory design, monitoring and enforcement, not just apparent 'toughness', have been found to make a significant difference to compliance outcomes (e.g. Bardach and Kagan 1982). For example, in Braithwaite's studies (e.g. 1984, 1985) the character of regulation that is most likely to lead to successful compliance programs is discussed in depth separately to the discussion of the internal factors that indicate better compliance programs. Not just the existence but also the nature and strategy of regulation makes a difference.

Self-regulation personnel

While management commitment and external regulatory pressure are significant, the studies show that without the linchpin of an internal compliance constituency, little is achieved. Rees' (1988) evaluation of the California OSHA experiment with the Cooperative Compliance Program between 1979 and 1984 found that the growth of safety management professionalism was crucial to compliance with regulatory goals. The program authorized labour-management safety committees on seven large construction sites to assume many of OSHA's regulatory responsibilities (such as conducting inspections and investigating complaints), while OSHA ceased routine compliance inspections. During the program, accident rates ranged from one-third lower to five times lower than comparable company projects, and the satisfaction of workers, management and government participants with the program was high. The evaluation found that this approach succeeded mainly because it strengthened the existing job site safety programs in ways that traditional regulatory strategies could not. The voluntary job site safety programs in turn had been promoted and implemented by safety management professionals, a professional specialization promoted by the American Society of Safety Engineers. The safety management professionals within the companies also acted as go-betweens and facilitated the labour-management and regulator-management communication necessary for the program to succeed (Rees 1988: 92, 98–9, 108). In smaller companies, like Haines' (1997) Australian construction contractors, a 'virtuous' general or safety manager may act as the internal compliance constituency.

McCaffrey and Hart (1998) concluded from their study of self-regulation in the US securities industry that the institutionalization of regulatory occupations within industry (in this case, financial compliance officers) is one of the main conditions in which self or 'shared' regulation is most likely to be effective so long as the law strengthens the position of the compliance staff. Valerie Braithwaite (1993) evaluated both substantive and procedural compliance with the Australian Affirmative Action Act, which requires companies to develop an equal opportunity policy for women, set objectives, monitor them and submit a report on their progress. She found that commitment to human resources management correlated highly with both procedural compliance with the eight steps required by the legislation, and with the more substantive compliance measure of reported implementation of practices accommodating to women. The degree of professionalism of EEO officers, especially their professional networking with other EEO professionals and with the EEO agency, was also positively correlated with procedural and substantive compliance with the requirements of the regulation (V. Braithwaite 1992).

Similarly in a study of corporate compliance with US civil rights laws, Edelman (1990) found that an important source of diffusion of due process protections was the professionalized practices of personnel officers and the establishment of personnel departments. These personnel officers saw compliance as part of their professional function and therefore provided a direct channel through which models of employee rights implementation could enter the organization and created an internal constituency for the elaboration and enforcement of employee rights. In a completely different situation, hospital neo-natal intensive care units, Heimer (1996: 37) concludes that the law's shadow is likely to be 'densest' within organizations when it 'largely coincides with the shadow cast by professional bodies'. She goes on to argue that 'professions are simultaneously the organizational participants responsible for altering the scripts or routines of organizations and the carriers of legitimacy'. They legitimize organizations by acting as 'sentinels' tracking the organization's external environment, including legal and regulatory messages, and adapting organizational systems to respond to those messages appropriately.

The studies summarized in Table 2.1 emphasize, however, that it is not the mere existence of a self-regulation function or compliance constituency within an organization that helps lead to the success of the self-regulation, but the 'autonomy and power' (Taylor 1984), 'clout' (J. Braithwaite 1984: 359) or organizational muscle given to this constituency by senior management, by the habits of decision-making practices and by employees in general (McCaffrey and Hart 1998: 173).

Integration into everyday operations

Those studies that have looked in depth at the internal functioning of companies in response to responsibility issues generally point to the importance of integration of social and legal responsibilities into operating procedures, everyday decision-making and functioning, ordinary performance appraisal systems and reward systems. These are the most sophisticated indicators of success of a compliance program. For example, John Braithwaite's (1985) study of the companies with the best mine safety records found that important factors of success were developing programs for safety training and performance, clearly defining safety performance requirements for line managers and holding them accountable for their performance. Haines (1997) identifies a 'harmonizing' management philosophy that is oriented towards putting safety and business together.

This fourth factor is generally the direct output of internal compliance constituencies' work. It is here we ought to be able to see the best measures of success. Yet it is here too that organizational cultures and structures are so different that evaluation is difficult and perfect recipes impossible to predict. Studies aimed at a management/practitioner audience also tend to focus on these sorts of factors (e.g. Pastin and Brecto 1995, who see it as important for all management to follow through on compliance/ethics concerns by including them in performance measurement systems and by not retaliating for reports of unethical or illegal conduct).

Public opinion

Few studies look at the issue of the extent to which companies feel community pressure as a factor in the implementation and effectiveness of self-regulatory programs. However, as we shall see, it can be quite crucial. One of the most striking studies is Hoffman's (1997) research on corporate environmentalism in the US chemical and petroleum industries. (His work is discussed further in Chapter 3.) Hoffman found that overall corporate expenditure on environmental issues and the implementation of environmental management systems over thirty years followed the rises and falls in public concern (as evidenced by media articles) about environmental issues, rather than waxing and waning with government policy. In particular, even as the Reagan government rolled back environmental regulation and enforcement, public concern rose and so did corporate concern with environmentalism (1997: 144–5).

Taylor (1984) mentions the significance of public interest groups' interest and involvement in the environmental impact statement (EIS) process, and DiMento (1986) sees community groups as an important independent source of information to both regulators and business about environmental issues. For Rees (1994), the success of INPO depended in part on the bad publicity given to the Three Mile Island accident and therefore industry belief that public opinion would turn completely against them if they did not effectively self-regulate each other. Thus, public opinion or social movement politics can create a climate in which management commitment is more likely to arise in response. The involvement of affected communities and stakeholders can also improve the quality of the program. For example, Valerie Braithwaite (1993) found that women employees were rarely included in consultation about EEO policies under the Affirmative Action legislation but when they were the program was likely to be better, and Rees (1988) found that labour involvement in cooperative compliance programs was also important.

Other factors

Most studies of factors affecting the implementation of compliance programs indicate that size is a significant factor. In the previous chapter we saw that the data on implementation show that larger companies are

more likely than smaller ones to have implemented compliance programs. Some of the factors that lead towards low compliance particularly affect smaller businesses, such as the complexity of regulation and
the costs of compliance with regulation (Genn 1993; Moses and Savage
1994). In their analysis of motivations for implementing occupational
risk management in large UK companies, Ashby and Diacon (1996: 241)
refine this analysis a little by finding that it is capital intensity (i.e. ratio
of net tangible assets to number of employees) rather than pure size that
is likely to be correlated positively, with companies attaching importance to occupational risk management.

A MODEL FOR CORPORATE SOCIAL RESPONSIVENESS

What, then, can we hypothesize about when a compliance program
might be successful at institutionalizing good corporate citizenship in
an organization? How do the five main factors identified above – management commitment, external regulatory pressures, compliance personnel, integration of responsibilities into company procedures, and
public opinion – inter-relate to explain why and with what success companies implement self-regulation systems? The key is in understanding
how each factor pushes external social and legal responsibility issues
into a higher place on formal and informal internal corporate decision-
making agendas. Each of the five factors increases the permeability of
internal corporate processes to external values and/or builds capacity
for companies to respond appropriately.

Two researchers of corporate responses to environmental issues
have suggested that there are three phases in the managerial process of
dealing with dilemmas raised by social issues (Chaganti and Phatak
1983: 187):[2]

1. The commitment to respond.
2. The acquisition of specialized skills and knowledge.
3. The institutionalization of purpose.

The beginning of each phase represents a strategic decision point at
which the opportunity for social responsibility issues to couple with
organizational processes occurs.[3] The three phases also correspond
roughly to three of the factors consistently identified as important in the
studies discussed above. The remaining two – external regulatory pressure and public opinion – can be applied at each of the three phases.

The first phase is the *commitment to respond* which is indicated by
the interest and involvement of the CEO in making statements about

the issue and setting aside resources to address it. This corresponds with *management commitment* as an important factor in explaining compliance program success.

The second phase is the *acquisition of specialized skills and knowledge* in which the corporation acquires the know-how and personnel to deal with the issue. This process often means that specialist functions and policies are set up to deal with compliance or social responsibility issues. Specialist employees are appointed, such as environmental managers, EEO officers, or compliance professionals, and are empowered to put the relevant issue on the agenda and to formulate procedures and policies to deal with it. This corresponds to the existence of *self-regulation personnel* within the organization and their responsibility for a compliance policy.

The third is the *institutionalization of purpose* in which the policy is made an integral part of corporate objectives, standard operating procedures are revised to make responsibility issues a part of everybody's job, and reward systems are changed so that managers are motivated to take responsibility issues into account. This corresponds to the factor of *integration of compliance responsibilities into procedures, operations, reward and performance review systems*.

These phases do not occur as a purely spontaneous internal measure within the organization. Rather, they are usually a response to external as well as internal pressures and can be shaped by external influences. Each of these phases in corporate responses to responsibility issues represents a critical point at which (a) external values can have some impact on internal corporate workings through the agency of regulators, public interest groups, the media and, most significantly in many instances, compliance professionals; and (b) internal management can make a difference to the accomplishment of social values through improved decision-making, rectification of wrongs, and action to improve outcomes for stakeholders.

Thus, the first phase – management commitment to respond to a particular social issue – can be prompted by external factors such as regulatory action through new regulations, a tougher enforcement policy or a particular regulatory incident, by private litigation (or the threat of it), by changes in public opinion and social movement politics and by modelling what competitors are doing.

At the second phase, the appointment of a specialist self-regulation function may be a response to regulatory suggestions or requirements, or copy-catting competitors. The self-regulation professional himself or herself usually acts as a conduit of information, skills and concerns from external groups such as regulators, public interest groups, and communities of professional experts that significantly shape the way in which the company handles legal compliance and social responsibility.

The self-regulation professionals within the organization will also have a big influence at the third phase by bringing in ideas and values about how self-regulation should be institutionalized. In this phase too, regulators, public interest groups and private management consultants, auditors and verifiers for groups such as standardization organizations have an influence through inspections, audits and verification systems. Employees, union representatives and local community representatives may also have an opportunity to input their personal or social values through involvement in decision-making processes and consultative bodies.

This theory of how values can be institutionalized within corporate decision-making processes and cultures can be diagrammatically represented as something that looks a bit like a fish skeleton (see Figure 2.3). The central spine of the fish represents the internal workings of the company (including formal and informal governance processes, standard operating procedures, ingrained culture, management systems, disciplinary processes, quality controls, and so on). Along the spine of the fish are the nodes at which it is strategic to incorporate regulatory values, ethical considerations or corporate responsibility issues into decision-making and internal corporate reform. In this simple diagram these are the three phases identified above. As we shall see in Chapters 8 and 9, after the third phase should be a further phase of evaluation of existing compliance functions, policies and procedures, either as part of an internal review or in response to the discovery of a problem which becomes a public issue through publicity or regulatory scrutiny. This can lead back to CEO commitment to respond and start the cycle of phases again.

The ribs represent the different external pressures that can be brought to bear on the internal workings of the company. These nodes of influence affect whether and how legal and ethical values are considered. 'Compliance-oriented' regulators and community groups will strategically focus monitoring and accountability on these nodes, as will effective local community groups or other stakeholders. The central spine, the internal workings of the company, is the receptor of these pressures, but it is not passive. There is a process of dialogue and deliberation in which management only receives the message and moves on to the next stage if it makes sure that its systems can actively engage

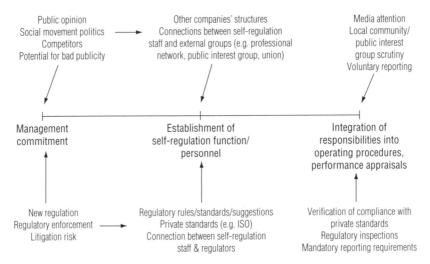

FIGURE 2.3 Institutionalization of social and legal responsibilities in organizations

with broader concerns. Compliance/self-regulation professionals will be key agents of this active engagement. They will both bear and exert pressures at all these points. Thus, there is an interaction effect whereby management commitment and external regulatory pressure can boost the effectiveness of self-regulation professionals, and vice versa.

CONCLUSION

This ideal does not imply an ever-expanding legalistic colonization of regulatory compliance over business decisions. Rather, the goal is that organizations should be effective self-regulators within the context of democratic deliberation over competing values and regulatory requirements. This may imply the need for dedicated staff to ensure this goal is met – that is, a self-regulation function. However, it may not be a legal compliance function that has the responsibility for ensuring this happens. At present, compliance units, or units like them, show a particular potential to be a focus of democratic self-regulatory activity within organizations. But it could just as easily be a business ethics unit, a social responsibility committee, a board audit committee, or a more traditional management function such as quality or risk management. The significant thing is that this function not simply behave as a mini adversarial regulator within the company. Rather, it should facilitate internal deliberation and self-criticism that takes into account environmental factors and values other than profitability and material considerations.

The success of corporate regulation depends crucially on a corporation's ability to institutionalize responsibility. This is a complex, and in some ways unnatural, task for organizational bureaucracies. In any particular situation their success will be the function of a nexus of management priorities, the permeation of legal and community values through legal incentives and regulatory pressures, the existence of empowered internal compliance constituencies, and their success at incorporating legal and social responsibilities into internal management. The following two chapters, Chapters 3 and 4, examine the external influences and corporate dynamics by which initial management commitment to compliance or self-regulatory programs are prompted. Chapters 5 and 7 will be concerned with the next phase: the acquisition of specialized skills and knowledge to institutionalize responsibility within the organization, specifically the role of compliance or self-regulation professionals. Chapter 6 identifies some of the pathologies of compliance systems that arise along the way. Chapter 8 moves on to the ongoing institutionalization of responsibility within the corporation, and its continuous improvement.

3 | Motivating top-management commitment to self-regulation

Top-management commitment is the first decision point for successful self-regulation system implementation. But what prompts this commitment in the first place? Compliance staff frequently discuss the need to make a 'business case' for corporate commitment to compliance to ensure management attention, interest and support.[1] The first section of this chapter juxtaposes the 'business case' for self-regulation with the deterrence theory view that organizations will only commit to comply to the extent that it is in their immediate self-interest to do so. As the second section of this chapter shows, both compliance managers and empirical deterrence research find that management motivations for compliance are more nuanced than the simple deterrence model allows. The final section examines more closely the multiplicity of motivations for the cultivation of leadership in good corporate citizenship by looking at early participants in a voluntary program for reducing greenhouse gas emissions: the Australian Greenhouse Challenge program.

Chapter 4 builds on this analysis to pose a general explanation for how compliance leadership and modelling explain the diffusion of compliance system implementation. As we shall see in this chapter and the next, top management most frequently focus on compliance when their attention is captured by an actual or potential crisis of publicity or litigation. Top-management attention opens a window of opportunity in which the corporation might become committed to compliance leadership, or at least to copying other compliance leaders. It is what happens when this window opens that determines whether there is ongoing implementation of an effective self-regulation system and, ultimately, the institutionalization of active, good corporate citizenship.

THE 'BUSINESS CASE' AND THE CASE FOR DETERRENCE

The business case

Most inhouse compliance managers are very aware of the general business opinion that 'the compliance function does not produce anything but only consumes company resources' (compliance lawyer, AssurOz). For external compliance consultants, it is hard work to sell compliance services to clients who see all legal services as 'grudge purchases' (Adviser Three). Inhouse compliance departments are often seen as the 'ministry for stopping business' (Compliance Manager at Alpine Insurance; see also Spangler 1986: 77 on the 'Department of Profit Prevention'). As a result, many compliance managers devote considerable attention to attempting to demonstrate that good compliance is good business. Weait (1994: 383) concluded from his study of compliance officers in London financial institutions that 'getting people to comply as a matter of principle ... means identifying to some extent with the dominant profit motive of the firm' (see McCaffrey and Hart 1998: 157–8 for a similar Wall Street perspective).

On the whole, compliance managers appeal to management concerns by seeking to convince them of 'the business case' for a good compliance program.[2] Consider the imagery used in the following list of professional development seminar topics for compliance professionals in Australia during 1997 and 1998:

- 'How to sell compliance to the board.'
- 'Selling to the board – using examples which the board can relate to.'
- 'Using compliance to enhance your business – the benefits of a positive compliance system.'
- 'How to sell compliance as a benefit not a burden.'
- 'The business case for compliance.'

There is an underlying reality to compliance managers' business case arguments. Compliance managers, regulators and scholars have assembled much evidence that good compliance can be good business in some circumstances. The Anti-Discrimination Board of New South Wales' *Anti-Discrimination and Equal Employment Opportunity Guidelines*

(1997) estimates the average cost of sorting out a relatively serious discrimination or harassment grievance within the organization at $35 000 and $50 000. The senior EEO officer at Aussie Dollars uses inhouse seminars deliberately to frighten senior management into a realization of how much harassment and discrimination problems can cost by quoting the recent very public and drawn-out sexual harassment case at Trustus (Australia) that is reputed to have cost $650 000 in damages and other costs combined. Other interviewees sold sexual harassment policies as a positive contributor to corporate competitiveness through the ability to compete to be 'the workplace of choice for keen, productive staff' (Good as Gold Australia). For occupational health and safety practitioners, 'total cost' methodology calculates lost productivity and management and staff downtime spent dealing with injury and illness (e.g. Hopkins 1995: 58–9). Some have developed accounting systems that can trace and quantify the 'value added' that corporate occupational safety and health units provide in prevention of injuries and accidents and maintenance of a healthy workforce (Mathews 1997; Oxenburgh 1991).

Michael Porter of Harvard Business School has been the leading economist proponent of the view that there are considerable opportunities for companies to innovate to add value through their environmental management systems. He shows how environmental improvement can benefit resource productivity both through process and product benefits. Potential process benefits include material savings resulting from re-use, or recycling, of production inputs, increases in process yields, less downtime through more careful monitoring and maintenance, better utilization of by-products, conversion of waste into valuable forms, lower energy consumption, and improvements in the product as a by-product of process control. Potential product benefits include higher quality, more consistent products, lower product costs (for instance, from material substitution), lower packaging costs, more efficient resource use, safer products, lower net costs of product disposal to customers, higher product resale and scrap value (Porter and van der Linde 1995: 126).

A taskforce of the World Business Council for Sustainable Development (WBCSD), made up of representatives from over fifty major companies (including Monsanto, Unilever, Johnson & Johnson and Sony), is working on common indicators for eco-efficiency and a framework for reporting them. This work leverages from the efforts of the Global Reporting Initiative, the ISO 14000 series and others attempting to harmonize indicators of the quality and extent of environmental management. The WBCSD eco-efficiency project links environmental indicators with indicators of economic success, and sees environmental efficiency as inextricably linked to business efficiency and performance (see Keffer and Lehni 1999). Similarly, the Global Environment Management Initiative (a non-profit organization set up by several very large US companies to promote environmental health and safety system excellence) report on metrics that environmental managers in their member companies have developed to demonstrate the value of environmental programs to management and shareholders in terms of income, savings and cost avoidance. For example, one DuPont subsidiary calculates the costs of spill cleanup, remediation, waste disposal, and water and air pollution control in cents per barrel of refined product, and seeks to achieve a decrease over time through spending money on the environmental program (GEMI 1998: 14–16).

An interviewee at a major European car manufacturing company illustrated well the importance of 'eco-efficiency' in practice. After describing the basics of the environmental management system for which he was responsible, he commented, 'We don't just do these things because we want to be more environmental. We want to get a competitive advantage and a more cost effective process.' He then went on to describe a process in the company in which environmental engineers and others were encouraged to think about environmental problems and ways to solve them, but the decision about which investments in improved environmental performance to make would be made on the basis of economics. He saw the WBCSD pilot study on eco-efficiency indicators as a very important initiative for his company to 'get the communication bridge between experts and management' linking environmental performance and general performance so that decision-making on environmental initiatives could be coordinated into general decision-making.

Consumer protection compliance is particularly amenable to a convincing sales pitch, since it easily translates into keeping consumers satisfied with the quality of service and products offered to them, as well as avoiding legal penalties and costs. The Australian Society of Consumer Affairs Professionals in Business (SOCAP) explicitly embraces the philosophy that what is good for the consumer is also good for the bottom line. It commissioned a study of consumer complaints-handling mechanisms in Australian industry and a survey of consumer attitudes towards them and found that where consumers were satisfied or more than satisfied with the way in which their complaints were handled, they were much more likely to repurchase than if they did not complain, or were dissatisfied or merely 'mollified' by how the complaint was handled (TARP 1995a, 1995b). Indeed, where complaint handling exceeded consumer expectations, the consumer was almost as likely to repurchase as if there had never been a problem (TARP 1995a: 18). According to members of the association, this data was very effective at creating much interest among larger companies in improving their consumer complaint-handling functions.

Derber (1998: 227) cites a body of research that 'supports the notion ... that a high-road corporate strategy in which companies work fairly with unions and treat the community and the environment respectfully – can be profitable, and often more profitable than low-road strategies'. A number of pilot investment funds or share indices testing the performance of socially screened investment funds have been set up and shown promising results (e.g. Joly *c.* 1997; Sauer 1997; Waddock et al. 1998). (However, it is by no means clear that corporate social responsibility is always profitable. Chapter 4 will consider more ambivalent studies.)

The corporation as amoral calculator

Talk about the 'business case' for compliance makes an implicit distinction between the business and the moral, ethical or social cases for compliance. The prominence of the 'business case' in their thinking suggests that compliance managers might see the primary motivation for managers' self-regulation commitment as a rational calculation about the possible costs of being caught in non-compliance versus the benefits of a breach. Compliance managers continually come up against the reality that top management might accept compliance in principle but do not see it as worthwhile to pursue self-regulation excellence with commitment because there are no profits in it:

> The biggest challenge in this area [sexual harassment] is getting the most senior level of management to take a stand that it is against the values of the bank. We're yet to do that properly ... They are very business case focused. At the end of the day in this area, you can't point to X% return ... While they will say that it is important to do the right thing, in reality they will focus more on bad debts. (Banksafe Australasia)

As the EEO officer at Pets & Health discovered when she hired a feminist consultant to train senior managers, it can be 'pretty disastrous' to push the 'feminist thing'. A more subtle approach must be taken to winning commitment: 'I feel very passionately that you can't push it as a feminist issue but have to see it as a good for business issue'.

Regulators and regulatory scholars also distinguish between potential motivations for obeying regulatory rules when they distinguish between 'compliance' and 'deterrence' approaches to regulatory enforcement. For example, Friedrichs (1996: 284) distinguishes 'compliance', which uses persuasion and cooperation, from 'deterrence', which involves prosecution and punishment (see also Baldwin et al. 1998: 18; Hawkins 1984; Hopkins 1995: 431–2; Reiss 1984). The term 'compliance' is used by the scholars here in a way that is too narrow and can therefore be confusing. They use 'compliance' to refer to a particular approach to securing compliance that relies primarily on persuasion and cooperation, rather than on sanctions and punishment. I use 'compliance' in a much broader sense throughout this book to apply to corporate accomplishment of regulatory objectives, whatever the enforcement or other regulatory strategies used to achieve it.

The deterrence approach assumes that corporate management will only do 'the right thing' to the extent it is in their self-interest to do so. For example, Pearce and Tombs (1990, 1997, 1998) argue that since all corporations have profit maximization as their main goal, they will always be 'amoral calculators' (Kagan and Scholz 1984) that only ever comply with regulatory requirements when the penalties are heavy enough to ensure their calculations come up with the correct answer. Law and economics theorists (see Ogus 1994: 90–2; see also Becker 1968; Stigler 1970) see compliance as the outcome of an equation: the benefits of non-compliance versus the probability of being discovered and punished, and the severity of the penalty.

At the 'compliance' end of the spectrum, Bardach and Kagan take the view, on the basis of largely anecdotal and unsystematic evidence, in their influential *Going by the Book* that 'good and bad apples are intermixed in the regulatory population' (1982: 66) and that 'the preponderance of regulated enterprises usually are good apples'. They argue that market pressure, legal liability and regulatory goals coincide so that compliance staff 'can use the threat of inspectors' visits to push for adherence to regulation; and a relatively small number of well-publicized severe punishments for regulatory noncompliance act as a sufficient deterrent' (1982: 162; see also Hopkins 1995: 77). In Kagan and Scholz's terms (1984: 67), most business organizations act as 'political citizens'. They are 'ordinarily inclined to comply with the law, partly because of belief in the rule of law, partly as a matter of long-term self-interest'. But their commitment is contingent on their own views as to proper public policy and business conduct, so that some law-breaking results from principled disagreement with regulatory rules and practices.

However, the compliance/deterrence distinction does not stand up to empirical examination. Nor does it reflect the practical experience of compliance managers. As the following quotation illustrates, for many compliance managers making the 'business case' means performing a finely nuanced balancing act of appeal to different motivations in different situations in order to secure the attention and commitment of top management to complying with the law:

> The manager shouldn't just be thinking of their selfish concerns, but thinking of other people and they should do that because (1) it's right and (2) it's good for business, because if you end up in court it costs a lot. So you have to move from social justice to business concerns. If you put up hard figures of how it could affect them, then they are more inclined to listen. You see them becoming more interested. That means both showing them that harassment and other problems do occur and cases do go to court, and giving them the dollar figures of what it costs. So that their unit is not just spending money. Some people will respond very quickly to social justice and others will only respond to the big stick of the law telling them they must behave lawfully. So you have to very carefully judge your audience and decide quickly what approach to take and then manage the debate. (Aussie Dollars)

This compliance manager designs redundancy into her advocacy of compliance. She appeals to what is 'right' as well as what is 'good for business'; she uses the dollar figures of what problems cost and manipulates the shame that people feel when their organization is involved in a court case. This allows her to present the arguments she thinks will be most useful in any one situation without committing herself to a single approach that might fail for a particular audience. Her strategy is a wise one in the context of the conclusions that can be drawn from scholarly studies of compliance and deterrence.

THE RESEARCH ON DETERRENCE AND COMPLIANCE

While the 'sheer deterrence' (Aalders and Wilthagen 1997: 416) approach holds some attraction as an explanation for how management decides whether to comply with regulation, it is clear that it will only apply in very narrow circumstances. One of the leading empirical researchers of deterrence and business regulation (Scholz 1997) has argued that the simple model of deterrence is only valid when the following assumptions are true: corporations are fully informed utility maximizers; legal statutes unambiguously define misbehaviour; legal punishment provides the primary incentive for corporate compliance; and enforcement agents optimally detect and punish misbehaviour given available resources. External regulatory conditions must make deterrence possible by ensuring that breaches are swiftly identified and punished sufficiently harshly.

Deterrence also depends on the assumption that corporate management is motivated to comply via a mechanism of fully informed rational calculation. Scholz (1997) has concluded from his empirical tests of the deterrence model that mostly this assumption does not hold true. The rational mechanisms of deterrence are usually confounded by the effects of bounded rationality and voluntary compliance. The research of compliance-oriented scholars also blurs the boundaries between deterrence and compliance. Indeed, the empirical research shows in at least five ways that mechanisms of 'voluntary compliance' and 'deterrence' are impossible to disentangle in most organizations' motivations to comply.

Firstly, most 'compliance'-oriented researchers find that deterrence is a necessary backup to voluntary compliance based on cooperation and goodwill. They do not find deterrence and voluntary compliance to be mutually exclusive. In models such as Ayres and Braithwaite's (1992) enforcement pyramid (see also Burby and Paterson 1993; Gunningham 1994; Gunningham and Grabosky 1998; Rees 1988, 1994), deterrence is an essential background threat helping to motivate potential defaulters to comply before sanctions are imposed. The research on voluntary compliance also finds that most companies and individuals will voluntarily comply with regulations perceived to benefit the market or society as long as the regulatory agency makes a credible effort to identify and punish hard-core non-compliers. Consensual compliance is thus generally contingent upon persuading those of goodwill that their compliance will not be exploited by free riders who will get away with the benefits of non-compliance without being held to account for it (see Levi 1988; Scholz 1997: 262). For example, people will pay their tax as long as they believe that those who do not pay will be caught.

Secondly, the research on deterrence has shown that, contrary to the assumption that corporations are fully informed utility maximizers, the bounded rationality of organizations and top management means that many do not make rational cost–benefit calculations about compliance until something happens to bring the risks of non-compliance to their attention. Economic costs which do not draw attention to themselves by generating some kind of crisis are often overlooked by busy management (see Hopkins 1995: 88–95). Thus, Scholz and Gray's (1990) comprehensive research into the effectiveness of OSHA enforcements based on a sample of nearly 7000 large manufacturing plants and using annual data on inspections, citations, penalties and injury experience for each plant from 1979 to 1985 found only a modest reduction in injury rates in all plants following an increase in enforcement activity. A 10 per cent increase in enforcement activity would decrease injury rates by 1 per cent. However, individual plants that were inspected and penalized experienced a 22 per cent decline in injuries over the next three years. These very substantial effects on firms that are inspected suggests that firms are not acting in purely rational ways. (According to the deterrence hypothesis, the fact that they have been inspected and penalized in a particular year should not have affected their cost–benefit calculations of the probability and costs of enforcement, although it might have a general deterrent effect on the whole population.) Rather, Scholz and Gray (1990) conclude that imposing penalties results in improved safety because penalties focus managerial attention on risks that may otherwise have been overlooked. As Scholz comments (1997: 256), 'Safety records improve after inspections that cite hazardous conditions for the same reason that safety increases after major accidents – because then management resolves problems that were overlooked while management was concerned elsewhere'.[3] Weil (1996) finds, also in relation to OSHA regulation, that despite a probability of inspection of 0.4 and an average fine per inspection of US$300, custom woodworking enterprises show a high level of compliance (between 42 and 51 per cent) during initial inspections, which increases markedly on subsequent inspections. He concludes that these enterprises are highly responsive to inspections despite few follow-up inspections and low expected fines. Similarly, McCaffrey and Hart (1998: 87) in their study of compliance systems on Wall Street find that firms will make heavier investments in compliance than they otherwise would, in the wake of a regulatory incident.

Scholz and Gray also concluded that the fact that injury reduction effects occurred over a three-year period suggests management do not just correct the cited violation but once attention is drawn to health and safety non-compliance, it triggers a broader review of performance. Thus, while general deterrence (the general expected probability of being inspected and fined) is not sufficient to motivate whole organizations to comply with all applicable laws and regulations, once management attention has been drawn to a particular breach via the direct experience of an inspection, they are more likely to seek a systematic solution to ensure broader compliance.

This dynamic has an impact on the implementation of compliance systems. In her investigation of health and safety programs in UK companies, Genn (1993: 223) finds that it is 'when there is a potential for a catastrophe of either an economic or political nature, and also where companies are large, well established, highly visible and thus mindful of their public image', that they are more likely to have an occupational health and safety system in place. They are also more likely to have implemented a system addressing that particular high-profile hazard or short-term possibility of disaster than they are to have a system addressing longer term health issues: a high motivation to improve and maintain standards is most obvious where poor standards might threaten the very existence of the site or health risks are very well established.

Thirdly, when they do think about the risks of non-compliance, top management frequently do not make a simple calculation based on the dollar costs of non-compliance. Rather, other factors, particularly the financial and moral costs of bad publicity, are very significant. Thus, Scholz and Gray (1990) found that although workplace safety in plants inspected by OSHA improves after penalties are imposed, the size of the penalty has little impact on safety improvements. This contradicts the basic premise of deterrence theory that larger expected penalties will produce greater compliance. Davidson and others (1995) measured the stock markets' reaction to OSHA announcements of sanctions on the companies receiving them (adjusting for overall stock-market movement). The study found a stock-market decline average of −0.46 per cent on the days immediately before and after the announcement. However, they could find no relationship at all between the size of the fine and the stock-market reaction, suggesting that negative publicity is seen as more significant than the size of a penalty by industry. Fisse and Braithwaite (1983) studied the impact of publicity on corporate offenders in seventeen high-profile cases in great detail. They found that 'Adverse publicity is of concern not so much by reason of its financial impacts but because of a variety of non-financial effects, the most important of which is loss of corporate prestige' and that 'corporations fear the sting of adverse publicity attacks on their reputations more than they fear the law itself' (Fisse and Braithwaite 1983: 247, 249). Indeed, a series of studies have found that maintaining or advancing the corporate reputation and counteracting negative publicity is an important reason for top-management interest in compliance activities (e.g. Bardach and Kagan 1982: 164; Genn 1993; but cf. Haines 1997: 188–90).

Fourthly, motivations to comply vary between persons and contexts. There are a wide variety of motivations likely to apply in different enterprises, in different parts of the same enterprise and at different times in the same enterprise. Fisse and Braithwaite's (1993) examination of internal corporate accountability systems finds that companies will frequently be responsive to weak sanctions, including publicity and shame, because there are usually various actors associated with any wrongdoing. Some will be 'hard targets' who cannot be deterred even by maximum penalties. But others will be 'vulnerable targets' who can be deterred by penalties, and still others will be 'soft targets who can be deterred by shame, by the mere exposure of the fact that they have failed to meet some responsibility they bear, even if that is not a matter of criminal responsibility' (Fisse and Braithwaite 1993: 220; see also Braithwaite 1985, 1989).

Paternoster and Simpson's (1996) findings support Fisse and Braithwaite's argument. Their study looked at intentions to commit four types of corporate crime by MBA students, and found that these intentions were affected by sanction threats (formal and informal), moral evaluations and organizational factors. They find that where people do hold personal moral codes, these will be more significant than rational calculations in predicting compliance. If moral inhibitions are high, then cost–benefit calculations are virtually superfluous. But when moral inhibitions are low, deterrence becomes relevant. Thus, the response of the whole organization may depend on the dispositions of those who hold strategic power (and how effective they are at having their way in the organization). Differing motivations and responses will also be partially determined by economic circumstances and place in the structure, as well as by the individual dispositions of particular corporate managers. A consistent research finding is that larger enterprises are more likely to implement compliance systems and to be more compliant than smaller enterprises.

Fifthly, the vulnerability of corporate management to negative impacts on their own or the organization's reputation shows that enterprises can sometimes be made permeable to external values through the need to seek and maintain legitimacy. The possibility of fines, sanctions and inspections acts less as a deterrent threat than as a way to focus management attention on broader institutional issues that may affect the legitimacy and operation of their enterprise. Deterrence theory, like much law and society research, 'sees organisations as unitary rational actors whose responses to law are instrumental, substantive, and largely confrontational' (Suchman and Edelman 1997: 917). The evidence of the 'new institutional' scholarship in organizational theory, by contrast, shows that companies can be responsive not just to profit maximisation but also to normative cognitive influences, including the symbolism of law (i.e. the fact that laws represent some sort of normative consensus, regardless of the sanctions attached to them). A variety of institutional factors can lead organizations to conform to social norms even when formal enforcement mechanisms are imperfect. These include historical legacies, cultural mores, cognitive scripts, and structural linkages to the professions and to the state. Each can displace 'single-minded profit-maximisation with a heightened sensitivity to the organisation's embed-dedness within a larger social environment' (Suchman and Edelman 1997: 919).

New institutionalists DiMaggio and Powell (1991) describe three ways in which organizations adopt practices and structures from their normative environments beyond what is required by the technical and financial parameters under which they operate: organizations copy the apparently successful practices of other, similar organizations; organi-zations submit to the demands of powerful external actors, such as the regulatory agencies of the state; and organizations import the practices of professionals and other organized value carriers.

These three mechanisms relate to Scott's (1995: 34ff) three pillars of institutions – regulative, normative and cognitive – that create the insti-tutional contexts in which organizations operate. These three pillars can form a hierarchy from the legally enforced to the taken for granted (see Hoffman 1997: 36–8). Regulative institutions are based on legal sanc-tions and coercion. Their logic is instrumental and their legitimacy based on law. Normative institutions are a matter of social obligation, and are based on values and social expectations. Cognitive institutions are taken for granted. They are seen as 'orthodox', deeply rooted in cul-tural assumptions and ways of seeing the world. They are a matter of unconscious compliance on the basis that it is almost unthinkable to do anything else. In any particular company's 'organizational field', these three pillars may be consistent or inconsistent with each other, and may affect different groups within the company differently. A regulative institution that fits pre-existing normative and cognitive institutions will be much more 'successful' at achieving compliance than one that is in conflict with them. For example, Prohibition in the USA did not fit the culture of the time. Equally, however, a company or industry may find that it has to change the cognitive institutions of its internal culture in order to avoid conflict with newly emerging normative and regulative institutions adopted by the society at large as these new influences enter its organizational field.

There is some empirical evidence that this theory does help to explain corporate adoption of compliance and good citizenship systems. Weaver and others' (1999b) survey of factors affecting corporate ethics programs in the US Fortune 1000 companies supports the theory that environmental factors significantly influence the scope of ethics and compliance programs implemented. Companies were more likely to have adopted more elements of a formal ethics or compliance program (i.e. codes of conduct or policy documents, specialised ethics or compliance officers, training programs, and so on) if management were aware of the US Sentencing Commission's Corporate Sentencing Guidelines (regulative institutions), if the company's ethical failures had been the subject of media attention (normative institutions), and/or corporate representatives regularly attended networking meetings on ethics (normative and cognitive institutions) (Weaver et al. 1999b: 50; see also Reichman 1992).[4]

Edelman and various co-authors (Dobbin et al. 1988; Edelman 1990; Edelman et al. 1993) have used neo-institutional theory to explain the growth of employee due process rights designed to protect against a wide spectrum of arbitrary management behaviour, including indiscriminate firing, failure to promote, safety violations, unequal discipline, sexual harassment and discriminatory employment opportunity structures in US companies. Edelman (1990) argues that the civil rights movement and legal mandates of the 1960s together created a normative environment that put pressure on employers to create formal protections of due process rights. She shows how initially novel models of due process were accepted by some companies as a matter of legitimacy and survival in an environment in which they felt strong public scrutiny and employee expectations of change. Those that were most exposed to public scrutiny and government control changed first. Others followed in an effort to remain 'up to date'. Due process rights that were unheard of for private companies early in the century eventually became institutionalized in the normal bureaucratic structure of the corporation in the role of the personnel department and the professionalism of personnel officers. Now few large companies lack programs for safeguarding basic employee rights; they are simply part of the basic operations of a company.

Hoffman's (1997) study of corporate environmentalism in the US petroleum and chemical industries demonstrates the power of institutions on corporate behaviour through the period 1960 to 1993. He concludes, 'The corporate environmental management function grew from a small subsection of the engineering department to a large department operating independently. Fundamentally, corporate environmentalism evolved from an ancillary aspect of corporate operations driven by industry considerations to a central aspect of corporate strategy driven by core business constituency' (1997: 143).

Hoffman's content analyses of industry journals show that corporate attention to environmental issues did not follow the linear trends in volume of environmental laws and regulation, nor growth in industrial expenditure on environmental issues. So corporate attention to environmental issues cannot be explained solely by the motivation to regain control of capital and operating expenditure in relation to the environment, nor as a response to the threat of regulatory penalties and punitive damages (see Hoffman 1997: 144). Rather, Hoffman's analysis of the up-and-down trends in public concerns for environmental issues between 1960 and 1993 matched exactly his analysis of corporate concerns with environmental issues from the trade journals. He also points to the way in which organizations made similar shifts in management structures for environmental issues at the same time as each other (not just technological shifts as required by regulation) to illustrate the influence of social factors (1997: 145).

Thus, Hoffman sees the history of corporate environmentalism over the last thirty years in the US petroleum and chemical industries as a 'story of institutional negotiation over corporations' rules, norms, and, ultimately, beliefs regarding legitimate environmental management' (1997: 152). The field moved from being dominated by cognitive institutions, in which industry defined its environmental actions in terms of engineering advances, through to regulative institutions with the establishment of the Environment Protection Agency (EPA). The EPA was weakened by Reagan, but the public backlash against this weakening showed that environmentalism had now emerged as a normative institution. The chemical and petroleum industries therefore adopted environmentalism as a matter of social obligation. By the first international Earth Day in 1988, insurance companies, investors and competitors entered the field and prominent environmental events and disasters sharpened public concerns. Environmentalism therefore moved from being a social to a strategic issue for corporations and reached new levels of cultural primacy, bringing it much closer to a cognitive institution: 'The heresy of the 1960s became the dogma of the 1990s' (Hoffman 1997: 143).

Similarly, Rees' (1997) study of the emergence of the self-regulatory Responsible Care program of the US Chemical Manufacturers' Association also finds that it was the imperatives of institutional legitimacy that forced chemical companies to begin to self-regulate. Responsible Care was introduced in 1988 after the industry realized that the public saw the chemical industry as the USA's 'leading environmental risk and second leading public health risk' (Rees 1997: 486), especially after Bhopal. Top executives in Rees' study described Bhopal as the 'wake-up call' (1997: 485) that put them on the path to Responsible Care. The introduction of the Toxics Release Inventory (a post-Bhopal US regulatory reform) was a second shock showing the chemical industry as by far the USA's worst polluter:

> Public opinion is the root of all public policy and regulation and legislation, and if that public opinion is so negative, your franchise to operate – literally, in the sense of zoning, approvals by various state, local or federal agencies – your ability to operate in terms of federal legislation, are all affected. (A top chemical company executive quoted in Rees 1997: 486)

The evidence suggests that purely 'voluntary' compliance or self-regulation is rare, or perhaps non-existent. But neither does a simple deterrence model explain corporate compliance behaviour. In summary the picture of the organization as an amoral calculator moved by appropriate deterrence to 'do the right thing' must be supplemented and nuanced by the facts that:

- organizations can sometimes be persuaded to do the right thing without a direct threat of sanctions if there is a threat for defaulters in the background;
- some influential actors within organizations will be highly motivated to be law-abiding or socially responsible for its own sake;
- the existence of deterrence threats will not necessarily be a feature of daily decision-making;
- many organizations will behave in ways that they feel maintain their legitimacy in the eyes of industry peers, customers or governments irrespective of individual cost and efficiency calculations; and

- even where formal sanctions are applied, it is their informal ramifications (shame and negative publicity) that are more effective deterrent threats.

Effective self-regulation is conceptually possible. But purely voluntary effective self-regulation is simply not an empirical reality. What is needed is an explanation for motivations to implement self-regulation that allows us to leave 'compliance' and deterrence-type motivations entangled, as they are in real life. The experience of early participants in Australia's Greenhouse Challenge illustrates the entangling responses to deterrent threats, cost–benefit calculations and moral obligation.

A CASE STUDY: EARLY PARTICIPANTS IN THE
GREENHOUSE CHALLENGE

Chapter 4 will consider motivations for self-regulation leadership where mandatory law exists. We begin here with a case study of self-regulation in a regime with only a vague threat of regulation in the future, to show that motivations for self-regulation leadership exist independently of the short-term possibility of legal sanction. The Greenhouse Challenge is a program of voluntary agreements between industry and government to reduce greenhouse gas emissions to meet Australia's emissions targets under the Kyoto Protocol on climate change. The idea was developed by a network of industry associations and large companies during lobbying and consultation in the leadup to the first Conference of the Parties to the UN Framework Convention on Climate Change in Berlin in 1995. At that time the possibility of a carbon tax was being discussed in Australia. Industry proposed the Greenhouse Challenge as an alternative to a tax, or mandatory emissions reduction targets. The program was implemented by the Commonwealth government in 1996 and operates with a joint industry–government steering committee, although the Greenhouse Challenge unit is part of a government department. Understanding the motivations of the early participants in the program gives us an insight into why top management might wish to go beyond legal compliance and become self-regulation leaders.

In the program, voluntary agreements to reduce emissions are not legally enforceable and participants can withdraw at any time without legal or any other formal sanction. However, if they do remain in the program they must report annually and may be subject to random verification audits to check that they have done what they said they were going to do. They can be expelled from the program for failing to meet these obligations.

Consider the following quotations from interviews with the people responsible for corporate Greenhouse Challenge action plans in six companies, each of which had been an early participant in the program:

> [Mine of Riches] took the position it wanted to be among the first to sign up. It is company policy not to be second best. (Mine of Riches)

> [W]e thought energy management is good and so is being socially responsible. We're one of the largest, or at least most profitable, companies in Australia. So we should be responsible for the environment. Everyone knocks banks so if we can do something good then that's good for our image. (Big Bucks Australia)

> We wanted to do our bit and there was no point doing it alone. Dare I say it, there were some moral as well as financial benefits … So we wanted to save money, get some kudos for ourselves and drag business down this path [i.e. the path of using voluntary agreements rather than a carbon tax]. (Holes in the Ground)

> We recognised greenhouse is one of the major issues facing our industry and [Power To Go] wants to be seen as being proactive. We wanted to be one of the first companies to sign up. (Power To Go)

There are a variety of motivations at work here: the potential of competitive advantage, a sense of responsibility under a social contract, the need to garner good publicity, and legitimacy in public eyes. It is impossible to separate more strategic thinking from the (perhaps) more public interest oriented view of the obligations of a social contract on a corporation to be a good corporate citizen. However, each of these four organizations wanted to be, or to be seen as, leaders. Indeed, three had been involved in lobbying the government and bringing industry together into the project from the very beginning.

Public image

A number of greenhouse managers described their company's participation in the program as part of their general strategic policy on environmental issues to be seen as an environmental responsibility leader. For example:

> [Chemola] recognizes it is amongst the largest petro-chemicals complexes in Australia, and it is very aware of the expectations in terms of

corporate citizenship that that means. Our owners [two global compa-
nies] require environmental standards and [name of one] in particular
demands the leading edge of us. (Chemola)

We did it for our image because we need to show people [that we're
environmentally responsible]. (Fuel for the Fire Australia)

Often this is seen as a need to actively counteract the negative image of
big business in general and of the environmental unfriendliness of business activities (especially mining and manufacturing) in particular. As
an industry association environmental management coordinator put it:

Usually these companies realize they are loathed and try to do things
before they are asked to, in order to make themselves smaller targets.
They don't like being driven to do something. (Industry Association
One)

Leadership

The history of the Greenhouse Challenge is one of a group of leading
companies and industry associations in different industries that felt
particularly concerned or threatened by the possibility of a carbon tax
and came together to lobby against the carbon tax, and then developed
the idea of the Greenhouse Challenge as an alternative based on voluntary ('no regrets')[5] action. This allowed the government to abandon the
carbon tax idea but still accomplish something that it could take with it
to international climate change negotiations (Worden 1998). Many of
the earliest participants and ones that had been diligent with their
reporting by the end of 1998 were ones that had been involved from this
early stage (both individually and through their industry associations).
They were thus seeking to avoid the threat and cost of a carbon tax.
Simultaneously, these organizations were also trying to show leadership and strategy to lead both government policy and the rest of business towards voluntary action as a viable alternative to the carbon tax.

Some companies had boards who had thought this through very
clearly. The following lengthy story illustrates how leadership in this
area grew out of board commitment to leadership:

For us the greenhouse started as in issue in 87/88 in Australia. In the
early 80s greenhouse had already been an issue in Europe, our center.
Australia was a bit of a backwater. When it hit us in the late 80s, we
went to London and said we're interested in thinking about this issue.
At that time they had done a survey of papers published on greenhouse

and found that interest had already peaked in 1981 to 1984. They said go slow as they did not know whether interest would peak again. But it did of course. For us when these issues arise, the first thing we do is look for opportunities. We don't see it as a threat. At that stage we did a study of alternative fuels, looking for any opportunities so that we could get in first. We found no fuel was sufficiently economic ... but we still needed a management approach to greenhouse. In 1993 we started auditing energy because what you don't measure you can't manage. We didn't know what we would do about it. But we added CO_2 into the existing audits we did for the EPA and others. In 1994 the Greens were promoting a carbon tax and there were discussions with government and industry. We thought a carbon tax would increase product prices without getting companies to actually do anything about energy efficiency ... So we took the view that no-regrets measures were best. We thought it was better to give a higher priority to energy efficiency ... In some areas that was easy because it was part and parcel of our normal activities. In other areas it was a new concept so we had to sell the concept because people don't accept the relationship of energy auditing with the bottom line.

Very early I went to the Board. The press were talking about a carbon tax. We put the view to the Board we should promote voluntary no-regrets actions. So then we [i.e. the interviewee and other industry representatives and associations] set up the Australian Industry Greenhouse Network ...

Then we had an interesting Board meeting. The Greenhouse Challenge was going to Cabinet in December. It was all agreed and just had to be approved by Cabinet. At the last minute the Department of Environment put up the idea of a carbon tax. (Clearly someone in the Department didn't like the Greenhouse Challenge.) ... Prior to that Cabinet meeting people like [the responsible government minister] were coming and saying to us, 'Are you really going to join up, if I put up the Greenhouse Challenge?' He didn't want to go out on a limb. So I made a presentation to the Board and made the recommendation we should agree to join. But there was the possibility we would get the carbon tax instead. So the Chair went around the Board one by one and asked what they thought, and they all said yes, yes, yes. They saw it as a political reality that we should do something about greenhouse. And the Chair said, 'Whatever the government does, we will pursue no-regrets actions'. That made my life easier because regardless of what the government did, we would do it anyway. That was the decision and from then on I had the Board's total support. (Fuel for the Fire)

Here the board accepted that reductions in greenhouse emissions would have to be made one way or another, then made a conscious decision as to what they thought was the best way for them as a business to achieve reductions ('no regrets' actions). Once that decision had been made, the company was committed to following that course of action and persuading the government and other companies to follow their lead if possible. It was not merely the case that the Greenhouse Challenge was passively accepted as the 'lesser of two evils' (as compared to a carbon tax), as one greenhouse manager put it. Environmental managers together with top management of companies like Fuel for the Fire came to their own conclusion about what a business with integrity would do to look after business and the environment, and then attempted to steer others to the same conclusion:

> We're proactive about EHS and try to steer new regulatory requirements in the direction we believe we're already committed. (Chemola)

> We saw it as an external relations issue with significant potential to shape the business we're in. Externally we saw woolly thinking going on. We thought the Greenhouse Challenge was an appropriate response. If we wanted the rest of industry to go down that route then we should be in it leading and pushing. (Holes in the Ground)

> There are a lot of advantages [for our member companies] in being proactive ... Greenhouse is very much a case of industry seeing something would happen and they should shape it ... A lot of our companies place a lot of emphasis on being proactive because (1) it's more efficient to be leading and (2) reputation. (Industry Association One)

Thus, participation in the Greenhouse Challenge was about leadership and influence, both in terms of government policy and the rest of business, as well as positive public relations to protect the legitimacy of the business enterprise. Many of the greenhouse managers interviewed personally felt that it was important to save energy for environmental reasons and some thought that top management agreed too. This did not, however, imply agreement with whatever the government and the environmentalists might wish to do to reduce greenhouse emissions. Rather, like Kagan and Scholz's (1984) category of business firms as 'political citizens', many of these companies had strong views about what policy directions to take and intended to do whatever they could to influence government, industry and the public at large to take their view. At the same time they recognized it was important to be seen to be doing the right thing in the interests of the long-term sustainability of their businesses. (Here 'sustainability' does not refer to the physical environmental conditions of their business, but the social legitimacy in which it is clothed.)

Cost–benefit analysis

Rational cost–benefit analyses, apart from the calculation that the Greenhouse Challenge would be better than a carbon tax, also played a part in backing up both the leaders' decision to be actively involved in the program, and the followers' decision that they had nothing to lose by following the lead:

> There are tangible greenhouse/environmental management incentives for members of Greenhouse Challenge in terms of promotions offered by the Federal Government, and promotion opportunities they can do themselves plus cost savings. So there are lots of pluses. (Industry Association Three)

> It was seen as low cost, plus there are the benefits of publicity. So it was a good option, plus it was voluntary so we can get out of it any time. (Credit4Oz)

> We wanted to save money, energy management consultants were talking up potential savings. However we haven't been able to make anything like ten per cent. (Holes in the Ground)

Indeed, according to the Greenhouse Challenge managers interviewed, the savings and benefits were so obvious that often their companies were already beginning to do the things required by the Greenhouse Challenge anyway. When they centralized their functions, Credit4Oz realized what a large proportion of their regular outgoings were energy costs and wanted to bring their costs down. They then joined the Greenhouse Challenge to get 'kudos' for what they were already doing, and to drive environmental benefits that they were beginning to see were possible through the crossovers between their energy management and health and safety programs. For other participants in the Greenhouse Challenge, the impetus may have already come from an international parent in a more advanced jurisdiction to do something about emissions for public image reasons: 'Our international parent had already said in 1995 that they were setting a 1% target reduction in energy usage' (Chemical Kings); 'The Greenhouse Challenge doesn't set the expectations. We already have a firm belief we're leading on this … [Our parent] already demands environmental management and had set a target of fifty per cent reduction in emissions worldwide' (Chemola).

CONCLUSION

The 'sheer deterrence' view of corporate responses to business regulation implies a single path to compliance: heavy enough sanctions coupled with a high enough chance of being caught. By contrast, the scholarly literature and the experience of participation in Australia's voluntary Greenhouse Challenge program show that top-management motivations for compliance come from a plurality of places and influences. This provides us with some hope that companies may be permeable to external values.

Some top managers seek to assume an identity of compliance leadership among industry peers, consumers, investors and government, and other companies follow their lead. The pursuit of compliance leadership is most frequently prompted when the attention of corporate executives is captured by an actual or potential crisis of publicity or litigation. But organizations may also be provoked to adopt habits of compliance leadership by obvious changes in community values, by changes in laws that threaten to affect the reputation and legitimacy of the organization, or to place it in danger of litigation or enforcement action and stakeholder requirements.

Regulators that want to prompt corporate commitment to, and implementation of, effective compliance management systems therefore need to understand internal corporate responses to regulation and external values first, and then tailor regulatory action to catalyse self-regulation and hold corporations accountable for their level of integrity. One conclusion of this chapter is that to get at behaviour within the organization means changing the balance of external influences vying for management attention, so that social and legal responsibilities get a higher priority. A crisis of publicity or regulatory enforcement action can achieve this. As I shall argue in later chapters, this can also be facilitated by strengthening the bargaining power of the stakeholders, and broadening who the relevant stakeholders are.

4 Cultivating self-regulation leadership

Management motivations for commitment to institutionalizing social and legal responsibility are complex. Some companies are spurred to leadership by multiple motivations for self-regulation, while others will follow only when compliance systems have become a 'taken for granted' part of doing business. The objection to good corporate citizenship that management would not, or perhaps should not, dilute economically rational decision-making with social and legal responsibility issues is therefore too simplistic. In fact, management often will voluntarily take such factors into account either because they think it is strategic to do so, or because it has become unthinkable to do anything else.

The first section of this chapter broadens out the analysis in the previous chapter using my general interviews with self-regulation professionals. Compliance managers are very clear that organizational commitment depends primarily on the commitment of the very top level of management (the CEO and sometimes the board). Compliance managers' analyses of top-management thinking reveal that the most robust commitment to the self-regulation system is motivated by strategic decisions to cultivate an identity of leadership. However, this motivation to become a self-regulation leader is rarely, if ever, spontaneous. It is most commonly prompted by the experience of a regulatory disaster or public relations crisis either within the company or close to it (a parent, associated company or close competitor). Firms that take the lead create models of self-regulation system implementation and excellence, sometimes in partnership with regulators or even public interest groups. These models of self-regulation leadership then attract other companies to emulate the leaders' habits and identity of good corporate citizenship through dynamics of peer pressure, competition, social pressure and the demands of regulators and powerful stakeholders (see Figure 4.1). These dynamics become particularly potent at further moments of regulatory or public relations crisis which may propel new companies into self-regulation innovation and leadership.

This analysis shows that state regulators and their actions are not the only means of nurturing self-regulation. Corporate commitment to self-regulation will depend on how state regulation interacts with formal and informal regulation of a variety of other actors. The second part of this chapter considers the internal and external agents of self-regulation commitment: CEOs, self-regulation professionals and external stakeholders. It is they who will determine when the corporate window of self-regulation opportunity opens, and what happens when it does.

THE DYNAMICS OF LEADERSHIP AND MODELLING

Self-regulation leadership

All my interviews were with compliance managers who were seen as best practice practitioners.[1] However, out of this select pool, an even smaller group stood out by describing their organizations and top management as priding themselves on keeping ahead of the law and being seen as leaders in compliance and good corporate citizenship. Consider the emphasis on leadership in the following quotation from a presentation by a chief compliance manager on how compliance professionals should persuade top managers to see compliance as a 'must have':

> The short-sighted person raising the problems [with implementing a compliance system] above may be a great sales person or a manager – but the views expressed are not those of a business *leader*! A leader will see beyond the basic survival of the business and its short term bottom line position and develop a strategy for continuing business efficiency, growth and prosperity. (Boxall 1998; emphasis in original)

The linkage of strong self-regulation to business leadership is echoed in the explanation of his company's compliance commitment by an Australian compliance manager in Alpine Insurance, a global insurance company:

> [Alpine] was the first insurance company to approach the ACCC [Australian Competition and Consumer Commission] and ask for help about ensuring compliance when the insurance codes of conduct were

coming in. They decided to get in first ... We're one of the few companies that sack advisers who aren't up to standard. We give them a fair
chance. We try to educate them if they fail the audits and so on. But we
will sack them if they're not up to standard ... We're trying to keep
ahead of the law. For example, we are already thinking about problems
with putting products on the internet and the regulatory problems we
might face ... At the moment compliance is being included in new
product development from the very beginning ... The changing regulatory environment is very good for the Compliance Unit, but also for
the organization. It means we can value add into our products by providing information people can understand and keeping ahead of the
law. It means that people might develop brand loyalty to [Alpine]
because we have better information earlier, even when another company might put out a superior product. We're trying to develop our
brand image at the moment and in this area you can really only do it
with add-ins or service, because all the products are basically the same.

This compliance manager saw his company's identity as incorporating
compliance leadership and a culture of good citizenship that led it to
keep ahead of the law in the standards it upheld. No direct coercion or
cost factor forced them to take this approach to compliance. Nor was
theirs a purist, 'holier than thou' approach to ethics: to him, cultivating
compliance leadership was seen as both prudent ('everybody's going to
have to live up to these standards eventually'), and strategic in differ-
entiating their brand name in a marketplace where products do not
differ very much and companies compete on service and add-ins. However, the Australian insurance codes of conduct, which this compliance
manager mentions, were introduced partially in response to a major
scandal involving agents of almost all insurance companies in Australia, including Alpine. The agents and companies were involved in
serious misconduct in the way products were sold to Aboriginal people
in remote communities in northern Australia, and were successfully
pursued by the Trade Practices Commission (Ducret 1993).

In the following quotation, another compliance manager also
describes his Australian company, GarbageRUs, as having a culture of
compliance leadership derived from its international parent. This time
the motivation comes again from prudence. The US parent had experienced massive losses and share price downturn when it was forced to
comply with superfund obligations to clean up previously contaminated land. This was enough to change the culture of the whole organization from the top down to see 'one hundred per cent compliance' as
a crucial goal. But the motivation for leadership also originated in a

current desire to influence government policy to help the company to reap the first-mover advantages of leading changes in the law:

> In the US, liability for past misdeeds in relation to landfill etc has really changed the culture of the organization. Now it is part of the mission statement to take the same perspective and live up to the same standards required in the US in every country in which they [the international parent] do business regardless of the local legislation because of the US experience. This is often very expensive at the moment in relation to the environment, but they believe it is worth it in the long run when Australia catches up in terms of regulatory requirements. We've already seen that happen in New South Wales where we were the only company that complied when new regulations for draining methane from landfill were introduced. (GarbageRUs)

For a company that makes money from contracting with councils and companies to deal with waste, brand image among the general public was not very significant. But keeping ahead of the law by applying US standards in all countries turned out to be a shrewd business investment. When the new laws came into effect in New South Wales, this company could reap the benefits of compliance immediately and without extra expenditure. Earlier the US parent had reaped just such an advantage in the USA by helping to develop new stricter landfill rules, spending tens of millions of dollars putting all their facilities in compliance with the new standards before they became law, and then teaming up with environmental groups to push the new law through when Congress delayed (see Cairncross 1995: 193; see also Braithwaite and Drahos 2000: 267–70 and Porter and van der Linde 1995 for further examples on how some companies attempt to use environmental regulation to gain first-mover advantages).

Another example of a company seeking to use compliance leadership in a dynamic regulatory and social environment as a market advantage was DuPont's development of the DuCare photograph development system. In this case the company did not attempt to raise barriers to entry through regulation, but envisioned a 'super-compliant' product as a way to carve out a special market by reducing environmental compliance costs for its film and photochemical customers. DuPont developed an 'environmental pressure map' of the USA that ranked different areas by regulatory stringency in relation to allowable silver concentrations and likelihood of enforcement. An analysis of DuPont's customer concentrations were laid on top of the map. The market opportunity arose because of the reality (and perception) of increasingly stringent environmental regulation. The company's financial and marketing analyses were based on the assumption that regulatory compliance and standards would continuously tighten to affect more and more graphic arts facilities. The target customer groups were those in areas that had been identified as strict or transitioning, and the profit potential was based on the idea that regulation was generally becoming more stringent (Boyd 1998: 31). In fact, the new processing system failed to be a market success, probably because of lax monitoring and enforcement of photochemical waste regulations by government agencies.

As these cases illustrate, several reasons may combine in any one case to motivate an organization to move beyond the mere implementation of a compliance system to the pursuit of self-regulation leadership:

- a general desire to actually be a good corporate citizen;
- the desire to take advantage of perceived first-mover competitive and efficiency advantages in compliance, including the ability to shape government/regulatory policy to suit the company early on rather than have a less suitable system forced upon it;
- the ability to advantage from regulatory barriers to entry; and
- a desire to be seen by prospective customers, staff, investors, regulators, government, local communities and/or other stakeholders with power to make decisions affecting the business as a good, legitimate corporate citizen.

However, the most common reason for organizations to adopt systematic and robust self-regulation systems is probably the experience of a regulatory or public relations disaster, or the imminent apprehension that one may occur.

The dynamics of leading and following

As illustrated in Figure 4.1, there are three broad dynamics by which the habits of compliance leaders are adopted. Firstly, if a company faces a *disaster* (for example, a major regulatory investigation, a penalty or an accident that becomes a matter of public concern), or sees its competitors face a regulatory or public relations disaster, it may decide to implement a self-regulation system to avert or soften the impact of the disaster. This experience will (a) prompt senior management of some organizations to think seriously about compliance and to decide to *innovate and become leaders*, and (b) motivate others to *model the innovations* developed by self-regulation leaders.

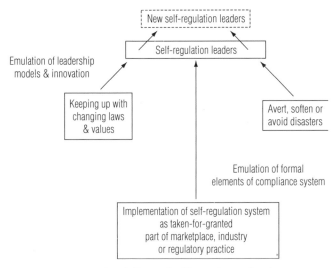

FIGURE 4.1 Modelling of self-regulation leaders

Secondly, in their attempts to keep up with changing law, changing community attitudes, and apparently successful ways of doing business to avoid the possibility of legitimacy or regulatory problems, (a) some companies will become compliance *leaders*, and (b) others will *emulate compliance leaders*.

Thirdly, these paths can eventually lead to the habits of the leaders becoming part of the taken-for-granted organization of business (a 'cognitive institution'), so that many companies copy the leaders because it seems to be *the natural thing to do to have a self-regulation system*. At this stage stakeholders, including investors, insurers, public interest groups and others, will expect all decent companies to have self-regulation systems.

These paths are not exclusive alternatives. As we have already seen, different motivations for self-regulation commitment can rarely be isolated from one another. One event or motivation will frequently trigger another, simply by directing attention towards social and legal responsibility issues. Similarly each dynamic will overlap with another, and modellers frequently become leaders, and vice versa.

While regulatory inspectors might be attempting to push organizational compliance upwards through inspections, citations and fines, the implementation of effective compliance systems is likely to be a result of the pull of corporate leaders who are already exhibiting successful compliance models. Figure 4.1 illustrates this dynamic by showing companies catching up with and overtaking compliance leaders' models of compliance systems in order to avert or soften regulatory disaster, or to keep up with changing community values and laws. At the bottom of the diagram, furthest away from the leaders, are those companies who catch up with habits of leadership only when self-regulation becomes a taken-for-granted part of their industry.

The limits of this analysis should be borne in mind in interpreting the results: firstly, the purpose here is to focus on motivations for commitment, not those motivations that might have led to non-compliance. Secondly, the analysis focuses on commitment to implementing a system, not on motivations in relation to individual instances of compliance or non-compliance. It is not difficult to imagine circumstances in which top management may be committed to the compliance system as a whole, but be motivated towards encouraging or ignoring non-compliance in a particular circumstance. Thirdly, while this analysis presents a typology of motivations for implementing a system, even a strong commitment towards implementing a good system does not mean that the result will be an effective system. Indeed, the arousal of the desire to implement a system is only the first step. An organization's compliance performance will depend on how that opportunity is utilized by internal and external actors to introduce compliance functions and procedures into the organization.

This analysis takes modelling of self-regulation leaders to be an important explanation for the diffusion of self-regulation practices (see Braithwaite and Drahos 2000: 539–43, 578–601, for further development of the theory of modelling in business regulation). However, this should not be taken as saying that modelling is the *primary* motivation for companies to implement a compliance system in the first place. Copying competitors is probably not an important motivation in itself. It was rarely mentioned as an independent motivation in my interviews and those quantitative studies that address the issue of motivation to implement a compliance system have not found it to be an important factor: the surveys either do not include it as a category (Apel 1995), or it is rated by respondents as of little importance (see Beckenstein and Gabel 1983). This may be partly because modelling is a more abstract concept which is unlikely to be identified in ordinary language. It is also because it is the motivations of leadership, of response to actual or potential disaster, to changing laws, stakeholder expectations and community opinions that are the primary motivators for interest in self-regulation.

But when management does decide to respond, it is the compliance ideas developed by leaders that they use. Thus, the modelling effect is indirect – the possibility of implementing a self-regulation system comes to management attention as an issue only because some companies (and regulators) already lead in this area, because some companies argued for compliance to be included as a mitigating factor in the US Federal Sentencing Guidelines or because a regulator such as the ACCC has successfully persuaded a number of large, well-known companies which were targeted for potential enforcement action to implement compliance systems.

Once such implementation reaches saturation point in an industry or geographical area, modelling remains more implicit than explicit. The expectation that companies will have a compliance system will have seeped into normal business operating procedures and relations, into the way in which regulators organize their inspections and pitch their educative efforts, and into stakeholder expectations. Corporate commitment to a compliance system seems to be a natural and inescapable part of doing business because 'everybody else is doing it'. Self-regulation practices follow the lead of those who normally set industry practice.

Leadership when disaster forebodes

The most common reason given for implementation, or renewed commitment, to a compliance system in the interviews was the experience of some sort of regulatory disaster in the recent past (or occasionally the not so recent past), or the imminent threat of one occurring in the future.[2]

Here the actual experience of disaster leads to a commitment and resolve not to let it happen again, resulting in a stronger-than-usual commitment to the compliance system and sometimes to self-regulation leadership. As Adviser Eight commented about those compliance managers who are members of the US Ethics Officer Association, 'I can go around the room at Ethics Officer Association meetings and say I know why each of you are here'. A compliance lawyer at Aussie Products, a mining and manufacturing company, described the genesis of his firm's trade practices compliance system in the following way:

> But I have to be completely honest. It started out as a matter of necessity because we were constantly getting into trouble with the ACCC [with particular types of breaches of the Act]. We had already responded to that and got the bones of the compliance program together before the very bad publicity in 1995 and big fines in the [name of case]. However, the publicity did mean that the general manager of [Aussie Products] and the board became very supportive of the compliance program.

Here it was a series of breaches that brought the company's lawyers into unpleasant encounters with the regulator and prompted them to introduce a compliance system. But it was not because of these low-level regulatory troubles that the compliance manager believes top management became committed to an excellent compliance system. It was only when the company faced an enforcement action for price-fixing that garnered very wide publicity and large fines that the compliance manager felt top management's full support.

At Trustus it was a sexual harassment case that took five years to settle and cost the company much in negative publicity that prompted commitment to an EEO system: 'The company probably didn't even think it was an issue before that. It was a very hard way to learn but it was probably one of the better things that has happened to our company in terms of the educational awareness that it has brought up' (Vice-President Human Resources). In response to this crisis the company eventually hired consultants to study the culture of the organization, and others to conduct workshops with staff to discover what values and quality of relationships they thought should be evident in their workplace. Then training on harassment was conducted combining the values developed from the ground up through the staff workshops with considerations of legal liability.

The new sexual harassment grievance-handling process went far beyond what the law required. It gave employees the option of not only an internal complaint mechanism, but also the ability to take their complaint to an external and independent ombudsman who could (a) help complainants to work out how to solve the problem themselves within the company, or (b) write a report to company management saying what ought to be done, or (c) advise complainants that they should seek external legal remedies. While this process was expensive, the Vice-President for Human Resources explained, 'It was not as expensive as the actual case and the humiliation of having trial through media. It was terrible for our reputation to customers and to staff. A lot of staff began to ask themselves whether they really wanted to work for a company that could do that to its employees.'

Here again it was the combination of the eventual financial costs of settlement and the costs of litigation, together with the public humiliation and reputational loss by negative publicity, that mainly pushed commitment to the policy. Also, the interviewee believed that management were previously unaware of the potential costs of a sexual harassment incident, illustrating Scholz's quantitative findings that corporate management often just does not think about calculating the potential costs and benefits of a compliance program until some disaster brings it to their attention. Unfortunately the loss of reputation among employees was so severe that the interviewee believed many still lacked trust and confidence in management's attempts to address the problem.

In the case of pharmaceutical company Pets & Health, the company hired an EEO officer and introduced sexual harassment and other EEO policies when it received a letter from the Australian Affirmative Action Agency saying that it was in danger of having its affirmative action report failed for not meeting the requirements of the Act. This prospect made the CEO and human resources director realize that they needed to pay attention to this issue and to advertise specifically for an EEO officer. At a compliance practitioners' conference, another compliance manager in a company that leases out gaming equipment described the way in which the denial of a licence to operate in a particular jurisdiction, a US$500 000 fine, and associated negative ramifications for the company's stock price, focused top-management attention on implementing an excellent compliance system.

While immediate experience of regulatory disaster is probably the strongest motivation for compliance system implementation, observing disasters faced by competitors can also increase management commitment. The five-year sexual harassment case faced by Trustus (Australia) was often mentioned by other EEO officers in the financial industry as an example of what their companies were trying to avoid. At Wonderchem (a company created by the merger of two chemical giants), at both antecedent organizations the existing environmental management systems were vastly improved in the immediate aftermath of the major dioxin gas pollution accident at competitor Roche's Seveso fragrance plant near Milan in 1976. In both companies the CEOs observed the regulatory and public relations consequences of this disaster for Roche, and asked their own heads of environment, health and safety whether they could be made personally responsible if such an accident occurred in their own firm. When the CEOs realized they could be liable, both ordered the implementation for the first time of systems for monitoring and auditing compliance with the companies' environment, health and safety policies.

Observation of other disasters in the industry seems to have been a particularly effective mechanism in the financial services industry globally. For example, a financial compliance manager in the New York office of Trustus referred to a number of insider trading scandals and derivatives problems and said he saw compliance in the financial services industry as a 'growth industry during the 1990s because everybody was looking at themselves and other firms and saying that could have happened to us'. Across the Atlantic in London, another financial services compliance manager also attributed a huge rise in interest in compliance to a 'fear factor post-Barings and BCCI [two collapses of financial institutions due to fraud]'.

In each of these cases, the avoidance of bad publicity and the wish to resolve matters internally rather than externally where they become public seems to be a major motivating factor: this can motivate a commitment beyond compliance to avoid bad publicity, not just technical breaches. A compliance manager in the financial sector in New York described it this way:

> In my view compliance is ethically oriented and you hire compliance people who know right from wrong ... At [Moneymachine] we don't care what the law says because we go further than the law. I don't analyse law although I'm a lawyer: I check the 'optics' are right. I ask, will it look right to people even if it's not illegal? I'm not doing law-smithing. I don't say do it this way rather than that way in order to make it legal. (Moneymachine)

Clearly the fear calculus, including the possibility of plummeting share values, is the (largely unspoken) looming possibility behind responses to disasters or potential disasters, but so is the corporate and potentially individual shame of publicity. Openness to shame and legitimacy crises opens up the possibility that costs and negative publicity deterrence may lead to a more positive commitment to the benefits of compliance. Consider the following explanation of why one safety, health and environment (SHE) manager believes that his CEO is committed to the company's environmental, health and safety program:

> Our CEO is very committed. He was the general manager of [name of another subsidiary of same company] in New Zealand before his current job. At that time he asked me to go to Auckland for a meeting to present a letter of assurance that Safety, Health and Environment standards were being met. I was annoyed that I had to go all the way there for only ten minutes worth in the meeting. But when I got there this guy invited me to the beginning of the meeting and we spent from 9 am until midday with all the managers discussing SHE [safety, health and environment] issues, and he knew more about all the incidents they had than they did, and he questioned them closely about them. They all went away very nervous about those issues.

I think it's because CEOs are just people. They have kids and don't want to be held responsible for problems that arise. Our CEO told me once that he was working in the UK when there was a chemical site explosion years ago, and he swore he never wanted to be in a situation like the CEO then and other managers who were grilled about what they didn't do by the media. Now we all look at Esso and the Longford plant and don't want to be in that situation. We all want to be loved. We don't want to be held responsible for these problems and the CEO is the one who will be on the TV. (Chemical Kings Australia)

More directly, implementation of a compliance system may occur because a regulator or court requires it as part of a settlement or judgment in the wake of a crisis or accident. However, the indirect effect on companies not the actual subject of proceedings is probably greater than the direct effect in these cases (see Chapter 9). The publicity that attends one case of a corporation being put on probation to implement a compliance system is likely to influence scores more to follow suit.

In his random stratified sample of 300 US companies with more than fifty employees, Apel (1995) found the top three motivations for compliance efforts to be: an intent to maintain an ethical reputation; general legal concerns, and a response to the US Federal Sentencing Guidelines for organizations; and fear of litigation. These results tend to confirm the primary importance of reputation and publicity as a motivator for compliance systems. A Price Waterhouse (1997) survey did not break down its motivational analysis into small enough categories to be very meaningful. It did find that 82 per cent of compliance programs were introduced to reduce liability exposure, and 27 per cent were in response to past problems. Forty-eight per cent also developed their compliance programs to respond to the Federal Sentencing Guidelines and 40 per cent to reflect specific industry guidelines. It is unclear whether firms in the first category were primarily motivated by the need to avoid the financial or the reputational costs of liability. The second figure does, however, confirm that the implementation of a compliance system is a response to a particular experience of regulatory disaster in a substantial minority of cases. On the whole the primary motivation for devoting resources to a compliance system seems to be directed towards avoiding the risks of non-compliance rather than a positive conception of good citizenship. An important but subordinate reason for compliance programs is in direct response to regulatory (or self-regulatory, i.e. industry association) guidelines and requirements such as the Federal Sentencing Guidelines, a regulator's direction or the Responsible Care scheme.

This is not to say that all companies will always respond to sanctions or horror stories. There are structural conditions that influence which organizations will become compliance leaders. Overall, large companies are much more likely than smaller ones to introduce compliance systems (e.g. Andersen 1996; Genn 1993; Gunningham 1998). In Haines' (1997) study of organizational occupational health and safety responses to the deaths of workers, larger and more profitable organizations were more likely to 'respond virtuously'. They re-evaluated organizational safety levels, altering workplaces or work practices and re-emphasizing current safety policy. She explains this by reference to the choices that competition offers them. Larger organizations with higher status in the 'contracting hierarchy' have greater choice and therefore more opportunity to see safety (compliance) as an integral part of success (see Haines 1997: 153, 216). For other organizations, whose choices are more limited, the relationship between profit and safety is more likely to be seen as negative.

Leadership to keep up with changing values and laws

Some compliance managers saw their organizations' top management as wanting to keep up with changes in community attitudes, law and regulation via the compliance system. They saw their companies' commitment to self-regulation in terms of a desire to be responsive to the regulatory and value changes they could see going on around them. Some organizations simply recognized the need to keep up with changing laws and values before any problems occurred. For example, the EEO officers in Aussie Dollars and Banksafe Australasia described the original genesis of their sexual harassment and EEO policies in changes in industrial relations legislation and the introduction of Sex Discrimination and Affirmative Action Acts in Australia. In one case, this was a result of a joint union–bank review of issues (Aussie Dollars). In the other case (Banksafe Australasia), employees themselves (perhaps as a result of awareness of their rights under the new legislation) were making a number of claims of harassment and unlawful termination.

Changes in the law or in community attitudes may be heralded by a dramatic accident, regulatory enforcement incident, court case or public scandal. The health, safety and environment head at Pharmarama, a Swiss-based pharmaceutical company, had worked his way up as an engineer over two decades and took a long view of how the corporate commitment to environment and safety had evolved with changes in community expectations over that time:

> Our [environment and safety] management system evolved and emerged over a long period. After World War Two there was a big industrial boom in Switzerland. There were some chemical explosions, some outside [Pharmarama] and some in [Pharmarama], so safety was seen as very important, but environment was a very small concern. Then in the 1960s people realized such damage cannot be done to nature. First people were concerned with wastewater and then air emissions ... You could smell it down here from the river. We didn't have any disasters then, but awareness was growing. You needed end of pipe controls. So the concern about the environment began to grow in addition to the existing concern with safety. In the 1990s environmental concern is very strong – it dominates ... In summary it is a gradual evolution. Awareness develops gradually, but you need key experiences of yourself or others like accidents or crises to push you to the next step when you are nearly ready anyway. For example, in the 1950s [Pharmarama] introduced safety engineers into *some* plants. Then there was an explosion in Pharmarama. So safety engineers were introduced in all plants and they got better support. Then there was a chemical reaction in [one division of Pharmarama] that caused dioxin poisoning. That was a signal that it was not enough to have a safety engineer specialist in each site. There must also be a corporate responsibility that can't be delegated. So we needed a systematic corporate management system.

In this safety and environment manager's analysis, his company had moved broadly with the changing values of the time, introducing small innovations and then being galvanized into further action by the spectre of disaster. Ultimately, then, the motivation to keep up with changing values and laws is about avoiding potential legitimacy crises or regulatory action.

The idea of implementing a compliance system generally comes from somewhere else. Thus, an impressive number of compliance managers described their company's compliance commitment as originating in the attitude of a new CEO who arrived on the scene enthused with values that were already widespread in the organization or culture where he or she had come from. For example, one EEO officer responsible for the sexual harassment and EEO program in a major Australian financial institution, Good as Gold Australia, believed that 'the impetus for our focus on diversity came from our CEO ... who came from the US and didn't believe the discrimination and lack of diversity in Good as

Gold Australia. He has been very public about it ... The program was not his initiative, but there was not the same commitment beforehand.' The phenomenon of new foreign CEOs bringing more progressive values with them is well known within the Australian financial industry. EEO officers in other companies looked on and regretted the lack of a US CEO to increase corporate commitment.

This can also occur on a broader scale, with whole national industries trying to catch up with the values and practices they perceive as institutionalized in leading nations. A compliance manager in Marks Bank, a German bank, attributed a new interest in and commitment to financial services compliance systems to a rapid improvement in regulation in Germany over the last seven years, the harmonization of European financial services regulation following the EU financial services directive and the regulator's requirement of audit of compliance system each year since 1994. He thought German banks were responding to the new regulatory area by working very hard 'to catch up' with US regulatory compliance practices.

A natural part of doing business

Finally, organizations may implement a self-regulation system simply because it has become a natural way of doing business in that industry, through a combination of regulatory action and the fact that a critical mass of other businesses has implemented such systems. This fits with the neo-institutional theory that norms begin as values that are ahead of community attitudes, then are embodied in social movements that successfully implement them into regulatory institutions such as laws, and finally become norms that everybody takes for granted. The fact that having a self-regulation function has become a part of the natural way of doing business in some areas was reflected in statements by compliance managers such as that their CEO saw compliance as 'a necessary evil. They think it's just the way the industry has gone that the compliance function has to be there' (Trustus Australia).

Implementing a self-regulation system may also occur almost as a condition of entering a new type of market, or doing business with larger companies. For example, one compliance manager in an investment bank (Trustus US) described how his bank had first taken compliance seriously when it had acquired a securities broking business. At that time traditional banks did not have compliance functions, but securities houses did.

Similarly the German compliance manager in Marks Bank, quoted above, saw European financial institutions following American compliance practices in financial services in order to be perceived as able to compete in the contemporary global financial services market. Regulators will also use widespread implementation of compliance systems as a natural part of the way in which they organize their inspections and other regulatory activities, although they may not formally mandate a compliance system. Other research has shown that contracting conditions can become an important mechanism in the diffusion of compliance functions. Larger organizations demand that their contracts only go to smaller organizations with appropriate self-regulation arrangements, and may even have systems for checking their contractors' compliance arrangements (e.g. Gunningham and Grabosky 1998: 109–13; Haines 1997: 235).[3]

OPENING THE WINDOW OF OPPORTUNITY: AGENTS OF CHANGE

Several actors can become agents of change by creating the crisis that draws management attention to compliance. Firstly, media attention and social movement activists can put pressure on top management and their public reputations to conform to values espoused by the public in order to avoid criticism. If top management constantly read in their newspapers that public attitudes towards their industry are plummeting, or see the misdeeds of themselves and their competitors catalogued regularly in the media, they are more likely than otherwise to be motivated to do something about potential problems. Secondly, regulatory enforcement blitzes, the introduction of new regulation, or government signals that new stricter regulation is being considered will create regulatory crises in top-management minds that may motivate interest in a compliance system.

But the creation of crises will have little ongoing effect if nobody inside the company takes responsibility for leveraging the maximum amount of corporate change from the opportunities they present. The most obvious potential internal agent of change is the CEO, the top manager himself or herself. When compliance managers were asked why their organization had implemented a compliance system and what factors they felt would make a system effective, they confirmed the importance of top-management commitment as a precondition to compliance system effectiveness. The US CEOs who brought a more proactive approach to preventing sexual harassment to the Australian financial industry, and the chemical company CEO described above, show how CEO commitment can be communicated effectively to other senior managers and encourage action on their part. This can also occur though a particular member of the board, perhaps a woman on a male-dominated board who takes an interest in harassment issues, or through an international parent that takes compliance issues very seriously and therefore forces the CEO of the subsidiary to do so.

The fish spine theory set out in Figure 2.3 illustrates how both external influences and internal receptiveness and capacity are necessary to institutionalize corporate responsibility. The balance of external influences vying for management attention will determine what priority is given to compliance. The internal constituents of the organization will determine how crises and opportunities for self-regulation will be handled. In the era of the new regulatory state, government agencies aim to work with these external and internal agents of self-regulation.

External change agents

A variety of external stakeholders, apart from regulators and governments, can and do permeate the veneer of corporate unresponsiveness (with varying impacts) to prompt commitment to implementation of a self-regulation system, to offer expertise, skills, comment or participation in the design and operation of a compliance management system, or to monitor and hold accountable its implementation and outcomes. External stakeholders who might seek to permeate corporations in this way can be divided into two categories:

- *Consumer and social movement activists*: Those whose interests are directly supposed to be protected by the compliance or self-regulation system, and those who claim to speak for those whose interests are directly at stake such as consumers, local communities, public interest groups, including environmental groups, and social movement activists. Internal stakeholders such as employees share much in common with this group.
- *Financial stakeholders*: Those with a financial stake in the company such as shareholders, investors, insurers, lenders and those who are deciding whether to purchase a financial stake in the company.

Consumers and social movement activists
Since the consumer revolution of the 1960s, US consumers and social movement campaigns have frequently targeted companies for social

responsibility shortcomings, and made a difference to corporate behaviour (Braithwaite and Drahos 2000: 597; Smith 1990). As a result some elements of corporate social responsibility do become part of the competitive structure of business (see Grabosky 1994). For example, Wheeler (1998: 14) cites a range of British survey evidence that consumers prefer to purchase products they perceive to be environmentally friendly. A 1994 US public opinion survey found that almost half of those polled were more likely to buy from a company with a good social reputation and almost 60 per cent would likely not buy from one with a bad reputation, while one-quarter would be willing to spend a premium of at least 6 per cent for products and packaging that were 'safe for the environment' (see also LeClair et al. 1998: 6).[4] Some concerned citizens have tried to boost the weight of their voice by buying shares in corporations they wish to influence in order to have the right to bring resolutions in general meetings. Others lobby investment schemes of which they are already members (such as church investors and pension funds/superannuation schemes) to take social responsibility issues into account in their investment decisions and proxy votes.

When the state brokers a means to monitor corporate behaviour, consumers do use it. For example, the US government has required companies to report all their emissions of pollutants and chemicals to air, water and land in the Toxics Release Inventory. The information was made available on the web, and consumers and a variety of public interest groups have made it one of the USA's most popular websites,[5] while regulatory officials have judged it 'one of the most effective instruments available' for reducing toxic emissions (Gunningham and Grabosky 1998: 64).

Some public interest groups, such as consumer groups and environmental groups, have developed a more focused interest, in comparing compliance system design and implementation and compliance outcomes so that they can discriminate between different companies in their consumer boycotts and socially informed investing. For example, in 1997 and 1998 the International Federation of Chemical, Energy, Mine and General Workers' Unions (ICEM 1997, 1998) published 'Stakeholders' Reports' on 'the world's most powerful mining corporation', Rio Tinto, in the tradition of the first social audits, which were externally generated reports disclosing social and environmental aspects of corporate business (Gray et al. 1996: 265–90). The Rio Tinto reports focus on the company's impacts on indigenous people, health, safety and workers rights, and the environment as well as financial and operational issues.

The most successful social action campaigns have resulted in voluntary schemes that set out codes of conduct or management system standards which companies must implement, combined with independent monitors to check compliance. Typically these schemes involve a code of conduct that has been agreed jointly between leading businesses and activists. The joining fee paid by member companies funds an independent inspectorate. Thus, the effectiveness of social movement politics at mobilizing media publicity and shame to prompt management attention to a social issue is institutionalized into an agreement setting out a code of conduct. It is the independent monitoring of compliance with the code of conduct that ultimately cashes out social concern into day-to-day accountability, since the monitors are supposed to be given regular access right inside the company and are able to monitor on a systematic and professional basis.

One of the most successful examples is the Rugmark Foundation that monitors compliance with a code which provides for the education of former child labourers and their replacement with adult labour in carpet manufacture in South Asia (Liubicic 1998: 130; Varley 1998: 451ff). Other similar initiatives include the FIFA (Federation Internationale de Football Association) program for the manufacture of soccer balls without child labour (see Liubicic 1998: 130–1, Varley 1998: 458ff), and forest stewardship councils in various countries, beginning in Canada, that provide independent certification of well-managed forests to timber and paper buyers (Gunningham and Grabosky 1998: 108).

On the whole, however, consumers and social movement activists lack the capacity to effectively monitor the claims of companies about the environmental and social responsibility of their products and internal management systems. In many cases they may not even be aware of which companies and their internal compliance systems should be of particular concern to them. As Liubicic (1998: 116) concluded from his review of voluntary corporate social responsibility codes, consumer pressure motivates only those multi-nationals that have a 'tarnishable image', generally those that manufacture or sell consumer goods for which they spend money advertising to create consumer goodwill.

Smith (1998) and Karliner (1997) have both published critiques of corporate environmentalism that show how easy it is to pull the wool over stakeholder eyes through 'greenwashing' an environmentally friendly veneer over an essentially unchanged production process (see Chapter 6). While consumer and social movement activists can have a significant impact on compliance, they generally have neither enough access nor enough clout to be effective on their own. The second category, financial stakeholders, is rather different.

Financial stakeholders

Potential investors in a company, such as those proposing to take over a business, intending to buy shares, lenders proposing to borrow money or insurers with a major amount at stake, can be interested in compliance outcomes. Their primary interest is ensuring that no scandals or breaches of legal obligations are about to be discovered and ruin their investment in the company. Increasingly such investors believe that a good way to get assurance that non-compliance will not become an issue is by checking whether the compliance system design is adequate to prevent future breaches, and that it is well implemented.

There already exist a variety of organizations aimed at encouraging and assisting institutional and other investors to use their investment decisions, and sometimes proxy votes, to promote corporate social responsibility.[6] For example, the Social Investment Forum is an organization based in Washington DC, with the object of promoting socially responsible investing and a membership of over 600 investment professionals and institutions.[7] It set up the Valdez principles, now administered by the Coalition for Environmentally Responsible Economies, as a code of environmental practice in the wake of the Exxon-Valdez disaster (Gray et al. 1996: 260). The Interfaith Center on Corporate Responsibility (ICCR) comprises more than 275 religious institutions, controlling US$100 billion in shares in the USA, that use their investments to promote social change.[8] It publishes principles for global corporate responsibility and has a history of encouraging churches and individuals to use their shareholdings to propose shareholder resolutions at meetings that highlight corporate social responsibility issues such as companies' activities in South Africa during the apartheid era, the marketing of breast-milk substitutes in third world countries (Simpson 1991: 6, 27) and genetically modified foods in the USA (Cowe 1999).

Various books on socially responsible investing are available to the socially conscious middle class with spare cash to invest (e.g. Hancock 1998; Miller 1991). The US 'ethical investment market' has been estimated to amount to roughly one out of every ten dollars in the market, and asset management and socially screened portfolios have grown at a rate of approximately 200 per cent over the last two years.[9] In 1997 the Social Investment Forum estimated that more than US$1 trillion in assets was under management in US portfolios that use screens linked to ethics, the environment or corporate social responsibility, an amount that would account for nearly 9 per cent of the US$13.7 trillion in investment assets under professional management in the USA (Social Investment Forum 1997). By the end of 1999 the Forum found that socially responsible investing in the USA had grown to US$2.16 trillion, amounting to one out of every eight dollars under professional management in the USA (Social Investment Forum 1999).[10] The Forum also found that the fastest growing element of socially responsible investing in the USA in 1999 was portfolios that utilize shareholder advocacy as well as screening.

In 1991 Simpson estimated that ethical investment funds amounted to US$500 billion in the USA and £100 billion in the UK. She was able to list twenty-nine ethical investment funds of various types operating in the UK (Simpson 1991: 1, 10). If single-issue social responsibility investment is considered, the amounts invested according to social responsibility principles may be higher. For example, Simpson (1991: 6) reports that £89 billion worth of UK pension funds (or 40 per cent of the total) in 1989 operated with some form of restriction relating to South Africa, with similar proportions in the USA.[11]

As Gray and co-authors (1996: 251) note, specialist ethical and environmental investment funds are likely to remain too small relative to the whole market to be a very potent agent of change. But the increasing interest in socially responsible investing from various institutional investors promises to be a more powerful avenue of change. (The figures above that estimate the extent of the social investment market do attempt to include such funds.) Gray and others cite evidence that US and UK pension funds, especially trade union, local authority and public service funds, are showing an increased interest in the social ramifications of their investments. For example, the Central American Union Federation AFL-CIO (through the development of social criteria for investment) and the California Public Employee Pension System (through its attempts to force a stronger environmental commitment from Exxon Corporation in the wake of the Exxon-Valdez disaster) each have reputations for socially responsible investments.

The *Times* of 24 November 1999 (p. 6) carried a report that Britain's largest life insurance company, Prudential, had announced that it had hired an ethical investment consultant to advise on the environmental and social responsibility practices of British business 'to screen all its investments in UK-quoted companies and flag up those which have no positive policies towards the environment, equal opportunities and health and safety of staff'. Mark Thompson, an investment director at the company, is quoted as saying, 'We're taking this approach for financial reasons, not moral ones. We believe that environmentally sound companies are better run and will make good investments in the long run.' His attitude suggests that social responsibility concerns are filtering into the marketplace. But, in relying on financial stakeholders such as institutional investors to leverage corporate operational responses to environmental and social responsibility issues, social responsibility remains subordinated to economic efficiency and profits.

In fact, the jury is still out on whether good corporate citizens are better investments than poor corporate citizens. Chapter 3 reviewed some of the evidence that 'ethical' investment strategies may be more profitable than investing in the general market. However, more broad-ranging and theoretically rigorous studies are ambivalent. Wheeler (1998: 14) cites an analysis of the results of twenty-one studies of this issue that come to the conclusion that firms with a social responsibility agenda certainly 'performed no worse and perhaps better' than others (Pava and Krausz 1995). Similarly Gray et al. (1996: 249) find from their review of the research that 'ethical investment portfolios, whether hypothetically constructed on the basis of particular criteria or comprising the actual shareholdings of the ethical trusts themselves, broadly produce returns in line with the market as whole'. However, the stricter the ethical criteria, the lesser the return (Gray et al. 1996: 249). The most recent studies tend to confirm this conclusion: that there is no clear evidence that socially responsible investing out-performs general market indices, and there is usually no significant difference in return at all (see D'Antonio et al. 1997; Dhrymes 1998; Kurtz 1997).

Simpson (1991: 85, 86) conducted a very thorough review of the studies available at that time and found that it was almost impossible to draw any conclusions at all on the performance of investment funds that focus on investing only in positively responsible companies, because of the diversity of criteria for investment, the inevitable variation in the performance of investment managers and the lack of data. It was only methodologically sound to try to draw conclusions on funds that screen out certain companies on negative grounds for irresponsible practices (such as companies with links to South Africa during apartheid, with nuclear weapons manufacture and tobacco production), although a variety of factors can complicate these studies too. On the whole the results seem to show that none of the screened investments studied has excluded enough investments to make a big difference to performance positive or negative.

However, an element of the self-fulfilling prophecy complicates this question. As Simpson (1991: 92) argues, using disinvestment in South Africa as her example:

> ... as sentiment grows against South Africa, and the health of the economy is weakened by selective sanctions and presents a risk for investors, the investor who supported the social movement will gain. The performance argument works in favor of the ethical investor while their concerns are beginning to have an effect on wider society. Likewise, as active socially responsible investors have pressed US companies to disinvest, so the pool of untainted companies grows and makes performance easier for other South Africa free investment vehicles. There is also a self-fulfilling element to these forms of investment which is due to weight of capital involved. If big investors decide that certain shares are 'good' – for example, certain well-identified green stocks – then their price will rise.

Ultimately share values relate to market perceptions, and as public perceptions change, this may affect share prices. In the end it is only because public interest groups and activists have exposed corporate wrongdoing that people have sued and governments have acted to introduce stricter regulations, that environmental and social responsibility affect corporate profits at all. The two sets of stakeholders are interdependent. The responsibility is everybody's in a democratic society to keep market perceptions of corporate value and profitability in kilter with social and environmental value.

Insurers and lenders too are beginning to make their decisions partially on the basis of corporate implementation of legal and social responsibility management systems (see Gray et al. 1996: 253–4; Gunningham and Grabosky 1998: 115–20). There may be a very direct link between the economic wisdom of the decision to insure/lend or not to insure/lend, and the existence of legal and social liabilities. Some lenders and insurers are making some effort to test the implementation and effectiveness of companies' self-regulatory systems, especially in relation to environmental, health and safety management. Frye (1998; see also Gunningham and Grabosky 1998: 115–18) reviews the way in which many US lenders have focused increasingly on the borrower's corporate environmental management system, often using ISO 14001 or EMAS (the European Union's standards for environmental management systems). He shows how US case law, which makes lenders potentially responsible for the environmental liabilities of their debtors, has encouraged this trend. Lenders also have an interest to avoid the strict cleanup responsibilities required under US law if they have to foreclose and, of course, are concerned that the borrower not default because of environmental liabilities. Frye (1998) points out that sometimes the identification of environmental risks during financing results in the lender bringing in an insurance company which becomes an additional stakeholder with an interest in minimizing environmental problems at the site.

Insurance companies most spectacularly showed their concern with their own possible liability for environmental disasters in the discussions at the Kyoto Climate Change Convention in 1997. At Kyoto, Greenpeace ran a campaign to persuade insurers to break ranks with manufacturing and energy interests. Insurers warned that they would unload the shares of companies that did not modify environmentally destructive practices, as they became increasingly concerned that natural disasters associated with uncontrolled climate change could wipe them out (Braithwaite and Drahos 2000: 275). As Joly (*c.* 1997), the senior vice-president of Storebrand, Norway's biggest insurance company, points out, insurance companies as an industry are at risk from the likely consequences of climate change. Loss prevention is therefore a major motivating factor in insurance companies arguing for global action on climate change (see, generally, Gunningham and Grabosky 1998: 106–21; Schmidheiny and Zorraquin 1996).

The aim of many investors, especially institutional ones, is to create a new relationship with their fund managers, 'to shift the balance away from the professionals who invest money, and towards the ultimate owners or trustees who are becoming actively involved in laying down investment strategy' (Simpson 1991: 8). This could mean that the juggernaut of short-termism is controlled. Consider Miller's (1991) account of his personal conversion to socially responsible investing from a view that companies and investment managers should manage purely in the interests of shareholders:

> Then it struck me that there really is no conflict between my social concerns over environmental degradation, racial discrimination, or political disenfranchisement on the one hand and my philosophical convictions that (1) corporations exist for the sake of their *stockholders*, not for the sake of their employees or communities or society at large, and (2) investment managers have fiduciary responsibilities to their *clients*, not to various other segments or all of society, on the other. And the resolution really was simple.
>
>   All I had to do was recognize that the legitimate interests of shareholders and investors are not necessarily limited simply to maximizing their short-term financial returns. Rather, they may – and often do –

encompass nonquantifiable and nonfinancial concerns for the *quality* of life itself – including the air they breathe, the water they drink, and the opportunity to live free. Thus, even if it is morally indefensible for a company's management to act otherwise than to maximize risk-adjusted returns for its shareholders in the absence of a mandate from them to do so, once granted such a mandate, that is precisely what a company's management *must* do. (Miller 1991: xii; emphasis in original)

Here Miller describes a paradigm shift: from the investor as purely concerned with being a rational economic actor, to restoring his integrity as a whole person with other beliefs and values and becoming a citizen in his stance towards his investments, not just a profit-maker.

What he does not do is take the next steps of recognizing that, as a citizen of a community, he might be under an obligation to care for his fellow citizens and their welfare and the well-being of their common environment. He does not see that he might have the responsibility in his shareholder status to deliberate with other shareholders about the values that should guide their business, and that perhaps this deliberation should be expanded to others who are directly affected by the business practice of 'his' company, including employees, managers, local communities, and so on. Furthermore he might need to recognize that just as he himself is a citizen with various values and obligations, so too is the corporate entity in which he invests (made up as it is of employees, shareholders, managers, and so on, who all have individual values and citizenship obligations) and that therefore the corporate entity as a whole may legitimately be required to pursue values other than short-term profit-making.

Internal change agents

As the most powerful manager in the company, the CEO is the most *influential* internal agent of change in compliance matters. But the most *strategic* agent of change is the compliance professional. This is because the compliance manager is a specialist devoted to analysing and addressing compliance risks for the sake of the company. Indeed, compliance staff can create a feedback loop for strengthening compliance, once a window of opportunity is opened, as follows:

1   A crisis occurs, so top management looks around for an appropriate way to respond.
2   Someone is aware that leading companies in their industry or in some other industry have compliance systems. They decide to

follow their lead and implement a compliance system and to appoint someone to the position of compliance manager (or 'environmental' manager or 'EEO' officer or Greenhouse coordinator). Indeed, McCaffrey and Hart (1998: 87) found that Wall Street firms often hired high-profile attorneys or former regulators as general counsel or compliance manager in the wake of regulatory disasters. One firm hired a prominent attorney in such circumstances and gave him a US$4 million signing bonus, which earned him the label the 'Darryl Strawberry of compliance' (a reference to a high-earning baseball star).

3   The new self-regulation function institutionalizes a permanent (at least as permanent as any function or office in intra-corporate politics can be) mechanism of communication of risks and business case arguments for compliance to top management, so that interest and commitment to compliance no longer rely solely on the haphazard regulatory events that occur externally and happen to come to CEO attention.

4   If self-regulation managers are effective and not sidelined within the organization, they will be able to prevent top management slipping back to complete ignorance of compliance issues and will gradually work on implementing a 'best practice' compliance system as modelled by other companies, utilizing any further crises (or potential crises) to make incremental gains.

Self-regulation managers' techniques for securing top-management commitment to implementing, researching and supporting compliance/social responsibility programs reflect this recursive structure. Maintaining management commitment is an ongoing (Sisyphean) task of 'grabbing attention' by reference to potential or actual disasters, then building commitment by defining compliance as an essential strategic issue for the business. The 'business case' for building commitment can incorporate the savings and the marketing opportunities self-regulation represents, a desire to enhance reputation and legitimacy or simply the need to keep up with commonly held views of good business practice.

Commitment is built on much more than a deterrent threat. It incorporates a wide variety of reasons for seeing self-regulation as strategic, both positive and negative. Yet as Figure 2.3 also implies, it is the regulator, and the public, who must deliver the ultimate 'sales pitch' to management by providing clear sanctions (formal or informal) for breaches of legal standards. While self-regulation professionals can sell the efficiency benefits and cost effectiveness of a program, they must have the full attention of senior management to do so. This means that frequently various stakeholder groups must prompt management motivation to compliance system implementation.

CONCLUSION

The results of the research summarized in this chapter, and the previous one, do not offer much succour to the 'true believer' who might hope that companies would automatically implement effective compliance systems out of a natural disposition to comply. This does not necessarily mean there is no widespread disposition to do so voluntarily. But if that disposition does exist, it is not sufficient to motivate the devotion of resources to implementation of a system to ensure compliance. The best chance for getting most companies to implement a systematic self-regulation program seems to be when there is a crisis of legitimacy brought about through a moral panic in the local community, a spectacular regulatory enforcement action, or a major accident. These events create a window of opportunity in which top-management attention is momentarily focused on the risks of non-compliance and on the benefits of attempting to systematically ensure compliance.

While the window is open, the nature and effectiveness of the system implemented depend on two things: what models are available, and what use internal company agents and external stakeholders make of the opportunity. When a crisis occurs, the organization which suffers, and many others who are watching their industry environment, are likely to respond to the crisis or potential crisis by implementing whatever self-regulation systems they see being modelled by leaders in their business environment or being promoted by regulators and other groups. The nature of the self-regulation field will depend on the models developed by those companies who have already become motivated to become leaders and by self-regulation professionals, regulators, and external interest groups before the window of opportunity opened. If there are some standards for self-regulation systems generally accepted by regulators and industry and if there are self-regulation professionals with integrity available, then management commitment may well fade when the crisis is over, but a decent system will be in place that institutionalizes the possibility for management commitment to be raised again.

That is, at least, the potential. The reality will often turn on what the self-regulation function does, once one is introduced into the organization. Community and regulatory values do not permeate organizational cultures and structures unembodied: internal actors, especially self-regulation practitioners, are key influences on the way in which a number of other important factors (internal and external) affect the corporation. They can foment change and response through their own dual allegiances to the organization and also to community or regulatory values. The integrity of the corporation will often depend (but not exclusively) on self-regulation practitioners and how they do their job – their personal and professional integrity. They can help to overcome bounded rationality and bounded imagination within organizational decision-making. Chapter 5 turns to the emergence of the self-regulation profession, and the methodology adopted by 'best practice' self-regulation professionals.

5 | Self-regulation methodology and social harmony

A crisis of social concern may spark the first phase of organizational institutionalization of responsible self-regulation – top-management interest and commitment. However, the initial response to social responsibility concerns will often be a general statement of policy lacking specific steps, standards or incentives for implementation by management (Weiss 1981: 412). Companies without a pre-existing self-regulation system rarely have the institutional capacity to act effectively on management commitment. The second phase of institutionalization of self-regulation is the acquisition of skills and expertise to act on that commitment, generally through the establishment of a self-regulation function.

This chapter analyses the methodology adopted by best practice practitioners. Compliance managers see the ideal compliance (or similar) function as a bridge from management commitment to institutionalization of legal and social responsibilities in all the business of organizational life. The (often naive) hope is that theirs will be a 'harmonizing' role (see Figure 5.1). Self-regulation staff aim to bridge the gap between the values of the wider society, including regulators, governments and public interest groups, and the pursuit of business. In practice, organizational self-regulators sit at the point of fracture between the business of profit and the various legal and social responsibilities that different members of the broader society legitimately (and sometimes illegitimately) hold for organizations. Self-regulation professionals will frequently face a choice between taking on organizational power structures to fight for legal and social responsibility, giving in to business pressure or giving up their self-regulation role. Chapters

6 and 7 look more closely at the potential for conflict in the self-regulation manager's role.

THE EMERGENCE OF THE SELF-REGULATION PROFESSION

Many corporate compliance and self-regulation programs are devised by corporate lawyers, particularly in the established areas of antitrust and securities regulation in the USA. Indeed, inhouse lawyers have grown in number and significance over the last twenty years (Liggio 1997: 1203–4).[1] Their 'professional project', particularly in the USA, has included the claim that they have an important role in advising on compliance with regulatory norms through the practice of preventive law (Rosen 1989: 487; see also Gruner 1997; Nelson and Nielsen 2000). However, the expansion of compliance and risk management programs in corporations has also opened a number of new professional 'jurisdictions' (Abbott 1988), specializing in the management of legal and ethical issues around securities, environment, health and safety.

The growth and 'professionalization' of compliance work are reflected in the development of a range of specialist groups of self-regulation professionals. Mostly these relate to areas where there is a history of significant regulation. They include:

- The Society of Consumer Affairs Professionals in Business in the USA, Australia and Europe was set up to provide professional culture, support and knowledge for people employed by organizations to handle *consumer complaints*.
- The Regulatory Affairs Professionals Society in the *pharmaceutical industry* with 4000 members worldwide is another example of such an organization.
- The US *Health Care Compliance* Association now has 3000 members and will soon offer them professional accreditation (Singer 1998, 2000: 13; see, generally, Heller et al. 2001).
- The US Privacy Officers Association was recently set up to cater for *privacy officers and advisers* in all industries and began with seventy members in its first month (Singer 2000).
- There are countless associations and meetings catering for *environmental and occupational health and safety* managers (see Farr et al. 1994; Futrell 1994: 834; Wren 1995; Wright 1998).
- Compliance officers in the US *securities industry* began to meet as early as the 1960s, with their 1996 conference having over

2200 participants (McCaffrey and Hart 1998: 84). The US Securities Institute Association holds a compliance meeting every year attended by hundreds of compliance managers, mainly from securities houses.

- The US National Society of Compliance Professionals is more inclusive of compliance professionals from *banks* that have broker-dealer services and the Investment Company Institute also has a very large compliance section.[2]
- In the UK the Compliance Institute (formerly known as the UK Association for Compliance Officers) and SHCOG (Securities Houses Compliance Officers Group) were both established as professional associations for compliance managers in the *finance and banking* area in the early 1990s and between them now have over 1000 members.[3] The introduction of a new regulatory system under the 1986 Financial Services Act encouraged most firms carrying on investment business to introduce a devoted compliance function (Weait 1994: 381). In the 1990s (the former) financial regulators such as the Securities and Futures Authority (SFA) and the Investment Management Regulatory Organisation (IMRO) both experienced high staff turnover as experienced regulatory staff were lured away to much higher paid jobs as compliance managers in financial institutions eager to ensure they were not the next Barings.[4]
- In Frankfurt an informal group of compliance officers from the biggest banks with *investment* businesses meets regularly to exchange opinions and the Bankers' Association includes a more formal compliance section.[5]

Most significant is the emergence of practitioners who identify themselves broadly as 'compliance professionals', rather than as lawyers, auditors or specialists in a substantive regulatory area. The new occupation spans non-lawyers, including human resource managers, auditors, ex-lawyers who now see themselves as compliance managers, and lawyers who specialize in compliance issues. The emergence of the new occupation is evident in a sprinkling of new professional associations and institutions that cater to their interests and concerns:

- The compliance section of the Practising Law Institute meets annually in New York and San Francisco, with about one hundred in attendance at each meeting.
- In the USA the Ethics Officer Association, a professional association for the exchange of information and strategies on corpo-

rate ethics, compliance and business conduct programs, was formed in 1992 and had grown from 30 to more than 500 members by 1998 (Driscoll et al. 1995: 117; Driscoll et al. 1998: 49; Morf et al. 1999), and to over 700 members in October 2000.[6]

• The membership of the Association for Compliance Professionals Australia (ACPA) illustrates how the compliance industry draws together people from many different occupational backgrounds into a new profession. ACPA has grown to well over 1000 members since it was established in mid-1996, and incorporates lawyers as well as auditors, regulators and ex-regulators, managers, trainers, human resource managers, and many others.

These are associations that are distinct from the legal profession (although the American Corporate Counsel Association has also taken an interest in compliance issues; see Rosen 1989). One study of ethics and compliance officers in the USA found that only one-third of the sample had a law degree (University of Tampa Center for Ethics 1997). Only 19 per cent of members of the Ethics Officer Association come from a legal background (Ethics Officer Association 1999). Another survey of 200 organizations with ethics or compliance programs found that, of those responsible for the program, the three most common areas of expertise were general business management (31 per cent), legal (26 per cent), and audit and finance (percentage not stated) (Petry 1995). Only about half of the membership of the ACPA work in law firms or inhouse legal departments (Compliance News 2001).

Clearly there is no one self-regulation profession. There are a variety of specialist occupations that perform self-regulation or regulatory compliance functions. In Australia and America, at least, there exist broad-ranging associations and networks that aim to bring together both specialists and those with responsibility for more generic compliance. However, whether these different occupations self-consciously identify with one another or not, they do perform similar functions and articulate very similar philosophies as to how self-regulation professionals should do their jobs.

THE METHODOLOGY OF SELF-REGULATION PRACTICE

The purpose of introducing a compliance or self-regulation function is ostensibly to integrate legal and social responsibilities into the day-to-day management and behaviour of the organization. My analysis of interviews with self-regulation professionals, their professional literature, and their conference and seminar presentations give a fairly consistent picture of the methodology by which practitioners in different industries, regulatory arenas and nations achieve this goal. This methodology can be summarized in the following steps:

- Secure *top-management commitment* to the compliance program and to the structure and status of the compliance function.
- Conduct a *review of the compliance/social responsibility risks* raised by the organization and its context (including legal, social, ethical or environmental issues as appropriate), and compile a list or register of laws, regulations, voluntary codes, and other provisions and principles with which the company ought to comply. These may be priority ranked.
- *Match risks, laws, and so on, to relevant businesses, units of operation and individual job descriptions* in order to make it clear which roles and units need to comply with which provisions and principles.
- *Design management structures, standard operating procedures, directives and guidance systems* to ensure that managers and workers comply with the identified provisions. This might include operating system redesign, product redesign, sign-offs and reporting requirements, new standard operating procedures, and changed job profiles, decision-making criteria for investments that include compliance criteria, and so on.
- Design *training programs and documentation* to communicate their particular compliance responsibilities to all employees, to secure senior and middle management commitment to the compliance program, and to change cultures and attitudes where necessary. Documentation can include manuals, handbooks, online documents, reminder cards, posters, newsletters and memos from the CEO or senior managers. Training programs may include computer-based training, work unit discussion groups, formal seminars led by compliance staff or external consultants, videos, and workbooks that employees must go through with their supervisors.
- Set up *auditing and monitoring systems* for discovering and responding to potential compliance problems. This can include implementing consumer and staff complaints-handling systems and hotlines, ensuring compliance staff are constantly available for queries and advice, and implementing monitoring, surveillance and auditing programs.

- Use performance reviews, disciplinary systems, promotions and bonuses to *hold staff accountable or reward them* in relation to their implementation of their compliance responsibilities.

The more sophisticated literature, including Australia's standard for compliance programs (AS 3806–1998), states that corporate compliance program methodology also ought to include another series of steps associated with the evaluation, review and improvement of the compliance program. But my data and other research have found that it is rare that even apparently best practice compliance professionals attempt to implement these steps in a systematic way (except in environmental management systems). Therefore these steps are omitted from this description of self-regulation methodology. (This issue will be further discussed in Chapters 8 and 9.)

In the implementation of these seven steps a few basic principles characterized the approach seen as most effective by those interviewed and observed, and in their literature. As with all my analysis of the data from self-regulation managers, this does not mean that all of the interviewees felt they had perfectly implemented these principles and elements. Rather, they concluded from their experiences of success or failure that these few principles would be important for success. These could be expressed in four 'mottoes':

- *Be commercially streetwise*: offer solutions, not prohibitions.
- *Make compliance easy and natural*: incorporate it into standard operating procedures and management practices.
- *Change hearts and minds*: use education and training backed up with disciplinary action.
- *Strive to incorporate compliance into the heart of corporate decision-making* about investments, strategies and accountability.

The first three principles met near-unanimous agreement among the self-regulation professionals interviewed and observed. The fourth is more rarely volunteered (although it is also rarely dissented from), but as I will argue below, it is the key in determining whether legal and social responsibility has actually been institutionalized effectively.

Be commercially streetwise

The one over-riding principle frequently mentioned as the hallmark of the effective compliance professional is the ability to accommodate compliance and business to achieve both regulatory and business goals simultaneously: an equitable workplace that attracts excellent staff; minimal paperwork and prohibitions; a plant with a good reputation with workers and local communities; satisfied, well-informed consumers; and so on. The 1998 meeting of the ACPA was told by a former compliance manager, now marketing manager in a major financial institution, that business managers 'want compliance to be invisible'. She reminded the audience that business managers want compliance managers who 'understand and focus on business objectives', who 'don't say no' but offer solutions and find ways of legally achieving business goals. Compliance managers are expected to 'facilitate business objectives' by being 'service providers not decision-makers'.[7] The work of harmonization of legal norms with organizational culture, corporate governance systems and business goals requires the compliance professional to act less 'in the role of a policeman ... than an ally in an effort to run the company profitably and legally' (Beckenstein and Gabel 1983: 477).

Compliance managers strive to avoid being seen as aloof and legalistic. They want to be seen to identify with business perspectives: 'They can't see you as a stuck up knowledge-bonce. You need to get a bond of trust with them. You need to get them to like you, to have a good working relationship so that they will come to you with questions' (Trustus UK). One compliance professional described it as a 'marketing exercise' to be visible and accessible and to help with any problems they have, 'because I want them to think I'm really helpful ... so they have confidence in me to come to me with a problem' (Trustus Australia). This principle for action identifies compliance professionals' role as loyal citizens of the corporation. They must be 'commercially streetwise' in seeking to align the 'business case' for compliance with the operation of the compliance system: 'We do a balancing act between making sure the company complies and there is still a business' (Alpine Insurance (Australia)). A handbook for UK financial services compliance officers sets out the concern behind this principle well:

> In order to ... succeed in breeding real commitment, however, you need to demonstrate the alignment of these compliance concerns with the long-term interests of the firm and its owners. In short, business success is built on reputation, and reputation is built by the firm through the protection of investors, through clean and orderly market conduct and through not posing a risk to the financial system. Your advice must further, and be sold on the basis that it furthers, these objectives. (Newton 1998: 139)

Indeed, the ability to integrate compliance with business is seen by many compliance managers as the chief innovation of their new profession. Many interviewees were at pains to contrast the business-oriented approach they took as compliance professionals with what they saw as the less effective and more obtrusive legalism of traditional lawyers (see Parker 2000b). Adviser Two, a compliance lawyer in private practice, was keen to point out that his firm took a 'management-oriented approach to legal services', in contrast to other law firms, by physically working in clients' offices. The compliance manager at Trustus Australia quoted above emphasized that it was important for her to put a lot of effort into 'getting close to the business, showing that you're commercial, helping to find solutions. Legal will come in and say, "You don't comply. It's your problem. See you later." We can't do that.' Adviser Seven offered a harsh criticism of lawyers' approach to compliance:

> Lawyers offer a numeric approach. They start with section forty and go onwards through the Act covering everything. It is better to not respect the law but people and jobs … The perception of compliance as a legal issue is a problem. Frequently the lawyer is only one hundredth of the answer. I know one company where the lawyer responsible for compliance has never even met the marketing manager and that compliance program is going to be useless.

The ultimate effect of an over-riding focus on harmonization can be that compliance staff try to avoid conflict:

> The compliance people who have been the most successful are the ones that don't go around beating up on business units. They keep commercial reality in their minds … They are the ones with the gentle approach who get business on side … Good compliance people have enough business acumen not to be too theoretical, but to give solutions. Otherwise you just have clashes all the time. (Convict Cash Australia)

As this compliance manager recognizes, effective compliance managers cannot be engaged in political stoushes all the time. However, an exclusive focus on being gentle on commercial reality is not always appropriate either. A compliance manager who cannot impose a compliance decision on a line manager, when necessary, is thoroughly ineffectual.

Make compliance easy and natural

The second principle follows naturally from the first: compliance managers try to make being compliant as easy and natural as possible for employees. Compliance professionals frequently claim that good compliance systems are about management ingenuity more than law (Sharpe 1996). It is about designing operating procedures and management systems for preventing breaches before they occur. This is the 'nuts and bolts' work of harmonization of business and compliance – the competence and skills analysis to identify the compliance tasks and responsibilities of every individual in the company, and management system design that might go right back to the basics of the business plan, or the operating procedure.

For example, standard operating procedure might specify what protective clothing should be worn when, safe procedures for operating machinery, what information should be given to customers or investors before completing a transaction, which documents should be checked by lawyers, what events should trigger a report to compliance, and so on. In factories this could also include equipment design to make non-compliance impossible or difficult, such as via technology that reduces or avoids pollution, safety barricades and automatic shut-downs.

In services industries, equivalent attempts to prevent non-compliance by design can be accomplished by computerized systems. Some securities houses use systems that will not allow traders to complete trades that would breach conflicts of interest rules, capital maintenance requirements and other rules. Alpine Insurance has a sophisticated computer system for checking all documents produced at any level of the company for any public purpose for breaches of the Trade Practices Act (such as false and misleading conduct), or any other relevant company policy. Whenever anybody (from sales agents to senior managers) produces a letter, advertisement or other document that will be seen outside the company, they must email that document to the system for sign-off by a compliance officer and a legal officer before they can send it out. The compliance and legal departments guarantee that all documents are processed within a certain time limit. The computer system creates a record of what documents have been approved, how long they took to gain approval and any issues that are raised. This is the heart and soul of preventive compliance systems – 'embedding' compliance systems in the management, culture and goals of the organization (Sharpe 1996).

Compliance is in part a creative task of thinking up systems for effectively ensuring compliance in all the nooks and crannies of the organization. These systems push the responsibility for compliance onto every worker and manager as a natural part of their jobs:

The biggest advantage of having an environmental management system is to make sure that environmental issues are dealt with in the ordinary management system – to make sure that people know their job has an environmental impact and what to do to avoid or minimize that impact. Previously the people in operations were thinking there were environmental issues in their work. But they would think the environmental office is in charge of those issues or the environmental officer will tell me what to do. He has to understand his task is to control the environmental impact. (Hot Rods)

The main objective of this principle, and of corporate compliance systems in general, is to facilitate and empower others in the business to 'do compliance', so that compliance is not solely the responsibility of the compliance function, but is a natural part of everybody's function. Compliance professionals continually attempt to 'cascade' responsibility for compliance down through line management, so that a culture of compliance commitment permeates the organization:

Our job is to supply the tools for compliance so that people know that they have to comply and know where to find out how to if they need to. At [name of another company] they had seventeen solicitors and they were checking absolutely everything. Then they realized that it wasn't their job to do compliance, but to provide the tools for everybody else to do it. (Alpine Insurance)

As a compliance manager at Trustus (Australia) put it, 'It is your job to educate business and let them take ownership and responsibility for compliance themselves. You are aiming at doing yourself out of a job.' At their most noble, this is the purpose of ethics and compliance programs: to push legal and ethical values so far down into organizational life that they become part of the everyday reflexes of the company. This emphasizes the inherent interdependence of self-regulation practice: the self-regulation professional is dependent on the members of the business to accomplish social and legally responsible actions, while the members of the business are dependent on the self-regulation manager to help them think through how to do this in practice.

Change hearts and minds

In order to make compliance easy and natural, compliance managers spend much of their time trying to change the behaviour and attitudes of employees and managers. The centrepiece of most compliance programs in trade practices, financial services and sexual harassment was the employee training and communications program. (In environmental management systems, training was less important, and technological innovation to reduce environmental impact more important.) These programs have two major aims: to train employees in standard operating procedures that embed compliance in the organization, and to engage with employees' values and change attitudes towards compliance.

The training and communication programs are frequently the major focus of compliance practice. But compliance managers also struggle to ensure that training is backed with discipline and rewards. These too have two purposes: to motivate employees and managers, since evaluations, rewards and potential discipline drive the rest of business conduct, and to distance the company from non-compliance and prove to regulators that non-compliance is taken seriously by dismissing or disciplining individuals identified as responsible. As we shall see, the ideal of backing up training with discipline and rewards is not always realized.

Compliance staff often focus much of their energy on training programs. Interviewees described compliance systems in which employees are required to attend induction courses that incorporate compliance elements, followed by regular update and training programs. The more traditional, and still widely used, form of program is the training session in groups of twelve to forty people, which involves interactive discussions of real-life problems and aims at equipping participants to understand the conduct that will get them into trouble. All interviewees rejected the archaic lecture approach to compliance training that focused on legal principles and definitions: 'We avoid using section numbers like the plague … We don't dazzle them with law. We've learnt that just puts them off. They are more interested in what they can do and why' (Aussie Products). Many companies used videos or simple manuals with cartoons and concrete examples in their training sessions.

One of the most popular new developments is computer-based training that staff members can complete at their desks in their own time. The latest technology not only uses video-clip scenarios and multiple-choice questions, but also records staff members' answers to test questions, affording the company a quantitative check of the compliance knowledge and 'awareness' of its staff. Staff can be required to complete training modules regularly, and the system will provide a documentary record of the fact that the organization has forced its staff to undergo training. This can be produced to regulators or courts if the company's compliance commitment comes into question at some later point.

Awareness education is not confined to face-to-face training programs. All the companies used a variety of different media to ensure

that the need to avoid non-compliance, and the possibility of being disciplined for engaging in it, were constantly before employees. Ways of
getting the message across included posters, pamphlets and stickers,
circulars and memoranda from senior management, propaganda
through the company's internal TV channel, and newsletters. One EEO
officer interviewed described the 'pre-Christmas party blitz', in which
pamphlets reminding people of the impermissibility of sexual harassment and what to do if it happened were sent out to all employees with
their payslips in November.

Some training programs were mostly operational, aimed at instructing
employees in how to follow operating procedures that seek to ensure
compliance. Yet most have some element of cultural and attitudinal
change as a desired outcome. This was most obvious in the sexual harassment programs discussed in my interviews. The primary aim of most of
the sexual harassment training seminars described was to confront pre-
suppositions and attitudes to win personal commitment to the sexual
harassment policy. As the EEO officer at Pets & Health described it, the
focus of preventive training is an attempt to 'win hearts and minds'[8]
to the anti-sexual harassment cause before discipline is necessary by
'persuading them it's a good idea'.

Using real-life case studies rather than abstract lectures on legal
responsibility or equal opportunity principles was seen as key to creating personal commitment to anti-harassment. Thus, at Credit4Oz the
'briefings' were judged a success when they used a case study which
started off innocuously and eventually became a rape, in order to produce a 'shocking and confrontational' reaction which 'made people talk
a lot afterwards'. Aussie Dollars were replacing their computer-based
training, which 'tended to ram the facts of the legislation down people's
throats', to a focus on 'changing behaviour and attitudes' by developing ten real-life scenarios with which employees would interact. A
video produced by four banks (including Banksafe Australasia and Big
Bucks Australia) begins and ends with vignettes showing a man going
home to tell his wife and daughter he has been accused of harassment
at work. In the second scene the wife angrily leaves him as he stands
distraught in the driveway moaning, 'What have I done?' The video
guide tells discussion leaders to invite employees to consider the effects
that workplace harassment can have on their personal, as well as their
working, life.

It is probably self-evident that effective compliance systems must
also use incentives and sanctions to achieve desired employee conduct.
For example, studies of correlates of illegal behaviour in organizations

have found that organizations which have both clear standards and expectations about inappropriate behaviours, and reward systems in place to monitor and reinforce expectations, probably reduce abuses (e.g. Mitchell et al. 1996). In another study, Pastin and Brecto (1995), business ethics consultants concluded from their sample that poor ethics compliance environments correlated significantly with performance measures or reward systems that employees saw as attaching financial incentives to behaviour inconsistent with ethical conduct. The interviewees frequently described detailed training and communications programs backed up with the potential of dismissal for serious compliance breaches. However, interviewees rarely described positive rewards and incentives for good compliance performance by employees. Nevertheless, when they theorize about their practice, reflective compliance practitioners do recognize that incentives and rewards are necessary and that a gradation of discipline is essential. For example, Joseph Murphy (1994) argues in one article in *Corporate Conduct Quarterly* that positive motivators are an essential part of an effective compliance management system, especially in any organization that uses incentives and evaluations as an integral way of achieving its other objectives such as sales and productivity targets or quality control. Murphy sees no reason in principle why compliance performance should be any harder to evaluate than other employee traits such as leadership or the ability to develop subordinates.

Compliance managers did more frequently report that poor compliance performance is disciplined or taken into account in employees' performance reviews. For example, in the USA, where generalized compliance systems are probably more advanced, Didier and Swenson (1995: 12) summarize surveys that showed 78 per cent of a survey of 'compliance aware' organizations claimed to consider employees' compliance track records during employee performance appraisals. In a more general sample, 68 per cent reported that they considered compliance track records in employee appraisals, while only 32 per cent of a survey of smaller companies (50–500 employees) did so. However, interviewees and survey respondents rarely describe sophisticated gradations of discipline for compliance breaches (cf. Lytton and Denton 1998). In practice, the only progression that most compliance practitioners can manage to incorporate into their compliance systems is the gradation from (a) training to change attitudes and educate employees on standard operating procedures that incorporate compliance standards, to (b) discipline, usually via dismissal (see Chapter 6 on scapegoating).

However, the business orientation of compliance practice is reflected in the fact that compliance practitioners do not rely most heavily on sanctions, but on changing attitudes and behaviours to prevent non-compliance before it happens. Where training and promotion efforts fail to teach employees to govern themselves in accordance with company policy, the internal discipline of the company becomes more concrete. Incentives and sanctions motivate compliance by making it a factor in annual performance reviews, and by sanctioning or dismissing employees for non-compliance. In some situations it is easier for an organization to discipline people for non-compliance that is discovered, than to put in place management and training programs that seek to prevent it. But on the whole, the objective was for the compliance function to do its utmost to avoid the nastiness and conflict of discipline by ensuring that people learnt how to be compliant and changed attitudes accordingly before a problem occurred.

Incorporate compliance into corporate decision-making

One of the main objectives of a self-regulation system is to incorporate compliance issues into internal decision-making agendas. The three mottoes discussed above are mostly aimed at ensuring that compliance becomes part of routine decisions and actions by middle managers and employees, decisions that are often made without people even realizing they are making them. Ultimately, however, compliance must be incorporated into top-level decisions on strategic planning, goal-setting and corporate investments.

Firstly, compliance must be part of the central coordination and accountability functions of the organization if middle managers and employees are to take it seriously. As one interviewee commented, 'Operations are going flat strap on the dollar and making a profit, so the CEO has to raise compliance if it's not going to be forgotten' (GarbageRUs). It is the CEO and top management who have the privilege of setting the goals and the luxury to think about them. Therefore it is they who are in the best position to sit back and reflect on compliance, and it is they who must ensure the message being sent down the line is that compliance is important and can be harmonized with making a profit. Most best practice compliance programs therefore include systems to ensure that compliance performance information is reported from operations to the centre. This may take the form of performance reports (regular reports on the implementation of compliance procedures and compliance rates, as appropriate) or 'exception' reporting (required reporting of non-compliance incidents and a regular sign-off that compliance procedures have been followed).

Accountability for self-regulation performance is only one element of putting compliance into corporate decision-making. The next step is that central strategic planning must set positive goals for compliance performance. For example, Novartis' doCOUNT system is a standardized database for environment health and safety performance management that integrates accountability and target setting.[9] Operations must report information about all aspects of their safety, health and environmental performance into the database so that group headquarters can hold business operations to account for their performance and so that the centre can be informed in setting performance targets and initiatives for the whole group.

At most major international chemical companies (e.g. Roche, Bayer, Orica), a management standard for environmental health and safety is set at corporate level together with performance goals. Business units are required to translate these principles into concrete goals and are held to account for them.[10] Most collect self-reported information. Some have very systematic auditing systems in addition. This approach is not limited to environmental, health and safety compliance. At Big Bucks Australia, for example, the centre sets a process that every business unit must go through to manage its own risk, including its financial services compliance risk, and then requires report-back on the implementation of that process. However, setting targets and holding businesses to account for them can be quite difficult for self-regulatory units at corporate group level in large multinational companies made up of separate businesses organized according to national or product lines. Many such groups have a culture of independence in these businesses that make them resistant to target setting from the centre.

The final step is to move beyond putting compliance into corporate goal-setting and accountability, and incorporate it into strategic decision-making on investments and other aspects of corporate planning. One example of a corporate attempt to ensure that environmental responsibilities are incorporated into high-level strategic planning and investment decisions is DuPont's approach. In 1999 it was reported in the *Economist* that DuPont CEO, Chad Holliday, is zealously embracing environmentalism for his business as 'a radically different way of defining growth'.[11] The corporation's initiatives include changing the criteria on which managers are assessed to include measures of environmental impacts and setting targets for reducing emissions and materials use. DuPont's Corporate Environmental Database and Plan integrates information about the performance of its businesses on a variety of environmental issues and also provides information about all proposed and existing projects within the corporation for reducing environmental damage that require capital investment. Business units have environmental performance targets they are expected to meet, and at the same time are also expected to propose plans for investment to reduce environmental damage with costs and potential savings. These proposals are then considered as part of the normal business investment planning process, and the most economically viable projects are selected for funding. Other proposals are abandoned or reworked until they are economically viable. This model attempts to use the comprehensive information available via the database and the environmental investment decision-making process to integrate environmental performance and goals right into business planning, instead of providing a separate set of (tenuous) funds for environmental improvement.

At Hot Rods too a similar system is in place. Fifteen or twenty years previously it was seen as the duty of environmental officers at operational level in the business units to look after environmental issues. The centre made decisions on finance at a high level, and the environment was an issue for the plants. This meant that even simple energy-saving projects that would clearly produce cost savings through an initial investment were not carried through. There was no finance available because they had not been considered part of the central group budgeting and investment process.

Now the chief environment, health and safety (EHS) manager describes Hot Rods' philosophy as trying to make 'the ecological and the economic work together', with technology as the key to doing this. Thus, business units are encouraged to identify environmental damage that is occurring and look for technological solutions. Feasibility studies for technological environmental projects are now financed by the centre, with a small contribution from the individual plant. Viable projects are thus identified and adequate funding is provided for the plant to implement them through the group financing plan. Indeed, Hot Rods is moving beyond this into trying to integrate environmental performance targets with financial performance targets so that environmental engineers and senior managers can communicate and deliberate effectively about what projects to take on. The aim of this whole approach was described by the chief EHS manager as trying to overcome the bounded rationality of central decision-making that does not consider environmental concerns: 'At the end of the day there might be a conflict of interest between the amount of money we have to spend and the environment. But what shouldn't happen is that high-up decisions on finance are made without reference to the environment.'

However, just because investing in pollution prevention will earn a payback or a profit does not make it a financially rational investment. Even if they are financially sustainable on their own terms, environmental projects must compete against other more profitable uses of the money. Thus, Boyd (1998) has concluded from detailed analysis of three case studies of environmental investment decisions by large multinational chemical companies (including DuPont, and also Dow and Monsanto) that the firms' decisions to not invest in pollution prevention that would have had a financial payback were still financially rational. The firms did not 'suffer from a myopic inability to appreciate cost-saving' opportunities of pollution prevention. Rather, 'significant unresolved technical difficulties, uncertain market conditions, and, in some cases, regulatory barriers or insufficient emissions enforcement rendered the investments financially unattractive' (Boyd 1998: 37).

As Boyd's study shows, not even the most financially attractive environmental projects will be guaranteed support if the decision is made on purely financial grounds. The 'triple bottom line' approach to corporate decision-making attempts to address this dilemma (Elkington 1998). The central idea of the triple bottom line is to place environmental and social sustainability on the same terms as financial stability in quantification for internal decision-making and external reporting. (Social and legal compliance responsibilities would be included in considerations of social sustainability.) At present the calculation of the triple bottom line is mainly a post-hoc calculation for the purposes of impressive external reporting, rather than a working tool for internal thinking. The aspirations of best practice corporate social responsibility proponents is to make the triple bottom line a tool for bringing values other than pure financial reasoning into the calculus of how the company should run.

Excellent self-regulation functions put regulatory goals and social values into top-level corporate strategy and planning where they can affect what the whole company can invest its resources in. Compliance managers' 'business case' arguments for self-regulation leadership particularly focus on finding strategic opportunities in compliance. For example, the president of ACPA at its first conference tried to press this home:

> I see the next model of compliance as being the enlightened self-interest cultural compliance version of compliance … This type of compliance will occur in a company that looks objectively and dispassionately at all its legal requirements on the one hand, yet at the same time looks at ways that it can turn these methods of compliance into a market advantage or a more effective way to run their particular organization. Such compliance requires vision, leadership, commitment, lateral thinking and imagination.[12]

As we saw in Chapter 3, bounded rationality frequently blinds management to the rationality of taking non-compliance costs and risks into account, let alone looking for strategic self-regulation investments. This approach to compliance is much coveted but little practised.

The holistic approach to self-regulation methodology is usually a matter of corporate evolution in industries and/or areas of regulation where public and regulatory pressure has been strongest, such as environmental, health and safety regulation in the chemical and mining industries. Interviewees who had worked in compliance for a long time saw the compliance function moving from a low level operational support to a higher level corporate control function in their own companies and across whole industries. At Trustus (UK) one compliance manager had been working in marketing (in a firm that Trustus has now acquired) when new rules promulgated under the 1988 UK Financial Services Act required the company to designate a compliance officer. Since this interviewee happened to have a law degree, she was given compliance responsibilities on top of her normal job. Ten years later compliance had grown into a central corporate function with a large staff.

Similarly, several environment, health and safety interviewees who had been with their companies many years described a process by which companies had first responded to environmental and safety risks by the ad hoc appointment of environmental officers at plant or business unit level – an engineer responsible for keeping pollution under control or making sure workers followed rules that kept them safe. When major disasters occurred, and CEOs and directors realized that the whole company's image might suffer or they themselves be held liable, environment, health and safety became a corporate-level function in most large chemical and mining companies. Compliance comes to be seen as a corporate function with strategic and coordinating elements. The existence of this evolutionary dynamic is supported by studies that take a broader sweep of the history and structure of corporate self-regulation (e.g. Hoffman 1997).

CONCLUSION

Internal compliance constituencies are often a linchpin of the organizational institutionalization of corporate social and legal responsibility
(see Sigler and Murphy 1988: 103–4). The emergence and growth of
compliance professionalism as an occupation (or set of occupations)
means that the relationship between corporate responsibility programs
and the character and position of self-regulation professionals is only
likely to become stronger. It is self-regulation professionals (whether
they explicitly identify themselves as compliance or ethics generalists
or whether they are specialists in a substantive area such as environmental management) who are often the only people employed explicitly to embody organizational responsibility and integrity. A designated
compliance role is a self-regulation toe-hold in the organization, with
the potential to grow.

Figure 2.3 illustrated the dynamics by which issues such as public
opinion, bad publicity, social movement politics, what competitors are
doing, new regulation, regulatory enforcement actions and potential litigation can all prompt management commitment to implementation of
a system to manage social and legal responsibility issues (Phase One of
the institutionalization of responsibility). It also showed that once a
self-regulation function is established (Phase Two), it becomes one of
the tasks of this function to monitor these external events and communicate them to workers and management. Thus, the self-regulation
function can help to sustain commitment to the implementation of the
compliance system as well as facilitate day-to-day organizational compliance with legal and social responsibilities. According to this theory,
self-regulation staff would be insider-outsiders who act as a bridge
between values expressed in law and legal institutions, social movements, the professional community of self-regulation professionals, and
the internal culture and management of companies. This harmonizing
ideal is illustrated in Figure 5.1.

This analysis of the potential harmonizing role of organizational
compliance functions in social solidarity between legal institutions,
broader society and business owes something to Durkheim's vision of
coordination between law, society and morality (1964, especially ch. 3,
Book One of *The Division of Labor in Society*). Cotterrell's (1995) re-read-
ing and rehabilitation of Durkheim's sociology of law proposes that
Durkheim's central contribution is to address the normative question of
how regulation can be effective in modern complex societies, 'and the

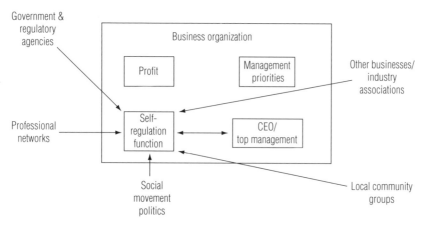

FIGURE 5.1 Harmonizing role of self-regulation units

regulated ... able, in some way, to participate as moral actors in a solidary society which is more than an economic free for all'. It is not a descriptive analysis of the nature of law in any existing society, but a moral inquiry into how law can support 'the condition of responsibility arising from interdependence of individuals or their commitment to a community' (Cotterrell 1995: 194, 202). Read in this way, Durkheim meets the empirical and normative concerns of scholars such as Stone (1975), Selznick (1992) and Braithwaite (Ayres and Braithwaite 1992; Fisse and Braithwaite 1993) with how (social and legal) responsibility can be institutionalized in business organizations.

Durkheim, like many socio-legal scholars who followed, was an analyst (and advocate) of regulatory pluralism. Regulatory pluralism means recognizing the 'moral distance' between state-law and the fields of social interaction it purports to regulate. For example, in his posthumously published lectures on *Professional Ethics and Civic Morals*, Durkheim proposed a form of associational democracy and government in which every area of industry would be responsible for its own ethics and self-regulation under the coordinating oversight of the state (1992: 13, 39). In *The Division of Labor in Society* Durkheim saw and advocated 'regulation at many "levels" and in different functional environments within society ... within the overall co-ordinating structure of the state ... [in order to] acquire the legitimacy that might be provided by the collective participation or concern of citizens in the processes of its creation, and by a conception of regulation as expressing the active moral commitment of the community' (Cotterrell 1995: 272). This normative argument has the attraction of being empirically realistic. Regulation already does occur at many levels through different social interactions. The state has no monopoly on regulation. Cotterell's summary of the normative challenge posed by Durkheim also sums up the challenge facing the new regulatory state that relies on enforced self-regulatory mechanisms:

> In these circumstances the empirical and theoretical study of law in society surely needs to consider how regulation can acquire the qualities of being simultaneously rationally planned and purposeful and also deeply rooted in social and cultural life. The task now may be to examine how modern regulation can *build afresh* some of the qualities that writers have long associated with pluralistic law and regulation. (Cotterell 1995: 308, emphasis in original)

In Durkheim's work, the professions and their ethical self-regulation are seen as crucial institutions for building social solidarity based on moral commitment. In *Professional Ethics and Civic Morals*, Durkheim argues that the modern pursuit of business exists 'outside the sphere of morals and ... almost entirely removed from the moderating effect of obligations' (1992: 10). Indeed, his diagnosis of how the roles required by business organizations tend to leave no room for social responsibilities is not dissimilar to the contemporary research reported in Chapter 2. He argues that, 'if a sense of duty is to take strong root in us, the very circumstances of our life must serve to keep it always in mind all the time and, as often happens, when we are tempted to turn a deaf ear' (Durkheim 1992: 12). His solution is a re-professionalization of the marketplace. Every citizen should be obliged to be a member of a professional community in which he or she would be socialized into a collective, but particular, morality that suited his or her particular industry or trade. Top-down state regulation should not displace the professional community's responsibility to self-regulate, that is to articulate its own specific rules and ethics from the bottom up. (Contemporary scholars, including Gordon and Simon (1992) and Wheeler and Wilson (1998), have drawn on the professional ideal in similar ways in proposals to re-moralize business.)

In the later sociological functionalism of Talcott Parsons, the moral coordination role of professionalism transmogrifies: from the ideal that everybody should be a member of a profession, into the theory that the established professions can play a mediating role that coordinates private individuals and entities and broader social values. The member of a profession, especially the legal profession, 'stands *between* two major aspects of our social structure; in the case of the law between public authority and its norms, and the private individual or group whose conduct or intentions may or may not be in accord with the law. In the case of the physician it is between the world of sickness and of health' (Parsons 1954: 381; emphasis in original). Thus, Parsons concludes that the professions may be regarded as 'mechanisms of social control':

> They either, like the teaching profession, help to 'socialise' the young, to bring them into accord with the expectations of full membership in the society, or they bring them *back* into accord when they have deviated, like the medical profession. The legal profession may be presumed to do this but also two other things, first to forestall deviance by advising the client in ways which will keep him better in line and … second, if it comes to a serious case, implementing the procedure by which a socially sanctioned decision about the status of the client is arrived at, in the dramatic cases of the criminal law, the determination of whether he is innocent or guilty of a crime. (1954: 382; emphasis in original)

At this point the professional harmonizing ideal proposed by the new self-regulation professionals meets the analysis of the past masters of the theory of social solidarity. Compliance practitioners on the whole see their role as to be professional in translating broader social and legal values into the particular and plural worlds of their organizations, and in turn to communicate the constraints of organizational life to regulators and government. Their task is to fit regulatory goals to organizational norms and thus make compliance strategies come alive – in a way that external regulators can never achieve alone – by making compliance programs that are contextually specific and demonstrate genuine organizational commitment from the inside out. Leading self-regulation professionals believe, on the whole, that it is possible to harmonize business and regulatory goals and therefore to assist good companies to be good citizens through their own two-way role in the regulatory effort as compliance professionals. The inchoate tendency is towards a Durkheimian faith in the possibility that social solidarity via moral commitment can be achieved if business organizations can self-regulate and establish their own rules in partnership with the state. Their faith in the feasibility of such a model of self-regulation is itself a major impetus for the continued development of the new regulatory state, as compliance professionals become involved in lobbying governments for appropriate regulatory regimes.

Experience shows this faith to be misplaced. Gordon and Simon (1992: 243) report that Adolph Berle, one of the architects of the New Deal, thought that the Roosevelt administration's regulatory programs would liberate the corporate bar to do social good, and make a good living at the same time, by allowing them to advocate the public good to their clients as compliance with law. Like the purported role of compliance professionals in the new regulatory state, the innovative business regulations created by the original regulatory state of the 1930s were supposed to secure for lawyers a structural role as the social conscience to business. In practice, 'this view has turned out to be astonishingly naive both in assuming that lawyers would come to regard regulation as uncontroversially legitimate and in predicting that public enforcement would eliminate client opportunities for self-interested deviance' (Gordon and Simon 1992: 243).

The growth of business regulation has spurred legal professionals and their corporate clients on to newer and more creative ways of avoiding social and legal responsibilities. For example, Dezalay (1996: 66) analyses the role of elite legal practitioners during the New Deal, at other times in history, and currently in the emerging global legal order, as 'double agents' in a political game, 'now public servants, now mercenaries, fashioning with one hand the rules which they were striving to evade with the other'. Elite corporate legal professionals create an image of themselves as statesmen virtuously assisting to construct effective regulatory regimes in order to market themselves all the more effectively to big multinational firms who want to twist those rules to their own purposes (Dezalay 1996: 68; see Dezalay and Garth 1996).

Similarly, the self-regulation professional is subject to powerful pressures to enhance corporate legitimacy without changing substance. Real corporate change would require fighting and winning too many corporate battles. The view of compliance practice as harmonization omits the structural contradictions and politics inherent in compliance managers' roles. As many critics have noted, the Durkheimian approach is deeply flawed in 'its conception of state and law as largely unproblematic expressions of moral consensus' (Cotterrell 1995: 194).[13]

Chapter 6 turns to the potential pathologies of compliance systems. In Chapter 7 I reconstruct an alternative ideal of professional integrity for compliance professionals that takes account of the conflict and politics inherent in the practice of permeable self-regulation.

6 | The pathologies of self-regulation

The self-regulation system may be able to help heal the rift between individual ethics, social values and the culture of business. But there are cracks in the façade of harmony. The very fact that compliance managers spend so long explaining their harmonizing function and the need to 'sell compliance' indicates that the just and seamless melding of legal/social responsibility and organizational management is a highly problematic accomplishment. A preliminary survey of occupational stress among US health care compliance officers concluded that they were 'more likely than most professional groups to experience stress associated with workload, role conflict, and role ambiguity'. Interviewees reported conflict between 'the government's and the board's expectations and the way business just gets done', being expected 'to ensure compliance with the deals and contracts that some senior management made and signed without input or review by the compliance officer', and feeling responsible for compliance problems they uncovered but could not solve (Heller and Guetter 1999: 47, 48, 50). These contradictions in the compliance function are structural. They relate to potential pathologies of compliance that have their origins in the techniques of the new regulatory state, and in the demands of organizations to make compliance problems disappear.

The first part of this chapter considers three contradictions implied in the encouragement of corporate self-regulation by the new regulatory state. The second part considers four potential pathologies in the corporate implementation of compliance systems. The chapter concludes by characterizing many of these pathologies as arising from the stance of 'risk management' taken by both the new regulatory state and corporations to problems of compliance with legal and social responsibilities. It is a challenge of institutional design to make risk management a positive, not a pathological, response to democratic responsibility.

COMPLIANCE CONTRADICTIONS IN THE NEW REGULATORY STATE

In part, the compliance-oriented techniques of the new regulatory state are a response to the burden of governance. They are an attempt to share the burden of regulation with the company and, in effect (frequently not acknowledged), with the compliance staff employed by the organization, and even other third parties, including industry associations that run self-regulatory schemes, professionals who are given gatekeeper responsibilities, and stakeholders who might be relied on to monitor corporate conduct. This leaves the new regulatory state open to at least three criticisms:

- Firstly, that it relies too heavily on companies' own assessment and management of compliance risks to achieve regulatory objectives.
- Secondly, that it puts an intolerable burden on the internal corporate staff responsible for self-regulation to resolve conflicts between business and regulatory goals.
- Thirdly, that it relies too heavily on third parties and the institutions of 'civil society' who have insufficient access, information and resources to regulate other than in a partial and piecemeal way.

Over-reliance on corporate management

The first of these criticisms is an argument that in relying on corporate self-regulation, the new regulatory state is especially vulnerable to perpetuating all the pathologies of corporate management of compliance spelled out in the second half of this chapter. The new regulatory state is criticized for being ineffectual in its reliance on arms-length monitoring and control (see Shearing 1993: 76–7). Commentators from the left (e.g. Pearce and Tombs 1998) criticize the new regulatory state for abrogating its responsibility to combat the injustices of private markets by entrusting it to those very corporate actors who ought to be regulated. In particular, regulatory innovations are frequently criticized for relying primarily on enforced self-regulation and 'process' regulation that displace conflict from the courts and the public arena to internal corporate management and dispute resolution.

This style of regulation is said to subordinate social values to management priorities and routines. For example, Chambliss (1996: 1) criticizes US anti-sex discrimination regulation for 'a series of displacements' of conflicts that deny conflict altogether. According to her, the regulation pushes conflicts away from the courts to informal and internalized organizational procedures that encourage scapegoating of individual employees. Other critics point to potential failures to deal with power imbalances between complainants and respondents, complainants' vulnerability to accepting lesser remedies than they might deserve, and the essential privacy, individualism and lack of public accountability of the process (Bacchi and Jose 1994; Devereux 1996; Scutt 1988; Thornton 1989, 1991). In the case of environment, health and safety management systems, large companies with sensitive public reputations will only put in place systems to manage urgent, large-scale potential disasters (Genn 1993; Pearce and Tombs 1998). In the case of consumer protection, they will only concern themselves with consumer safety and information provision to the extent that brand value and loyalty may be affected.

An intolerable burden on self-regulation staff

The second criticism is that the new regulatory state's reliance on internal corporate compliance management only appears to be effective because it pushes the real responsibility for handling the tough parts of regulation onto corporate compliance professionals. The co-option of compliance staff, lawyers, auditors and other professionals as (private) agents of regulation is one of the characteristics of the new regulatory state (see Braithwaite 1997; Grabosky 1990; Power 1997: 32). For example, Halliday and Carruthers' (1996: 407) study of the UK government's reforms of insolvency regulation showed that failures of the 'state's capacity for surveillance will provoke efforts by the state either to create new professions to extend public intervention into private markets, or more likely, to demand new public responsibilities of private professions'. Professions, according to Halliday and Carruthers, represent 'a convenient and arms-length' way to monitor powerful economic actors. These actors' professional integrity, reputation and ultimately livelihood theoretically lie in assiduously fulfilling their gatekeeper responsibilities.

From a regulator's viewpoint, the hope is that an effective internal corporate compliance unit will avoid the need to prosecute a company in the future by ensuring compliance in the present. For the regulator, then, the role of the compliance unit is to work the requirements of the law into the corporate heart and mind in order to avoid conflict before it starts or, where conflict is unavoidable, to ensure that it is resolved at the earliest possible level by acting as a mini-court or regulator within the company. Ideally the self-regulation system would effectively implement the harmonizing methodology described in Chapter 5. The compliance function would change how new products are developed, how employees are rewarded and disciplined, and how standard operations are carried out so that non-compliance does not occur. Conflict would be resolved in favour of compliance at the product development meeting (where the compliance officer is present), through internal disciplinary proceedings and in a multitude of other interactions at all levels of the company. When this fails, the compliance unit would take responsibility for having out whatever conflict is necessary within the company. Regulators hope that compliance officers will receive reports of non-compliance from whistle-blowers inside the company and that, if necessary, the compliance officer himself or herself will turn whistle-blower to the regulator, so that enforcement action can be taken.

On the one hand, this opens the new regulatory state to the criticism that it co-opts professionals, especially legal professionals, with social responsibilities that can potentially destroy their ethical autonomy and undermine their advocacy and representational function (Combs 1994; Partlett and Szweda 1991; cf. Parker 2000b). These professionals become part of a 'Foucauldian' web of state control over clients, all the more insidious because of how self-regulation appears to be a voluntary response to state incentives (see Grabosky 1995: 543). On the other hand, an urgent threat that is regularly discussed by compliance professionals is the likelihood that compliance people will be sacked or sidelined when powerful players within their organizations do not want to seriously address legal and social responsibilities. A regulatory strategy that depends on corporate employees being willing to sacrifice their jobs seems doomed to fail most of the time.

The new regulatory state can create a direct conflict for compliance officers by giving them whistle-blowing rights and obligations. For example, under the UK financial services regulation regime, designated compliance officers in firms must report certain breaches to the regulator after they have reported them to senior management and nothing has been done. In 1998, IMRO (a former self-regulatory organization under the UK Financial Services Act) disciplined a compliance officer for failing to report non-compliance to it in just such circumstances. Michael

Wheatley was banned from holding a compliance position again.[1] Even where compliance officers have no formal whistle-blowing obligations, the mere existence of an area of regulation creates a conflict between a general right (or duty) to prevent and report illegal conduct, and the duty of loyalty and confidentiality to an organizational employer. At the US Practising Law Institute's 1999 corporate compliance conference, one presenter highlighted the conflicts faced by compliance staff by entitling his talk, 'Some organizations call it "compliance officer" – Some call it "designated felon"' (Zinn 1999: 545; see also Parker 2001).

The potential for the compliance professional to lose his or her job is not a distant one. The secretary of the Association for Compliance Professionals Australia (ACPA) believed that even within the first year or two of the Association's existence, he had seen people become compliance officers and then lose their jobs in corporate 'restructures' that were really about dismantling a meddlesome compliance unit.

Chambliss (1996) analyses a number of US cases of EEO officers suing their former employers for compensation after losing their jobs for championing EEO against their superiors' will. She shows that the US courts have enforced the employee's duty of loyalty to the employer, but ignored the probability and actuality of organizational non-compliance and resistance to the compliance role. The result is to give EEO officers who wish to uphold EEO values no protection against sacking.[2] In effect, Chambliss (1996: 23) argues, the 'courts pretend that regulation can occur *without* conflict – that there is no such thing as a resistant employer'. In certain circumstances then, the new regulatory state stands accused of placing a conflict (or at least a contradiction) within the person of the self-regulation manager and then refusing to acknowledge it.

The growing number of people employed by organizations to be responsible for internal self-regulation will frequently find themselves in the dilemma of choosing between their livelihood and their integrity or self-respect. This should not, however, be seen as a 'fault' exclusive to the new regulatory state. Indeed, as Chapter 2 argued, it is a contradiction that we all face at one time or another in the course of our membership of organizations. How can we uphold broader values and personal integrity when our livelihoods are dependent on loyalty to organizations that do not necessarily share our values? By using regulatory techniques that formalize the requirement for organizations to self-regulate, the new regulatory state merely sharpens the conflict by increasing the number of people who are employed specifically to handle the interface between business and social values.

Piecemeal regulatory efforts by third parties

Self-regulation professionals are just one of the third parties, albeit the most obvious, on whom the new regulatory state places some of the burden of business regulation. The main progressive innovation of the new regulatory state is its explicit analysis of and reliance on the possibility of working with and relying on non-state regulation to improve the effectiveness and efficiency of state regulation. Grabosky (1995; see also Grabosky 1994) has categorized ways in which governments are increasingly relying on pre-existing non-governmental institutions and resources (including both civil society and markets) to support regulatory compliance with policy objectives, including:

- *Conscription:* Governments command third parties to assist with the processes of compliance (see Gilboy 1998) – for example, cash transaction reporting requirements.
- *Required private interface:* Governments require that targets of regulation use specified machinery of private institutions – for example, independent certification of an environmental management system to ISO 14000 or some other standard.
- *Required record-keeping and disclosure:* Governments require disclosure of certain aspects of regulatees' activities – for example, greenhouse gas emissions.
- *Co-optation of organized interests:* The representation of interests in tripartite or corporatist policy processes in order to gain further information and build support for policy outcomes.
- *Conferring entitlements:* Governments create certain specified rights, confer them upon private parties and leave it to those parties to enforce – for example, patent, trademark and copyright laws – or empower third parties to undertake enforcement actions on behalf of the state. This category might also include the creation of trading regimes for rights to certain amounts of emissions.
- *Incentives:* Governments offer incentives to regulatees to induce compliance or to third parties for production of regulatory services – for example, relaxing regulatory requirements for companies with exemplary compliance records, and rewards/ bounties for surveillance activity.
- *Contracting out:* Governments contract out one or more regulatory functions – for example, contracting out of motor vehicles emissions testing on a user-pays basis.

- *Delegation or deference to private parties:* Governments rely on regulatory activity being carried out in the private sector rather than duplicating it – for example, standards developed by private standards-setting organizations are adopted by government regulatory agencies, the US Securities and Exchange Commission delegates rule-making to self-regulatory organizations such as stock exchanges.
- *Abdication:* Governments abdicate their regulatory role and leave allocative and ordering decisions to the market.

The reality of regulatory pluralism means that this approach is an essential deepening and corrective to the technique of command and control. Thus, for example, The Netherlands Ministry of Justice in collaboration with Dr Dick Ruimschotel and the Rotterdam Erasmus University, developed the 'T11' for use as a standard checklist for public agencies in assessing new regulatory proposals and reviewing enforcement and other issues in relation to existing regulation (see Parker 1999d: 40; Ruimschotel et al. 1999). The T11 is intended to be a coherent enumeration of eleven factors that determine compliance by target populations with laws and regulations in order to design more effective regulation.

The T11 factors are divided into three main categories:

- *Spontaneous compliance dimensions:* Factors that affect the incidence of voluntary compliance – that is, compliance which would occur in the absence of enforcement. These factors are knowledge of rules, cost–benefit considerations, level of acceptance, normative commitment and informal control.
- *Control dimensions:* The influence of enforcement on compliance. These factors are informal report probability, control probability, detection probability, and selectivity.
- *Sanctions dimensions:* The influence of sanctions on compliance. These factors are sanction probability, and sanction severity.

The factors in each category seek to help regulatory agencies quantify the likely impacts of both state action, inherent ability and willingness to comply by the target population, and the likelihood of third parties encouraging compliance by exercising market or other controls and enforcing non-state sanctions (including negative publicity). These factors help to identify where regulatory design is likely to be most effective at accomplishing compliance, and where additional work with the target population or third parties may be required, or additional sanctions and enforcement necessary.

A number of government agencies in different countries are experimenting with voluntary agreements with individual companies or industry associations to replace proposed government regulation with self-regulation, and are even brokering opportunities for social movement activists and companies or industry associations to decide together on self-regulatory responses to identified problems that include third party monitoring and review. A good example is the US White House Apparel Industry Partnership (see Varley 1998: 464–7), which is aimed at preventing the use of 'sweatshop' labour (including child labour) in the manufacture of fashionable clothes and shoes by US-based companies at sites outside the USA. Under this scheme, apparel companies that meet certain criteria are allowed to join a non-profit association. They must follow a code of conduct and must arrange for some form of external code-compliance monitoring by either an auditing firm or an organization completely independent of the company (such as a human rights organization).

The potential pathology of 'regulating' via an agreement like this is that agencies of the new regulatory state will place a higher burden on third parties than they can bear. In voluntary programs, companies often set their own standards, but fail to give the information and access that consumers and social activists hope for in order to monitor whether standards have been met. For example, labour and activist groups have criticized the White House Apparel Industry Partnership for merely giving 'the Good Housekeeping seal of approval to a kinder, gentler sweatshop' (quoted by Varley 1998: 466). One of the concerns of these groups was that third party monitors would not be granted adequate access to factory sites, and that their reports on compliance with the code would only be reported to the company, not to the association running the scheme, and certainly not to the wider public.

While some US companies with factories or outsourcing facilities in third world countries already engage third party monitors (Nike engages Ernst and Young to perform audits in Indonesia, Thailand and Vietnam, and Price Waterhouse to audit facilities in China; Wal-Mart hires Cal Safety Compliance Corp, a specialist company, to audit some manufacturers), companies tend to resist completely independent monitoring because they believe independent monitors (including activists) lack skills, are eager to find fault, will give embarrassing information to the media and create an adversarial relationship between the clothing company and the supplier (Varley 1998: 438–9).

The history of information that has become public when monitoring reports are leaked to public interest groups suggests that there is good reason for activists to be suspicious of information that is not public. After a consumer boycott and social campaign against the mistreatment of workers in outsourced factories, Nike introduced a voluntary code of conduct and hired accounting firm Ernst and Young to audit each site's compliance with the code. In 1996 an Ernst and Young audit of a Nike contractor facility in Vietnam was leaked to the Transnational Research and Action Center in San Francisco. The audit had found that workers were exposed to carcinogens that exceeded local legal standards by 177 times in parts of the plant and that more than 100 workers at one section of the facility had respiratory ailments. Although the report found Nike in compliance with its own code of conduct, it documented a series of unjust and hazardous work conditions that contradicted the findings of an earlier report on allegations of worker abuse that Nike had made public (Mokhiber and Weissman 1997: 13–14).

Similarly a number of environmental regulators are experimenting with giving special recognition to companies that comply with the ISO 14000 series that sets standards for environmental management systems.[3] ISO 14000 is a powerful self-regulatory tool, but its limits illustrate some of the potential problems with abrogating responsibility for monitoring self-regulation to third parties. Sites may seek third party verification of compliance with the ISO 14000 series, but the standard itself does not demand independent verification as a condition of having a good environmental management system. Although information generated by processes required in the ISO 14000 series may be helpful to local communities in judging environmental performance (Gunningham and Sinclair 1999: 8), there is no requirement to report to local communities or to meet their expectations. Indeed, the International Organization for Standardization is an essentially technical organization and is therefore not set up to be democratic. In fact it is dominated by large corporations and developed countries.

In their study of the making of ISO 14001 and its content, Krut and Gleckman (1998: 28) comment that, 'although ISO 14001 started out with a broad mandate, it ended up being written by a small group of business executives, hand in hand not with nature, but often with lawyers concerned about the legal obligations ISO 14001 may create in their home countries'. The ISO 14000 series does not set specific goals or performance levels, only process goals (Gunningham and Sinclair 1999: 9; Krut and Gleckman 1998), and there is ambiguity about whether the continual improvement that it does require is for continuous improvement of the management system or its environmental outcomes.[4]

Ultimately the pathology is that the new regulatory state will fail to exercise adequate control and oversight over third party efforts at regulation to ensure they are effective and coordinated. The temptation will be to shirk the responsibility of maintaining an overview of where they are working and where they are not. This means failure in the fundamental responsibility of the state for social justice by failing to be aware of patterns of abuse, injustice or neglect, and by failing to take coordinated and concerted action, through regulatory enforcement, the enactment of new rights and liabilities, and/or the promulgation or clarification of regulatory standards. In most of these circumstances only states have the power and legitimacy to perform that action or broker the type of discussion in which such action can occur.

The greatest potential of the new regulatory state is that it will avoid fruitless expenditure of government and business resources on the vain hope of using command-and-control techniques to accomplish corporate compliance with technical rules, and concentrate on accomplishing substantive compliance with regulatory goals by whatever means is appropriate and feasible (Baldwin 1997; Grabosky 1995; Manning 1987; Sparrow 1994, 2000). The greatest danger is that the new regulatory state often descends into a neo-liberalism that subordinates democracy and public policy objectives to market forces, or to supposed free markets that are really a masquerade for big business domination (see Hutton 1996; Korten 1995; Pusey 1991).

ORGANIZATIONAL IMPERATIVES: MAKING COMPLIANCE CONFLICT DISAPPEAR

The primary hope of a company that puts in place a self-regulation unit is that the compliance staff will be a lightning rod, defusing conflict and ensuring the company avoids public scandals, litigation, enforcement action and harsher regulation. Perhaps the outcome will be consistent with the regulator's ideal vision of the role of internal compliance. Perhaps top management are genuinely prepared to embrace regulatory (and social responsibility) goals throughout the organization, and to support the self-regulation unit in working out how to achieve that in partnership with regulators and stakeholders. More likely, in most cases, the natural concern to not spend too much on peripheral functions, such as compliance, and the inherent tendency for central policies on anything but profit-directed activities to be under-valued will prevail. Conflict between compliance and business goals is likely to arise regularly and persistently, if not frequently.

In practice, all companies with compliance systems will tend (to a greater or lesser extent) to use and abuse compliance systems and staff to absorb and deflect conflict that would otherwise lead to challenge and change in one or more of the following ways:

- Firstly, companies will tend to use the compliance system for symbolic purposes for bolstering legitimacy but making no substantive change, if not necessary.
- Secondly, the implementation of compliance systems via employee discipline can displace conflict and shift the risk of liability onto the individual employee and away from corporate management.
- Thirdly, the compliance system and staff can also be used to evade legal responsibility by obscuring organizational and senior responsibility for non-compliance, and scapegoating employees or compliance staff themselves for problems for which the organization and senior management would otherwise be held responsible.
- Fourthly, the company can use stakeholder outreach strategies to strategically contain dissent from external stakeholders without necessarily modifying corporate behaviour.

Compliance as symbolism

One of the major motivations for the introduction of self-regulation systems is to preserve legitimacy in the wake of a scandal or legal action (or potential scandal or action). Commitment to preserving legitimacy might be strong, but this does not mean that commitment to substantive change is strong. As Edelman and co-authors (1991: 75) comment, 'organizations create symbolic structures as visible efforts to comply with law, but their normative value does not depend on effectiveness so they do not guarantee substantive change'.[5] The organizational imperative will often be to tame or avoid conflict by accomplishing enough symbolic change for 'business as usual' to continue with little disruption. Indeed, all 'compliance' with the law is to a greater or lesser extent a manipulation of symbols and resources associated with rules.

The most potent means for a company to ostensibly comply, while avoiding substantive change, is through hiring lawyers and others expert in the techniques of 'creative compliance' (McBarnet 1994). It is well known that lawyers are expert in creating legal techniques for complying with the formal requirements of taxation and corporate law, while evading engagement with its substance, spirit and soul (Cain 1994; McBarnet 1994; McBarnet and Whelan 1997). Similarly companies can hire legal and compliance staff to develop paper systems that are merely about filling in forms, ticking checklists and distributing manuals. These give 'business as usual' the veneer of responsibility.

Some compliance 'leaders', who implement their own internal self-regulatory systems before regulators and legislators have a chance to spell out compliance standards, may in fact gazump democratic debate and regulatory policy by imposing their version of best practice compliance on regulators and courts before others have a chance to have a say.[6] Australian companies' initiative in developing the Greenhouse Challenge program of voluntary agreements to reduce greenhouse gas emissions (see Chapter 3) before the government could prescribe more onerous compliance requirements is a classic example of this strategy. Similarly Karliner (1997: 51) argues that those transnational companies who were responsible for selling chlorofluorocarbons (CFCs) in the first place that created the hole in the ozone layer (e.g. DuPont, ICI, Hoechst) later co-opted the Montreal Protocol which banned CFCs. They marketed profitable alternatives to CFCs ahead of the Protocol schedule and were thus able to be seen as environmental leaders, to make a profit, and to influence the interpretation of the Protocol. Meanwhile the alternatives to CFCs that they themselves sold contributed to ozone depletion (HCFCs) and global warming (HFCs), although less virulently than CFCs. By defining the parameters of the debate, compliance 'leaders' can ensure that little substantive change is required. Indeed, powerful corporations often have suasive or symbolic power, as well as economic power (Sitkin and Bies 1994: 30). What amounts to compliance is always constructed and negotiated between regulators, regulatees and sometimes other stakeholders to a greater or lesser extent (Hutter 1997; Reichman 1992).

Companies can also use the positive symbolism of very specific compliance and social responsibility efforts that generate good publicity to distract attention from more serious ongoing problems. It is easy for companies to make donations or to implement trivial environmental projects that generate good public relations, but either do not achieve the significant benefits that they claim or deflect attention from the much more serious environmental damage caused by other parts of company operations. Critics of corporate domination have revealed the other side of corporate campaigns publicizing their own good for business/good for environment programs (Beder 1997: 128–30; Karliner 1997: 168–96; Smith 1998: 124–58). For example, Beder cites evidence that one oil company, Chevron, spends five times as much publicizing its environmental action as it does on the actions themselves (see also Karliner 1997: 172–4 on Chevron), that Dow Chemical received favourable publicity for a US$3 million wetland protection program while downstream from its factories birds had dioxin-related deformities, and that 3M's well-publicized 3P ('pollution prevention pays') program has saved it US$500 million while its emissions of toxic chemicals remain among the worst in the USA (Beder 1997: 128–30).

Smith (1998: 124–58) analyses the text and images used in advertising campaigns by IBM, Shell and McDonald's to portray themselves as environmentally concerned and responsible companies in the context of: (a) IBM's well-documented 'foot-dragging on cleanup of soil and ground water contamination' in Silicon Valley, and its reluctance to phase out CFCs; (b) Shell's activities in Nigeria (see segment on 'stakeholder containment' below), including the alleged spilling of 1.5 million gallons of oil, continued use of gas flaring even after being fined for the practice, and a 50-day delay in stopping a particular crude-oil spill from a pipeline rupture; and (c) McDonald's decision to re-introduce paper packaging in order to appear more environmentally friendly in response to public pressure, despite their own independent research that showed their use of polystyrene packaging actually used less energy, produced less landfill volume and was easier to recycle (because paper coated in food cannot be recycled easily). In each case Smith shows how the glossy images of corporate advertising successfully overcame the sour taste of social and environmental irresponsibility.

Empirical evidence on the implementation of self-regulatory policies within companies suggests that legal principles and social values are inevitably overwhelmed by management priorities. In their survey of ethics programs in US Fortune 1000 firms, Weaver and co-authors (1999a: 283) find that 'the vast majority of firms have committed to the lower cost, possibly more symbolic side of ethics activity: the promulgation of ethics policies and codes. But firms differ substantially in their efforts to see that those policies or codes actually are put into practice by organization members.' Even good compliance programs are likely to suspend the law, while appearing to extend it into corporate domains. For example, Edelman's study of ten US corporations found that anti-discrimination complaints were consistently seen as examples of poor management or personality clashes, rather than indicators of practices of discrimination that should be identified and eliminated, as the law intended (Edelman et al. 1993).

Tombs (1992) comes to similar conclusions from his study of corporate self-regulation in six best practice safety companies in the UK chemicals industry (all among the top fifteen multinational corporations in the UK). All six had recently instituted, or were about to institute, programs giving top-management backing to a higher profile for safety and highly formalized safety auditing programs. However, Tombs found that the promise of these compliance system changes was not borne out in practice. Each company had a devolved organizational structure, with a separate corporate safety services unit. These units performed only advisory and facilitating functions, rather than systematically checking and forcing compliance performance. He concluded that while the policies sounded impressive and the safety staff had greater technical capacity to prevent or identify safety crimes, they completely lacked adequate power to enforce their advice (Tombs 1992: 81).

Another commentator notes that, despite a mountain of successes in corporate environmental management, 'the "green wall" … – those institutional barriers that segregate environmental professionals from core business functions – still stands in many companies' (Ditz 1998: 54). One survey suggests that most corporate environmental initiatives are running into this wall (Shelton and Shopley 1997: 120). Only 4 per cent of the surveyed companies self-reported that environmental issues were 'a fully-fledged part of their business management approach'. Shelton and Shopley (1997: 121) report that the attempt to include environmental issues as an element of strategic management is frequently frustrated by factors such as corporate downsizing, tight financial controls and increased scrutiny of the bottom-line contribution for all organizations in the company, and new management paradigms (e.g. re-engineering, total quality management) that redirect management priorities.

In my own fieldwork there was plenty of evidence that compliance staff frequently face a latent conflict within their organizations. Top levels of management say they support compliance and/or social responsibility and issue policies and statements to that effect. But in practice senior managers require inconsistent things of middle managers that are passed on to low-level employees. One compliance practitioner explained this latent conflict well in a seminar presentation:

... it is not uncommon to find executive management and front-line employees committed to 'doing the right thing,' but that line management is not so committed, because of a conflict of accountabilities. Often, line management is charged with a responsibility of meeting deadlines within budget. In concept, folding in compliance can slow down progress and cost money. Therefore there is a built-in bias against compliance that means the manager may not satisfy these other expectations. (Zinn 1999: 539)

Adviser One, an independent compliance consultant, frequently faced the frustration of being hired by senior management of medium-sized companies to solve their compliance programs, only to run into the opposition of middle management who would 'run interference'. Senior management who mouth support for compliance, but do not sack unsupportive middle managers, place the conflict on the shoulders of the external compliance adviser to absorb.

However, the extent to which the drive to legitimacy will require organizations to achieve substantive compliance rather than symbolic change is an empirical question. In some areas organizations may be forced by accountability to make more substantive changes than in others. This empirical variation raises a normative challenge. How can we ensure that the normative value to organizations of implementing a self-regulation system in the first place does depend on its ultimate effectiveness (not just empty symbolism)? How can regulators and other stakeholders in a democracy ensure that companies only receive kudos for compliance if they engage in self-regulation with integrity? How can we move along the timeline (Figure 2.3) from prompting management commitment to do *something* (i.e. *anything*) about compliance, to prompting management commitment to do something *effective and substantive*?

Shifting responsibility and risk

In a series of surveys of corporate ethics programs, Weaver and Trevino and colleagues (Trevino et al. 1999; Weaver and Trevino 1999; Weaver et al. 1999a) have identified two different approaches to formal ethics management.[7] The *compliance orientation* focuses on rules, detection and discipline of offences by employers. It suggests that 'employees cannot be trusted, or are in some other way ethically incompetent', and 'whatever salience they create for an ethical role identity is created by the fear of discipline for non-conformity'. By contrast, a *values-oriented program* emphasizes support for employees' ethical aspirations and shared values. It 'suggests that employees already are committed to ethical behavior' (Weaver and Trevino 1999: 320, 323).

The compliance orientation imposes rules on the employee from outside, rather than building up personal integrity by working with those values employees already hold. It assumes a 'calculative, self-interested response to the ethics program', one that may be effective at producing appropriate behaviour but is unlikely 'to enhance organizational commitment or communication' (Weaver and Trevino 1999: 323). This disciplinary approach inherently raises the potential that the compliance system will unjustly dominate employees by simply shifting the risk and responsibility of compliance to them. This creates a paradox. Normally a holistic corporate compliance system should include systems to avoid unjust treatment of employees by the corporate employer, through due process guarantees for hiring, firing and discipline, anti-discrimination measures, training and equipment to prevent injury and accidents, and fair salaries and promotion opportunities (cf. Henry 1983; Selznick 1969). At the same time, compliance systems are often dependent on employee discipline for their effectiveness.

If the compliance system is not unjust in its approach to discipline of employees, it may still dominate in the way it constructs the appropriate personal behaviour and attitudes of employees. Chapter 2 has already outlined the ways in which organizational life tends to dull and dominate people's sensitivity to values other than those required by the particular role they play in the organization. The contemporary corporation's interest in nurturing a distinctive 'corporate culture' can also colonize the personalities, values and actions of its workers. For example, Casey's (1995: 139) ethnographic research on employees' sense of personal identity in a major US technology services company, code-named 'Hephaestus', found that the 'psychostructure' of the workplace selects and shapes employees' orientations and characters to suit the organizational culture and the corporation's desired character type.

The 'Hephaestus' character also transfers to employees' lives outside work so that employees do not just take on a corporate organizational role but also internalize the values and practices of the new culture and identifications, as their 'older forms of identification are displaced' (Casey 1995: 140). An active, best practice compliance management system is itself aimed at creating a corporate 'culture of compliance' (or if it is more symbolic and less effective, an 'image' of compliance) through managing and disciplining employees. It is itself a program of corporate colonization of employee psyches and values.

Nowhere are these dangers more obvious than in those compliance measures that are supposed to protect employees from injustices such as health and safety hazards or sexual harassment. For example, sexual harassment grievance-handling processes often do operate as an avenue of empowerment for employees who believe they have been harassed. But companies also often choose to emphasize the negative, disciplinary aspect of their sexual harassment policies to employees, rather than their empowering, protective aspects; for example, the title of Big Bucks Australia's brochure, 'Sexual Harassment – Off Limits', and the memo sent to all staff from the acting managing director at AssurOz stating that '[AssurOz] will not tolerate sexual harassment – no excuses, no exceptions. If anyone is found to be sexually harassing another person in the workplace their employment or agency will be terminated' (see Parker 1999c: 27–8). Indeed, the message that employees will be swiftly dismissed for harassment is so strong that in the experience of at least one EEO officer interviewed (at Aussie Dollars), once a formal investigation has begun, the alleged harasser usually gets 'spooked' and resigns.

Corporate handling of sexual harassment allegations may be more punitive than remedies available in external agencies, since the company has the power to hire and fire, or make everyday life miserable. It is not only perpetrators of harassment who can be subject to strong discipline. Most policies also warned that mischievous or unfounded complaints were a 'serious breach' of the corporate code of conduct (Credit4Oz), which could themselves lead to disciplinary action or even defamation proceedings (Big Bucks Australia). Employees were therefore well advised to think carefully about whether they were likely to succeed before airing a grievance, rather than encouraged to bring potential problems to management attention.

Occupational health and safety management systems too are a frequent source of rules, management and discipline for employees in certain industries. Chemical Kings' occupational health and safety management system in Australia and elsewhere contains hundreds of safety rules, including how to walk down the office stairs safely:

> Every time there is an injury somewhere, the CEO leaves a voicemail about it and there are newsletters with graphic descriptions of incidents and how they happened. The philosophy is that every injury is absolutely inexcusable and could be prevented. In this building there has been over a year since the last medically treated injury and no one wants to be the first one. There are all these rules. When you start, you think it's ridiculous and we're not in school. But it really gets into your psyche. (Junior legal compliance officer at Chemical Kings Australia)

In a number of systems, including Chemical Kings', the number of days that have passed without any 'lost time injuries' is prominently displayed and nobody wants to be the worker who breaks the count by taking time off for an injury. In one award-winning occupational health and safety management system, employees in each bakery of a chain were promised a bonus that increased with the number of days the whole bakery went without a 'lost time injury' (Murphy 1994: 43). These systems create incentives for individual employees to take responsibility for their own injuries by not taking time off to treat those that do occur, and via pressure to themselves prevent their own injuries to avoid letting down the team. This takes the onus away from senior management to devise safe workplaces and safe work systems. In effect, it may also punish victims of injury at work for their own injuries. Twenty-five per cent of respondents to a staff survey on British Rail's health and safety systems spontaneously stated that although the aims of the policies were good, they believed their most important function was to move responsibility away from the board and 'pass the buck' to staff (Hutter 2001: 145–7).

A further example of the way in which self-regulation systems can dominate employees is through the tendency for companies to focus on employee fraud as one of the first and most important issues for internal compliance and control systems. A fraud audit and investigation system is often one of the first elements of a compliance system to be put in place and often the most thoroughly implemented element of the compliance systems (see Friedrichs 1996: 115–21 on employee crime). Fraud control is essential to protect customers, especially for companies in the financial services industry. However, when companies expend overwhelmingly greater effort implementing internal employee fraud control systems than employee protection compliance systems, it suggests that corporate management's basic compliance stance towards employees is more adversarial than engaged (see Levi 1987: 132–3 for estimates of the extent of corporate self-regulation of employee fraud). Fraud control pits employers against employees.

The most common subjects of corporate compliance systems and codes of conduct are the control of conduct that is harmful to the company itself, such as employee theft, improper book-keeping, conflicts of interest, and corruption. A KPMG (1997) survey of business ethics practices sent to chief executives of the top 1000 public and private Canadian companies found that the ethics issue rated 'very important' most often by respondents was 'integrity of books and records'. The Price

Waterhouse Survey (1997) of corporate compliance practices found that the most popular area covered by compliance programs was 'ethics, conflicts of interest and gifts', with 86 per cent of respondents saying that their program covered this area – far ahead of environmental health and safety, employment law, consumer protection and other areas to benefit customers, communities or employees. Forcese (1997: 14) finds that corporate codes of conduct in the USA and Canada generally contain provisions aimed at protecting the firm from wrongful acts by its employees, while corporate social responsibility ranks low on the list of priorities.

The 'good citizen corporation' movement can be seen as an exercise in risk management which 'flips' liability for corporate non-compliance from the vicarious liability of the entity and its managers to the personal liability of 'wayward' employees. Laufer (1999: 1409ff) argues that the survey evidence available on the corporate implementation of compliance systems show that companies introduce formal codes, but not necessarily adequate systems for implementing them. They implement rule systems, but not value and integrity-based systems. They offer lip service to policies of compliance but simultaneously 'wink' at non-compliance: 'organizations simply select compliance purchases at the minimum level of expenditure necessary to shift liability to the agent' (Laufer 1999: 1403). Employee non-compliance is a risk that is bound to occur. The purchase of a compliance system may be a form of self-insurance so that liability for non-compliance attaches to the individual and not to the entity. Thus, compliance systems often institutionalize an inherent structural conflict in which the institution tries simultaneously 'to eliminate sexual harassment from the work and academic environment, and to insulate itself from liability' (Kihnley 2000: 70).

Scapegoating

The third primary way in which a corporate compliance system may be used to deflect conflict is by creating a trail or formal system that obscures top-management or entity responsibility for breaches, and/or scapegoats particular individuals or business units as legally responsible for non-compliance. For example, John Braithwaite (1984: 308) reported from his fieldwork on corporate crime in the global pharmaceutical industry that, to his amazement, 'two American executives I interviewed explained that they held the position of "vice-president responsible for going to jail" ... Lines of accountability had been drawn in the organization such that if there were a problem and someone's head had to go on the chopping block', it would be theirs.

In the case of the 'vice-president responsible for going to jail', the scapegoat consents to his or her treatment (and is later rewarded for it with a promotion). More pernicious is the use of the compliance system to scapegoat powerless employees without their consent. A particularly obvious example occurred in the aftermath of the 1998 Longford explosion in Australia. A huge explosion at Esso's (a jointly owned Australian subsidiary of Exxon) gas plant killed two workers and closed down all gas supplies in the state of Victoria for two weeks. At the Royal Commission into the circumstances of the incident, Esso's lawyers blamed the explosion on the employees who were at the site at the time, including the two dead workers, and accused one of the survivors of being defensive, evasive, contradictory, inconsistent and subject to convenient memory lapses in his evidence to the commission. The Royal Commission's report cleared the workers and put the responsibility squarely on the company (see Hopkins 2000). In the meantime, investigative journalists uncovered evidence of several other accidents around the world involving Exxon subsidiaries where a similar strategy of deflecting responsibility had been attempted. The local newspaper published a report that argued that part of Exxon's global environmental and safety management system, 'Operational Integrity Management System' (OIMS), which is otherwise regarded well, aims to suppress evidence of its culpability in disasters, by making systematic use of its inhouse lawyers to conceal and fabricate evidence.[8]

This is not an isolated incident. Braithwaite concluded from his data on corporate crime in the pharmaceutical industry that large pharmaceutical companies plan very carefully how to set up structures for allocating blame, including through the use of contractors to do the 'dirty work'. He also found that companies have two kinds of records: those designed to allocate guilt, for internal purposes, and those designed to obscure guilt and diffuse responsibility, for external consumption (Braithwaite 1984: 138, 308).

As Laufer and Robertson (1997) argue, the research on corporate ethics and compliance systems has so far failed to normatively evaluate the extent of social control and domination exercised by top management over employees through compliance systems. Indeed, the ever-present compliance control and surveillance of some organizations' employees – from the computer-based training they are required to do when they arrive, to the poster in the toilet informing them that sexual harassment is against company policy, to the managing director's circular addressing conflicts of interest or reminding them of the rules governing their screensavers – could paint a picture straight from Foucault's (1977) *Discipline and Punish* of employees made subject to the discipline of best practice compliance management.

One compliance manager (the EEO officer at Pets & Health) voluntarily showed some sensitivity to the problems corporate disciplinary processes might raise when she said (slightly defensively):

> We're not trying to stamp out people's fun and make this into a military type operation. We think we are a successful company because we are open and we want that to continue … We are not trying to smash people.

Indeed, all the EEO officers interviewed about sexual harassment policies were not coy about stating that one of their main objectives was to avoid the interference and supervision of external agencies, whether anti-discrimination regulators or courts, in disputes and grievances that arose within the company. The chief EEO officer at Aussie Dollars in a training seminar that I attended was clear that the purpose of the bank's grievance-handling policies was 'to marginalize third parties as much as we can. Because it is the bank's responsibility and we should fix it.' EEO officers describe their purpose as 'to ensure that complaints are not taken externally and that if they are, we have a defendable position because we have investigated them thoroughly' (Big Bucks Australia). In this context, self-regulation professionals assume a special importance as double dealers in social control, specializing both in ensuring corporate compliance with the law (or at least enough compliance to minimize risk of liability) and in ensuring employee compliance with company policy.

Compliance managers have an interest in what one interviewee called 'virtuous delegation'. This means that the compliance unit can point to a chain of controls that leads to a particular employee or unit being held responsible for doing the wrong thing, rather than responsibility being able to be clearly assigned to the top, to the entity as a whole (or indeed to the compliance manager). Compliance professionals themselves have an interest in distancing themselves from whatever goes wrong to avoid having to resign their job, be sacked or get in trouble with the regulators. As one solicitor put it, 'For many organizations the compliance officer is seen as an opportunity to set up a fall guy'.[9] For example, in his interviews with UK financial services compliance officers (who had clearly defined responsibilities to the regulators), Weait (1994: 384) found that 'compliance officers are unanimous that they are not responsible for compliance, merely responsible for ensuring that people have the means to comply. They are keen to forestall potential scape-goating [of themselves] and emphasise individual [employee] responsibility.' Thus, management pressure to shift compliance responsibility to employees is reinforced by self-regulation professionals' interest in managing the conflict they themselves face (and avoiding being made scapegoats themselves).

Stakeholder containment

We have seen that companies often dominate internal stakeholders (employees, including compliance staff), even through the implementation of compliance systems in which employee rights, concerns and values are ostensibly supported. The final pathology concerns corporate relations with external stakeholders. As we saw in Chapter 4, there is evidence that a variety of external stakeholders can and do permeate the veneer of corporate unresponsiveness (with varying impacts) to prompt commitment to implementation of a self-regulation system. They might also offer expertise, skills, comment or participation in the design and operation of a compliance management system, or seek to monitor and hold accountable its implementation and outcomes. Rhetoric about the 'stakeholder corporation' is now commonplace among corporate social responsibility strategists (e.g. Elkington 1998; Wheeler and Sillanpaa 1997; World Business Council for Sustainable Development 1999). Yet systems that purport to incorporate consultation and dialogue with stakeholders succumb to their own pathologies.

From the perspective of ethical theory, at best it is morally neutral for a company to identify relevant stakeholders and how their interests or views intersect with corporate action or decision-making (Goodpaster 1991: 87–8). The corporate management of stakeholder relations is of ethical consequence only when people in the company decide what to do on the basis of the stakeholder perspectives identified. Corporate management might conduct a stakeholder analysis merely to identify potential resistance and retaliation to corporate plans, not because of any ethical concern for stakeholders. The corporate response to stakeholder perspectives might involve substantive action to address stakeholder concerns, public relations or nothing, depending on the corporate judgment of what difference the particular group of stakeholders might make.

The danger here is that corporate management turns citizens with legitimate opinions on corporate actions into the target of a corporate strategy that has traditionally been aimed at another category of 'stakeholder': competitors and contractual partners in the supply chain. As Gilbert (1996) argues, the traditional concern of corporate strategizing is the 'stakeholder containment imperative'. The aim is to colonize and control a particular segment of the marketplace through partnership with a few strong stakeholders, and the domination of others: 'The Stakeholder Containment Imperative is an ethics of bullying stakeholders. Indeed, the Stakeholder Containment Imperative honors strategic bullies' (Gilbert 1996: 51). Current corporate models of stakeholder outreach are generally aimed at consulting with stakeholders in order to analyse their perspectives so that the company can decide what to do to manage the risk that stakeholder action might harm the company, rather than engaging with their concerns and opening the corporation up to democratic accountability.

Some critics of the 'stakeholder corporation' argue that stakeholder consultation and dialogue tend to define people with concerns about corporate activities and social responsibility as 'stakeholders' in the corporate economy, rather than as 'citizens' with legitimate rights to hold corporate governments accountable. For example, Karliner (1997: 41–2) argues that shareholders, customers and employees become 'first class' stakeholders, while advocacy groups and local communities are merely 'third class'. The consequence, according to Karliner, is that 'the designation of "stakeholder" tends to remove citizens from the realm of political power achieved through participation in democratic institutions … it redefines citizens and their communities as constituencies of transnational corporations in the world economy – virtually defining them as residents in a global version of the "company town".'

Certainly different categories of stakeholders have different levels of impact at different points of the compliance management process. The following two stories, of Monsanto and Shell, illustrate the problems and possibilities of stakeholder engagement.

Firstly, the story of Monsanto's failure to engage seriously with stakeholder concerns with genetically modified crops which were flagged by its own employees and consultants, and the stakeholder actions that eventually forced them to take the issue seriously, illustrates the problems and possibilities of stakeholder engagement in corporate self-regulation. Monsanto has an audited internal environmental management system. In March 1997 the company retained SustainAbility, a well-respected London-based non-profit environmental and social responsibility consultancy firm, to provide ongoing advice on sustainable development, agriculture and corporate reporting.[10] Through 1997 and 1998 SustainAbility worked with Monsanto environment, health and safety staff to organize meetings with retailers, farmers' organizations and public interest groups who were critical of Monsanto's introduction of genetically modified food technology to Europe. SustainAbility advised Monsanto senior management to define their core values and ethical principles in regard to biotechnology, and gave specific advice on how to do so. Despite the fact that a state-of-the-art environment management system was in place, internal staff with enthusiasm and integrity had been appointed, and creative and knowledgeable consultants hired, this advice was not followed. SustainAbility felt that 'we have seen little change, and the [operating] companies tend to do what they have always done. The legalistic "we know best" mentality has actually become stronger, rather than the more consultative model we were hoping to encourage.'[11] In December 1998, SustainAbility did what they felt integrity demanded and decided (after consulting all fifty of their network members around the world) to end their retainer with Monsanto.

By the beginning of 1999, the protests of activists and consumers had made genetically modified crops a major European and global news story. Protest focused on:

- Monsanto's proposal to market weed-resistant crop seeds that utilized the 'terminator' gene: the seeds would grow into plants that would show superior resistance to weeds when used in combination with Monsanto chemical products. But in order to re-coup Monsanto's investment in the crops, the 'terminator' gene would ensure that the plants produce only infertile seeds, thus ensuring that farmers would have to continually buy new seed from Monsanto. It was argued that this technology could make farmers dependent on Monsanto and more prone to unmanageable debt, and would reduce crop diversity;
- concerns that the use of genetically modified organisms in human food had not been adequately tested for safety and might have unforeseen consequences on human health; and
- concerns that genetically modified crops might have unforeseen environmental consequences via inadvertent cross-pollination and their presence in the food chain.

Initially Monsanto brushed off criticism from environmental and consumer groups. However, European supermarkets and processed food brands, especially in Britain, were much more vulnerable to consumer pressure than Monsanto (which markets mainly to farmers and to other companies). Supermarket chains such as Tesco and Sainsbury started trying to ensure that the foods they sold did not use genetically modified ingredients. India and Zimbabwe banned the technology, and agricultural research organizations condemned it. US corn exports to the EU were reported to have dropped by 96 per cent in a year, and farmers themselves indicated that they would be reluctant to buy Monsanto products, since they might have no market for their crops if they used them. When activists in the USA started to protest against genetically modified crops, the Clinton administration backed down from its aggressive free trade approach. In May 1999, Deutsche Bank recommended that institutional investors sell Monsanto shares, and the price dropped. By the time Deutsche repeated the advice in September, other analysts joined in, and Monsanto stock had lost 35 per cent of its value in a year (Wall Street as a whole went up 30 per cent).[12]

According to newspaper reports, the final straw was the attitude of one very powerful stakeholder, Dr Gordon Conway, president of the Rockefeller Foundation.[13] The Rockefeller Foundation had invested more than US$100 million in Monsanto to develop new varieties of genetically modified rice. Conway was called in for consultation by the Monsanto board as a part of their initial response to activism and protests. By appearing to engage with stakeholders, Monsanto was hoping to convince its investors not to be put off by the protests. Conway was expected to be an ally, given the millions he had put into Monsanto's development of genetically modified food technology. The board's willingness to meet with him was hardly an example of democratic engagement with critical stakeholders. However, the board were surprised: Professor Conway stated that he deplored the corporation's style and global strategy, and advised them to change their approach and commit to prompt, full and honest sharing of data.[14]

Monsanto's attempt to manage the damage being caused by social protest by appearing open was revealed for what it was by a multi-million dollar investor who turned out to be unmanageable. Conway had informed the press of what he would tell the board: '"It was like a boil had been lanced," said one person who was party to the talks. "Someone in authority had for the first time held this monolithic corporation up to public accountability".' Monsanto CEO, Shapiro, publicly admitted that 'we have irritated and antagonized more people than we have persuaded ... our confidence in biotechnology has been widely seen as arrogance and condescension'. In October 1999, Monsanto undertook not to develop and sell the terminator gene, the most controversial aspect of its biotechnology program.[15]

In December 1999 it announced a proposed merger with Pharmacia and Upjohn in which at least 20 per cent of the genetically modified crops business was to be spun off into a separate business. In the wake of Monsanto's mishandling of the genetic modification issue, the merger agreement valued Monsanto shares at US$13 a share less than they had been valued in a similar merger proposal only a year earlier (Martinson 1999).

In the absence of strong regulatory action at a global level over a newly emerging technological innovation, Monsanto was only brought to heel via a chain of informal action that started with environmental activists and spread to consumers, supermarkets and processed food companies, and ultimately to investors. It was the investors who wielded the power to demand action, but they only did so because of the protest of activists, retailers and farmers.

On the whole, companies will often not be responsive to consumers and social activists until investors and shareholders begin to show their concern. Monsanto changed only when its share price dropped and a hundred million dollar investor questioned its approach. Yet even a corporate acceptance of social responsibilities in response to a crisis of public legitimacy, brand value and share price may only mean that the corporation learns to manage the risk of adverse stakeholder reaction, not to open itself to democratic deliberation. Royal Dutch Shell, a global petro-chemical group based in London and Amsterdam, has walked this fine line after facing two major social action campaigns in 1995.

The first was a Greenpeace campaign against Shell's plan to tow a disused oil platform, the Brent Spar, to the North Sea, dynamite it, and then sink it in a deep ocean trench. Shell's environmental assessment procedures had identified this as less expensive to accomplish with less environmental risk than bringing it to shore for break-up and disposal. The proposal had been approved by the UK government. Greenpeace was concerned about pollution that could be caused by leaving the Brent Spar on the seabed, and also claimed that there were 5550 tonnes of contaminated oil on board. (After the most dramatic episodes of the campaign, Greenpeace scientists discovered that this estimate was a mistake and publicly admitted so.)

The second issue involved Shell's oil activities in Nigeria.[16] Its oil exploration, the continuous flaring of the gas that escapes from the earth as oil is mined, and leaks from uncovered high-pressure oil pipes had gradually ruined the Ogoni people's farmland over a period of years. Shell's royalty payments for use of the land, however, went to the national government which gave very little to the minority Ogoni people. The Ogoni started a political campaign against the government, claiming self-determination and control over their traditional lands and the rich oil rights attached to it (see Osaghae 1995). As the protests against the government's commercial dealings with Shell (and also with Chevron) became more direct, the Nigerian government used force to clear them away from both oil companies' land. It was alleged by human rights groups that the government abused human rights to protect the oil companies and to silence dissent, and that the police and military even used cars and helicopters provided by the oil companies to round up and arrest protesters. In 1995 world attention focused on the issue when environmental and human rights activists, Ken Sara-Wiwa and eight colleagues, were summarily executed by the Nigerian government after being arrested for protesting against Shell on Shell land.[17]

The Brent Spar campaign sparked massive consumer boycotts in Europe. Fifty Shell service stations in Germany were damaged (including two that were fire-bombed and one that was raked with bullets). A number of European governments protested Shell's proposal (see Brown 1998; Ledgerwood 1997: 194–6), and retail sales in Germany and other continental European countries dropped by 30 per cent (Ledgerwood 1997: 196). (This now made dumping the platform at sea much more expensive than the very expensive procedures required for controlling ecological risk while dumping on shore.) After Ken Sara-Wiwa's execution, leaders, including Nelson Mandela, called for Shell to disinvest in Nigeria, and at one stage the US administration proposed implementing economic sanctions against Nigeria that would have also damaged Shell.

In response to both events, Shell's brand value dropped rapidly, especially in Europe. The company's own public opinion polling found that it was viewed as 'worse than average' on environmental and human rights issues, and that this was as true among 'experts' as among the general public. At the same time, the general context of lowering oil prices and more competition was driving share prices down anyway. In response, Shell had to do something to rehabilitate its image, its brand value and perhaps its share price, to avoid potential future liability for environmental and human rights issues, to make itself more attractive to good quality staff and to make itself a credible participant in discussions with governments and third parties about emerging regulatory issues.

Rather than sinking the Brent Spar, Shell had it towed to a Norway fjord in 1995 to await a resolution. Early in 1998 Shell announced that the Brent Spar was to be sliced into six pieces and used in the foundations for a roll-on, roll-off ferry terminal on the Norwegian coast at a cost of US$35 million (compared with £4.5 million for their original proposal) (Brown 1998). The tripartite relations between Shell, the Nigerian government and traditional land-owners were less satisfactorily resolved. Shell eventually offered to clean up the oil spills on Ogoni land, to restart local development projects, and to stop continuous flaring on all its sites by 2008 (Shell 1998: 13), a practice that has long been outlawed in most first world countries. However, similar confrontations with traditional land-owners continued to occur on other oil fields operated by Shell and Chevron.[18]

Starting in 1996, Shell massively changed the delivery of its environment, health and safety management system, hired SustainAbility to implement a global stakeholder consultation program and indulged in a massive public relations campaign to advertise its new 'open' approach to listening to stakeholders. As Shell's vice-president for environment, health and safety put it, at Shell 'the acute was always managed well. The chronic was not managed so well' until social responsibility issues impacted on 'brand value' through consumer action and social movement politics. Previously environmental issues had been a matter for each separate national company in the group. Now the central Shell group requires adherence to stricter and more standardized environment, health and safety management practices. Each must have an EHS management system which must be certified against a recognized independent systems standard, such as ISO 14000 or EMAS. Each must also report health, safety and environment performance data and have it verified and meet certain centrally imposed targets by certain dates for reducing Shell's environmental impact, including the phasing out of flaring and the elimination of CFCs and halons (Shell 1998: 20–1).[19]

The second prong of Shell's response was its 'stakeholder dialogues', and associated advertising campaign. Stakeholder dialogue is aimed at developing new key performance indicators for environmental and social responsibility to be used in Shell's external reporting, in an attempt to forestall criticism. The huge advertising campaign associated with the dialogue exercise gave Shell a chance to 'green up' its image. One set of advertisements appears in magazines such as the *Economist* and the London *Financial Times*, clearly aimed at leaders in opinion-making and those deciding whether to invest in Shell shares, rather than at social activists. These advertisements are a series of full-colour double-page images of lush rainforest, a tiny tree frog, an obviously diverse blend of people of different ages and races, and so on, and they ask questions such as 'Exploit or explore?', 'Cloud the issue or clear the air?', and 'Protect endangered species or become one?'. The text of each advertisement refers to one of the environmental or social responsibility issues that Shell is seeking to address. Each also contains a careful disclaimer that the advertisement is a Shell group initiative and does not necessarily reflect the views of any Shell operating business. The disclaimer clearly illustrates the difficulties of centralizing control on compliance management issues across a huge corporate group.

In another more detailed backup advertising pamphlet, 'Listening and Responding: Dialogue with our stakeholders', the Shell group uses cute graphics and the following text to say that it is 'no longer solely accountable to our shareholders' but to 'our customers and our people, to other companies with whom we work, to government and non-governmental groups, and to all those affected by our operations and products'. It states that Shell must not only comply with law but also 'understand the currents of social opinion and strive to meet societal expectations that are not reflected in legislation'. The pamphlet goes on to describe their focus group and survey methodology and commits Shell to continue to engage employees, the public and peer companies in dialogue about 'the three legs of sustainable development: economic progress, environmental care and social responsibility'. They invite people to visit their interactive website and to receive and comment on Shell's social responsibility reports.

Shell's new systems seem to have made a real difference to its attitude to communication with its external stakeholders. For example, in Australia in mid-1999, a non-Shell ship bringing oil to Shell's refinery spilt ten gallons of oil in Sydney harbour.[20] In comparison to Esso's non-transparent and scapegoating response to the Longford explosion a few months earlier (described above), Shell immediately issued an apology and began to clean up the spill, despite the fact that, by the letter of the law, it may have been able to escape any responsibility for it. However, one of the few attempts by activist stakeholders to systematically assess the company's social responsibility management tells a slightly different story. On the 'Corporate Watch' website,[21] an independent site that rates multinational corporations along a number of dimensions of social responsibility, Shell was rated very well for its openness to stakeholders, but its actual environment management system did not rate so well, even after three years of 'stakeholder engagement'. (In comparison, Exxon, Esso Australia's parent, rates badly on openness but well on its actual system for managing the environment.) There is no necessary connection between fancy programs for consulting stakeholders, and stakeholder concerns being incorporated into how a company regulates itself.

CONCLUSION

Shell learnt from the Brent Spar that its traditional, technical approach to environmental risk management was not effective at controlling the risk that people would perceive its actions as environmentally unfriendly and contrary to community values. Shell's new consultants, SustainAbility, have written about how Shell's well-respected and sophisticated 'scenario planning' exercises were blind to community perceptions as a source of risk (Elkington and Trisoglio 1996). Michael Power (2000) explains that the '*new*' risk management sees people's values and perceptions as a new, but so far largely unquantified and unquantifiable, source of uncertainty about the results of corporate action. The new risk management seeks to holistically integrate analysis of all sorts of risk to top-level corporate strategy, then use top-down internal control systems to control it. Technical risk management is no longer separate from internal control functions (see also Laufer 1999).

Focus groups are used to gather information on how corporate action is likely to be perceived as meshing with, or contravening, people's values. Indeed, it is now recognized in mainstream risk management methodologies, including risk management standards (e.g. AS/NZS 4360), that focus groups and research on stakeholder opinions are important sources of analysis of potential risk (Baldwin and Cave 1999: 141; Power 2000). A body of research on the psychology of risk perception has found that people's perceptions of the seriousness of risk are affected by factors such as 'catastrophic potential; degree of personal control over the size and probability of the risk; familiarity with the risk; degree of perceived equity in sharing risks and benefits; visibility of the benefits of risk taking; potential to impose blame on risk creators; delay in manifestation of harm; voluntariness with which the risk is undertaken' (Baldwin and Cave 1999: 141). As Monsanto and

Shell both discovered, risk assessments based on technical evaluations of the level of risk can be poor predictors of individual and social actions that are affected by people's perceptions of issues and their values. If Shell had conducted focus groups as part of its risk assessment of different options for the Brent Spar, it might well have chosen a different option.

The new risk management shows great promise in its inclusion of people's values and perceptions in the risk assessment process. As Heyvaert (1999a: 140) comments, a fundamental problem of traditional environmental risk assessment is that it is 'undemocratic' because it takes into account only technical scientific considerations, not people's values and perceptions (see also Baldwin and Cave 1999: 142). The new approach is potentially a way that stakeholders' voices can be heard at the phase of detecting potential crises, and therefore prompting management commitment to respond by implementing an internal control system. Indeed, it is often only a crisis of legitimacy brought about by publicity and public attention that will prompt top-management interest in, and commitment to, implementation of a corporate self-regulation system.

Yet the fact is that public attention to any particular issue or company is cyclical and short. It is simply unsustainable to expect the politics of activism and media investigation to be able to constantly prompt the ongoing commitment that is necessary for effective self-regulation (see Braithwaite and Drahos 2000: 319; Downs 1972). New corporate risk assessment methodologies have the capacity to institutionalize an awareness of potential corporate legitimacy crises and therefore build commitment. CEO awareness that the cycle of public attention can turn to their industry or company at any time, and probably will at some time over a period of decades, combined with risk assessment of stakeholder perceptions and values as a standard risk management methodology, can help prompt a commitment to solving legitimacy crises before they occur.

However, the danger of the new risk management methodology is that if it *analyses* seriousness of risk in terms of people's 'perceptions', this will naturally lead to *controlling* risk through communication that changes 'perceptions' without changing facts. There is a great danger that once external (and internal) stakeholders' values and perceptions are identified, they will be managed by public relations exercises that neutralize the possibility of protest and consumer boycott, rather than actively prompting internal organizational commitment to real change. For example, both SustainAbility (an independent non-profit consultancy) and the World Business Council for Sustainable Development (a membership organization of big business, originally set up to lobby for self-regulatory approaches to environmental issues at the Rio Summit) in their leading approaches to corporate stakeholder engagement are mainly concerned with helping companies to organize focus groups, forums, open days and glossy social responsibility reports. They will encourage companies to engage in dialogue, but it is unclear whether they will facilitate stakeholder involvement in the implementation of compliance and responsibility measures in the daily operations of the company. Their stakeholder consultation systems are attractive to companies as tools for managing the risk of consumer action and social movement politics negatively impacting on image, brand value and ultimately share price.

Corporate communication to ensure that stakeholder perceptions reflect reality, not psychological biases, may be appropriate. But the risk management approach to stakeholders runs the very real potential of public relations and information-gathering that does not tie into systems to make sure stakeholders' concerns are actually taken into account and acted upon. Stakeholder consultation systems, such as Shell's, do not give interested groups and individuals any rights 'to participation and to discussion, a right to be involved in debate and a right to be considered as groups, and even individuals, with needs and agendas that are not necessarily satisfied by profit accumulation' (Wheeler 1998: 15). There is a need to find ways to empower otherwise powerless stakeholders, rather than allowing companies to 'manage' them. If risks are perceived and felt by differentiated groups with different sources of information (including public authorities, the scientific community, industry, consumers, interest groups, and so on), the effectiveness of risk management and regulation will depend on securing the participation of these groups (Heyvaert 1999b: 38; see also Heyvaert 1999a). However, 'participatory procedures' for goal-oriented, profit-making companies may be very different from the participatory democracy usually advocated for state institutions (see Chapter 8).

If these are the potential criticisms of companies' 'compliance' efforts, then they apply doubly to the techniques of the new regulatory state. Regulatory agencies increasingly rely on the compliance risk management of regulated companies to manage and prevent regulatory risks – 'meta-risk management'. One of the clearest examples of this approach is the proposal (currently not implemented) that the Basle Accord (which sets international standards for regulating bank capitalization) would require national regulators to use credit-rating agencies' measures of risk and banks' internal (risk management) models for allocating capital to credit risks to determine how much capital regulation should require the banks to hold.[22] This does not address the very real risk of conflict between regulatory goals and business practices, or even the need for regulated business to receive authoritative guidance.

Figure 5.1 illustrated the way in which ideally the business concerns of the organization reach out and embrace values and norms coming from external communities and politics through the harmonizing role of the self-regulation function. However, the harmonizing conception of the compliance role ignores the fact that people, and even regulators, disagree on appropriate responsibility goals for business. In particular, different regulators, different businesses and different individuals draw the balance very differently between short-term profit maximization and social responsibility. In practice, both regulators and corporate management expect the compliance unit and compliance system to defuse these compliance–business conflicts, but often in very different ways. Either way the compliance staff must live with an inherent structural conflict in their role, and with tensions that put obstacles in the way of a smooth embrace between responsibility goals and business goals.

7 | Model corporate citizens: The role of self-regulation professionals

In his 'how-to' book on compliance in financial services in the UK, experienced compliance manager Andrew Newton poses the central dilemma that faces all compliance (and other self-regulation) staff:

> [O]n the one hand, to work closely enough with the business it serves such that it understands and anticipates the needs of the business for compliant solutions that take the business further, so contributing to the sense of common purpose and the development of the right culture; on the other hand to maintain sufficient independence and objectivity to recognize, where it is the case, that the most creatively formulated compliant solution may not be capable of accommodating the immediate desires of the business. (Newton 1998: 91)

There are at least two competing visions of the work of compliance functions in this passage, two different ideas of where the ultimate loyalty of self-regulation professionals lies (to employer, or to regulators and external social values), and two potential modus operandi for compliance work (a 'harmonizing' role and a 'political' role).

Both the new regulatory state, and corporate top management, will tend to abdicate responsibility for reconciling the practice of business with social and legal responsibility to self-regulation functions. This chapter argues that self-regulation staff should not absorb and deflect conflict. Rather, they should use conflict to facilitate self-criticism, internal deliberation about integrity, and internal–external dialogue with and consideration of 'stakeholder' views by internal players. Their job is to help to resolve conflict within the organization, and between the organization and the external world, through:

168

- acknowledging and dealing with conflict between an organizational practice or event, and the demands of the law or of social responsibility; and/or
- defining and passing on the conflict to appropriate decision-making organs within the organization for decision and action; and/or
- facilitating escalation of the conflict to a regulator or to some other external accountability mechanism, if it cannot be resolved internally.

This chapter outlines the conditions in which, first, the harmonizing role of self-regulation functions is most successful and, second, the political, conflict-handling role (the 'clout') of the compliance function is likely to be effective. These two faces of the compliance role cannot be separated – each lacks integrity without the other. Integrity cannot, however, be achieved in isolation. The harmonizing role only flourishes in the context of the self-regulation professional's connection to regulatory communities, broader civic communities and professional communities. The political, conflict-handling role is only possible with the support of the nurture of personal skills and commitment in the self-regulation profession, internal corporate systems that demonstrate compliance commitment, and external support from regulators and broader communities.

THE HARMONIZING ROLE

Mainstreaming external values within the organization

In Chapter 2 we saw that a number of evaluative studies do indicate that the existence and institutionalization of self-regulation professionals of various types were significant factors in the success of corporate compliance and self-regulation in occupational health and safety (Rees 1988), financial services (McCaffrey and Hart 1998; see also Weait 1994) and equal employment opportunity (Edelman 1990). Many of the self-regulation managers interviewed saw in their role the creative task of weaving external values with management practices – making law come alive in organizational life. As an EEO officer at Aussie Dollars put it, her aim was to 'mainstream' EEO compliance so that it would become 'second nature to managers'. Many self-regulation managers are conscious of operating at two levels: the level of values, and the level of management practice. One seminar speaker raised a wry laugh from the audience by beginning his presentation with the observation that, in compliance work: 'At one level you have a "pious hope" and on the other you have the dry, difficult task of making it work'.[1] A US commentator uses the colourful metaphor of having 'one foot planted firmly in the shifting, treacherous terrain of the law, and the other planted just as firmly in the oozing swamp of business' (Terrell 1997: 1005). In a more serious consideration of what compliance work involves, three leading US compliance practitioners state that the role of inhouse compliance staff is to 'internalize the external integrity standards they are charged with implementing throughout the company'. They go on to reflect: 'The values and commitment of the ethics and integrity program become part of their personal missions, often with an enthusiasm that cannot be explained merely as the product of their company paycheck' (Driscoll et al. 1998: 48).

However, this does not mean that effective self-regulation managers must be individuals who are inherently and uniformly more 'ethical' or 'virtuous' than any other member of their organization. Indeed, many of the people I met in my fieldwork did not talk naturally and explicitly about their own personal normative commitments (although some did). It is hard to say whether this was out of shyness, an exaggerated sensitivity to commercial values, or complete lack of normative commitment. Nevertheless, even for those who shied away from raising issues of their individual integrity and ethics, the harmonization of organizational life with external values infused their descriptions of their work.

In any firm many individuals (probably all) are inherently capable of ethical judgment and law-abiding behaviour. The reason for the self-regulation manager's special focus on personal and organizational integrity is structural: 'People in compliance are more interested in ethics because they have the luxury to do so' (Eurostock UK compliance manager). The self-regulation function is charged with being the 'conscience or consciousness of the firm' (Trustus US compliance manager) by the CEO and senior management. Once a compliance function gains a toe-hold in an organization, then there is at least one person, the compliance manager, who has a personal and professional stake in pursuing organizational integrity.

Indeed, the self-regulation manager ought to be a model of integrity. There ought to be a wholeness between his or her obligation to the organization to do the job of compliance, and his or her normative commitments from the rest of life, whatever they may be, to abide by the spirit of the law, to pursue environmental sustainability, to value health and safety from accidents, fairness to minorities, an equitable balance between work and family life, or fair operations of the market. Other individuals in the firm will be asked to play out functional roles that do not require them to consider personal or external social values. They may even implicitly be required to abandon their personal values while at work. But the job of self-regulation always involves the bringing together of business practice and some set of external values (at least as they are institutionalized in the law). In a consistently hostile environment, of course, this task will be unsustainable. The compliance person will be put in the terrible position of having to choose between giving in to tokenism, resigning from the organization, or whistle-blowing.

My fieldwork uncovered some self-regulation managers who seemed completely absorbed with business concerns to the exclusion of other values.[2] Most, however, expressed some broader normative commitments and interest in integrity. For example, seven of the twelve EEO officers interviewed explicitly expressed such commitment to the value of sexual harassment and EEO policies. Most seemed to have more progressive views in relation to gender equality than did senior management. This is supported by Valerie Braithwaite's (1992: 48) study of Australian affirmative action contact persons that found that most reported having more progressive views than their senior managers. Like Eisenstein's (1996) 'femocrats' within the public bureaucracy, some were even committed feminists following a career path that was both personally rewarding and altruistically oriented. The EEO officer at Good as Gold Australia described herself (and other members of the financial EEO officers' network of which she was a part) as 'a little bit of a social change agent in the business world'.

Among the trade practices and financial services compliance professionals interviewed, several explicitly stated that they had chosen to work in a particular company specifically because of its commitment to good corporate citizenship. Others I met at conferences and seminars said that they were looking for new jobs where compliance was taken more seriously, or compared earlier compliance positions unfavourably with their current ones. Others explicitly described the personal moral commitment they believed compliance managers must bring to their jobs: 'Your ethics cannot be questioned. You cannot tell others what to do if you are unethical or you will be a hypocrite. You must have absolute integrity' (Big Bucks Australia compliance officer). For some interviewees, this integrity was seen as a feature that distinguished compliance professionals from other professionals, especially lawyers:

You need a fair and just outlook in how a business should be operated ... There must be an underlying sense of fairness in your character ... that you shouldn't be overly opportunistic, smart and technical. It needs to be in your character to go looking for fair solutions to problems rather than just technical legal ones. A lot of lawyers love to be wise guys and to hit people over the head with the technical stuff. But in this work it is not a question of whether something is right or wrong in the legal sense but of whether it could be perceived to be right or wrong. In a competitive industry it is to our detriment in the long run if we are seen as a bunch of wise guys. (GarbageRUs compliance officer)

Adviser Ten, an Australian consultant who worked mainly in financial services and telecommunications compliance advising, described his career (from student to regulator to financial services firm to consultant) in terms of his ongoing commitment to values and ethics in law. Unlike legal practice, 'which is just making sure transactions go through', he saw compliance as attractive because it asks 'what is the point of the law? It is about what people should think about values, laws and ethics.'

Self-regulation professionals and integrity

Their personal and professional integrity as individuals and as a business unit is crucial to any success a self-regulation function might have. Against the tendency of organizations to fragment ethical and socially responsible selves from business selves, self-regulation professionals are placed in the organization with the explicit task of pulling these various selves together at three different levels: they must maintain their own personal integrity (and that of the compliance or self-regulation group); they must help others (individuals and business units) in the organization to also act with integrity; and they must do both these things with the aim of leading towards integrity at the organizational level. In his seminal work on social theory and professional ethics in an age of organizations, Larry May sees personal identity 'as a web knit from the various identifications and commitments that one makes with various social groups' (1996: 13). Integrity is about being responsive to all the social groups and concerns that have formed you as a person, not just playing out the one-dimensional role morality associated with membership of a particular group (e.g. parent, corporate lawyer, shop assistant).

Fiona Haines' (1997) recent work on organizational occupational health and safety responses to worker deaths illustrates this point nicely. She divided her sample of thirty-seven firms that had experienced a worker death into: (a) those who several years after the event had responded 'virtuously' by re-evaluating organizational safety levels, altering workplaces or work practices, and re-emphasizing current safety policy; (b) those who had displayed a 'blinkered' response, limited to isolating and altering those visible and specific factors that led to the death in question; and (c) those who displayed no change. Her data showed that those which displayed a virtuous response also had a 'virtuous culture' – that is, one that 'seeks to harmonise and "blend" the various demands it faces, rather than one which dichotomises and forces choices'. The virtuous culture sees 'safety as integral to organisational activity, while the culture lacking in virtue would tend to push safety into the background in order to focus on short-term demands'. Again 'integrity' is important here. Virtuous managers 'integrate' safety and health concerns into the '"hard-nosed" business concerns of time, money and productivity' (Haines 1997: 69, 94–5, 100–1, 123).

In 1993 Toni Makkai and Valerie Braithwaite tested the hypothesis that professional role orientation, values and autonomy would contribute to greater compliance. They compared nursing directors' levels of professional orientation and commitment to organizational values with data on the level of their nursing homes' compliance with government standards. They found, against their hypothesis, that professional orientations, values and autonomy did not have a significant independent effect on nursing home compliance. One of their conclusions was that they may have been wrong to sharply dichotomize professional and business orientations in their survey instrument. Directors of nursing may need strong orientations towards both professionalism and business efficiency to be effective in improving compliance (Makkai and Braithwaite 1993: 55). Their data are consistent with the integrity hypothesis. Self-regulation professionals are responsible for institutionalizing responsibility in organizations. Therefore in order to be successful they must exhibit not only the appropriate 'professional' values to have the motivation to improve compliance, but also a commitment to the organization and its efficiency in order to be able to put those values into action. Makkai and Braithwaite's study suggests that it is false to see professional autonomy and business orientation as always antipathetic. Rather, we can hypothesize that compliance professionals' integrity should be proved in their dual dependencies and loyalties to company and regulatory goals.

Most self-regulation professionals sit at the intersection of government regulation, broader public concerns, and professional community with organizational life. As an empirical matter, it is through their engagement with three communities – regulatory community, broader public communities, and professional community – that their awareness and commitment to external values are nurtured. It is the influence of these three communities (often through self-regulation staff) that makes integrity an issue within organizational life. As a normative prescription, it is therefore through these three mechanisms that integrity must be built.

The regulatory community
Firstly, and most clearly, self-regulation managers frequently act as a source of communication between regulatory agencies and their employer firms. Their job is to help the organization to know what it needs to do to comply with what the regulator requires. They can also inform and negotiate with regulators about what is reasonable to expect of their organization, how objectives can best be accomplished and what rules are not working well. As one compliance practitioner put it (more bluntly than most), 'compliance represents both the regulator and the firm' (Trustus US). Another commented that being a compliance manager was 'a real balancing act', with 'a foot in each camp'. He went on to vividly describe a situation he had faced where a regulator insisted that the CEO of one of his company's businesses be dismissed as part of the settlement of potential regulatory enforcement action. This compliance manager first argued with the regulator against losing the CEO, and then reasoned with the board that they must dismiss the CEO. His conclusion was that because his compliance unit dealt with regulators 'on a daily basis', they must see it 'as a partnership at all levels'.[3]

At Wonderchem, a major European chemical company, a long-term environmental management specialist described the excitement of working in pollution control in the 1980s as environmental legislation and environmental management technology developed in parallel with a 'challenging competition between legislative development and technological development' in leading countries like Germany and Canada: 'every new technological development you made became a new legislative marker'. He spent hours on the phone to legislators, discussing what level of emissions reduction could be achieved by the new technologies constantly coming on line and therefore what could be put in regulation. While pollution control is no longer progressing so quickly, compliance officers in other areas, especially financial services, must also now work with regulators to negotiate regulatory standards.

Indeed, there is a general movement among leaders of the profession towards the view that compliance is a 'partnership' between the regulator and the compliance function working together.[4]

The existence of some degree of partnership or community between regulators and regulatees is a precondition for effective regulatory activity in any area. In her examination of *Rules and Regulators*, Black (1997) has argued that whenever regulators use rules they must overcome potential problems of over- or under- inclusiveness, indeterminacy and interpretation in order to be effective. One important way in which these problems can be addressed is by ensuring that the context in which the rule is 'formed, followed, and enforced' is that of an 'interpretive community'. Interpretive communities are 'constituted by institutional practices which may exist in the form of shared cultures, norms, goals, definitions, [which] can be created through, for example, training and education'. In such communities, Black proposes that 'conversational' regulation that overcomes many of the inherent limitations of conventional rule-making such as 'uncertainty and honest perplexity and the problem of explicitness' is possible. Interpretive regulatory communities could also address creative compliance and instead create 'instinctive compliance' through 'the development of a tacit knowledge and understanding which can inform the application of the rules; [and] by overcoming the opportunistic approach to rules which is the basis of creative compliance' (Black 1997: 6, 30, 31–2, 38).

Similarly Meidinger (1987) sees all regulatory action as taking place within regulatory communities which, in their dialogues and disagreements, constitute, define and redefine appropriate norms of behaviour:

> ... members of regulatory communities have ongoing relationships with each other. In those relationships, they both pursue their own, often inconsistent interests and struggle to define a shared vision of the collective good. Because they live significant parts of their lives with each other, members of the community frequently influence each other, act with reference to each other, and desire each other's respect. Therefore, as well as being arenas for the pursuit of pre-existent interests, regulatory communities appear to have the capacity to be 'constitutive' – that is, to be forums in which appropriate individual and collective behaviour (and interests) are defined and redefined. (Meidinger 1987: 365)

Meidinger's thesis is backed up by empirical research on the way in which the interactions between inspectors and businesses construct the meaning of compliance (e.g. Hawkins and Hutter 1993). Similarly, John

Braithwaite's influential theories of compliance and regulation generally rely on the assumption that regulatory messages are communicated into a world of shared bonds and understandings in which companies can effectively respond to regulatory signals, and the parties deliberate effectively about their responses to them. This in turn creates shared commitments to regulatory goals. It assumes that regulators and regulatees are part of the same 'community', that they have continuing relationships and the same basic understanding of the meanings and goals of regulatory enactments. For example, Ayres and Braithwaite's (1992) theory of responsive regulation relies on a tripartite regulatory community made up of regulators, regulatees and public interest groups, who will deliberate together about the use of regulatory pyramids. Fisse and Braithwaite's (1993) corporate accountability model relies on corporate responsiveness to broad, weak, informal sanctions on the many individuals who can pull the strings of informal control and trigger bonds of responsibility within corporate communities.

As Black (1997: 33) points out, interpretive community for ensuring mutuality in the interpretation of legal rules has often been achieved by using legal professionals trained in judicial rules of interpretation for both the formulation and application of rules. Corporate self-regulation professionals, even more than legal professionals, show the capacity to specialize in being agents of regulatory community, through the negotiation of the meaning of compliance with regulatory rules, the translation of regulatory messages to organizational life, and the communication of the extent to which organizational compliance is possible to regulators.

Broader communities
Secondly, self-regulation managers can communicate to organizational members the values expressed in the media and by social movements, public interest groups, local community groups, and other groups and individuals. They may do this through monitoring media and public attention to issues touching how the corporation carries on business, by receiving reports on what customers and others complain to the company about, or by more proactive means such as stakeholder consultations and dialogues via focus groups or surveys. Here the compliance manager acts as a bridge between 'stakeholders' or broader communities and the organization. This makes the self-regulation function an important way of opening up the previously private corporate sphere to democratic deliberation in the public sphere, a topic that will be discussed in detail in Chapters 8 and 9.

Professional communities

Thirdly, self-regulation managers are frequently members of a professional network or community that can nurture their integrity and sense
of commitment to external values as well as organizational loyalty. In
an important book advocating and analysing corporate compliance systems, Sigler and Murphy (an academic and a leading US compliance
practitioner) make this clear in relation to the role that corporate
lawyers should play in compliance:

> Corporate lawyers have dual obligations to the firm they serve and to
> the profession they pursue. Their professional obligations make them
> more responsive to the demands of public agencies than other
> employees or managers of the corporation. Without betraying their
> employers, while still honoring the principles of the attorney–client
> relationship, they must try to act as agents of change within the cor-
> poration ... The American private enterprise system and the American
> corporation have had social responsibilities thrust upon them. The
> corporate lawyer must serve as translator (not merely as advocate) of
> those public responsibilities and also convey to government the point
> of view of his corporation regarding those responsibilities. (Sigler and
> Murphy 1988: 95–6)

When Sigler and Murphy wrote their book, they probably did not realize the extent to which compliance would begin to emerge as a distinct
profession in the 1990s with its own professional communities overlapping with, but independent of, the legal profession.

My interviewees did not provide a wealth of data on the significance
of their networking with other self-regulation professionals and how
that related to their values. However, most were very definite, when
asked, that they valued the opportunity to meet with colleagues at
meetings, seminars and conferences. Several financial services compliance managers in New York and London commented on the importance of the various formal meetings of networks of compliance
managers they attended as well as 'how important it is to be able to contact colleagues in other firms' (Trustus UK). A number of compliance
managers described how they would ring colleagues in other firms to
find out how to address a problem they were facing, or to congratulate
colleagues on how they had dealt with a problem. The one compliance
manager interviewed who thought the formal professional network
meetings were not important had been working in the area for many
years and said he already kept in contact with many compliance managers informally. The environmental managers I interviewed in Europe

all regularly met with one another. Indeed, some already knew which other companies I was visiting when I walked in the door for the interview, through their regular sessions with colleagues. The EEO officers at Pet and Health Care, Good as Gold Australia and Credit4Oz explicitly referred to networks of EEO officers from different companies, and their links with anti-discrimination regulators or industry association EEO advisers, as helpful sources of support.

Indeed, most compliance practitioners I observed showed a real hunger to attend meetings and seminars where ideas on skills and techniques might be passed on. Although they did not necessarily use the explicit language of building professional community, they certainly wanted to join professional networks, meet informally with colleagues from other firms, and acquire values and skills independent from the pure business of their organizations. Some associations of compliance professionals are now introducing accreditation for their members if they attend appropriate courses and pass tests.[5] Others are defining standards of practice for compliance professionals without going so far as proposing professional accreditation. For example, the Australian association was involved in developing the Standards Australia standard for compliance programs: AS 3806–1998.[6]

Valerie Braithwaite's (1992) quantitative work on Australian affirmative action (AA) officers offers a more systematic evaluation of the significance of professional networks in supporting the work of compliance professionals, as we have already seen in Chapter 2. She interviewed AA officers and evaluated both the procedural and substantive compliance of their organizations with the Australian AA legislation. Firstly, she found that AA officers were most effective when they were well networked with other AA officers and with the Affirmative Action Agency. Although AA officers generally reported more progressive attitudes than senior management, they drifted towards senior management views where they had little contact with others interested in EEO (Braithwaite 1992: 48, 95; see also Slovak 1981). Similarly Edelman and co-authors (1991: 91–2) in their study of the strategies used by AA officers found that their professional self-identity and network ties were a significant component of their capacity to institutionalize EEO/AA measures through the exchange, negotiation and standardization of affirmative action plans, programs and rules.

As Braithwaite (1992: 95) suggests, this fits well with social psychological research which shows that people need social validation of their views (as well as help in problem-solving and ideas) in order to retain their commitment. Indeed, the psychological research has shown that when people identify with a group or accept its values, their sense of self is linked to acting in compliance with group norms, including norms about ethical behaviour. The motivation is internal: it is not linked to judgments of risk in the environment (Tyler 1996; Tyler and Dawes 1993). Therefore well-integrated group members can act altruistically and independently to uphold group norms even in hostile environments. This is how professions are supposed to work, according to theorists of professional socialization. Where a practitioner identifies sufficiently with his or her professional community through socialization, he or she is supposed to naturally follow professional ethical norms (as well as cognitive skills) even in work for powerful and rapacious clients (see Durkheim 1992; May 1996: 63). Thus, an engineer relying on both cognitive and affective factors institutionalized in his or her professional identity, and assuming the support of professional colleagues, might blow the whistle on the use of unsafe construction materials in his firm, despite short-term organizational interests in doing the job more cheaply.

THE POLITICAL ROLE

The significance of clout

As we have seen, self-regulation professionals will not always be able to make harmonies. Evaluative studies of what makes corporate self-regulation effective, as well as compliance managers' own folklore, find that self-regulation professionals' political resources, status and clout within an organization make a significant difference to effectiveness. McCaffrey and Hart (1998: 241) note that 'anyone who looks at broker-dealer firms [internal compliance systems] in any detail will be struck by how internal politics and managerial styles produce regulatory differences across them'. They go on to conclude that differences can be attributed largely to how well those working in legal and compliance offices succeed at being 'taken seriously' within the firm, which in turn depends on 'first, how well do they convince enough powerful actors in the firm that legal and compliance "adds value" to it? Second, do they establish a reputation as competent, reasonable, and respectable "insiders"? Third, how strongly does upper management support them and internal controls generally?'

McCaffrey and Hart's first two questions relate to how they fulfil their 'harmonizing' role. But they place this harmonizing role in the context of a third condition of success that emphasizes top-management backing and the way in which the harmony-making role is used to support political influence and management controls. In one sense then, the harmonizing role is the pleasant face that makes the political reality more palatable, or as one compliance professional put it, 'the iron fist in the velvet glove'.[7] As Taylor (1984: 257) found, in relation to government environmental analysts, self-regulation staff 'have to work in a spirit of mitigation on most projects in order to gain credit to challenge the occasional "dogs" it is legitimate for them to advocate killing, and to change basic premises and procedures of design over the long term'. McCaffrey and Hart (1998: 157) note that compliance and legal officers often have a 'personal and professional' stake in accomplishing this degree of influence. This should not imply that the harmony-making role is just a matter of 'image' to sweeten the bitter medicine of clout. Rather, the two faces of self-regulation professionalism (harmony and conflict) must stick together. Often peaceful harmony will only reign when the just conflict has been fought and won; and conflict can more easily be resolved where there has been a previous commitment to harmony.

In their research, Edelman and co-authors find that, once in place, AA officers will 'form alliances with various constituencies, and take actions that generate new tensions'. They will tend to develop their own agendas that involve significant internal political activity and are 'significantly influenced by conflict, bargaining, and coalition-building among individuals or groups with diverse interests, by the diffusion of ideas among organizations, and especially by the structural contradictions inherent in their position' (Edelman et al. 1991: 75; see also Rees 1988: 231 on safety professionals).

The crossover between what the scholars find and what compliance managers experience and pass on as compliance 'best practice' comes full circle in John Braithwaite's work. In his study of corporate crime in the pharmaceutical industry, he concluded that one of the conditions for making corporate self-regulation work was ensuring 'that pro-public interest constituencies within the corporation are given organizational clout'. In this context, he suggested that examples of strengthening clout for pro-public interest constituencies would include:

> giving the international medical director an unqualified right to veto any promotional materials from a subsidiary which do not meet corporate standards of full disclosure of product hazards, having the plant safety officer answerable to a head office safety director rather than subject to the authority of the plant manager whom s/he might

> need to pull up for a safety violation, having quality control indepen-
> dent from marketing or production pressures, having an international
> compliance group answerable only to the chief executive officer.
> (Braithwaite 1984: 302)

Again, in his study of the internal compliance systems of the five
American coal mining companies with the lowest accident rates for the
industry at the time, Braithwaite (1985: 63) showed that one of the factors they had in common was that they gave a lot of informal clout to
their safety personnel, so that in practice line managers were unwilling
to ignore the advice of safety staff. Joe Murphy, leading US compliance
expert and advocate of compliance to both regulators and industry, read
Braithwaite's work. He found the concept of 'clout' rang true to his own
experience as a compliance lawyer, and he thought it should be further
discussed in the compliance community. Murphy asked Braithwaite to
write a paper with him on the significance of clout, which was published
in the journal *Corporate Conduct Quarterly* aimed at US compliance
practitioners (and also read widely around the world).

Braithwaite and Murphy proposed a number of factors as tests of
compliance staff's clout, such as sufficient resources, senior status,
direct lines of communication between compliance staff and line personnel and chief executive/board audit committee, a history of backing
compliance staff against line managers, a history of discipline of line
managers who ignore compliance advice, and rewards, incentives and
promotions for compliance staff (Braithwaite and Murphy 1993: 53, 62).
Murphy uses the word 'clout' extensively in his own writing and speaking, so that it has now become a common term in the USA, UK and Australia that compliance officers use to describe their role (e.g. Hutter
2001: 175 (UK); Sharpe 1996: 37 (Australia)).

In my fieldwork, compliance officers explicitly saw the clout to make
things happen, and the willingness to use it, as crucial:

> A compliance officer has to be seen as independent. They have to be
> seen to be able to stand apart from anyone who can really bully them.
> Generally they are on the Board or close to the Board. This is written
> into the rulebooks, that they have to have a direct line to the man at the
> top, so there is no question about it. (Trustus UK)

> In compliance clout is everything. If you assign compliance to an indi-
> vidual in the organization who is not well-regarded, or who does not
> exercise independent management responsibility, or is viewed in real-
> ity as a lackey or subordinate for some other real agenda that everyone

knows about, you cannot expect satisfying results from your compliance function. From the earliest stages of the compliance initiative in the organization, executive management at the highest levels must express its unconditional commitment to and seriousness about compliance – and must vest in the selected CO [compliance officer], unconditional responsibility and authority to address the issue as it rolls out throughout the organization. (Zinn 1999: 539)

The head of compliance for equities and corporate financing in a major trading bank had thought through, in particular depth, the implications of the structural contradictions of compliance practice:

[Y]ou have to approach [compliance] from the viewpoint of understanding the business, how it is transacted, structured … It is too easy to apply a rule. You can either go round checking that the business is safe or you can add value. Adding value creates its own challenge because to add value you must be close to the business. So you run the risk of business capture: Compliance is not independent if it always 'finds for' business. You must protect business from itself and from the outside world without compromise. You must maintain independence. (Eurostock)

His basic premise was that his job was to protect the business 'from itself and from the outside world' by keeping it responsible from the inside out, and thus avoiding problems. This means that compliance needs to have the clout to force issues onto the agenda at the highest level, the savvy to raise them at middle management level, and the support to educate for and enforce them at lower levels.

Conditions for accomplishing clout

Serge Taylor (1984: 3) finds that it is relatively easy to accomplish formal (or symbolic) integration of environmental analysis into government departmental decision-making, especially if those government organizations already have well-structured planning processes. But more is required in order for environmental impact assessment to have a substantive impact on the 'social intelligence' of the organization, that is the 'social thinking necessary for intelligent trade-offs between different goals in environmental decisions'. Taylor (1984: 252) proposes that institutionalization of 'social intelligence' requires that the organization vest resources (or clout) in those committed to the particular value. According to Taylor, this means the existence of four conditions: a group inside the organization committed to the value; goals clear enough to provide guidance for action; autonomy and power for this group so that they can protect the value; and outside support for the inside group's goals.

My own research and interviews with self-regulation professionals about what techniques they found effective, and other fieldwork, also found that the 'clout' of the self-regulation unit depends on the personal approach and skills of the self-regulation manager, the structure of the organization, and the strategy of regulatory agencies and law. Disregarding Taylor's second condition (which relates to the clarity of management commitment and the design of the law), I use my research to adjust Taylor's remaining three conditions to determine those in which internal self-regulation staff will acquire the influence to make a difference:

- *Personal skills and commitment:* Self-regulation staff must have appropriate skills, personal and/or professional commitment to legal and social responsibility values and an ability to champion compliance/self-regulation through a combination of value-adding (harmonizing) and playing politics (persuading, negotiating and sometimes fighting).
- *Internal support and commitment:* Self-regulation staff should enjoy (a) effective reporting and feedback mechanisms, (b) top-management backing to win employee commitment, and (c) the ability to quickly escalate conflict up to somewhere where it can be appropriately dealt with.
- *External support from regulators and broader community:* Self-regulation staff must be backed up by (a) external legal protection so that they can afford to take an unpopular line, (b) the ability for compliance officers and stakeholders to appeal to external accountability mechanisms when internal processes are failing to appropriately deal with conflict, and (c) social movement activism that mobilizes negative publicity, consumer action, stockholder resolutions, and so on, to grab management attention and leverage organizational change.

Personal skills and commitment

When external social values conflict with business practices or events, it is essential that self-regulation staff have a commitment to integrity if they are to make a difference. But this is not enough on its own. They must also have the personal skills and status to champion those values without completely alienating themselves from the business. One very senior compliance manager in a leading international bank described the complex inter-relationship between integrity, clout and business commitment:

> Compliance needs people with stature and standing, otherwise they will have no clout … It helps to have a professional background of one sort or another partly because then you're used to dealing with complex issues and partly because of the ethical underpinning of the professions. You need to be able to absorb issues quickly and to know when to put your foot down. But you've got to like the business otherwise it will come across. (GloboBucks)[8]

Some compliance managers stand out as showing a particular ability as individuals to play politics and wrest some self-regulation influence in the company:[9] For example, the innovative 'customer' introduced by AAMI in Australia was championed by a consumer activist turned consumer protection professional. AAMI was an organization that had faced persistent consumer problems in the past with the Australian Competition and Consumer Commission (ACCC) and consumer advocates, and was seeking to remake itself in a more consumer-friendly image. During consultations on the terms of a new mandatory code of conduct for the insurance industry, AAMI management challenged a prominent consumer activist to tell them exactly what he wanted AAMI to do for consumers. The activist replied that AAMI should ask Simon Smith, a lawyer who had worked in community legal services and later as an insurance ombudsman. They did, and ended up hiring him as a permanent consultant.

Smith drew on his experiences and skills as a consumer advocate lawyer, as an ombudsman and in a stint working in the UK, where Citizens' Charters were being introduced in government. He implemented a 'consumer charter' that sets out what customers can expect in terms of service and complaint resolution from AAMI, that promises a penalty payment to a customer when any of those promises are broken, and that publishes an independently audited annual report on compliance with the charter (see Chapter 8 for further description of the charter). In this case, two consumer activists – one outside the organization and one who was hired to work inside it – used their personal skills, commitment and experience to command respect and leverage change out of the introduction of new regulation of the Australian insurance industry.

In Chemcloud, a major European-based chemicals manufacturer, the environment, health and safety director was another internal self-regulation professional of tremendous commitment and political skill who had almost single-handedly waged a campaign over five or six years to force the board to take their own statement of principles seriously. The EHS director decided to force the board into moving from symbolism to concrete action by simply working on the assumption that it had intended him to come up with an action plan to put its own statement of environment, health and safety principles into action. Therefore, over a period of two or three years he produced a series of papers and resolutions for board approval on the difficulties Chemcloud faced in operationalizing the principles, and what they could do to overcome them.

His lobbying and sheer obstinacy eventually paid off, with board approval for an extremely wide-ranging set of standards for environment, health and safety, and a centrally controlled auditing program to make sure they were met. In the context of an otherwise highly decentralized company with tiny corporate group services functions, he was able to put together a central team that would roll out a substantial program, with major potential to change the way in which separate business units operated with full board support. By having the board set out 'expectations' for EHS performance in a very comprehensive standard, and by instituting a rigorous auditing program, this one man put himself in a good position to persuade business heads to take him seriously and made a huge difference to the status of EHS issues in the company.

Not all self-regulation professionals are naturally outstanding political players or imbued with the skills and experience that give them the ideas to implement company-changing reforms. However, even compliance managers who do not start out with outstanding skills, commitment and experience can acquire some of them within a professional community. We have already shown that participation in such a network can help to maintain the value commitment, integrity and self-identity of compliance staff. Professional networking can also be an important factor in increasing their clout, status and standing, through: learning skills and building up value commitments; providing guidance and modelling on ethics, mobilization of clout, and best practice with respect to their own employment contracts, internal structures for ensuring clout, and so on; and supplying the concrete support or safety net of fellow professionals when things get tough, through financial assistance, lobbying, and a network of possible new job opportunities.

The skills and abilities passed on by professional networks can be formalized through the offering of accreditation. For example, the US Health Care Compliance Association (HCCA) and the UK Compliance Institute (for financial services compliance officers) are both introducing accreditation via courses for members, and it is a matter of active discussion in the Association for Compliance Professionals Australia (ACPA). In both the health care industry and financial services, most senior staff have professional qualifications and accreditations. Therefore the introduction of accreditation for compliance managers in these areas might mean they are taken more seriously.

Indeed, a major strand of the sociology of professions explores how it is that new or existing occupations try to credential themselves as professions in order to improve their status in the marketplace and in the broader society (e.g. Abel 1988, 1989; Larson 1977). This literature is largely critical of these 'professional projects' (Larson 1977) as built on flimsy claims to special expertise and attempts at market control. Yet this literature also shows that the building of professions is not just about neutral skills, but also about politics and gaining social power. Vis-a-vis individual clients, we may deplore professional politics that set up doctors or lawyers as unaccountable and unintelligible experts. But vis-a-vis the power of multinationals, the politics and status enhancement projects of professionals are useful checks and balances that may ultimately benefit individuals and communities.

As professional networks develop, they can also provide more formal support and guidance through the promulgation and advocacy of models of best practice that support compliance clout. For example, the ACPA has been involved in promulgating and promoting AS 3806–1998, the Australian standard on compliance programs. Their advocacy and promotion of this standard make it more likely that more organizations will follow higher standards in the implementation of compliance systems and, specifically, the conditions in which compliance managers work (see below on appropriate internal structures). Professional associations can also promulgate codes of ethics or principles that provide guidance to members on when it is necessary to fight and when to accommodate. The US HCCA, for example, has introduced a code of ethics (see Meaney 2001). Clearly the usefulness and effectiveness of such a code depends on the extent to which it provides practical guidance grounded in real experiences, as opposed to unrealistic, vague or symbolic principles that are designed to impress rather than to guide action. The HCCA code does provide some useful guidelines for compliance managers attempting to deal with the tensions of their role. For example, it sets out the following 'obligations to the public' as the first four rules:[10]

R1.1   HCCPs [health care compliance professionals] shall not aid, abet or participate in misconduct.

R1.2   HCCPs shall take such steps as are necessary to prevent misconduct by their employing organizations.

R1.3   HCCPs shall cooperate with all official and legitimate government investigations of or inquiries concerning their employing organization.

R1.4   If, in the course of their work, HCCPs become aware of any decision by their employing organization which, if implemented, would constitute misconduct and which will adversely affect the health of patients, residents or clients, the professional shall: (a) refuse to consent to the decision; (b) escalate to the highest governing authority, as appropriate; (c) if serious issues remain unresolved, consider resignation; and (d) report the decision to public officials when required by law.

Further guidance is offered in the terms of the following commentary:

> The duty of a compliance professional goes beyond other professionals in an organizational context, inasmuch as his/her duty to the public includes prevention of organizational misconduct. The compliance professional should exhaust all internal means available to deter his/her employing organization, its employees and agents from engaging in misconduct. HCCPs should consider resignation only as a last resort, since compliance professionals may be the only remaining barrier to misconduct. In the event that resignation becomes necessary, however, the duty to the public takes priority over any duty of confidentiality to the employing organization. A letter of resignation should set forth to senior management and the highest governing body of the employing organization the precise conditions that necessitate his/her action. In complex organizations, the highest governing body may be the highest governing body of a parent corporation.

These rules and commentary provide helpful and concrete guidance on exactly what integrity requires. Larry May (1996) suggests that professional associations should support professional integrity by giving concrete support to members who risk their livelihoods by standing up for values to which they are committed. For example, if a company undermines or sacks a compliance manager for advocating that money be spent on safety, the professional association could issue press releases about what has happened and offer financial support to the professional who has lost his or her job. Certainly ACPA leaders have seriously considered the possibility of offering some sort of income insurance for members precisely because of the likelihood of compliance professionals finding themselves in such a situation. More realistically, the existence of a professional association also provides a network of potential alternative job opportunities for self-regulation professionals unhappy with the support offered in their current jobs, or facing dismissal as the price of their integrity.

Internal structures
Personal skills and commitment, no matter how well supported by professional networks, are not enough to give self-regulation professionals the clout to make a difference. The second and most important condition for their ability to resolve conflict is that they have formal and/or informal support from within the company, particularly from top management. Self-regulation professionals can maintain their professional integrity by: ensuring their independence by reporting to the CEO rather than to business unit heads; having the possibility of dotted-line reporting direct to a board audit, compliance or social responsibility committee, and to the board of directors itself; and having the authority to investigate and intervene at any level of a company. For example, among the 'structural' elements of compliance programs, AS 3806–1998 (para. 3.2.4) sees adequate compliance staff as a significant resource for compliance and maintains that the professional integrity and ability of those staff should be protected and nurtured by ensuring they have high status and authority, access to all levels of the organization including senior decision-makers, and a record of integrity and commitment to compliance, as well as the skills necessary to implement behavioural and procedural controls. The US Federal Sentencing Guidelines provide that specific individuals must be assigned responsibility to oversee compliance within the organization and that they must be of a high level (United States Sentencing Commission 1992).

Self-regulation staff ought to have strong top-down support from senior management. At the most basic level this means being appointed at a senior enough level to earn respect within the hierarchical structure of the corporation. Many of the interviewees made this point and attributed what success they had partially to their seniority. For example, the EEO officer at Good as Gold Australia noted that she had been appointed at a more senior level than her predecessor and had been concomitantly more successful. A compliance consultant, Adviser Ten, told me that he always referred to compliance managers as 'compliance executives' when speaking to clients in order to get the message across that they ought to be appointed at a very senior level.

In formal terms, clout and seniority also usually mean a reporting structure that makes self-regulation managers responsible to top management, CEO, board, or board audit or compliance committees, not to any line manager. This means that the self-regulation person can quickly escalate unresolved conflicts to a level in the company where they can be authoritatively resolved. For example, the environmental and safety manager at GarbageRUs, an Australian subsidiary of a multinational, pointed out that his direct reporting relationship with the EHS manager at the international head office meant that he could go 'head to head' with the Australian CEO, if necessary. Indeed, his first international boss had expected him to do so often. Such a reporting relationship means that if there are competing messages about social and legal responsibility and profit-making/production goals being sent down the line from on high, the self-regulation person can make sure that top managers address that. If it is a matter of an individual doing the wrong thing against company policy, they can be quickly held accountable by higher management at the instigation of the compliance officer.

Just as various conventions have grown up to protect the independence of auditors and general counsel, so should the place of other constituencies within the corporation who might hold it to important public values be protected. This means that it is important to institutionalize the self-regulation function – through the role of general counsel, the chief compliance executive or EHS vice-president, board committees, and so on. Some regulators have begun to set standards for the formal clout accorded to compliance executives. For example, in Australia the Managed Investments Act requires Australian funds managers to implement a compliance program and a compliance committee that is responsible for it. In the UK financial services regulations require that if the designated compliance officer is not a partner or director of the firm, they must report directly to a partner or director (Newton 1998: 73, 82ff). Chapters 8 and 9 will consider regulatory strategies for accomplishing appropriate internal compliance systems.

In at least one company, Convict Cash Australia, the chief compliance manager shares the same protection in employment as the chief financial officer: the compliance manager cannot be sacked or even resign voluntarily without the matter going to a meeting of the board, where directors can satisfy themselves that the sacking or resignation is not occurring for the wrong reasons. Similarly in that company, the chief compliance manager must report to the board as to the circumstances in which any of his/her staff resign or are sacked from their compliance positions. In the USA, where the doctrine of 'at-will employment' makes all employees less secure than in Australia, one author has gone so far as to propose a standard employment contract for compliance officers to protect their independence (Murphy 1998).

In practical terms, top-down clout means that line managers and employees know from experience that the self-regulation person's advice is likely to be backed up by top management and that if they go against it, they are likely to be over-ruled (Braithwaite and Murphy 1993: 52). Clearly the best way to achieve clout is through the direct support of senior management, preferably the CEO himself or herself. Skilful self-regulation professionals can also supplement what formal clout they do have with informal means of appropriating clout to their cause. For example, the head EEO officer at Aussie Dollars, like a number of other self-regulation managers I interviewed, always ensures that before she does training in a work area, she has won the support of the most senior person in that area. On one occasion she gave a presentation to a business unit in which many of those present were more senior than her. For fifteen minutes, debate raged out of control about the fact that law regulated business far too much. Her strategy paid off, however, when the general manager (whose support she had garnered before arranging to do the presentation) put a stop to the debate by saying that 'it didn't matter what they thought and the bank didn't care if they went home and kicked the dog and abused their family, but while they were at work the law had to be obeyed and EEO had to be in place'. Other compliance managers told stories of overcoming youth and inexperience by working with more senior colleagues who did command formal and informal status within the organization.

Clout is also a matter of adequate financial and staffing resources being available to the self-regulation unit to do the job, and of self-regulation staff being accorded a senior enough status to be taken seriously by other senior decision-makers. One author (Desio 1998: 11) has suggested that compliance officers test their clout level by asking the following questions:

- Does the compliance officer have ready access to the corridors of power, or must he or she wait for an annual summons to give a presentation?

- Do key decision-makers in the organization know the name of the compliance officer without referring to their phone directory?
- Do they ever have lunch or other collegial contact with the compliance officer apart from structured meetings?

There is also a bottom-up aspect to clout – that self-regulation staff will be able to report non-compliance, or potential conflicts between business practices and responsibility goals, to a level of the company where they can be authoritatively resolved, and corporate practice, structure and culture changed. This means self-regulation staff must be part of an adequate information dissemination and reporting system within the organization. Best practice compliance staff should have adequate access to information dissemination channels within the corporation to ensure their message reaches employees and middle managers. Even more crucial is the ability to get important information upwards so that senior management and the board are convinced of the need to support the unit and give it resources. For example, at Banksafe in previous years it had been difficult to get management support for improving EEO, because the only information the CEO ever got about internal EEO matters was the report that was to be submitted to the Affirmative Action Agency. This report, naturally, presented the issue in the best possible light. A corporate restructure that gave the EEO unit a direct reporting relationship to the CEO allowed them to garner his support for improvements much more easily, and the EEO program was transformed.

External support
Finally, in order to have clout, self-regulation managers must be not only influential political players within internal organizational power structures, but also able to appeal convincingly to an external normative environment that might apply sanctions of shame, publicity or financial penalty to the company. Indeed, the threat of an externally imposed disaster may be the only effective clout-enhancing mechanism when the self-regulation person needs to confront the board or the top manager. Fundamentally, then, any organization's self-regulation performance must always be subject to the possibility (and preferably the reality) of deliberative responsibility through the legal system, media publicity, and formal and informal political processes in order for it to be internally effective. This should not just be a matter of relying on regulators to be

proactive. Everyone who has any stake in the compliance performance of the organization, from employees to consumers to public interest groups, must have the ability to be informed of, consulted on and/or challenge relevant corporate decision-making. Wherever abuse of power and injustice are possible via internal corporate self-regulation, there should always be the possibility of invoking legal sanctions through recourse to a court or regulator that can enunciate standards, grant rights and remedies, and reveal the unlawfulness of business practices. As we have seen, even without financial penalties that are heavy enough to act as economically rational deterrents, a skilful compliance professional can do a lot with the possibility of moderate or even weak sanctions. It is crucial that regulators and stakeholders be involved in developing standards for regulatory compliance and self-regulation systems and monitoring the programs and structures that are being put in place, if corporate self-regulation is not to be a sham.

Self-regulation professionalism and corporate citizenship

On the one hand, companies use the self-regulation role as a tool to help them to be seen as socially responsible, without substantially changing pre-existing business paradigms. On the other hand, there is a fear that compliance implies a potential for quite dramatic change to everyday business. When managers complain that compliance systems 'stop' business or try to colonize business decisions, they are not wrong. When it is effective, the self-regulation function is a tool for checking and changing corporate goals and commitments. Self-regulation managers become significant political players within the corporations they serve (Rosen 1989: 503). As we have seen, this requires skills in harmonizing corporate processes with corporate responsibilities, and also in heading off or handling conflict between the requirements of responsibility and ordinary organizational impetuses. This suggests that self-regulation professionals must not only be indubitably citizens of the organization, but also that they must maintain their compliance agenda against competing corporate concerns. How can self-regulation professionals put together the two faces of the self-regulation role? Can there be a theoretical rationale that accounts for both its harmonizing and political features that over-emphasizes neither one nor the other?

The most obvious path to synthesis is the path of 'professionalism'. Here self-regulation managers would attempt to manage their position by claiming detachment from both business and stakeholder/regulatory commitments. They succeed by giving cool, level-headed advice that neutrally accommodates various interests and concerns, and by providing tough but calm advice where necessary in potential conflicts. They are passionate about nothing, neither business goals nor regulatory outcomes. Rather, they define themselves as experts in the techniques of accommodation of the business to compliance ('streetwise' solutions) and of compliance to the business ('creative compliance'), and also at knowing where to draw the line because accommodation is no longer possible. In this picture the compliance manager copies the traditional (and successful) claims of the established professions to special technical expertise that deserves status, respect and trust (see Abbott 1988; Larson 1977; Parker 1997b).

Is the ideal of neutral, detached professionalism a suitable rationale for guidance in the self-regulation role? Certainly the empirical evidence suggests that self-regulation managers find it useful to claim a professional status. In their work on affirmative action, Edelman and co-authors (1991) found that AA officers used either 'neutral' or 'partisan' strategies to handle their inherently conflictual positions. Partisan AA officers became advocates for their employers or for disenfranchised employees. Neutral AA officers were either indifferent to the politics of their situation, or worked hard at mediating between different interests in a detached way. Edelman and co-authors (1991: 91) conclude that neutral, detached 'professionalism' is the most stable approach to handling and reconciling the inherent contradictions in the compliance role. My fieldwork shows that, in practice, self-regulation practitioners do seek professional status because it can provide them with a measure of status and autonomy that allows them to handle both the conflict and the harmonizing aspects of their role.

The traditional ideal of autonomous, neutral professionalism is not, however, a good model for staff in an internal corporate self-regulatory unit. Edelman and co-authors (1991: 92) conclude from their research that 'the thrust of the Professional approach is to accommodate competing interests, [therefore] they will not evoke striking reform'. By contrast, the 'clout' element of self-regulation practice must evoke substantive change through politics, skills and powerful internal support, if it is to live up to its ideal. Clout involves neither detachment nor neutrality. Clout is about playing politics to force organizations (and ultimately regulators) to deal with conflict appropriately. Nor is the harmonizing role particularly neutral and detached. Full-blooded loyalty to and immersion in organizational goals is necessary for effective harmonization.

Detached, neutral professionalism is an unrealistic conception of the daily work of self-regulation practitioners. They work in intimate inter-relationship with their corporate clients. They are often full-time employees and therefore constituent members of a larger corporate actor. They can no more take the high moral ground of forcing their own opinion on the client organization, regardless of business concerns, than they can credibly claim to be morally untainted by acting for the client regardless of the ethics or legality of what it does. Self-regulation practitioners cannot avoid daily and routinely taking part in, and responsibility for, decisions that keep the company running smoothly. Nor can they choose to act as internal mini-regulators who simply impose their view of social and legal responsibilities on their clients. Unlike individual clients who always retain in some sense an indepen-dent capability to make their own decisions regardless of professional advice, corporate decisions are always made by individuals standing in for the entity as a whole. Inhouse corporate lawyers and self-regulation practitioners cannot choose not to 'participate in making clients' deci-sions, but [only] what type of participation theirs will be' (Painter 1994: 520). They are not neutral and detached, but involved and partisan. They are constituent members of the organization and must harmonize that membership with whatever other 'selves' they have.

Furthermore, autonomous, detached professionalism does not pre-scribe a role that is likely to be effective in institutionalizing ethical and legal responsibility in organizations. In order to permeate organiza-tional cultures and decision-making, internal corporate actors who understand the business, the risks it faces and the way it operates must act as advocates and facilitators of ethical responsibility within the organization. It is a matter of common sense and of empirical evidence (see Haines 1997; Makkai and V. Braithwaite 1993) that compliance managers are only likely to be effective if they both know the business and are sympathetic to its overall goals. Only in those circumstances can they be persuasively relevant, and sufficiently committed for people to listen when they put their foot down or suggest different ways of doing things. The most effective change agent is an insider with stature, clout and respect. This prescribes a model of dialogue, of accommodation, and of day-to-day, hour-by-hour involvement in the politics, business and management of the 'client' organization, not of detached neutrality. Self-regulation practitioners should have clout, but theirs is the integrative clout of the yeast within the bread dough, not the external force of the knife that cuts the loaf.

Active citizenship is a better model for self-regulation professionalism than detached autonomy and neutrality. Citizenship incorporates ideals of debate and conflict over values and politics, together with interdependence, involvement and shared objectives. It does not focus solely on the harmony-making and social coordination role of self-regulation practitioners. But neither does it deny the importance and potential of attempting to engage and agree on values and the task of self-regulation. The concept of citizenship also allows more precision in defining the role of self-regulation staff: every individual and, as I have argued, every organization is a citizen of a broader national and global society. In that sense self-regulation staff have no special values or commitment that should make them different from anyone else in organizational life. What they do have is a special facilitating role in prompting organizational citizenship.

Good self-regulation professionals should see themselves both as citizens of the corporation and as citizens of a broader ethical community of compliance professionals, regulators and stakeholders. Their job is to dynamically bring these citizenships into alignment by contributing to the good corporate citizenship of the whole organization from the inside out. Good self-regulation is a political accomplishment, and attempts to achieve it frequently (perhaps commonly) fail. Self-regulation professionals are asked to live with the constant tension that harmonization and reconciliation between business goals and social values will fail, and they will have to resign (on principle), be dismissed (if non-compliance has occurred or if an unscrupulous manager wants to rid the company of a principled compliance manager), or face the constant potential of regulatory action for corporate non-compliance. But then so must every individual member of an organization who has any engagement with any values at all that are external to the organization. It is just that these tensions are so much more acute for someone whose job it is to manage social and legal responsibilities.

Is it legitimate for the new regulatory state and corporate managements to ask self-regulation practitioners to play this complex, potentially dangerous role? The effective compliance role is absolutely impossible, an idyllic fantasy, in the absence of appropriate internal and external systems supports. It is *only* legitimate to expect compliance professionals (and other self-regulation functionaries) to play the role outlined in this chapter if corporate managements, governments, regulators and civil society back up their integrity. It is a conception of self-regulation practice that is only worth pursuing if regulators, governments and broader communities are simultaneously making organizations permeable to democratic accountability and responsibility. For it is only in a democracy that supports and makes accountable democratic self-regulation of corporations that corporate employees (whether specialist self-regulation practitioners or not) can reasonably be expected to risk such bold action. It is only in such a democracy that self-regulation practitioners can be expected to receive the support from regulators and stakeholders that will either give them clout or give them support when they have to resign. How then can corporate self-regulation systems be linked to a broader deliberative democracy, and what is the role of stakeholders and regulators in accomplishing this? In Chapters 8 and 9 we turn to the institutional (corporate and regulatory) design required to make effective self-regulation a real possibility.

8 | The three strategies of 'permeability' in the open corporation

The previous chapters followed through the first two phases of corporate responsiveness to social and legal responsibility issues: management commitment, and the acquisition of self-regulatory skills and knowledge. This chapter moves to the third phase: the institutionalization of responsibility in corporate self-regulation. Responsible companies do not simply layer a compliance system onto pre-existing management processes and corporate cultures. Rather, responsibility is internalized when the whole corporation is opened up to a broader deliberative democracy. This is not to say that business corporations should be democratic. Their management should, however, be permeable to democracy through three strategies:

- *Strategy One:* Responsible corporate self-regulators use employees' cultures, values and self-identities to build organizational integrity. This is a *'bottom-up'* approach to self-regulation.
- *Strategy Two:* Responsible corporate self-regulators find it is strategic to take legitimate stakeholder perspectives and external values into account, by reporting information about self-regulation processes and performance to stakeholders, by consulting with stakeholders, and by giving those affected by corporate power the ability to challenge corporate decisions and actions. This is an *'opening-out'* approach to self-regulation in which stakeholder concerns and values have become an internal issue to be decisively addressed, not an externality to be ignored.
- *Strategy Three:* Responsible corporate self-regulators integrate into their routine management systems institutions and decision-making processes that ensure that the company becomes

aware of, learns from and responds to social and legal responsibility issues. This is a '*systems approach*' to corporate responsibility that emphasizes the importance of internal discipline, justice, self-regulation and self-evaluation systems within the whole self-management of the organization. (Systems are so important for the integration of self-regulation management that both of the above two principles also include a systems element – systems for learning from disciplinary issues – and Justice Plans.)

This chapter can be read as a guide to the three 'best practice' strategies necessary for managers and self-regulation professionals to institutionalize social and legal responsibility. They are not, however, a blueprint. Each organization must develop its own ways of engaging with employees, stakeholders and systems. Moreover, responsible 'self-regulation' is not the accomplishment of the corporation alone. It is found only in the embrace of management with the values and concerns represented by external and internal stakeholders. Therefore, for each of the three strategies above, this chapter also provides some suggestions as to what stakeholders (including professional associations, industry associations, financial and social stakeholders, and the media) and the law/regulatory agencies can do to turn these best practice principles into reality. Table 8.1 sets out a summary guide to the strategies and policy recommendations in this chapter.

The ideal of democratic permeability of corporate management may sound rather naive. Generally companies are democratic neither in their internal functioning nor in their external goals. Broad participation in important strategic decisions is not encouraged. Nor are those decisions necessarily transparent and accountable to outsiders, or even most insiders. Indeed, corporate strategy and innovation frequently rely on entrepreneurship and leadership by individuals and small groups with freedom to pursue their ideas, and quite often to impose those ideas on others. Can strategic corporate action be compatible with 'democratic' corporate citizenship? Is it the case that to the extent that a company *self*-regulates it must determine its actions by participatory procedures of decision-making that give employees and stakeholders rights of representation and/or consultation? Surely it is unreasonable to expect profit-oriented organizations to engage in this level of democratic engagement?

TABLE 8.1 *Strategies of permeable self-management*

	Connecting with employee values	Strategic stakeholder engagement	Social responsibility systems
Role of management	1. Dialogic, 'bottom-up' methodology and general approach to design and implementation of self-regulation program. 2. Design and integration of social responsibility into employee discipline and reward systems.	1. Disclosure of information on which stakeholders can engage corporate management. 2. Consultation with stakeholders on decision-making, on criteria for social reporting, implementation and performance of self-regulation processes. 3. Systematic policies and procedures for allowing stakeholders to contest corporate decisions that affect them (Justice Plans).	1. Clearly defined responsibility for self-regulation shared between self-regulation function, senior management, board, line management and employees (reflected in reporting lines, job descriptions, appraisals, and so on) in order to ensure that: • the places of internal voices for external values are institutionalised; • strategic stakeholder information flows through to appropriate levels; • conflicts are pushed through to the level at which they can be resolved authoritatively. 2. Self-evaluation and reporting of self-regulation performance and processes. 3. Discipline and reward systems integrated with self-regulation (column one). 4. Stakeholder contestation policies (column two) (Justice Plans).

TABLE 8.1 (cont.) *Strategies of permeable self-management*

	Connecting with employee values	**Strategic stakeholder engagement**	**Social responsibility systems**
Potential roles of civil society/ stakeholders (including industry and professional associations)	1. Employee associations and sub-group representation in groups to develop compliance arrangements and discipline arrangements. 2. Compliance professional associations disseminate best practice.	1. The 'penumbra' of democracy, including media scrutiny, social activism, ask for and read information, involvement in interest groups and consultative groups for specific sites (where corporate management makes the opportunity available). 2. Exercise rights by complaining to company and pursuing rights to complain to regulators, consult with regulators, enforce rights in courts and tribunals. 3. Offer codes of practice and accreditation to standards for self-regulation programs. 4. Regulate/accredit social reporting standards.	1. Everything in columns one and two. 2. Disseminate best practice and research on what works. 3. Develop principles of good practice and exhort their implementation. 4. Offer accreditation to codes of practice.

Potential roles of law/ regulators	1. Design of law could leave space for ground-up decisions about compliance arrangements (e.g. standards, not rules). 2. Laws and tribunals oversee basic rights of fairness in discipline.	1. Mandate disclosure of information about self-regulation and regulate its quality. 2. Broker opportunities for dialogue between management and stakeholders as part of regulatory process or in special forums. 3. Give particular stakeholders rights to receive information, be heard, to sue, seek orders, and so on. 4. Indirectly provide incentives for Justice Plans or directly mandate them as licence conditions, and so on.	1. Exhort implementation of a best practice code for self-regulation programs. 2. Mandate reporting of implementation of code of best practice. 3. Liability incentives for implementation of effective self-regulation programs. 4. Mandate implementation of effective self-regulation program (e.g. as licence condition).

It is not the *idea* of democratic responsiveness that is inapplicable to corporate management. It is the current *institutions and practices* of democracy that are unhelpful. Traditionally, political theorists emphasized achieving the democracy of *states* through formal participation in public political decision-making: the vote, standing for election, the courts. These cumbersome procedures are put in place to prevent nation-states becoming too 'strategic' about conquering new territory or unjustifiably interfering in people's lives. Traditional notions of democracy are, however, too inflexible and exclusive even for contemporary state democracies (and are even more unwieldy when applied to corporate management).

Thus, feminists and others have re-formed the understanding of participation in deliberative forums to include informal political participation in social movements, community groups and the institutions of civil society (Lister 1995: 8–9). Similarly, Habermas (1996: 359–87) has argued that democracy means that the formal public political sphere must be 'porous' to the protests and contributions of individual citizens and social movements, not restricted to their involvement through elected representatives. There must be enough participation by a wide enough diversity of citizens in a wide enough diversity of communicative styles to ensure all of the relevant considerations become part of the deliberation (Bohman 1994: 918; Young 1993). Newer ideas of (deliberative) democracy therefore focus on the possibility of contestation and participation in ways appropriate both to the institution and to the people who should be able to contest decision-making in that institution, whether they are seen as 'stakeholders' or as 'citizens'.

We are yet to step beyond the bounds of traditional electoral democracy to fully imagine and create the means of participation and contestation that fit the unique features of corporate business organizations. Democratic *permeability* does not require the slavish translation of state democratic institutions to private business organizations. It does not necessarily require 'public directors', majority voting, inclusive voting rights in general meetings, industrial democracy, worker cooperatives, or many other suggested applications of democratic theory to corporate governance (although some of these institutions may suit particular companies in particular circumstances). Nor must those institutions proposed to improve the democratic accountability of corporations necessarily be 'constitutionalized', or mandated by law. The requirements of democracy in relation to corporations are very unlikely to be satisfied by law alone. Rather, the three management strategies discussed in this chapter are a contextually sensitive way of making business organizations democratically responsive.

Bottom-up: Corporate culture

Connecting with employees

The democratic ideal applies to business organizations because they are social (and political) entities. They are microcosms of a broader society in which democracy is generally accepted as a normative ideal. They are made up of individuals. Most, if not all, of those individuals have an interest in one or more of those generally recognized values that include worker health and safety, environmental sustainability, reduction in social inequality, consumer safety, and market integrity. Many of them may also have an interest in other emerging values that are the topic of debate outside the company (and hopefully within it too). The best corporate approaches to self-regulation use the values, self-identity and social commitments of the members of the organization as a resource, to keep connection with external social values and to ensure that members comply with those obligations that have been accepted by the company.

For exactly the same reasons that external command-and-control regulation will fail, a legalistic, top-down approach to compliance management *within* the company will also be a weak guarantee of compliance. At the simplest level, this is because a corporate compliance management system that fails to enter employees' 'zone of meanings' will not be effective at teaching them or convincing them of what it actually means to comply (d'Arville and Duffy 2000). At a deeper level, a self-regulation program that fails to connect with people's values and identities will fail to connect with anything that offers a robust motivation to commit to compliance – it will be dependent on extrinsic sanctions and rewards for success only, not intrinsic ones (see Kohn 1993). Also, a compliance management approach that does not seriously engage with employee opinions, concerns and experiences about compliance will mean that employees distrust management's approach to compliance. There will be no bond that convinces them it is worthwhile to comply to help the company. Finally, engaging with employee concerns and values about self-regulation builds up the integrity of the whole organization by building up personal integrity, individual by individual. This is a bottom-up resource of connection with and permeability to the broader culture and its values.

Empirical evidence supports the case that self-regulation systems are ineffectual unless they connect to corporate culture and seek to engage employee commitment, participation, values and identity. For example, Shaw and Blewett (1996: 189) cite a tranche of empirical research comparing the features of occupational health and safety management in enterprises with high and low injury (claims) rates. This research finds that 'management concern for the workforce, participation in decision making and participative problem-solving in relation to OHS', workforce empowerment, a belief that occupational health and safety is an important issue in the workplace, workforce trust that management is committed to occupational health and safety, and a workforce belief that workers have some degree of control over the nature of their work were all linked to lower injury rates. Their review of the research also finds that, in the absence of effective employee participation, some of the commonly recommended bureaucratic approaches to occupational health and safety management were not necessarily associated with lower injury rates, including senior management representation on occupational health and safety committees, and written safety rules.

Similarly, in her study of compliance with Australian affirmative action law, Valerie Braithwaite found that connections between EEO officers and the corporate constituents they hoped to benefit, the women of the company, significantly improved compliance. Yet her study found that EEO officers rarely used formal or informal meetings and contact to seek out women's support or opinions on EEO issues. For example, 80 per cent had had no meetings with only female employees in the previous twelve months, and a further 11 per cent had only had one such meeting. However, her data showed that participation and cooperation of female employees in the program, when it was present, was strongly correlated with effective procedural and substantive implementation of affirmative action policies under the Act (V. Braithwaite 1992: 51–2, 53).

We have already seen in Chapter 6 that a series of studies by Weaver and Trevino (1999) differentiate 'compliance' and 'value' orientations towards corporate ethics management. Their measures of employee perception of a 'values' orientation in the ethics management system included counselling and helping employees to make their own ethical decisions, encouraging shared values, and supporting employee goals and aspirations. In the one organization studied in depth, they found that employee perceptions of both orientations contributed to 'reduced unethical behavior, ethical advice seeking, awareness of ethical issues, and perceptions of better decision making' (Weaver and Trevino 1999: 329). But in each case the 'values' orientation (either alone or in combination with the 'compliance' orientation) had greater explanatory power than the 'compliance' orientation.[1] The values orientation also correlated better with employee commitment to the organization, integrity, and willingness to report bad news to superiors. By focusing on participation and shared values, the values orientation reduced conflict between the organizational role and the extra-organizational role. This approach helped the employee to feel that not only was their personal integrity intact, but also that the organization supported their personal goals and therefore they could support its goals (1999: 320–2). As Trevino and co-authors (1999: 149) conclude in another summary of the same data, the values-based approach works effectively when it motivates 'employees to aspire to ethical conduct, [encourages] them to question authority when ethics are at stake, and [holds] them accountable for rule violations'.

Connection with employee values, cultures and self-identities in an organization's management of compliance should be achieved in two main ways:

- through the *methodology and general approach* that self-regulation professionals and senior management take to design and implementation of the self-regulation system (this will also have implications for what the law/regulators require of corporate compliance systems); and
- in particular, through the design and integration of compliance into employee *discipline and reward systems,* since this is the place at which the organization most explicitly exercises its power over employees.

Methodology and approach

It is sometimes suggested that corporate social responsibility implies industrial democracy: worker cooperatives, worker participation in corporate governance processes through employee representation on boards (compare the German system of employee representation on one tier of a two-tier board), mandated worker votes on important issues, or mandated worker representation on particular company committees (such as health and safety, or equal opportunity committees) (see Graham 1989: 205–7; Parkinson 1993: 383–6; Selznick 1992: 314–18). This is not the argument here. Generally it will be the ultimate responsibility of corporate management, not employees, to systematically address social and legal responsibilities. In most cases it is unrealistic, inefficient and unwise to expect companies to have elaborate worker participation procedures as part of their formal governance and strategic decision-making processes (although in some cases it may be extremely effective). Instead, top management should take responsibility for an appropriate compliance or self-regulation *system* (see below). However, in the implementation of that system, management should always use an approach or style that seeks to connect with employee values, self-identify and corporate culture to the greatest extent possible.

This means that individual self-regulation professionals, and other managers with self-regulation responsibilities, should use a bottom-up methodology. They should, where possible, try to enter the 'zone of meanings' of employees in specific contexts, aim to build on pre-existing employee value commitments, and where inappropriate value commitments hold sway, and use dialogue and persuasion to try to transform corporate culture. This approach to compliance implementation could include the following (all of these ideas are real examples gleaned from self-regulation practitioners interviewed for this study):

- compliance training that includes ample opportunity for discussion and dialogue in order to gauge the values, concerns and opinions of employees, address their questions and concerns, and engage with those concerns, build on them and transform them where necessary;
- self-regulation managers who allocate plenty of time to getting alongside and understanding corporate cultures by spending time with different groups of employees as they do their jobs in their own workplaces, so that self-regulation managers understand how compliance concerns connect with day-to-day workplace reality;
- using the information and experience gained from the above activities to design and responsively change self-regulation procedures and management systems in response to employee criticisms, concerns and priorities, and to make it easy to comply in the reality of everyday life (see discussion below on discipline systems for a specific instance of how this might occur);
- using every opportunity (whether in training, promotional material or informal conversation) to emphasize the way in

which the self-regulation system connects with employees' existing self-identities (e.g. as someone concerned about environmental issues, as someone who cares about their colleagues and their safety/rights, as a customer themselves, as an engineer who likes to think of ways to do things efficiently and with as little waste as possible, as professionals who are proud of their work, who owe duties to the community). For example, consumer protection training might begin with the employees' own experiences of being a consumer and explain their own rights in that situation; environmentally conscious employees might be rewarded for thinking of ideas to prevent waste and pollution, and so on;

- making sure the self-regulation rules, rewards and discipline are applied equally at all levels of the organization, rather than just imposed from above on lower levels;
- using hotlines, whistle-blower policies, and prizes and incentives for good practices to ensure that employees know that their opinions and ideas on appropriate self-regulation policies are valued, and that their knowledge and ideas do filter up to officers in the organization where they can be used appropriately;
- wherever possible, using teams of employees and managers to design the self-regulation operating procedures for their own worksite within principles and outcomes set (or approved) by the centre of the organization, so that each operating unit's procedures are contextually appropriate and well accepted by the people who have to follow them; and
- wherever possible, encouraging teams from each business unit or work team to set their own goals for compliance performance and procedures, within the broad principles set by the organization as a whole, so that they will own them and compliance creativity and responsibility will be encouraged.

This is a matter of style and methodology. These are not principles that can be legislated for or mandated. Managers will mostly garner ideas about how to connect with corporate culture and employee self-identities by reading popular management books (e.g. Deal and Kennedy 1999; Pinchot and Pinchot 1994; Senge 1992), and by modelling the experiences of other managers. However, examples of how to achieve these practices (and many others of a similar ilk that I have not been able to list here) can be promulgated in best practice guidance, model regulatory compliance plans, educational seminars, and voluntary standards and codes by compliance professionals' associations, industry or stakeholder groups, and regulators (see below and Chapter 9).

It may be that the best thing the formal law and regulators can do to enable bottom-up corporate compliance management is to *refrain* from regulating the details of corporate compliance systems. This is because law cannot define what good corporate citizenship means in every organizational context. Law needs to leave space for corporate management to make good faith efforts to find their own way to self-regulation through connections with corporate culture. In this way, law can model the possibility for connection with 'ground-up' values.[2]

Employee discipline

Unfortunately one of the potential pathologies of corporate self-regulation systems is that they attempt to do the exact opposite of using the integrity of employees as a resource for organizational integrity. They often attempt to shift the responsibility for, and risk of, non-compliance to individual employees (see Chapter 6). How can an organization be a good corporate citizen when it constantly pushes the responsibility for compliance onto individual micro-behaviours, rather than changing business systems and cultures that institutionalize irresponsibility on a grand scale (Nielsen 1996: 214–15)? The whole point of using a compliance system to prompt self-regulation and integrity is supposedly to address cultural and systemic causes of non-compliance. On the other hand, effective and fair discipline for non-compliance is essential, otherwise employees will not trust the system enough to blow the whistle. They will feel that they can get away with non-compliance, that no-one really cares about breaches, and, if senior people who flout the system are allowed to get away with it, that there are different rules for different folks and so the company is not worthy of their trust or commitment.

Nielsen (1996: 157–86; see also Nielsen 2000) has developed a helpful typology of employee discipline and grievance-handling systems that illustrates the various possibilities for focus on different objectives of such systems, including '(1) correcting and punishing policy violations, (2) fairly processing cases, and (3) continuing individual and organizational learning and development' (Nielsen 1996: 157). From his empirical research he identifies four ideal types that emphasize each of these objectives to different degrees:

1   *Investigation-punishment systems:* Management conduct a top-down investigation of complaints; senior management makes a decision and findings and punishment are announced to the offender.

2   *Grievance arbitration systems:* Employees file a complaint with an employee representative (e.g. for unfair discipline), and both present their objections to their supervisors. If the grievance is not resolved, it is taken to upper-level management and then to a jointly chosen external arbitrator who decides within the existing policy framework of the organization.

These two systems both investigate, punish and control deviation from existing corporate policies, and thus focus on the first and second objectives. System One focuses on due process, while System Two focuses on speedy correction and punishment of violations. Both allow little scope for feedback, discussion or challenge of broader corporate policies or cultures.

3   *Mediator-counsellor systems:* An employee contacts a counsellor to discuss a problem and, with the employee's permission and as much confidentiality as possible, the counsellor clarifies the facts and discusses the issue with those involved. Policy and other implications of the case are discussed confidentially with employee relations staff and upper management, and the counsellor advises, mediates and persuades with no authority to make decisions or punishments.

4   *Employee board systems:* An employee files a complaint with an employee representative and they both discuss the problem with the employee's supervisor, then with an upper-level manager if it has not been resolved, and finally take it to an employee board which decides the case within the organization's policy framework and which can also make recommendations about policy changes.

These two systems focus more on discussion, criticism and reform and thus emphasize the third objective, but also the second objective. Nielsen (1996: 186) finds, however, that the best mediator-counsellor systems rely on the individual qualities of the mediator or counsellor, rather than on system strengths, and thus are hard to reproduce, so that employee board type systems are generally the best systems.

Systems One and Two institutionalize essentially 'single-loop' learning in which a particular deviation from company policy is corrected, but little 'double-loop' learning at either an individual or an organizational level occurs. Systems Three and Four do better at double-loop learning, using employee discipline and grievance systems, customer complaints and non-compliance incidents to identify patterns of compliance and ethical problems and to understand how company policies and corporate traditions, systems and informal cultures are contributing to unethical and irresponsible practices. Systems One and Two may punish someone who was caught out responding to latent conflicting messages from upper management, for example product safety versus production targets. At the same time these systems protect management from having to institute real change. It might force changes in individual behaviour, but not in whole cultures. It might result in a fair outcome, but the organization might learn how to make the wrong outcome appear fair next time by extra documentation. Systems One and Two do not consider double-loop issues such as changing company policies to be more effective or fairer, or 'triple-loop biases' within traditions, cultures or systems. Nielsen (1996: 186) makes the empirical finding that the 'worst system, investigation-punishment, is the most common. The best system, employee board with outside arbitration, is the least common.'

Recognition of corporate culture and connection to employee values and self-identity need not mean that the 'civic space' within organizations must be modelled on attempts at civic space in public politics. Bottom-up self-regulation can be achieved through management style and approach, better than it can be accomplished by mandating particular participatory decision-making processes. Trustus' sexual harassment policy (introduced after a case that took five years to settle; see Chapter 4) is an example of an attempt to move beyond discipline to connect with employee values, to ensure utmost fairness, and to learn from problems at an individual and corporate level. The new sexual harassment policy and grievance-handling process were set up as a general 'workplace values and relationships' policy which went far beyond sexual harassment. The new policy and training workshops were grounded in staff ideas about what values and quality of relationships they thought should be evident in their workplace. The new grievance-handling process gave each employee the choice to take a complaint direct to company management (where a traditional investigation, decision and enforcement process could be activated at management discretion) or to utilize an external ombudsman at any stage (either before or after a management decision is made). The ombudsman's role was framed with maximal flexibility to improve or complement what was possible through management decision-making systems. The ombudsman could conduct his or her own analysis and investigation of the situation to determine whether to help the employee to resolve the problem for themselves (individual empowerment and learning), to recommend changes to management (a review of a decision that had already been made or a recommendation that a particular course of action be taken to resolve the problem), or to advise the employee to sidestep internal corporate justice all together and pursue their rights in the formal legal system.[3]

However, as Nielsen (1996: 216) recognizes, individual and organizational learning 'depend upon a reasonable quality of protected civic space within our organizational communities', and this is a fundamental problem in most organizations. There are few or no protected civil liberties for employees. Even within internal due process systems, legalistic procedural rights may be protected, but employees are rarely empowered to discuss and critique current organizational practice. Even companies that follow all the principles discussed in this chapter will still, on the whole, be bad at double-loop and triple-loop learning. The new regulatory state must therefore develop a major role in collecting and 'meta-evaluating' information about the performance of compliance systems. It is the (new regulatory) state that must take ultimate responsibility for looking for patterns and problems at a system, culture and tradition level in order to continually prompt corporate governments to improve their own management of responsibility issues.

Finally, corporate self-regulation programs that are effective at connecting with employee values will rely more on the general methodology and approach to compliance described above as the frontline in self-regulation, and less on discipline as an enforcement mechanism. The methodology described above (and also that described below in 'systems approaches') requires management to create positive opportunities for employees and managers to exercise self-regulation responsibility, not just to discipline them for failures. Here the 'enforcement' of compliance on employees is turned upside down to empower employees to contribute with 'active responsibility' to self-regulation, rather than the 'passive responsibility' of punishment (Braithwaite and Roche

2001). This implies that self-regulation managers should rely on coercive approaches, such as discipline, only as a last resort once they have failed to connect with employee identities and values.

OPENING-OUT: THE STRATEGIC STAKEHOLDER ENVIRONMENT

The penumbra of democracy

In the day-to-day practice of self-regulation, stakeholder pressure can be a good counter-weight to the daily press of short-term business concerns. External scrutiny and engagement can mobilize shame, publicity and other sanctions, and nurture skills and independence to make internal self-regulation work, as we have seen in previous chapters. In general terms, *consumer and social movement* activist stakeholders tend to be good at prompting commitment through publicity and shame (Phase One of the institutionalization of social and legal responsibility). On the other hand, certain *financial* stakeholders, such as insurers and lenders, will have great leverage in demanding implementation of a self-regulation system and will also have more capacity to influence the design of compliance management systems (Phase Three). (They may also have a competing interest in covering up the possibility of liability which is stronger than their interest in prevention.) Since the whole point of internal self-regulation systems is to mitigate some of the injustices companies might perpetrate on various 'stakeholders' in the course of business, as a matter of principle, self-regulation ought to be accountable to those who it is supposed to benefit. However, the self-regulation managers interviewed for this book had little experience of attempting to engage stakeholders in the self-regulation management process.[4]

   In the 1970s the classic works of 'stakeholder pluralism' by Christopher Stone (1975) and Ralph Nader (Nader et al. 1976) advocated that professional corporate managers could and should take into account in decision-making a range of interests wider than those of shareholders.[5] The main institutional reforms proposed to achieve stakeholder accountability included: appointing 'public directors' to corporate boards to represent the public interest (see Parkinson 1993: 386–93; Stone 1975: 152–83; Weiss 1981); mandatory social impact statements and/or audits (Dierkes 1985; Parkinson 1993: 372–83; Sheikh 1996; Stone 1975: 221–7); and mandatory stakeholder consultation mechanisms (Stone 1975: 219–21). These proposed institutions, like the institutions of industrial democracy mentioned above, have been criticized for hampering corporate innovation and goal-oriented rationalism with the cumbersome pre-set procedures of representative democracy. Tripartism and collaborative regulatory processes have also been criticized for being inherently unachievable – processes that claim to implement such philosophies do not meet the criteria (see Seidenfeld 2000).

By seeing the company as an 'entity', we are forced to recognize that it has its own regulatory (i.e. management) mechanisms that (frequently at least) have their own integrity. Blair and Stout's (1999) 'team production theory' (discussed in Chapter 1) sees the internal governance structure (the 'mediated hierarchy') of a corporation as one of its main functional attractions. The central insight here is that members of the corporate team give up control rights over the output of the enterprise and also their firm-specific inputs to a firm structure and board of directors. They do this to work together for mutual gain by allowing the hierarchy to mediate disputes about the allocation of duties and rewards. Thus, 'the directors are trustees for the corporation itself – mediating hierarchs whose job is to balance team members' competing interests in a fashion that keeps everyone happy enough that the productive coalition stays together' (Blair and Stout 1999: 771, 773–4). At their broadest, Blair and Stout suggest that creditors and local community members may be included, for some purposes, as 'members' of the team.

The argument of this book is that once the corporation becomes its own entity, it will generally encompass a broad range of stakeholders. Because it encompasses a broad range of stakeholders (many of whom had little choice in becoming part of the corporate 'team' in the first place), and because it entails a governance structure that makes decisions affecting those people's rights and entitlements, its decision-making processes are a legitimate subject of democratic theory (which is focused on improving the social, economic and environmental justice of decision-making). This fits well with the 'stewardship theory' of management (Donaldson 1990; Donaldson and Davis 1991; also discussed in Chapter 1), which argues that it should not be assumed that managers will act only opportunistically in their own interests. Because of fear of loss of reputation, most of the time managers are forced to make decisions that really do balance the interests of stakeholders inside and outside the organization. The decisions they make will, however, be conservative in the sense that they will generally reflect the existing balance of power between different stakeholders. As Herbert Simon (1952) put it in his theory of 'satisficing', managers will try to achieve satisfactory profits within the constraints that various constituencies place upon an organization (see also Nielsen 2000).

Mandatory adherence to particular democratic procedures is unlikely to inject dynamism and life into the self-regulation system. Rather, it is the appropriate strategic stakeholder environment that can motivate company management to do the right thing. It is external influences that prompt responsibility when they reach into the organization and are embraced in internal responses across the three phases of the process of management of corporate responsibility (illustrated in Figure 2.3). The institutionalization of self-regulation will lack dynamism and 'grip' on real life if the company's external environment is not making compliance a strategic issue.[6]

This means that the external regulation of corporate management processes must always be indirect to an extent. Neither the new regulatory state nor any potential democratic agency can prescribe to companies in any detail how to manage and implement their self-regulation systems. To change the behaviour within the organization, the balance of the bargaining power of its stakeholders must be changed and, indeed, the group of stakeholders with bargaining power broadened. Sceptics often raise the problem of identification of a sufficiently narrow range of stakeholders and/or the balancing of their (competing) interests as an objection to corporate social responsibility. The argument here is that the group of stakeholders whose interests are considered by management should be made as broad as possible in order to make strategic corporate decision-making reflect the broader deliberative democracy as well as possible. (Currently only a few stakeholders usually have a privileged bargaining position in corporate decision-making.) This allows the problem of identification of 'legitimate' stakeholders and appropriate balancing of their interests to be handled in broader democratic forums, not by management or shareholders alone. It should be up to the local community, the nation-state and/or the international community to determine who are legitimate stakeholders by making sure they have appropriate power.

Thus, the primary prescription for improving corporate self-regulation management is changing the power of 'external' agents to influence internal behaviour. The paradox is that, once permeability has been accomplished, these 'external agents' are no longer purely external. Now the organization is understood empirically and normatively as an 'open system' that is 'characterized by a continuous cycle of input, internal transformation (throughout), output, and feedback (whereby one element of experience influences the next)' (Morgan 1997: 40). The (democratic) environment and the organizational system are in a state of mutual interaction, exchange and interdependence. (Figures 2.2 and 2.3 represent this opening-out.) Ultimately this can affect not just the board of directors and upper-management decisions about broad policies, but ultimately also get inside the corporation and change internal structures and everyday behaviour. Corporate–stakeholder relations are more 'democratic' without denying the reality of corporate strategy as a driving motivator.

Corporate permeability to the strategic stakeholder environment can and should be achieved by corporate management in the following three ways (in order of increasing intensity):

- *Disclosure of information* on which stakeholders can engage corporate management – that is, public reporting of information about self-management processes and performance.
- *Consultation* with stakeholders on how to make decisions and how to implement self-regulation processes, including consultation on criteria for social reporting (above), and management of social and legal responsibility issues.
- Systematic policies and procedures for allowing stakeholders to *contest* corporate decisions that affect them on the basis of either legal rights, or standards the company has voluntarily adopted ('Justice Plans').

These three principles are discussed below. Not every principle must necessarily be fulfilled on every aspect of social responsibility self-regulation. As shall become apparent, empirical evidence of the effects of systematic stakeholder engagement are scant because stakeholder engagement is rarely practised systematically by corporate management. Therefore, these principles are preliminary and experimental.

The Monsanto and Shell case studies in Chapter 6 showed that issues of social responsibility can become internal issues for corporate government when stakeholders have sufficient clout. The law is not the only or best tool to achieve the permeability. The vitality of the penumbra of democracy is every citizen's responsibility, not the government's. However, the entitlements of stakeholders that represent various social responsibility concerns are often fragile, so that they have insufficient internal impact to make a difference. The extent to which stakeholder consultation occurs will often depend on the vitality of stakeholder groups – the extent to which they are well organized and well informed and have some well-recognized entitlement (either socially or legally recognized) that requires them to be heard. In the case of each of the three principles above, non-government organizations and civil society will have a role in opening-out the corporation.

In some circumstances it may be necessary for government regulation to directly or indirectly put stakeholders into a position where they have rights and entitlements that make it strategic for corporate management to adopt these principles. Government regulation might accomplish this through: (direct or indirect) regulation of self-regulation reporting requirements (information disclosure); brokering dialogue opportunities; and providing rights and liabilities, forums for contestation and (direct or indirect) regulation of Justice Plans.

Shareholders are the beneficiaries of a significant number of default rules that are pre-contractually biased in their favour. However, relations vis-a-vis shareholders and other stakeholders, and between different stakeholders, can be altered if the law puts certain stakeholders into a stronger bargaining position by giving them rights to sue, receive information or hold accountable in other ways (see Millon 1995: 23). It is one of the urgent, ongoing tasks of state (and global) democracy in the era of the new regulatory state to consider which stakeholders should have more (or less) bargaining power than they currently do to influence corporate power.

Information disclosure

Company reporting and disclosure of information (voluntary or mandatory) is one aspect of corporate governance which has the potential to make a significant difference to ordinary citizens' ability to make companies responsible for failures of social responsibility. The principle is simple in theory: companies should disclose high-quality (i.e. relevant and reliable) internal information about their own processes for managing legal and social responsibilities, and their performance or outcomes, to those stakeholders affected by their actions. This will put those stakeholders in a good position to hold them accountable through the markets for their securities, products and services, reputations, insurance and debt, and through accountability in the courts and other regulatory processes (if the information discloses the basis for a legal liability or sanction).

The disclosure of such information is consistent with the principle of allowing shareholders with social responsibility concerns to improve the efficiency of markets with socially responsible investing. It also gives consumers and activists information on which they can base dialogue with corporate management, and wage campaigns that utilize sanctions and rewards of publicity and shame. Social reporting can help 'create a regulatory system more in line with, and responsive to, any corporation's unique situation, while also reflecting society's expectations' – a form of 'regulated autonomy' (Hess 1999: 46, 50). It can help the business to understand stakeholder expectations better, make decisions in a more fully informed way and increase public accountability (see Hess 1999). In practice, of course, these advantages will fail to materialize if companies have no incentives to voluntarily disclose information, and if they do not disclose reliable or meaningful information, or it is only disclosed to a small group (e.g. certain financial stakeholders, such as insurers or institutional investors). Government action or industry-level self-regulation may be able to coordinate or regulate corporate disclosure to help to prevent some of these failures, including through the identification of those stakeholders to whom disclosure is expected (and to what extent).

Globally, many companies do now voluntarily publish information about their social and legal responsibility practices. Most commonly this is in the form of annual environmental reports, and, for some companies, more general social responsibility reports. In their review of global corporate social and environmental reporting practices, Gray and co-authors (1996) find a global trend towards increased social and environmental disclosure, with the USA leading in the 1970s, and Europe catching up in the 1980s and 1990s. Reporting of issues relating to responsibility towards employees was stronger from the 1970s. Disclosure of environmental issues became more popular in the early 1990s. A 1997 Canadian study found that 60 per cent of major Canadian companies had voluntarily started to incorporate sustainable development management and reporting into their operations (up from 45 per cent in 1992).[7]

The Investor Responsibility Resource Center in the USA has found that 61 per cent of Standard and Poor 500 companies published an environmental report in 1997.

However, voluntary social and environmental reporting is likely to be limited in its scope and biased towards positive information.[8] For example, in Australia a series of well-designed surveys by Deegan and co-authors find a trend towards greater voluntary environmental reporting and disclosure throughout the 1990s (Deegan 1996; Deegan and Gordon

1996; Deegan and Rankin 1996). However, Australian companies are much more likely to make positive environmental disclosures than negative ones. In a random sample of 197 Australian companies, the average amount of positive disclosure for each company was 180 words. The average of negative disclosures was only six words. Only fourteen companies provided any negative disclosures at all (Deegan 1996: 123). Deegan and Rankin (1996) studied a sample of twenty companies that had been successfully prosecuted for environmental offences in the period 1990–93 and had also reported on their environmental performance for that period. They found that, even in that sample, only two of the twenty reported the environmental offence during the period. In all the reports positive information far outweighed negative information. In their global study of social reporting, Gray and his co-authors warn that even the most popular point of corporate social responsibility reporting – that is, environmental disclosures in Western Europe – is 'close to its voluntary peak in terms of both its extent and the development of innovative methods of reporting' (Gray et al. 1996: 212), and that it is now essential that government policy address issues of accountability. As the Australian case illustrates, in the absence of clear standards in relation to reporting, the material voluntarily disclosed can be quite misleading.

Secondly, even where social responsibility reporting is widely adopted, corporate reports vary so considerably in the conventions used to report performance that stakeholders find them difficult to interpret intelligently, to compare and to be assured of their significance and reliability. This suggests that not only should organizations report their self-regulation impacts and achievements, but there also ought to be some regulation of the quality of the reported information. There may be a role for either civil society or state agencies to develop standards in relation to key social and legal responsibility performance indicators, so that interested people can intelligently compare how different companies perform against each other and across time; and also to develop routines and practices for audit or other quality review of social reporting.

Globally, there are a variety of industry-based groups working on developing voluntary standard frameworks and protocols for social, and especially environmental, reporting (see White and Zinkl 1998: 34). These include the New Economics Foundation and the Institute of Social and Ethical AccountAbility's Quality Scoring Framework for assessing companies' social-accounting processes and how well they meet company and stakeholder needs; the 'Sunshine Standards for Corporate Reporting to Stakeholders', proposed in 1996 by the US-based

Stakeholder Alliance to set out the information companies should routinely provide to stakeholders in annual reports;[9] the 'Global Reporting Initiative' (draft guidelines for reporting on sustainability, prepared by a broad consortium of multi-nationals and industry groups), launched by the Coalition for Environmentally Responsible Economies (Plender 1999);[10] the UN Financial Institutions Initiative on the Environment; and the World Business Council for Sustainable Development's eco-efficiency indicators and reporting taskforce which is also working towards broad social reporting indicators (Keffer and Lehni 1999).

The content and quality of corporate social and environmental reporting can be regulated through a combination of some or all of: general corporate law requirements (government regulation); securities exchange listing rules (co-regulation) that mandate reporting and quality assurance; and accounting standards (gatekeeper regulation) that set out content and audit requirements. Regulation of disclosure could have several advantages: firstly, mandatory rules can create certain quality standards of information disclosure by audit and content requirements. Secondly, they can help to set standard guidelines to make reporting meaningful and comparable. Thirdly, mandated reporting of social and environmental responsibility issues assumes corporate self-knowledge of its own way of dealing with responsibility issues. In order to report meaningfully, companies must have conducted social responsibility and compliance reviews. They must have implemented compliance and social responsibility management systems and they must have evaluated how those systems work. Thus, a requirement to report can prompt improved internal processes of decision-making.

The new regulatory state is yet to develop appropriate standards for corporate social responsibility reporting and for 'meta-evaluating' audits, evaluations and certifications by third party monitors. Yet the presence of this capacity will often make the difference between state abdication of regulatory responsibility to management priorities and open, permeable corporate self-regulation. While current financial reporting requirements (which typically rely on general mandatory disclosure rules in company law and securities exchange listing rules filled out by accounting standards) are by no means ideal (see McBarnet and Whelan 1999), they do at least provide a basis for discussion and critique, and for harmonization between different countries and industries. This framework is currently lacking for social and environmental reporting.

Already a number of jurisdictions are beginning to require reporting of material environmental performance and compliance issues as a matter of course (Deegan 1996). In the UK, occupational pension schemes are now required to declare their policy on socially responsible investments.[11] In certain industry sectors Danish companies must produce annual environmental reports to the Danish Commerce and Companies Agency, and The Netherlands, New Zealand and Sweden are also experimenting with similar programs (White and Zinkl 1998: 34). The UK Company Law Review Steering Group has proposed that at least listed companies should include in their full annual report an 'Operating and Financial Review' (OFR) to 'cover the qualitative, or "soft", or intangible, and forward looking information which the modern market and modern business decision making requires' (Company Law Review Steering Group 2000a: 180–6; 2000b: 45–50). This would generally include, among other things:

- discussion of key stakeholder relations – that is, 'an account of the company's key relationships, with employees, customers, suppliers and others on which its success depends';
- 'environmental policies and performance, including compliance with relevant laws and regulations';
- 'policies and performance on community, social, ethical and reputational issues'; and
- the 'dynamics of the business', which could include risks, opportunities and related responses in relation to health, safety and environmental costs.

The US Financial Accounting Board also proposed in 1998 that companies include more non-financial information in their annual reports, including ethical issues related to the company.[12]

These requirements are all steps in the right direction, but they do not provide sufficiently concrete and holistic guidance to corporations as to what information they should collect and report. Indeed, mandatory requirements to report social and environmental responsibility issues are criticized for being too vague. In Australia, for example, a requirement to report on environmental issues was introduced into the Corporations Law and will soon be repealed because of vagueness (Deegan 1999). The requirement to report responsibility issues is only useful as an integrating framework within which specific regulatory regimes develop specific requirements and standards and provide sufficient incentives and sanctions. The remainder of this chapter (and the next) includes specific proposals that organizations should be required to report on:

- their implementation of 'Justice Plans' (i.e. policies for contestation by stakeholders);
- the implementation and evaluation of 'systems' aspects of their self-regulation programs (i.e. the implementation of the 'Self-Regulation Principles' suggested below); and
- the outcomes or performance of these systems.

Regulatory agencies should take a role in helping to frame standards for and meta-evaluating corporate self-evaluations of these processes (see Chapter 9).

Consultation

Good corporate self-regulation may also include some consultation between management and stakeholders on corporate decision-making. In some stakeholder theories of business ethics, stakeholder consultation is proposed as the main means to ethical business decision-making (see Goodpaster 1991). The proposal is that before making substantive decisions, management will bring relevant stakeholders in, find out what their interests are and try to make a decision that compromises between business interests and stakeholder interests (Wheeler and Sillanpaa 1997: 141–66), or will involve stakeholders in determining and implementing shared goals and agendas for non-profit oriented community development (Wheeler 1998). The standard criticism is that this model is cumbersome, unrealistic and unsympathetic to the normal rational economic ways of corporate decision-making.

Here I propose a more modest meaning for 'consultation'. The other two stakeholder engagement principles (discussed above and below) state that information ought to be disclosed to stakeholders about self-regulation processes and performance, and that stakeholders ought to be able to contest corporate decisions that affect their interests on the basis of law or other voluntarily adopted corporate standards. The principle of consultation fills in the gap between these two by stating that good corporate self-regulation involves management *proactively taking into account stakeholder concerns and considerations* in decision-making. There are as many ways to accomplish consultation as there are potential social responsibility issues in individual companies. They range from active stakeholder representation on decision-making bodies, through to management simply taking into account available information about likely negative customer or community reaction when calculating the costs and benefits of a particular course of action. When should management engage in more participatory and less participatory stakeholder consultation?

Firstly, at all levels of the organization, information about stakeholder impacts, concerns and values should be ascertained and used in decision-making about particular courses of action. This may be as simple as keeping up with media reports on relevant issues, or it may be as complex as commissioning focus group research on company products and their environmental or social reputation. In most situations it will not be necessary to engage in very onerous, participatory stakeholder consultation in relation to general decisions. The requirement is simply that the organization collect publicly available information about stakeholder concerns and values, and make sure that that information feeds up and down the organization so that it can be taken into account in decision-making.

I have argued in previous chapters that the role of the self-regulation unit, in particular, ought to be to act as a sensor and communicator of community values, legal changes and regulatory risks that might impact on corporate decision-making. This means that the self-regulation function should make sure that someone is keeping track of changing laws, regulatory expectations, customer and community expectations and concerns (as evidenced by customer complaints, newspaper articles, and so on), and reviewing products and operations for changing compliance risks. The stakeholder 'consultation' principle will frequently be satisfied simply by ensuring that such information does indeed flow through the organization. In practice this will also mean that when conflict arises (as it will) because lower-level managers do not wish to change their actions to respond to those values, the conflict can be escalated to a level of decision-making where it can be authoritatively resolved.

Secondly, more participatory methods of stakeholder consultation should be used when the organization is focusing on reviewing or implementing its self-regulation processes and systems. Corporate decisions about processes and objectives of self-regulation programs that seek to manage impacts on stakeholders (e.g. site environmental management plans; safety features in pharmaceutical products) will justify more participatory stakeholder consultation processes than other 'run of the mill' business decision-making. It would be foolish not to consult well with stakeholders in relation to the self-regulation program itself, since legitimacy in their eyes is one of the main reasons for having such a program. Unlike proposals that call for generalized stakeholder democracy in corporate governance, this is a flexible yet focused principle that concentrates stakeholder participation where it is most significant and most valuable for management. For example, stakeholder participation is highly desirable in deciding on the contents of social reports. Thus, Shell's stakeholder consultation program (introduced after the Brent Spar publicity crisis; see Chapter 6) focuses on seeking stakeholder feedback on social and environmental reports. It uses that feedback to make the reporting categories and information given fit more closely with what stakeholders want (Elkington and Trisoglio 1996).

One major opportunity for stakeholder input into self-regulation processes and performance is when companies receive third party accreditation or recognition of the quality of their programs. This may be pursued voluntarily by the company for competitive advantage in the marketplace of reputation, or it might be required by investors or contractual partners. The promulgation of voluntary management standards, together with provision for accreditation via independent audit of implementation of the standard, is becoming a common response to public and market concern with corporate social responsibility. Accreditation to some of these standards is increasingly demanded by financial stakeholders such as insurers, contracting partners and lenders. In certain industry sectors certification to a particular standard may become a condition of standard contracts so that the standard is 'enforced' by the market and by third party certifiers and compliance specialists. The ISO 14000 series of standards for environmental management systems has had a huge impact in the European market and prompted the growth of an industry of privately hired certification specialists. Other similar standards include BS 7750 (a British Standards Institute standard promulgated in 1994) for environmental management systems, BS 8800 (British Standards Institute 1996) for occupational health and safety management systems, and AS 3806 (Standards Australia 1998) for compliance programs.

Joining a scheme like this may provide a highly systematized and transparent mechanism for stakeholder consultation and monitoring of self-regulation processes and performance, through the agency of independent auditors or through direct requirements for stakeholder consultation and participation. A study by the US Department of Labor and the State of California on the prevention of child labour in the apparel industry concluded that independent third party monitoring may be superior to state regulation and inspection in some situations. This is because of a greater risk of protest and publicity from independent monitors than from state regulation. Indeed, one study found that even in domestic US garment shops in San Francisco, where the Department of Labor had engaged in a targeted enforcement campaign for two years, the addition of private labour monitoring still made a big difference to compliance. There was a compliance rate of 87 per cent for privately monitored shops, and 68 per cent for shops that were only regulated by the Department of Labor (Varley 1998: 433, 435).

In practice, independent monitoring will often need to be brokered by government action. Furthermore, there are serious limits to what can be achieved by the audit methodology used by many monitors. There are questions about the extent to which they measure substance rather than procedure implementation, whether audits motivate the right kind of behaviour, whether anybody learns anything from the information generated and whether they actually act on what has been learned (see Power 1997). Finally, of course, third party monitors generally only operate in the first place because some other stakeholder demands that they be appointed.

Industry-based standards and codes of practice can also provide mechanisms for stakeholder consultation and accountability. Indeed, the evidence is that they are most effective at accomplishing policy objectives that might otherwise have been the subject of regulation where there is strong stakeholder involvement and independent monitoring. One is the Chemical Industry Association's Responsible Care scheme that started with the Canadian Chemical Producers' Association and now operates in forty-two countries and reaches around 87 per cent of the global chemical industry (International Council of Chemical Associations 1998: 2; see, generally, Gunningham 1995; Rees 1997). National Responsible Care schemes each involve chemical industry representatives working with community panels to develop codes of conduct on issues such as community awareness and emergency responses, pollution prevention, process safety, employee health and safety, product stewardship, and hazardous waste management (see International Council of Chemical Associations 1998). Companies must report on implementation and performance under the codes.

Since 1987 the US chemical industry claims to have used Responsible Care to reduce releases of toxic chemicals to the environment by 49 per cent, disposal in deep wells by 46 per cent, and off-site transfer for treatment and disposal by 56 per cent (Gunningham 1998). In Australia, the USA and Canada, national chemical industry associations have determined that the credibility and legitimacy of the program will be enhanced by independent external verification and monitoring of member companies' progress in implementation of the codes (see International Council of Chemical Associations 1998: 14–16; OECD 1997e: 17). For example, in Canada since 1993, once a company has completed its initial three-year implementation process, it goes through a verification process which involves a visit by a team comprising two industry experts, an activist (usually from the community advisory panel), and a local citizen (chosen by the site). The team interviews management, workers, neighbours, customers, carriers and others as well as reviewing documents, and issues a consensus report on whether or not the firm has fully implemented Responsible Care. If it is unsatisfied with the company's performance, it schedules repeat visits until confirmation is achieved. This process will be repeated after a further three years and the results must be publicly reported (International Council of Chemical Associations 1998: 15; OECD 1997e: 17–18). This process provides a high level of stakeholder consultation at the formulation and evaluation of a self-regulation program.[13]

The Ethical Trading Initiative in the UK, and the Social Accountability (SA 8000) standard developed by the Council on Economic Priorities Accreditation Association based in the USA (Liubicic 1998: 126–8), are both attempts at general codes and monitoring systems for corporate social responsibility. SA 8000 sets out standards for measuring the performance of multinational corporations and their suppliers in child labour, forced labour, occupational health and safety, freedom of association, discrimination, disciplinary practices, working hours, compensation and management (Liubicic 1998: 127). The Council of Economic Priorities accreditation agency would accredit monitoring firms to accredit companies and monitor their compliance with the standards. The company can choose its own monitoring firm, as long as the firm has been accredited by the association, but the monitoring firms are briefed by local unions and human rights organizations on issues present at specific sites they monitor, and interested parties can challenge certification.[14]

We cannot always rely on engagement between management and stakeholders to occur spontaneously, either through industry codes or in daily decision-making. It will also be necessary for government to facilitate moments of dialogue at which the bargaining power and legitimate interests and values of stakeholders become real. Stakeholders might come to these encounters with substantive rights, consultation rights, information rights, or only the informal possibility of publicity and social action. But, in any case, government agencies might be able to act as an honest broker. Thus, government might help broker self-regulation codes or standards and accreditation schemes that bring together industry and stakeholders. For example, the White House Apparel Industry Partnership mentioned in Chapter 6 is a self-regulatory scheme that was brokered by government. A government agency prepared a report on the problems of exploitation of child labour at overseas manufacturing sites for the US apparel industry. The government then set up a meeting between relevant companies and stakeholder groups. The result was a self-regulatory scheme, with independent monitoring of compliance. A risk assessment program ranks factories according to likelihood of code or legal violations (using thirty-seven factors) and then uses this to assign the type and frequency of monitoring. Each member of the scheme expects at least one factory audit per year for each of their sites around the world (Jeffcott and Yanz 1998; Varley 1998).

It is not impractical to broker stakeholder dialogue opportunities on an individual company level either. The Victorian Environment Protection Authority's (EPA) approach to environmental improvement plans (EIPs) is an example of a requirement backed up by the regulator that a company go through a process of decent engagement with stakeholders (EPA 1993a; 1996: 13; 1999a). In that process those stakeholders are given the ability to comment on every aspect of the implementation of an internal compliance management system from target-setting to implementation, and then to hold the company accountable for its performance on those targets.

The program was introduced because there had been significant conflict between local communities and facilities on environmental issues, with many local communities not happy with the level of environmental improvement achieved by the EPA working with local facilities. In one particular area, Altona, two potentially catastrophic accidents had occurred over a ten-year period. Because the residents were constantly annoyed and fearful, they opposed every application brought by local facilities for developments or changes. The EPA appointed a 'community liaison officer' to facilitate consultation between senior plant management and local communities to solve these problems and set objectives for environmental improvement in Altona facilities. She began to organize consultative groups for each plant. The groups include local community representatives, people who had previously complained to the EPA about the plant, and top management of the plant. These consultative groups meet approximately monthly to understand the environmental issues facing the plant, and to agree on an improvement plan to address those issues. The EPA is often called upon to provide advice in and to facilitate such meetings. Once the group has agreed on an EIP, the consultative group meets quarterly to hear reports of the implementation of the plan and to address new issues. After two years the whole process is reviewed and begun again.[15]

Contestation: Corporate Justice Plans

The traditional and most direct mechanisms for giving stakeholders the ability to be heard by corporate management is by making their concerns enforceable in law. The legal approach balances stakeholder rights and concerns against management priorities by stakeholders' rights to sue for damage, or by including stakeholder consultation and participation as part of licence conditions, and so on. However, the creation of rights is generally a blunt instrument for improving self-regulation within corporations. It does not necessarily make much difference at all to dialogue and accountability to particular stakeholders *within* corporate management.

Nor is a vague commitment to stakeholder 'consultation' sufficient. Consultation with employees, citizens, consumers and local communities is a valid part of the way in which a company should meet its social and legal responsibilities. But it is easy to consult without granting stakeholders their legitimate entitlements to justice. It is when people have a grievance about a company decision or action that the true 'stakeholder relations' become obvious. One of the most significant things that companies could do to make themselves good 'stakeholder corporations' is to ensure they give real rights, including rights to external review, to stakeholders (and stakeholder groups) with legitimate complaints about the company. The right to access justice – to be able to make claims against individuals and institutions in order to advance shared ideals of social and political life and to rectify relations that have gone wrong – is an essential part of citizenship in a contemporary democracy. I have proposed previously (Parker 1999b: 174–204) that companies above a certain size should be required to have 'access to justice plans' for those affected by their power. Each Justice Plan would incorporate means of handling disputes relating to all the company's legal responsibilities under various regimes, as well as other social values that the company has freely chosen.

The Justice Plan is a system that would ensure permeability to stakeholder contestation – the 'justice' element of self-regulation management.

This should include allowing stakeholders who represent broader interests (e.g. public interest groups) to contest corporate decision-making. The other 'systems' proposals (discussed below) aim to institutionalize an element of proactive corporate thinking about social and legal responsibilities. Corporate Justice Plans facilitate more reactive rectification of the mishandling of social and legal responsibility. It is neither appropriate nor possible for management to satisfy all stakeholder concerns in proactive decision-making. It is not only appropriate but just and right that corporate management be required to remedy specific wrongs done to particular stakeholders in breach of existing legal obligations (whether laid down in regimes of business regulation or in the general law of torts, equity or contract), and other obligations voluntarily accepted by the company (e.g. by signing on to an industry code of practice or promulgating their own codes of conduct). This is not much more than the whole of the law already requires. However, as is well known, the realities and technicalities of the corporate form and its governance (Dan-Cohen 1986), and of inequality of access to the formal court system (Parker 1999b: 174–204), often make it hard to hold companies accountable for their wrongs.

The Justice Plan idea is not as radical as it seems at first glance.[16] It is not a right to participate in normal corporate management processes. It is merely a way to enforce rights that are already recognized by law or that the company has chosen to accept. This is not a matter of incorporating into company law new obligations to stakeholders that change the principles of corporate purpose and governance. It is simply a matter of operationalizing the legal rights that diverse stakeholders already have, by ensuring the company has processes for adjudicating those rights internally, and referring them to external tribunals if they cannot be resolved internally.

Enforced self-regulatory activities in the domains of the environment, occupational health and safety, affirmative action and other substantive regulatory regimes already provide partial models for public and private organizations to comprehensively audit the ways in which they provide access to justice for customers, employees, shareholders, creditors and others, and then to improve them. For example, under anti-discrimination legislation, companies need to have systems for handling grievances about sexual harassment if they are to avoid vicarious liability for work-related harassment (Parker 1999c). One element of consumer protection compliance systems is customer dispute resolution mechanisms that allow companies to resolve customer complaints before they are taken to an external body. Almost all companies have some practices for dealing with grievances, complaints and claims to justice from a variety of stakeholders and citizens, even if these are partial and inchoate.

The 'Justice Plan' proposal is that companies critically examine these pre-existing dispute resolution mechanisms, discuss them with stakeholders, consider whether they do justice or injustice, identify where they have gaps, and implement more comprehensive policies and procedures. It would give institutions responsibility for the effects of their own power by insisting that they audit their own justice practices and develop policies with their stakeholders about how they will ensure access to justice for all (whether customers, creditors, employees, students or anyone else) who may suffer domination within their institutional network. Thus, a corporation or government department might introduce consumer complaints schemes, natural justice for employees in danger of losing their jobs, grievance processes for employees who experience discrimination or harassment and for debtors who feel they are being aggressively hounded for their debts. It might join an independent industry ombudsman scheme to which a grievant could appeal if their grievance was not resolved internally in a satisfactory way. It might even decide to pay for legal advice or representation for citizens who were unhappy with the justice meted out in informal and semi-formal forums.

Consider the 'Customer Charter' developed by the Australian branch of international home and vehicle insurer, AAMI. It provides an example of a Justice Plan, of reporting to stakeholders, and of stakeholder consultation (see Smith 1997; see also Chapter 7 above).[17] The Customer Charter (which is updated each year) sets out AAMI's standards of customer service in eighteen promises, under the headings: (1) accessibility, (2) personal information-privacy, (3) access and correction, (4) claims service guarantees, (5) premiums, (6) penalties, (7) redress, and (8) consultation, accountability and audit. Customers receive a payment of a $30 penalty if any of these promises is broken.

In 1998–99, 690 penalty payments were made and 96.2 per cent of these were initiated by AAMI staff. AAMI publicize an internal 'Consumer Appeals' service for clients, and also prepare an annual public report on their compliance with their Charter. The Charter report is audited each year by KPMG, and includes public reporting of figures of all complaints made internally to the Consumer Appeals service and those that are disputed further in the external Insurance Enquiries and

Complaints Claims Review Panel. The internal Consumer Appeals process complies with AS 4269, the Standards Australia standard on complaints handling. Most of the promises made are very specific, for example that AAMI will post a bank cheque within three days of agreeing to settle a motor vehicle total loss claim. A few are more vague, for example that AAMI promises to take 'all reasonable precautions' to prevent unauthorized access to personal information.

This Consumer Charter process provides engagement with customer-stakeholders at several different levels:

- The promises are very clear statements of the obligations that AAMI accepts in relation to its customers, both to comply with the law and to go beyond the law.
- Each year AAMI sets up 'Charter Teams' to review the Charter and to research and test possible new promises or revisions to the existing ones. These teams include not only senior management and line management, but also regulators and consumer advocates. This is a defined point at which stakeholders can influence service standards and management thinking.
- The Consumer Appeals process provides a forum for customer contestation of organizational decisions. The clear promises in the Charter and the existence of the $30 penalty 'cuts through bureaucracy, breaks down barriers, creates a sense of shared mission, and sharply refocuses corporate priorities on those elements that most need fixing' (Smith 1997: 139) by creating a focus for staff and customers alike and clearly translating customer dissatisfaction into corporate pain.
- The audited annual public report of compliance with the Charter's promises, including the number of penalties paid, complaints made and brief summary of organizational processes implemented to ensure compliance, gives customers a very concrete idea of the performance of the company on key customer service aspirations.

This is a partial Justice Plan (customers only). An improved Charter might extend similar principles and rights to employees (e.g. specific charter guarantees of equal employment opportunity, flexible, family-friendly working conditions, disputes resolved quickly and fairly) and to other stakeholders (e.g. vehicle repairers, other insurers, suppliers, road users groups).

A crucial aspect of an effective internal access to justice mechanism will be that the organization provides access to an external mechanism, and ultimately to the law, if claimants do not feel that justice has been done internally. Since internal institutional justice schemes can be criticized for being inherently biased in favour of the powerful organization that operates them, it will be no use introducing internal justice schemes if they are cut off from pyramids of access to justice strategies (see Parker 1999b). In the first instance, after unsuccessful internal dispute resolution, it might be necessary for institutions to ensure that citizens can go to an independent informal tribunal, ombudsman or industry complaints scheme. Membership of an association that provides tribunals or an ombudsman may be an access to justice requirement, as membership of the Telecommunications Industry Ombudsman scheme is for Australian telecommunications carriers. Ultimately institutional access to justice must be subject to the justice of law.

It will also be important that internal access to justice policies comply with benchmarks from external law, that they be transparent to the state, the legal profession and citizens by being subject to public reporting of justice processes and outcomes. In order to facilitate this, an element of institutional access to justice policies might be that the institution provide finances to assist dissatisfied grievants access legal advice and the court system. However, it is important that judicial review of organizational access to justice policies be 'flexible, strategic and contextual' (Black 1996: 51). Rather than forcing rigid and legalistic interpretations of principles of natural justice, proportionality and illegitimacy on organizations, judges and lawyers should take a reflexive approach in pointing out where the organization has failed and sending the matter back to the organization to internally come up with its own way to respect rule of law values and implement a solution (see Black 1996).

The Justice Plan requirement could be enforced in a pyramid of mechanisms, by requiring disclosure of what Justice Plan the company has, by monitoring market/reputation incentives for voluntarily adopted self-regulation, by liability and damages incentives, or finally by mandating it. Because the requirements of doing justice vary so much depending on the particular context – the type of industry, the social and economic status of the claimant to justice and their relationship with the company, and the requirements of the law relating to that particular area – it is inappropriate to prescribe strict rules about what access to justice procedures would be necessary in particular circumstances. It may be more appropriate to mandate Justice Plans indirectly and in phases:

- Firstly, companies might be required to report on their Justice Plans as part of the requirements for reporting generally on their compliance/social responsibility functions as detailed above.
- Secondly, once companies have become accustomed to this requirement, sanctions for failures to have an effective Justice Plan might be introduced. A particularly relevant sanction for failure to implement an effective Justice Plan might be the award of exemplary damages against organizations where an injustice occurs that should have been prevented and/or resolved by a suitable policy. Governments and courts are already willing to use awards of costs to discourage a party causing unnecessary cost and delay. Extra damages might be awarded in a court action arising out of a matter that the court thinks should have been dealt with internally by the losing organization. The extra damages might compensate the plaintiff for the fact that they have had to spend more time and money getting the matter resolved by going to court than if it had been dealt with internally in the first place, and will also be an incentive for plaintiffs to make institutions accountable in court for the way they do justice. If it were felt that letting plaintiffs keep the excess would give them a windfall benefit, the excess could be assigned to legal aid or to some other access to justice funding.
- Finally, once well established in leading firms and those who follow them, Justice Plans could be mandated. The most interventionist option is to make it an offence to fail to have a Justice Plan, ultimately punishable by corporate capital punishment – withdrawal of the firm's licence or charter. As draconian as this sounds, enforcement action up to licence revocation can already be taken in relation to a variety of types of business (including professionals such as lawyers) for lack of Justice Plan type processes. For example, some US states effectively do this with justice for nursing home residents: unless nursing homes come up with effective plans for improving residents' rights such as freedom of movement and choice of treatment, enforcement action up to licence revocation can be taken (Fogg 1994: 200).

A criticism of internal organizational justice schemes (as with informal justice generally) is that it individualizes and depoliticizes conflict and claims (see, for example, Edelman et al. 1993: 528). Internal corporate justice need not privatize disputes unduly if it is placed within a context of concern for and awareness of more structural issues. Like employee discipline systems, Justice Plans should not be used merely as single-loop learning mechanisms by the company. A company should learn from patterns of complaints and problems to improve its future decision-making and actions. The new regulatory state must have a role in holding internal corporate self-regulation (including Justice Plans) accountable by re-politicizing and resolving structures and patterns of injustice that arise from intra-corporate management of justice.

RESPONSIBILITY AND SELF-EVALUATION

Systems approach

Corporate culture (Strategy One) is important to building compliance from the ground up, and external pressures for accountability (Strategy Two) are crucial to keeping commitment to compliance strong. But large organizations must also have management systems in place that link the top to the bottom and provide something central for stakeholder concerns and employee integrity to hook into. This type of hierarchical and centralized system is necessary if democratic responsibility is going to affect how the whole organization conducts itself. All companies (over a certain size) should have a basic self-regulation system that articulates with a suitable disciplinary system and Justice Plans (as argued above) and that is seamlessly integrated into the corporate governance system. I have already discussed the two 'system' elements that should be put in place:

- The company's internal *discipline system* must articulate with the self-regulation system and be designed in such a way that it respects employees' integrity and connects with their values, and allows the company as a whole to learn from individual mistakes and misbehaviours in order to prevent them re-occurring.
- A *Justice Plan* for engagement with external stakeholders – every company above a certain size ought to have systems for identifying its obligations under law, and any others it wishes to adopt voluntarily, and have systems that allow external

stakeholders to use those rights to contest corporate actions and decision-making, including at the very least a complaints-handling system with a capacity to identify patterns of complaint and to report those issues to someone who can resolve them.

This section broadens out this discussion to include two more system elements for permeable self-regulation management:

- *Clearly defined responsibility for self-regulation* that is shared between the self-regulation function, senior management, the board, line management and employees (reflected in reporting lines, job descriptions, appraisals, and so on) in order to ensure that: the places of internal voices for external values are institutionalised; strategic stakeholder information flows through to appropriate levels; and conflicts over responsibility issues are pushed through to the level at which they can be resolved authoritatively.
- Regular *evaluation of corporate self-regulation processes and performance*, including the extent of implementation of self-regulation processes, whether their scope and strategy remain appropriate for the organization, verification of reports of activity and performance produced internally, and assessment of performance and outcomes of the whole approach to self-regulation within the corporation.

Clearly defined, shared responsibility for self-regulation

Most effective self-regulation management systems do and should include:

- a *self-regulation function* with clout to determine strategies and priorities for legal and social responsibility issues, to monitor compliance, to receive complaints from internal and external stakeholders, and to be responsible for coordinating reporting on the company's social responsibility performance to government agencies and the public. The chief self-regulation staff member should generally have a certain level of seniority (e.g. direct reporting line to board or board committee) and employment protections (e.g. no termination of the contract without a board review).

However, the self-regulation function should not be left with sole responsibility for self-regulation. Compliance with social and legal responsibilities should be a shared management responsibility. Institutional elements of the shared responsibility for self-regulation management might include:

- *A clear board-level self-regulation oversight agenda.* This might be achieved by a board audit or compliance committee, a designated board member (as is the custom in Germany), or simply by making the self-regulation program a standing agenda item on normal board meetings. The board should receive reports on social and legal responsibility issues, review self-regulation strategy and priorities, and act on policy issues raised by self-regulation activity. Certain categories of stakeholder might be represented on a board audit, compliance or social responsibility committee.
- *Reporting lines and job descriptions that make self-regulation part of everybody's job and make clear pathways for self-regulation performance and problems to be taken direct to the top through a reporting line independent of line management.* All employees and managers should have clear access to the self-regulation function in order to receive advice and raise issues. The chief self-regulation person needs to have senior management status, and a direct reporting line to the CEO and the board. This means that the self-regulation function can bypass uncooperative line management, has access to intelligence about conflicts and problems at every level, and the power to put them on the agenda at the highest level.

Some authors have suggested that separations of powers ought to be institutionalized within corporate decision-making (Bottomley 1997: 307; Braithwaite 1997; Handy 1992). Separations of existing intra-corporate powers might help to open up decision-making to the possibility of critique and alternative perspectives, but it will generally only strengthen the countervailing powers of functions that already exercise influence within most corporations, and increase the potential for adversarial confrontation between them. Instead, what is required is decision-making structures in which some different voices – voices that represent the values and integrity of employees and citizens – have some influence, but do not set up unnecessary adversarial conflicts. A corporate governance structure that rests on conflict between different values for decision-making is not very stable in business (and probably not in national governments either) (cf. Dunsire 1996).

The principles stated above set up a situation in which clearly defined responsibility for self-regulation is shared around all decision-makers in the organization at their appropriate level of decision-making. Frequently corporate decision-making processes are not open to information and values about social and legal responsibilities that might change behaviour. This failure leaves space for reckless and intentionally irresponsible actions to flourish, because each manager and employee settles for a bounded rationality that excludes responsibility for considering and acting on social and legal values. The reporting and responsibility lines suggested above attempt to ensure that information about social and legal responsibilities goes to everybody who needs that information for decision-making. This helps to prompt commitment and improve corporate decision-making by:

- making the CEO and managers aware of stakeholders and the environment of responsibility relating to their corporate decisions;
- empowering the board with more information about corporate management to make better strategic and policy decisions, and to review and assist management decision-making; and
- providing the potential to resolve conflict either by forcing a deliberation about the conflict at CEO or board level (or, in the worst case, trumping a decision) where management might otherwise have been reluctant to face the conflicts, or might have lacked the perspective to see it as an issue.

Chapter 7 cited Convict Cash Australia as a company where the chief compliance manager cannot be sacked or even resign voluntarily without the matter going to a meeting of the board. This is just one element of a compliance governance system at Convict Cash that attempts to implement the principles of clear, shared responsibility for self-regulation between the Group Board, the Group Board Compliance and Audit Committee, the boards and compliance and audit committees for each of the three or four separate businesses, management, and the compliance function:

- The Group Board Compliance and Audit Committee meets at least five times per year, consists of five non-executive directors of the company's principal board plus the Group CEO, and is attended by the chief compliance manager and the heads of each of the subsidiary businesses who must be available to take questions.

- Each subsidiary business also has an equivalent board compliance and audit committee, as well as a management compliance committee which has oversight of operational and policy issues in compliance.

- The compliance function prepares a 'Compliance Action Statement' for each meeting of the above board compliance and audit committees. This statement is based on the 'Compliance Register' which sets out all the group of companies' compliance requirements, prioritized according to risk and broken down operational area by area, with the people responsible for implementing each requirement and what they must do clearly identified. The Compliance Action Statement sets out all breaches of these requirements, who is responsible for fixing the problem, what they need to do, and the agreed date by which it must be done (signed by the relevant business unit head). This is one of the main agenda items for the compliance and audit committees of each subsidiary business. Higher risk issues are discussed at the Group Committee (although it does receive all reports and minutes of the subsidiary committees).

- The Compliance Action Statement is based on a 'sign-off' process of monthly questionnaires on compliance performance that every business unit head must answer. It is also based on a compliance review process that continues all year round, during which compliance personnel independently review the compliance performance of each business unit. (The issues for review each year are determined via a risk analysis and agreement with each business unit.)

- The board compliance and audit committees also review the minutes of the management compliance committees and other reports on the performance of the compliance function. They report all these matters for ultimate decision by the Group Board. It is the Group Board that is responsible for performance reviews of the compliance function.

This sets up a system in which the most senior management of the company (the CEO and subsidiary company heads) must personally attend reasonably frequent meetings in which their compliance performance is reviewed and discussed in detail. This lifts the profile of the compliance function with senior management and feeds the results of compliance reviews directly into high-level decision-making processes. It also gives the chief compliance manager (and others) a chance to identify emerging issues and to receive advice and authority to act on them. The Compliance Action Statements and monthly questionnaires also make it very clear who is responsible for what aspects of self-regulation, and should help to identify patterns of problems. Since the results are reported direct to board committees, they have a high degree of salience within the company since management and staff see that they are taken seriously. Yet the system is not inherently adversarial. At each stage – the planning of reviews for each year, the resolution of problems, and the reporting to board committees – agreement and input from the relevant business unit head is sought and, indeed, required. It is a system that attempts to maximize the possibility for a positive, cooperative approach to compliance – even as problems are identified, the main focus of the system is to identify solutions and to document their completion.

Self-evaluation

Effective corporate self-regulation depends on the company obtaining adequate information about its responsibilities in the context of its social and legal environment, relating that information to decision-making processes and operating norms, detecting significant deviations and taking corrective action.[18] Self-regulation is not self-regulation at all if it does not include regular self-evaluation to determine whether the organization is accomplishing the objectives it set out to achieve. How can an organization claim to have a serious self-regulation system if it never, or rarely, assesses answers to the following questions?

- What evidence is there that the design of the self-regulation system meets appropriate standards and is relevant to the risks facing the organization?
- What evidence is there that the self-regulation systems and policies have actually been implemented throughout the organization?
- What evidence is there to show the extent to which the self-regulation system has actually made a difference to people's behaviour, attitudes, the number of breaches, how decisions are made, and so on?

- What evidence is there to show that the company's self-regulation program actually contributes to accomplishing the substantive social values or outcomes that are inherent in the law
  and the voluntary codes and standards the company has
  adopted – for example, improvements in or preservation of
  environmental quality in the surrounding area, well-informed
  consumers, a healthy and safe workplace, lack of discrimination
  and harassment?

It is not the fact that someone in the organization has answers to
these questions that makes self-evaluation important. Rather, it is how
the organization uses that information to learn to improve its self-regulation performance. At one level, self-evaluation is essential to determining whether the organization and its employees are deviating from
the standards set down in its self-regulation procedures and policies, so
that the company can take corrective action in response to those deviations (including discipline, complaints resolution and compensation,
reports to regulators if necessary, and so on).

At a deeper level, effective self-regulation also requires double-loop
learning (see discussion above on discipline systems). This means being
able to detect and correct errors in the policies, procedures, cultures and
traditions of the whole organization (see Morgan 1997: 78–94). For the
organization, the self-regulation function is only useful if it helps to
constantly redesign management, procedures and culture to avoid non-
compliance with existing and emerging social and legal responsibilities.
This adds a fourth phase – self-evaluation and organizational learning
– to the institutionalization of social and legal responsibilities within the
organization (set out in Figure 2.3). Without this fourth phase, there is
nothing intelligent or dynamic about the institutionalization of responsibility, and therefore it fundamentally lacks the robustness that self-
regulation implies.

The little quantitative data available on the implementation of corporate compliance and self-regulation programs show that this is one of
their weakest spots. Beckenstein and Gabel's (1983) survey of US corporate antitrust compliance programs in 1983 found that audits were
under-utilized. A 1991 study of compliance efforts at more than 700 US
companies found that 45 per cent had no ethics auditing systems
(Kaplan 1991). Weaver and co-authors' (1999a: 288–9) study of ethics
programs in US Fortune 1000 companies found that 22 per cent never
compared their ethical performance with other companies (while only

23 per cent said they did so frequently or very frequently). Only 10 per cent surveyed external stakeholders frequently or very frequently regarding the firm's ethics and values and 46 per cent never did so. Only 10 per cent reported asking external parties to help them to evaluate the ethics program and 51 per cent never did so. Morf and co-authors' (1999: 269) survey of organizations that were members of the Ethics Officer Association found that 78 per cent had never conducted a 'moral audit', 30 per cent did not attempt to measure improvement in the ethical and moral standards of the corporations, and those that did, did so mainly via surveys (41 per cent); only 18 per cent had internal audit reports prepared.[19]

In Chapter 9 I will argue that one of the most strategic foci for regulators in the new regulatory state should be to enforce a procedural requirement that companies that claim to self-regulate must audit, review and improve the performance of their programs – the 'meta-evaluation' of self-evaluation. Below, I set out more broadly what regulators and other stakeholders might be able to do to help companies to implement effective systems approaches to self-regulation.

CONCLUSION

There are four potential steps that can be taken by professional, stakeholder or industry groups and governments in 'meta-regulating' corporate self-regulation systems to ensure implementation of the four system elements (discipline, Justice Plans, shared responsibility, and self-evaluation).[20] They are presented below, from the least coercive to the most coercive. These might be introduced sequentially over time, with the least coercive introduced first and more coercive elements introduced later as companies get used to the requirement; or a patchwork approach could be taken, with elements from each proposal used to back each other up:

- *First* is exhortation to implement best practice principles of corporate self-governance, with market and reputational incentives alone for enforcement. Like the OECD Principles for Corporate Governance (OECD Ad Hoc Taskforce on Corporate Governance 1999), government or non-government organizations might promulgate a set of basic, broad principles for effective governance of self-regulation.[21]
- These 'Principles for Corporate Self-Regulation' would set a baseline for voluntary reporting of self-regulation practices, for

third party monitoring, for educative activity by regulators (e.g. model guidelines), for best practice principles and voluntary or mandatory codes of practice for compliance management. Thus, they would be enforced only by the market (e.g. by contractors, investors, insurers) or via reputation (publicity in the media and among consumers). These principles would be very broad and flexible. Even AS 3806–1998, the Australian Standard for Compliance Programs (Standards Australia 1998) that appears to meet some of these objectives is probably too detailed. For the same reasons that it is worthwhile for government to be involved in helping to broker the harmonization of accounting and reporting standards for corporate social reports, it may be useful for government, or better still a multi-government organization such as the OECD, to be involved in brokering broad principles for self-regulation. Indeed, developments like this are not so far away (see below).

- *Second*, corporate reporting requirements (see above) could require disclosure of whether the company has a self-regulation system or not, what standards it reaches and what outcomes it achieves. This would build on the first step, and also on the disclosure policies suggested above in relation to stakeholder engagement. Here the requirement would be similar to the UK's Cadbury Code of Corporate Governance (Belcher 1995; Pettet 1998). Either the corporate law or securities exchange listing rules would require companies to state the extent to which they complied with the 'Principles for Corporate Self-Regulation', and the outcomes they were achieving. This would be subject to the same quality regulation as other financial reports. Again here, reliance is primarily placed on stakeholders to enforce the principles via reputation and market incentives.

- *Third*, liability incentives for a good self-regulation system (i.e. compliance with the 'Principles for Corporate Self-Regulation') could be introduced. These might include sentencing incentives (i.e. lesser damages or penalties for companies that have in place a self-regulation system that meets basic principles of good practice), reactive liability (extent of liability depends on extent to which the system discovered and rectified the problem before legal action was taken), corporate probation (enforcement action and/or court orders require companies to implement or improve their self-regulation system in accord with the principles), and regulatory incentives (a lighter regulatory burden for companies that show excellence in commitment to and implementation of a compliance system, for example less onerous licence conditions) (all discussed in Chapter 9). Here the expectation that companies above a certain size will have self-regulation systems shapes all regulatory, civil and criminal liability of companies. The proposal is not to introduce new substantive requirements that companies must positively implement self-regulation systems in all sorts of substantive regulatory areas. Rather, enforcement and compliance with current laws affecting companies would recognize that all companies have an inherent capacity for self-regulation, and that they are unlikely to effectively comply with their social and legal responsibilities unless they exercise that capacity.

- The *final*, and most coercive, step that could be taken to try to ensure corporate implementation of the principles of effective self-regulation management would be for company law to mandate all companies of a certain size and above to implement the systems principles. Again, this proposal recognizes that effective self-regulation must seep into all of corporate management and should therefore also shape company law, since it is company law that attempts to set out the basic expectations for corporate structure and the duties and responsibilities of various officers. Ultimately the basic expectation that companies have effective self-regulation systems should shape the contours of directors' duties (liability for loss caused by lack of internal controls; see Hill 1999), corporate liability in company law generally (self-regulation systems as a factor in determining the extent of liability), periodic reporting requirements (see above on reporting requirements), and the model corporate constitutions set out and assumed in company law. Most radically, the reporting and structural requirements for the company might be changed to incorporate an assumption or requirement that each company have a senior officer who is explicitly responsible for self-regulation management, including reporting on self-regulation systems (i.e. a similar position with similar obligations as the company secretary or appointed auditor).

These principles would have to be enforceable primarily by regulatory agencies, in particular the regulator responsible for supervising incorporation and financial reporting. However, in special circumstances they could also be enforceable by industry or other specific regulators (e.g. where they contribute to a substantive regulatory breach), by shareholders (where the company suffers a loss as a result of their breach) and perhaps by creditors (including employees) on winding up. This is not a proposal for a new general stakeholder remedy to be included in company law beyond shareholders and creditors (including employees). It is more appropriate for other stakeholders' rights to be part of specific regulatory regimes (e.g. industry-based or environment, health and safety, discrimination) where they can be identified and balanced democratically by those with experience, expertise and specific knowledge in the area.

These principles, and the proposals for their meta-regulation (above and also in Chapter 9), may seem onerous. In fact, they should provide a more efficient rationalization of what most respectable companies are trying to do anyway. In general a basic system of self-regulation is already required by so many areas of substantive regulation that there is probably something fundamentally wrong with the management of a large company that does not have a self-regulation management system to cover at least a couple of specific areas. The legal reforms I propose above as potential mechanisms to 'enforce' these principles are sensible ways of changing the law to fully respond to the fact that corporations are complex organizational systems, reforms that probably should be considered anyway.

There are positive advantages for implementing such principles. For companies, they would create a general structure in every company of significant size into which specific compliance plans under specific regulatory regimes would fit and could be integrated into a whole corporate integrity program. They provide a framework and build a capacity for self-regulation that cannot be achieved within the framework of any one specific regulatory regime (such as environmental, financial services or anti-discrimination regulation). It is difficult for stakeholders, regulators or legislators to achieve in each substantive regulatory regime the basic conditions which we have seen are necessary for an effective compliance program. While the Australian Managed Investments Act may require implementation of a compliance plan, appointment of a compliance officer and of a board-level compliance committee, it is unlikely and undesirable that each of the Australian environmental regulation, health and safety regulation, anti-discrimination regulation, insurance regulation, food safety legislation, and so on, should each provide for their own slightly different versions of the same thing. More likely in each regime a few, sometimes inconsistent, compliance system requirements will be introduced and varied over time. Much better that a basic code for corporate self-regulation systems should institutionalize a few common standards, providing a single framework into which different compliance plans can fit and therefore combining the power of publicity and sanctions in several regimes into a stronger movement for corporate self-regulation.

Implementing a basic code of principles for corporate self-regulation systems requires government agencies to work together to develop a small number of consistent standards for corporate self-regulation processes. Later on, government agencies might be willing to accredit combined compliance systems (say, covering both environmental and health and safety issues, as many in fact do in the global chemicals, mining, petroleum and manufacturing industries) as adequate under different governmental regimes of environment and health and safety, and to work together to eliminate inconsistencies and duplications. This innovation also ought to be attractive for corporate management as it holds the promise of harmonizing and clarifying various corporate self-regulation process requirements into an integrated system, with associated gains in efficiency and ease of gaining governmental accreditation and public recognition for their efforts – all this without significantly changing existing, substantive legal obligations. However, self-regulatory company constitutions cannot replace substantive regulatory regimes in environment, health and safety, discrimination, tax, prudential regulation, and so on. It merely provides a framework in which substantive regulatory regimes can more easily influence and interact with internal corporate decision-making processes.

9 | Meta-regulation: The regulation of self-regulation

Despite the dominance of organizations in contemporary social life, law is desperately short of techniques, doctrines and institutions that adequately respond to the social features of organizational entities, their impacts on stakeholders, their internal capacity for self-management, their capacity for diffusion and avoidance of accountability (see Dan-Cohen 1986: 13–14). Lack of corporate social and legal responsibility is not just a failure of corporate management. It is also a failure of legal regulatory institutions to interact with corporate organizations to make them open and permeable. Similarly, community action often fails to permeate the corporate shell and engage with corporation's self-governance capacity. Corporate responsibility, or citizenship, is constituted in interaction between formal regulation (through the state), informal social action (the penumbra of democracy and institutions of civil society) and corporate self-regulation.

The role of corporate citizens is *to use permeable, responsible self-regulatory mechanisms* (which meet all the requirements of Chapter 8) in order to determine for themselves how to instantiate regulatory responsibilities, and what values to follow within the grey areas where sufficient consensus has not yet been reached in the broader polity. The role of legal and regulatory strategies is to add the 'triple loop' that forces companies to evaluate and report on their own self-regulation strategies so that regulatory agencies can determine whether the ultimate substantive objectives of regulation are being met (safe workplaces, equal opportunity, improved natural environments, sustainable development, market strength, and so on) (see Figure 9.3 for a diagrammatic representation of the triple loop). The regulator's role is therefore one of 'meta-regulation' (Grabosky 1995: 543), and regulators and rule-makers will themselves have to revise and improve their strategies constantly in light of the experience and evaluation of corporate self-regulation. There are two main principles that law and legal institutions need to follow in order to keep the loops turning:

- Firstly, law and regulators must help *to connect the internal capacity for corporate self-regulation with internal commitment to self-regulate*, by motivating and facilitating moral or socially responsible reasoning within organizations. This is done by inducing corporate crises of conscience through regulatory enforcement action, legal liability and public access to information about corporate social and legal responsibility. But crises of conscience are not enough – legal liability and disclosure standards must be tied to incentives for, and guidance on, appropriate standards for self-regulation processes through *restorative justice*.
- Secondly, law and regulators should hold corporate self-regulation accountable, and facilitate the potential for other institutions of civil society to hold it accountable, by *connecting the private justice of internal management systems to the public justice of legal accountability, regulatory coordination and action, public debate and dialogue*. This can be done through providing self-regulation standards against which law can judge responsibility, companies can report and stakeholders can debate. This allows private management issues to become matters of public judgment. The most important standards for corporate self-regulation processes allow regulators, the public and the law to judge the companies' own evaluations of their performance, and whether they have improved it on the basis of those evaluations – *meta-evaluation*.

The successful combination of these two features (or their absence) – corporate crises of conscience tied to restorative justice and meta-evaluation – will be the hallmark of whether the new regulatory state holds corporations democratically accountable, or caves in to empty neo-liberalism.

Too often, emerging techniques of 'neo-liberal' governance are not tied adequately, in concept or in practice, to institutions of democracy. The neo-liberal state is good at recognizing that the state should work with markets and industry self-regulation in governance, if possible. Neo-liberal governance, as currently practised, too often forgets to facilitate scrutiny and accountability to institutions of civil society and even to the law (Pearce and Tombs 1998). The neo-liberal state shares some strategies in common with the ideal meta-regulating new regulatory state, but fails where it really matters – in completing the loop by connecting private self-regulation and market mechanisms to public justice and debate. The concept of 'permeable self-regulation' is not one in which the state resigns the right to determine all substantive values to which corporations should subscribe to corporate management. Rather, law must continue to set out minimum regulatory requirements (as it already does in a variety of regulatory arenas), and to facilitate further specific and contextual corporate dialogue with stakeholders on additional responsibilities.

In the new regulatory state, laws, policies and regulatory strategies for corporations should also always aim to maximize the possibilities for permeable self-regulation as a primary design principle from the beginning of the policy and law-making processes. The design of law and the choice of regulatory tools should always be capable of catalysing and holding accountable all phases of internal compliance system implementation, and of being responsive to different responses at each of those phases (see Ayres and Braithwaite 1992 on 'responsive regulation'; Selznick 1992: 463–75 on 'responsive law'; and Teubner 1987 on 'reflexive' law).

This chapter proposes principles for doing this at each of the three phases of institutionalization of social and legal responsibilities (Figure 2.3). There is a smorgasbord of options. Appropriate ones must be chosen on the basis of evidence about what might work, and must be regularly reviewed in the triple loop of regulators' evaluation of companies' self-regulation and self-evaluation. Table 9.1 sets out a summary guide to the principles and proposals in this chapter. In order to illustrate some of the possibilities, let us first consider a case study of one regulator that has attempted to take its role in regulating self-regulation seriously.

A CASE STUDY: AUSTRALIAN COMPETITION AND
CONSUMER COMMISSION

In Australia, antitrust and consumer protection regulation are combined in the federal Trade Practices Act (1974) which is administered by the Australian Competition and Consumer Commission (ACCC).[1] The ACCC has attempted to surmount the challenge of 'meta-regulating' corporate self-regulation in four ways:

TABLE 9.1 *Principles for meta-regulation at the three phases of corporate institutionalization of responsibility*

Phase	Aim of legal regulation	Legal and regulatory strategies
Phase One: *Prompting management commitment*	Tie crises of conscience to commitment to self-regulation – *restorative justice*.	1. Seek to identify and hold accountable all who are responsible for wrongdoing. 2. Adjusting liability by reference to self-regulation program – reactive liability. 3. Require self-regulation as part of response to or penalty for breach – corporate probation.
Phase Two: *Acquisition of skills and knowledge*	Foster and harness dynamic of leadership and innovation by some companies that is modelled by others to continuously improve skills and knowledge.	1. Initiatives to build compliance leadership. 2. Process regulation – regulation leads business in acquisition of skills and knowledge. 3. Education, advice and development of market for self-regulation expertise. 4. Building commitment through clear standards for liability and enforcement – i.e. flip back to Phase One regulatory strategies for those with no commitment to learning how to self-regulate.
Phase Three: *Institutionalization of purpose*	Check that the policy of self-regulation is robustly institutionalized throughout the company and has the desired effect without destroying integrity of self-regulation – *meta-evaluation*.	1. Reporting and verification requirements. 2. Meta-evaluation of self-evaluation as a regulatory requirement. 3. Immunities for self-disclosure and self-correction.

- *Industry self-regulation:* During the 1980s the ACCC became both more strategic in the cases it chose to investigate and enforce, and simultaneously more focused on nurturing compliance through industry codes of practice and individual corporate compliance systems (see below). It strategically used threats of enforcement action for breaches against particular industries to back up requests to develop effective self-regulation and to oversee the quality of self-regulatory codes (Tamblyn 1993: 160–2).[2] For example, in the fruit juice industry, investigators noted that manufacturers could add water or sugar to drinks labelled '100% juice', with little chance of being caught because investigations were scientifically difficult. At five or six cases a year, this had become a serious, but not major, problem. The ACCC responded by drafting a code of practice for fruit juice manufacturers that included a self-monitoring mechanism. Each fruit juice manufacturer had to contribute to a fund which would pay for the random testing of members' juices bought in the marketplace. The manager of the scheme would give the manufacturer a chance to put the problem right if a problem was found, before reporting recalcitrant manufacturers to the ACCC, which had made it clear it was ready to move against them in the courts. In 1998, Part IVB was added to the Trade Practices Act (partly at the instigation of the ACCC) and now allows the ACCC to register voluntary industry codes so that a contravention automatically becomes a contravention of the Trade Practices Act as well, and gives the Commission power to mandate an industry code if a voluntary one is not put in place under the Act.
- *Settlements that motivate corporate compliance programs:* Since 1979 the Federal Court had seen the extent to which an individual corporation has attempted to ensure its own compliance with the Act as an important factor in assessing the amount of criminal and civil penalties when breaches occurred (Fisse 1989; Parker 1999a). From the late 1980s ACCC staff have coaxed the courts to go a little bit further in each case in ordering companies to rectify damage done and put in place internal compliance systems to prevent it happening again. In settlement discussions ACCC staff found that they could trade on the fact that companies were willing to do more than was strictly necessary under the penalty provisions of the Act to

save the costs and diversion of litigation, and the scandal of a trial. The ACCC developed a practice of requiring companies that had breached the Act to implement corporate compliance programs (as a condition of settlement) to give added bite to the tiny penalties available under the Act (a maximum of A$100 000 in consumer matters, where a criminal standard of proof was applied, and A$250 000 in anti-trust matters, with a civil onus of proof). Even when penalties were increased in 1993 (up to A$10 million for anti-competitive conduct), the new penalties were used to reinforce the capacity to require compliance programs. In 1993, s. 87B was added to the Act (again partly at the instigation of the ACCC), making settlement undertakings enforceable in court (see Trade Practices Commission 1995). Further amendments to the Act in 2000 have given the court the power to make probation orders, community service orders, an order requiring disclosure of information and an order requiring an advertisement to be published. Probation orders are aimed at achieving a change in organizational culture to prevent repetition of the conduct and ensure self-regulation in the future. It can include an order requiring the company to develop a compliance plan, provide education and training for employees and managers in relation to compliance obligations and/or requiring the company to undertake a revision of their internal operations and control systems.

- *Nurturing compliance skills, knowledge and professionalism in business:* The ACCC has also nurtured compliance skills, knowledge and professionalism in business. It formed a Compliance Education Unit to foster compliance expertise in industry by developing the 'Best and Fairest' manual, a model compliance program and a set of training modules for companies to use with managers and staff. The Unit was also available to act as compliance consultants for companies who had entered into s. 87B undertakings or voluntarily wished to set up a compliance program.[3] While the Unit concentrated on compliance education, the ACCC backed its compliance focus by proving its willingness to launch big prosecutions and seek quick injunctions against unlawful conduct (Fisse 1989; Grabosky and Braithwaite 1986: 91–4; Tamblyn 1993). The focus is now on equipping external compliance professionals through units concerned with industry self-regulation, compliance strategies, and liaison with consumers and industry. The Society of Consumer Affairs Professionals in Business was started in 1993 with heavy ACCC involvement and subsidy. The Association for Compliance Professionals Australia (ACPA) was begun in 1996 in the hope of emulating its success, also partially at the instigation of the ACCC. Each association now has memberships of over 1000, and hold highly successful annual conferences.

- *Standards:* The ACCC has developed some standards by which industry self-regulatory schemes and compliance programs can be judged. In 1991, it published a guideline to good codes of conduct, and in 1996 all federal, state and territory consumer ministers adopted a guideline for fair trading codes of conduct based on it.[4]
- In 1995, the ACCC was involved in the development of a Standards Australia (the Australian body affiliated to the International Organization for Standardization) standard on complaints handling (AS 4269). In 1998 the Australian Standard on Compliance Programmes (AS 3806) was launched. In this case the ACCC, together with the ACPA, developed the standard under the processes of Standards Australia, together with representatives from the Australian Institute of Criminology, the Consumers' Federation of Australia, the Federal Bureau of Consumer Affairs and the Public Interest Advocacy Centre.

The ACCC has not collected the evidence or statistics that would allow a rigorous evaluation of the effects of their strategies. However, the anecdotal evidence suggests that the ACCC's approach has resulted in a much greater awareness and acceptance in a number of industry sectors of the need for trade practices compliance programs as a part of ordinary business.[5] The main weakness is that the ACCC has not regularly monitored the quality of corporate compliance programs or industry self-regulatory schemes. In particular, it has made only one application to court to enforce a s. 87B undertaking and has no systematic way of monitoring compliance with the undertakings. Nor are the circumstances in which self-regulatory industry schemes should be amended or scrapped in favour of government regulation very clear. As I shall argue, the fulfilment of the meta-regulatory triple loop should put a heavy responsibility on the regulators to collect data, analyse and report on the impacts of their activity and on patterns of corporate self-regulation so that both companies and regulators are accountable.

By making the implementation of self-regulation an explicit factor in settlement and enforcement policies, in penalty determinations in court and a condition of enforceable undertakings, the ACCC conditioned legal and regulatory responsibilities according to self-regulation responsibilities. In each case the strategies developed by the regulator were encouraged and supported by legislative and case law changes that better recognised corporate responsibility and capacity for self-regulation. In summary the ACCC developed strategies to:

- identify patterns in complaints by individuals, and serious breaches, and use strategic enforcement threats to motivate industry and corporate level self-regulation initiatives to address those problems (*Phase One – Prompting commitment*);
- nurture compliance skills, knowledge and professionalism, in order to facilitate organizational learning about compliance (*Phase Two – Acquisition of skills and knowledge*); and
- by making a duty of audit one of the conditions for s. 87B enforceable undertakings and by helping to develop standards by which industry codes of conduct, corporate complaints handling systems and compliance systems could be judged, the ACCC encouraged and, to a modest extent, enforced corporate self-evaluation of self-regulation performance (*Phase Three – Institutionalisation of purpose*).

PHASE ONE: PROMPTING COMMITMENT THROUGH RESTORATIVE JUSTICE

Law and regulation can help to prompt management commitment through enforcement action, liability to third parties, and by giving stakeholders rights to information through reporting requirements (that provides the ability to turn the spotlight of public attention on corporate behaviour). In fact, however, law and regulatory action frequently fail to adequately motivate the right people within the organization to detect, correct and prevent wrongdoing. Liability or negative publicity alone can have unpredictable effects on internal self-governance. Rather than prompting commitment to implementation of permeable self-regulation, it can create incentives to insure against liability, outsource risks, to follow internal guidelines by the letter instead of flexible approaches to suit the circumstances, or to silence whistle-blowers (Black 1999).

Prompting commitment to institutionalization of social and legal responsibility requires more than just a crisis of liability or publicity. It requires mechanisms that link legal and public responsibility to individual and organizational sub-unit motivation to change corporate cultures and self-management systems. Law/regulation should provide signals and incentives that permeable self-regulation is an appropriate response. This is a form of 'restorative justice' – putting right corporate wrongdoing by addressing both the particular injustice and the organizational processes that allowed it to happen. It is not merely liability, but a type of liability that identifies those who are responsible for doing or failing to prevent the conduct and motivates them to commit to setting up systems that ensure it does not happen again.

Restorative justice

'Restorative justice' is not intended to imply that the (corporate) offender ever had everything right in the first place and that justice can be done by restoring the status quo. Rather, the central idea is that the purpose of intervention is to give the offender a chance to proactively put things right. The virtue of active responsibility for the future is even more important than taking passive responsibility for the past (Braithwaite and Roche 2001). In criminal process, restorative justice requires an offender to confront his/her responsibility for wrongdoing by facing his/her victim/s and together resolving how to put the wrong right (for example by paying restitution or doing community service). The aim is not only to provide a better remedy and healing for the victim than imprisonment or a fine would provide, but also to help to transform the offender into a more law-abiding person in the future (Cragg 1992; Galaway and Hudson 1990; Marshall 1985; Messmer and Otto 1992; Van Ness 1986).

The 'justice' in restorative justice is strong (see Braithwaite 1999). Corporate restorative justice could include the following dimensions:

- *Restitution:* This involves putting right whatever went wrong in the particular case, for example compensating an injured worker, cleaning up toxic waste, or promoting an employee who has suffered discrimination.
- *Prevention (corporate 'rehabilitation'):* This involves putting the organization and its stakeholders in a position where the wrong will not occur again, by identifying how it happened and putting in place systems and safeguards to prevent, detect and correct wrongdoing in the future. This could include sacking managers who fail to take legal compliance seriously; redesigning a

manufacturing process to reduce or eliminate pollution; introducing an equal employment policy that involves training,
checklists for job interviews and promotions, and regular
review of gender and race statistics within the firm; or redesigning work processes with workers to eliminate safety hazards.

• *Social justice and democracy:* The plan for restorative justice
should be done on the basis of deliberation and inclusion of the
perspectives of relevant stakeholders and/or regulators who
have a broader view of problems and issues that arise frequently in other organizations, and are a matter of particular
social or economic concern. For example, unions may be
included in the discussion of safety issues and point out ways
in which problems have been solved in other companies or
additional safety problems that frequently arise in that industry and should be addressed; local residents may be given
ongoing access to information about what pollutants and other
by-products a factory site is producing and their research might
show as yet unregulated dangers that the company chooses to
take into account.

The first step in restorative justice is to identify and motivate all those
individuals and sub-units who can make a difference in corporate cultures to do so through legal or public responsibility. Traditional methods of corporate responsibility attribution in law are preoccupied with
trying to identify an individual who is at fault and determining
whether that person's fault can be attributed to the corporation as a
whole (see Wells 1998: 657–9; see also Arlen and Kraakman 1997; Coffee
1981; Fisse and Braithwaite 1993; Schlegel 1990). The 'vicarious liability'
theory makes the employer responsible as principal for all acts of
employees. The 'alter ego' or 'identification' theory makes the company
responsible for the acts of those people who make up its 'directing mind
and will', usually a fairly narrowly defined group of senior managers.
Both these theories create problems if the fault is one of omission and
carelessness by the whole organization, or one to which a number of
individuals and units contributed, but none with a high enough degree
of individual fault (see Bovens 1998 for a comprehensive analysis of this
problem). As we saw in Chapter 2, this type of diffused irresponsibility
is exactly the sort of problem that arises frequently in organizations and
creates the potential for ethical and legal problems in its own right, or
allows space for intentional evil to flourish. Law and regulatory action
needs 'to escape from company liability derivative on the wrongdoing

of one individual' and instead 'to capture the "corporateness" of corporate conduct' (Wells 1998: 659).

As Fisse and Braithwaite (1993) point out, much corporate non-compliance is probably 'over-determined'. It is caused or not prevented by a number of actors, both individuals and business units, within the organization. Fisse and Braithwaite sensibly propose that corporate accountability should be based on the principle: 'Seek to identify all who are responsible and hold them responsible, whether the responsible actors are individuals, corporations, corporate subunits, gatekeepers, industry associations or regulatory agencies themselves' (1993: 140). In general, senior officers (i.e. directors and senior executives) should be held personally liable for all that goes wrong within the corporation without need to prove intention or knowledge of the wrong, unless they had put in place an adequate self-regulation system (see discussion of adjusting liability below). Similar liability should be extended to any managers within whose unit or area of responsibility the misconduct took place. Other individuals and sub-groups would be responsible as appropriate.

It will usually be difficult for a court or regulator to identify who and what structures in the organization are responsible for any particular wrongdoing because of lack of access and information. It is for this reason that probation orders and settlements that require corporations to do their own internal investigation and correction are valuable (see below). The only way that law and regulators can adequately comprehend the complexity of corporate responsibility is by reflexively putting the onus on the corporation itself to identify responsibility when something goes wrong (the signal this sends is that organizations should proactively ensure responsibility beforehand). Fisse and Braithwaite (1993) demonstrate how regulatory enforcement action should be tailored to catalyse internal corporate justice systems to define who or which groupings are responsible for wrongdoing in the organization and in what degrees, then giving them a chance to rectify the wrong and learn ways to prevent similar wrongdoing in the future – responsibility enhancing regulation (see also Black 1999: 118; DeMott 1997; Gray 1998). By identifying a number of people and units who are culpable, the probability is increased that at least one of them will respond to the crisis by being motivated to improve.

Formal law

A variety of strategies that regulators use already trade on the wisdom of using cooperative and persuasive strategies in combination with deterrence and coercion to build commitment to compliance. Mixes and pyramids of regulatory strategies to promote compliance and self-regulation have been well explored by other researchers (see Ayres and Braithwaite 1992; J. Braithwaite 1984, 1985; Braithwaite and Makkai 1991, 1994; Grabosky and Braithwaite 1986).[6] Much of this work focuses at the level of regulatory agency activity within the discretion of individual inspectors and regulatory officials (e.g. Parker 1999d; Sparrow 1994, 2000). However, we urgently need to re-design formal law and regulatory strategy to build up commitment (and capacity, i.e. Phase Two) for self-regulation. It is rightly a tradition of law and society scholarship to focus on the grassroots of everyday experience of law: the inspectors' visits (e.g. Hutter 1997), the management response to the symbolism of law (e.g. Edelman 1990), and the way in which the aspirations of law break down in ignorance, lack of enforcement and creative compliance (e.g. McBarnet and Whelan 1997). Nevertheless, the symbolism of formal law has a capacity to affect the (much more voluminous) discretions of regulatory officials, the implementation of, and compliance with, law by corporations, and even public and internal organizational debates with stakeholders. Indeed, the many innovations of individual regulatory agencies and inspectors, and of individual corporations, will rarely have a broader impact unless they filter upwards to be reflected in the structure of corporate regulation laws that are applied more widely.

Furthermore, often regulatory or voluntary corporate initiatives that seem to have the potential to prompt better permeable self-regulation fail to have an impact beyond a few firms because of significant public and industry doubts about their fairness and justice. They are seen as discretionary concessions provided by unaccountable regulatory officials to self-serving corporations in defiance of the letter of the law, and possibly of procedural justice as well. Formal legal tools need to be designed better to recognise the potential for self-regulation so that it is held accountable under the law. Innovative self-regulation oriented regulatory strategies should not be left hiding in the shadows. Paradoxically, appropriate recognition of permeable self-regulation in *formal* law can create more space for corporate self-regulation to be tried effectively *outside* the formal legal arena.

There are two main ways to connect liability to commitment to self-regulation. One is through *adjusting liability* (either legal responsibility or amount of penalty) through reference to whether the company had in place an effective self-regulation program, and whether that program detected and corrected the breach – a broadened form of 'reactive liability'. In other words liability for both the corporation and its individual members is determined in part by reference to corporate and organizational factors. In practice, legal reform of this type is most effective when it flows on to affect prosecution policies, regulatory inspection priorities and decisions by stakeholders about the likely success and legitimacy of bringing suit or drawing attention to corporate failure.

The second tool is more proactive. It would make the implementation of effective self-regulation a required part of *the response to, or penalty for, breach*. In response to a breach the regulator or court would require a company to implement a system to prevent, detect, correct and report on future non-compliance. Usually this would also require the company to conduct an internal investigation and prepare a report on the breach that gave rise to the liability or potential liability in the current case. In effect this is a broadened form of corporate probation, since it requires supervision of the 'rehabilitation' of the company. One of the difficulties in current regulatory regimes is that regulatory officials often informally expect companies to implement or improve self-regulation in response to breaches or alleged breaches. Indeed, enforcement of penalties is often forgone on this basis. Yet there is little systematic oversight of the way in which regulators use their discretion in this area since it is so informal. Again, then, the impact of legal changes will depend on the effect they have on regulatory inspection practices, settlement policies and regulatory brokering of dialogue between stakeholders and corporate management.

Reactive liability

Reactive liability by reference to self-regulation can occur either by adjusting the determination of liability itself, or the determination of the penalty. The Delaware Court of Chancery's well-known *Caremark* decision is an example of directors' liability for corporate non-compliance conditioned upon the existence of an effective internal self-regulation system. In *Caremark* the court assessed the fairness of a proposed settlement in a shareholders' derivative action arising out of Caremark's criminal indictment on multiple felony counts of Medicare and Medicaid fraud which had resulted in payouts totalling US$250 million in civil and criminal litigation. The court held the directors could be held liable to the company for the amount paid, since the directors should:

> ... assure themselves that information and reporting systems exist in
> the organization that are reasonably designed to provide to senior
> management and to the Board itself timely, accurate information suf-
> ficient to allow management and the Board, each within its scope, to
> reach informed judgments concerning both the corporation's compli-
> ance with law and its business performance. (*In Re Caremark Interna-
> tional Inc. Derivative Litigation*, 1996 WL 549894 (Del. Ch. Sept. 25,
> 1996))

The *Caremark* decision effectively suggested that there is a duty upon
'directors to install and operate a corporate system of espionage to
ferret out wrongdoing which they have no reason to suspect exists'
(Barnard 1999: 987). Anecdotally, it is believed by US compliance professionals to have had a large effect on promoting the idea of good
compliance systems among directors.

Similarly in Australia, the *AWA* case made a huge impact on broadening Australian directors' perceptions of their responsibility for corporate governance (see Parker and Connolly forthcoming).[7] The
Supreme Court of New South Wales found that both the CEO and the
non-executive directors of a company could be found negligent for failing to ensure that adequate internal controls were in place to protect
against losses due to foreign exchange dealings.[8] The case made it very
clear that directors are individually responsible, not just for setting
broad policy but also for taking an active interest in ensuring adequate
corporate governance systems to effectively bring the company into
compliance with board policy.

Directors and managers are also being held accountable for social
responsibilities via strict vicarious liability for regulatory offences coupled with the availability of 'due diligence' defences or damages discounts for having in place a system to prevent breaches (Parker 1999d).
While the *Caremark* and *AWA* cases rely on general principles of company law to hold senior officers liable to shareholders for breach of their
duties, here the liability is under regulatory law and can potentially
make them subject to criminal or civil suit by either a regulator or
affected stakeholder. 'Due diligence' defences occur where directors and
top management are made personally liable for a regulatory offence
committed by an agent of the corporation, but can escape liability if they
can show they had in place an effective internal control or compliance
system to prevent the breach occurring. For example, many pieces of
environmental legislation deem directors and managers directly liable
for high financial penalties, or even prison sentences, for environmental

offences if the company is found guilty, unless they can prove a due diligence defence applies (e.g. Streets 1998). As we have seen in the ACCC case study above, in Australian trade practices regulation, for example, the courts have repeatedly discounted damages for breach where an effective compliance system exists, and the ACCC regularly negotiates settlements and/or damages on this basis (Parker 1999a).

It is neither efficient nor fair to rely on negligence law/directors' duties or glosses on specific areas of regulatory law to spell out the extent to which various corporate officers and employees can have their liability adjusted by reference to self-regulation systems. In Chapter 8 I argued that there ought to be a basic set of Principles for Self-Regulation set out by an international organization such as the OECD and/or by national governments, perhaps in the main company law of each country, that could be a guide for corporate self-regulation in all regulatory regimes. Here my proposal is that these principles ought to be explicitly made to have an application to *all* areas of civil and criminal liability in which an organization might be defendant.

One of the best-known ways in which something like this has been attempted has been through the US Sentencing Commission's Federal Sentencing Guidelines for organizations (USSC 1992; see also Fiorelli 1993; Gruner 1994; Kaplan et al. 2000). This is an example of a regulatory design that provides incentives for high voluntary compliance by providing that the existence of an effective compliance system will provide companies or individuals with a reduction of penalty if they are found to have breached the law. These guidelines were promulgated by the US Sentencing Commission (a judicial agency) and went into effect in absence of congressional action. The Guidelines define what makes up the basic elements of a good compliance program:

1 Compliance standards and procedures reasonably capable of reducing the prospect of criminal conduct.
2 Specific high-level personnel assigned responsibility to oversee compliance.
3 Due care not to delegate to individuals who had a propensity to engage in illegal activities.
4 Steps to communicate effectively its standards and procedures to all employees and other agents, e.g. training programs and publications.
5 Reasonable steps to achieve compliance with its standards, e.g. monitoring, auditing and reporting systems.

6   Standards consistently enforced through disciplinary mechanisms.

7   After an offence detected, organization takes all reasonable steps to respond appropriately and prevent further similar offences, including modifications to compliance program.

Those organizations that have a compliance program that meet the criteria are given decreased fines when they commit an offence. Those that do not have in place a compliance program are placed on probation, and required to implement one.

The Federal Sentencing Guidelines are a good example of the impact that legal tools that attempt to tie crises to commitment can reasonably be expected to have. The direct impact of the guidelines has been quite small – few organizations have claimed to have an effective compliance program in a sentencing hearing, and even fewer have been judged to have one for the purpose of a sentence discount. Parker and Atkins (1999: 444–5) compared post-Guidelines data on corporate sentencing from 1992 to 1995 with pre-Guidelines data for corporations sentenced in 1988. The data (from the USSC) indicated that in that time 27 companies had been found to have an effective program for the purposes of receiving a discount, while 166 were assessed by the court as not having one. This would indicate a near doubling of compliance program incidence from 1998 to 1992–95 (i.e. from 4.3 per cent to 8.3 per cent, and possibly a more significant difference if one took into account whether or not the corporation's compliance system was actively enforced and otherwise 'effective').[9]

The deeper impact of the Federal Sentencing Guidelines has been on corporate perceptions of acceptable practices and in regulators' prosecution and settlement policies. Firstly, the Guidelines approach has spread to many other regulators who are now willing to not prosecute at all if an enterprise can show it has a program in place that meets the USSC Guidelines and/or voluntarily disclose breaches discovered through that program. Several US agencies, including the Department of Health and Human Services (health care fraud compliance),[10] the Environment Protection Agency,[11] the Department of Defense (defense contractors)[12] and Department of Justice (for antitrust and environmental offences and now more generally in relation to all prosecutions of corporations),[13] have guidelines that require them to consider the quality and effectiveness of a regulated company's compliance mechanisms in deciding whether to initiate civil or criminal proceedings.

Secondly, the Guidelines have had a significant impact on the implementation of compliance policies among US companies generally (irrespective of whether they have had any contact with a regulator). Surveys have found that up to 20 per cent of companies surveyed introduced an internal system for ensuring regulatory compliance for the first time because of the Guidelines, and up to 45 per cent added vigour to an existing internal compliance system because of them (Harvard Law Review 1996; Price Waterhouse 1997; both discussed in Chapter 1).

The reactive liability approach can be taken one step further by tailoring regulatory inspection programs on the basis of the risk presented by different firms, which can be calculated by reference to whether they have an effective self-regulation or compliance system in place. For example, if the enterprise has conducted its own risk analysis and put in place its own compliance system, it may be a lower priority for inspection than an enterprise that has not. Further, when the self-regulating enterprise is inspected, the inspection may occur on the basis of checking the functions and outcomes of the enterprise's own compliance system (and, especially, its self-evaluation – see discussion of meta-evaluation in Phase Three below), rather than fragmented and specific regulatory rules (see Parker 1999d: 33–5 for examples).

A number of financial regulators have developed quite sophisticated models for tiering regulatory and inspection requirements for financial institutions according to assessments of *risk* that include an assessment of the compliance and risk management systems the entities themselves have decided to put in place (e.g. IMRO 1997). This approach is being actively encouraged by international associations of financial regulators such as the Basle Committee on Banking Supervision and the International Organization of Securities Commissions (Braithwaite and Drahos 2000: 141). These systems are more accountable and clearer where there is a basis in the law for adjusting the liability of companies with an effective self-regulation system, especially where the law sets out some consistent simple guidelines for what an effective self-regulation system must contain.

Corporate 'probation'

The second strategy is to use the coercive powers of the court or regulator, or the threat of such action, to require or encourage a company to implement a self-regulation system when a breach has been alleged or held to have occurred. The suggestions above looked backwards to condition liability on whether the company had or has an effective self-regulation system in place. Here we look forward and use liability and regulatory leverage to force companies to implement a self-regulation program for the future. This places the company on 'probation' since, if the program is not implemented, or not implemented effectively, further liability may ensue. There is no necessity that such an order should attach only to corporate criminal liability. It is equally suitable for civil liability, or as a condition of settlement or amnesty for potential regulatory action at the administrative level.

A number of scholars have suggested that a corporation could be given a probation order when it is found to be in breach of some regulatory compliance obligation. This might require them to rectify the problem, to implement a compliance system and/or to employ a compliance officer (e.g. Foster et al. 1998; Friedrichs 1996: 347; Fisse and Braithwaite 1993: 147–53). The USSC Guidelines do include, as we have seen, a provision that, in criminal cases, corporations which do not already have an effective compliance system should be put on probation to implement one (see Coffee et al. 1988). As Foster and co-authors (1998) argue, court-ordered implementation of a compliance program is a superior alternative to punitive damages (which are used extensively by US courts) in civil cases. While punitive damages rely on economic deterrence (that may or may not affect individual employee behaviour), probation orders actually have some hope of modifying and improving corporate behaviour, and serve as models that other organizations can follow to prevent breaches. (See Foster et al. 1998: 263–5 for a number of cases and pieces of legislation in which probationary type orders have been made or authorized in the USA.) As the ACCC case study at the beginning of this chapter indicated, in Australia the Federal Court is now being given explicit power to make corporate probation orders in relation to trade practices breaches.

Again, the actual incidence of court-ordered implementation of a compliance or self-regulation system is unlikely to make a huge practical difference, given the small proportion of corporations that are ever held liable in criminal or civil proceedings for breaches. Rather, it is the effect that legal recognition of the concept has on regulators' settlement policies and the way in which individual regulatory officials decide how to exercise their discretion that is important. Warin and Schwartz (1998: 72) quote USSC figures that show that, under the Guidelines in 1995 and 1996, 13.4 and 11.9 per cent, respectively, of organizational defendants were actually ordered to implement a compliance program. However,

Warin and Schwartz also find that settlement agreements by a number of regulatory agencies regularly require the implementation of compliance systems that can include the following elements: significant involvement from the board of directors; designation of a corporate compliance officer or committee; inspection of company books and records by the government; voluntary disclosure of wrongdoing to the government; waiver of any applicable privileges; and provision of training to company employees, managers and executives. Specific legislative authorization of regulators to use settlements that require implementation of self-regulation systems and that set out some guidelines on how to do so and what they should include make this discretion more accountable. In Australia the ACCC's enforceable undertakings powers have been very successful (Fels 2000). Because they are enforceable in court, they are more powerful than informal settlements, but also potentially subject to judicial oversight and accountability.

Finally, where the law and/or the regulator generally recognizes that implementation of a self-regulation program is an appropriate response to wrongdoing, regulators can also use it as a bargaining chip in brokering dialogue with stakeholders. For example, many anti-discrimination 'regulators' use the introduction of an anti-discrimination program as a bargaining chip in the conciliation of complaints between individual complainants and organizations. The study of forty discrimination conciliation files in Australia (from the Human Rights and Equal Opportunity Commission) by Devereux (1996) suggested that the existence of the hearing mechanism had been used to advantage in ensuring that respondents acceded to proposed conciliated settlements, especially in Sex Discrimination Act cases. In employment cases commission staff often encouraged settlements that included not only remedies for the individuals involved but also undertakings to implement EEO or sexual harassment training programs which might engender wider cultural change within the organization.[14]

Phase One of the corporate institutionalization of legal and social responsibility involves a sophisticated legal design. Liability needs to be tailored to motivate self-regulation by crises of conscience among as many people and units within the organization who can take responsibility as possible. Liability alone is not enough. It must be tied to signals and incentives that promote implementation of effective self-regulation. Otherwise crises of conscience peter out as the crisis passes. Restorative justice, on the other hand, motivates ongoing commitment to act on a pricked conscience by moving forward to Phases Two and Three of the institutionalization of responsibility.

Phase Two: Acquisition of skills and knowledge

What role can law and regulators play in the acquisition of self-regulation skills and knowledge by corporations? Understanding the details and technicalities of business processes and systems is not necessarily a great strength of regulatory institutions. Lack of such expertise is one of the primary criticisms of command-and-control regulation, and one of the main arguments in favour of more flexible self-regulation oriented regulatory instruments. Rather, the acquisition of skills and knowledge often occurs as part of a dynamic of leadership and innovation by some companies that is modelled and diffused to others.

Consider the level of acquisition of self-regulation skills and knowledge by companies as occurring along a normal curve (see Figure 9.1). Ideally, the movement occurs in two ways: firstly, the practices of the leading edge are modelled by those closest to them, and diffused throughout the curve as they become standard industry practice – through the professional expertise and networking of self-regulation professionals who are hired by more and more firms, and through the normal expectations of regulators, co-contractors, investors, customers and the general public. Secondly, the leading edge will creep forward as companies innovate in self-regulation processes and skills (usually in response to crises faced by themselves or their competitors). The effect is that the whole normal curve undulates forward. The role of government is to foster innovation and movement in this process to avoid stagnation. However, government generally cannot expect to directly impose appropriate skills and knowledge.

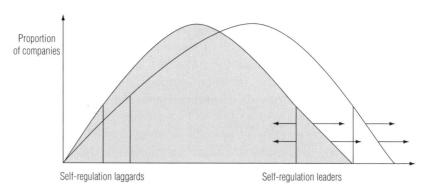

Proportion of companies

Self-regulation laggards   Self-regulation leaders

Level of acquisition of self-regulation skills, and implementation of self-regulation processes

Figure 9.1 Acquisition of self-regulation skills

Some commentators have suggested that this requires governments to formally tier their regulatory efforts in various areas. For example, Gunningham and Grabosky (1998: 402) discuss the possibility of offering distinct but standardized regulatory paths to enterprises with different credentials, characteristics and histories of compliance (see also Gunningham and Johnstone 1999: 92–172). The track offered to 'leaders' would be more flexible and attractive than that offered to the average enterprise, while another track with greater monitoring and reporting requirements might be required for 'laggards' or those 'on probation' after a serious non-compliance episode. For example, Cruickshanks-Boyd and Mantle (1996) propose the following four 'tracks' for regulation of the chemical industry:[15]

1   *Companies wishing to lead the field in health, safety and environment management:* These companies will have taken advantage of the incentives of the category below and will now be leading industry and working in partnership with government.

2   *Companies that have adequate health, safety and environment systems in place* (through involvement in the chemical industry's self-regulatory Responsible Care program): They should be encouraged by regulatory recognition of their Responsible Care achievements and observed benefits.

3   *Companies that are basically willing to comply but require clear information on how to do so with minimum standards:* They should be encouraged through education.

4   *Companies that do not comply:* Compliance should be forced by penalties.

These four categories move from the strongest to the weakest companies on health, safety and environment awareness, intent, know-how and capability; and from facilitation to enforcement in terms of the proposed government stance towards them.

The aim is for the regulatory responses to provide motivation and incentives for companies in each category to move up one notch. Companies in the fourth category have not even started the journey of institutionalization of social and legal responsibility. The appropriate response is for regulators to use strategies of accountability (described above in Phase One) that attempt to motivate them to self-regulate. In the third category, companies have some commitment to compliance but little knowledge and skills. The appropriate response is for regulators to guide and educate them on compliance. In the second category, companies have approximately equal health, safety and environment management skills and knowledge as regulators do. The appropriate regulatory response is therefore to judge, recognize and reward companies that put those skills and knowledge into practice. In the first category, companies have greater knowledge and skills of corporate management processes than regulators do. Regulators can learn in partnership with these companies, experiment with new ideas for improving compliance with regulatory goals and use this experience to change laws, regulatory standards and education programs that apply to all companies. The second, and especially first, category of companies may receive concessions or exemptions from the ordinary rules and penalties that apply to first and second category companies. Their exemplary performance will be reinforced through praise by regulators, which seems to work for them (see Makkai and J. Braithwaite 1993).

Regulatory strategies for moving forward the snail of acquisition of self-regulation skills and expertise may or may not involve formal regulatory tracks. However, they certainly must involve some flexibility in the range of enforcement responses available for different companies and a place for review and change over time, in order to respond to and improve different levels of skill and capacity for self-regulation. It is helpful to be aware of the following four regulatory toolkits for companies with different capacities.

Category One: Building compliance leadership

The promotion of permeable self-management requires legal and regulatory institutions that are not satisfied with rule compliance but which foster integrity and responsibility 'beyond the law' within a broader democracy. This will usually require either technological or management innovation (see, for example, Porter and van der Linde 1995 on environmental regulation). Category One applies to those (very few) leading companies who have acquired outstanding self-regulation skills and expertise, or at least have the commitment and capacity to do so with appropriate incentives. They only require liability in relation to broad outcome standards and reporting requirements to ensure they continue to evaluate their own performance (i.e. Phase Three regulation). Smart regulatory agencies look for innovative solutions to regulatory problems that go beyond compliance in the best firms and encourage them, test them, get community input and involvement, and then use them as a basis for understanding what can be required of other firms. The aim of Category One approaches to regulating self-regulation is to foster, create and identify compliance leaders who provide the models of skills and knowledge that can then be passed on to others (albeit perhaps only when a crisis hits).

This does not mean that regulators should just sit and wait to harness voluntary corporate innovations in self-regulation. Regulators can look for opportunities to foster innovation themselves by focusing on:

- companies that are having intractable problems and are therefore open to innovative solutions. For example, Chapter 8 discussed the example of the Victorian EPA's initiative with the Altona plant to develop an environmental improvement plan (with community involvement in dialogues brokered by the regulator) to solve constant community opposition. This initiative later became the basis for a series of environmental improvement plans brokered in a similar way at other sites, which were in turn the basis for the 'accredited licensee' concept – a more flexible licensing regime for sites with proven records of community consultation and self-regulation; and
- market leaders with a far-sighted view (or those who want to be!), who want to reap first-mover advantages in relation to potential new areas of regulatory activity and social concern. Australia's Greenhouse Challenge (discussed in Chapter 3) is a good example of this approach. A government agency signs up a dozen leading companies to audit and reduce greenhouse emissions in return for positive publicity benefits and free consultancy services. The voluntary agreement then spreads to hundreds of other companies of varying sizes, and it is possible to use this as a basis for compulsory reporting and verification audit requirements.

In this approach government uses rewards and incentives to encourage a small group of 'compliance leaders' to enter experimental programs for new regulatory approaches (such as moving from rule-based to a standard- or process-based regulation). In this way the enterprises receive rewards for high compliance with policy objectives under the experimental regime. Governments learn from them how to practically reform existing regulatory approaches and what is feasible to expect of business. Rewards for effective innovation in permeable self-regulation could include a reduced burden of routine inspections, penalty discounts for minor incidents of non-compliance, simplified licences and permits, permission to use a label or mark certifying a high level of compliance, and indemnities for voluntary disclosure and correction of non-fraudulent non-compliance. Indeed, at least one of these mechanisms – a label or mark certifying a high level of compliance – could also be used by non-government organizations, even where national governments do not adequately regulate corporate activities.

Category Two: Process regulation

The second regulatory approach to improving capacity for self-regulation is for government to lead industry via process regulation. This is suitable where there is a large proportion of businesses that have not yet developed the skills and capacity for self-regulation in the relevant area. Government can teach them something about how to self-regulate by forcing them to go through a *process* of self-regulation. Process regulations are based on a systematic approach to controlling and minimizing risks. Process-based regulation includes mandating 'best available technology' in environmental regulation for pollution reduction. This is an example of regulation that builds on innovations developed by leaders (Category One above). As new technologies to improve outcomes are developed, they become binding on firms lower down the curve.

Process regulations can also be based on requiring organizations to take a systematic approach to identifying, controlling and minimizing risks. This form of regulation forces companies to go through their own internal learning process about the risks or hazards they face and how to control them. Thus it facilitates and enforces internal capacity-building. For example, there is a movement in both occupational health and safety and food regulation towards requiring firms to engage in their own process of hazard identification, risk assessment and risk control to achieve safety outcomes. Regulatory systems that use the HACCP (hazard analysis critical control points) system place the responsibility to determine and control for problems with the individual firms, allowing for a tailored approach to addressing risk rather than a one-size-fits-all regulatory strategy. HACCP systems require the identification of likely hazards and of critical control points in the production process where preventative measures are essential to avoid those hazards. Critical limits are established and monitored for the critical control points and corrective action is taken if the critical limits are passed (OECD 1997e: ch. 4).

Process regulations give firms the opportunity to incorporate regulatory goals into other business goals and operating procedures, and their flexibility may make controversial regulation more politically palatable. For example, Australia's affirmative action regime fits in with the business goals of good human resource management, rather than imposing particular targets for equal employment. The Australian Affirmative Action Act requires employers with over one hundred employees to develop an EEO policy, set objectives, monitor them and submit a report on their progress to the federal Affirmative Action Agency each year. It also requires assigning responsibility to a senior officer, consulting with trade unions, consulting with employees, particularly women, and the collection of statistics to observe the gender by job classification breakdown. It does not require businesses to meet any outcome standard in terms of gender representation in employment (although other laws do prohibit discrimination).

An evaluation of compliance with the Affirmative Action Act found that 96 per cent of those businesses registered with the Affirmative Action Agency had submitted a report to it as required by the Act. Other research has shown that women's managerial representation has increased at a significantly higher rate in firms covered by the legislation than in those that are not, and that affirmative action programs in general have steadily improved since the regime was introduced (Affirmative Action Agency 1997; V. Braithwaite 1993).

Category Three: Education and advice

The third approach addresses the problem of lack of commitment while still building capacity. Here regulators give advice and education for accomplishing compliance by publishing best practice guides, running seminars, setting up networks and seminars for compliance professionals, and being involved in developing voluntary management system standards. This is only useful where regulators have access to more expertise and skills on self-regulation processes than the target businesses do. It can work well in an arena where there is a stable body of compliance/self-regulation know-how, and the regulator helps to transfer that knowledge from the leaders (generally larger companies) to the laggards (which usually include the smaller companies). For example, a number of regulators find that offering education and advice is a particular priority for improving compliance by small and medium-sized enterprises (SMEs) (e.g. Weinberg 1996).

A more innovative way to add education and advice to regulatory regimes is for regulators to foster private markets for self-regulation consultancy services and compliance professionals. We saw in the case study at the beginning of this chapter that originally the ACCC set up a

Compliance Education Unit to offer consultancy and other services to industry. Yet government funding of compliance advice for enterprises is often not necessary, as private markets in compliance professionals develop. Regulators can nurture these private markets by recognizing and working with self-regulation professionals. This is one of the strategies that the ACCC has used to great effect. Encouraging the development of associations for compliance professionals can solidify and legitimate self-regulation skills and knowledge as a distinctive and important body of knowledge in its own right. This is a more proactive, long-lasting strategy than the mere transfer of static knowledge through seminars and best practice guidance.

Category Four: Building commitment

Companies in this category have not moved into the second phase on acquisition of skills and knowledge because they still have not developed commitment to implement a permeable self-regulation system. Therefore the fourth approach flips them back to the techniques described above in relation to Phase One, to try to awaken commitment through enforcement action, liability or publicity. The Phase One regulatory tools themselves lead into acquisition of skills and knowledge by attempting to tie some basic standards for self-regulation to liability.

Using combinations of the four categories

Generally some combination of these approaches will be appropriate in any particular regulatory regime at any particular time. The choices might change quite dramatically as industry motivation and skills change and develop, or slip backwards. Indeed, Categories One to Three could be used as a timeline for developing corporate regulation in a particular area. In the first place, regulators or policy makers might work with industry leaders to experiment and learn as to what level and processes of, say, greenhouse gas emissions reductions are feasible through purely voluntary initiatives. These leaders might be given special recognition through a tax incentive, a right to trade emissions reductions (in the future), or positive publicity. Using what they have learnt, the government might introduce a law or a licence condition that requires certain companies to go through a process of greenhouse gas emissions audit, consideration of reduction measures and public reporting on the results. Once a significant number of companies have become familiar with the process of emissions audit and reduction, in the third phase emissions reduction standards for all companies might be introduced with penalties for non-compliance. Companies who needed it would be given education by the regulator on how to comply. (Those who came in earlier might be able to now sell their surplus emissions reductions.) In the fourth phase, the penalties for non-compliance become stricter and more rigorously enforced. Guidance on best practice self-regulation processes become standards for probation orders for non-compliers.

Alternatively, different approaches could be used for different categories of companies simultaneously, through techniques such as:

- *Differential licensing:* Licence conditions often require companies to implement certain elements of self-regulation (e.g. internal monitoring and controls in securities dealers' licences, environmental management for industrial sites). Some regulators are experimenting with programs that give licensees a more flexible licence which allows them a greater degree of self-regulation and more lenient enforcement policies if they meet a higher standard of self-regulation than average (see Aalders 1993; Aalders and Wilthagen 1997; Environment Protection Authority 1993b).

- *Exemptions from normal regulation:* Regulators might be given a discretion to exempt particular companies that meet high standards of self-regulation from the need to comply with the full letter of the law. Or they might reward these companies by exempting them from the full load of regulatory inspections and enforcement. One well-established example of how this can improve socially desirable outcomes is the Voluntary Protection Program (VPP) of the US Occupational Safety and Health Administration (OSHA). Under this program OSHA recognizes outstanding achievement by companies that successfully integrate a comprehensive safety and health program into their total management system.[16] Applicants to VPP must demonstrate in writing that their occupational safety and health compliance program includes management commitment and employee involvement, worksite-based job hazard analysis including baseline surveys of working conditions throughout the facility, hazard prevention and control, and safety and health training. The process also requires follow-up using annual program evaluations, verified by OSHA on-site every one to five years. Employers with exceptional programs receive special recognition, including: the lowest priority for enforcement inspections, the highest priority for assistance, appropriate regulatory relief, and penalty reductions of up to 100 per cent. For other firms a sliding scale of incentives is offered. The outcomes have been quite impressive (see Feitshans with Oliver 1997; see also Geltman and Skroback 1998 for an analysis of various similar programs developed by the US Environment Protection Agency).

- *Outcome standards combined with safe harbours:* Here trustworthy companies, or companies in an industry where self-regulation capacity is well developed and privately available, can be made responsible for outcomes, rather than having self-regulation processes regulated. The aim is to be as flexible as possible about the processes allowed for achieving compliance with the outcomes, while also providing the option of complying with a set of detailed guidelines or using a certain technology to ensure the required performance. Outcome standards can improve compliance by reducing the costs of compliance with technical rules and encouraging innovation to find the most effective ways to reach socially desired outcomes. One well-known example of the advantages that can be gained from broader, more flexible outcome regulation is the Amoco Yorktown experiment. In 1990 Amoco and the US EPA formed a partnership to study pollution reduction possibilities at the Yorktown refinery. They found that Amoco would be able to achieve the same level of emissions reduction required under the US Clean Air Act for a quarter of the cost (US$10 million instead of US$40 million) if the EPA would allow Amoco to decide where the money should be spent through innovations in process engineering, rather than applying specific rules mandating smokestack technology. However, the whole exercise cost US$2.3 million and, although the EPA paid 30 per cent of that cost, other Amoco plants and other companies in the refining business did not want to spend that amount of money looking for money-saving options. Nor could the EPA actually change its rules to be more outcome-based without legislative action (see Schmitt 1994; Howard 1994: 7–8 for descriptions of the experiment). When performance-based regulation is used, *safe harbours* can meet the needs of SMEs or other enterprises that do not have the capacity to engage in the innovation necessary to meet outcome-based standards on their own. For example, occupational safety and health legislation in the UK sets broad performance standards but also detailed codes of practice for guidance, which regulated entities can follow in order to meet the standards.

In each of these cases, there is a primary regulatory scheme and the regulator (or others) is given discretion to help reinforce self-regulation by adjusting the way in which the regulation applies to companies in different categories.

The problem of regulatory accountability

All these strategies raise issues about the accountability of the use of regulators' discretion to decide which companies fall into which category. On the one hand, flexibility is required in order to allow adequate opportunity for companies to take advantage of the incentives to move through the regulatory tiers. On the other hand, if this is achieved by giving regulators a lot of discretion, then their accountability for the use of that discretion will be at issue. This is likely to be especially problematic where some companies are subject to penalties and rules from which others are given dispensations. Alternatively, if the formal law sets out the tiers and their requirements in too much detail, there will be little flexibility for partnership and learning from industry about what works best.

A good example of both the benefits and problems of a regulatory tiering strategy is US OSHA's Maine 200 program and its proposed expansion into the Cooperative Compliance Program (CCP). The Maine OSHA office used workers compensation databases to identify the 200 employers with the highest number (not rate) of injuries and illnesses in their area. OSHA requested their cooperation in improving work conditions by committing to a comprehensive safety and health program that included employee participation, self-inspections, identification of worksite hazards, training programs, other strategies to reduce and prevent hazards, and quarterly reporting to OSHA. Employers who chose to accept OSHA's request received a significantly lower priority for inspections and a higher priority for technical assistance. The others would be targeted for inspection due to their risk prioritization. All but five of the firms chose to join the voluntary program. As of

December 1995 (nearly two years into the program), participating firms had identified 180 000 hazards and abated over 128 000 of those hazards (in comparison with the 36 780 that OSHA inspectors had discovered and cited in the previous eight years at those sites). Total workers compensation claims dropped by 47.3 per cent in those worksites during the program between 1991 and 1994 (see Parker 1999d: 17–19; see also Gunningham and Johnstone 1999: 82). [17]

The CCP would have extended nationally to 12 500 workplaces. Participation in the program involved identifying and correcting hazards, and establishing a comprehensive safety and health program that went beyond OSHA standards. The proposed program was very controversial. The US Chamber of Commerce and others challenged it in court and won on the grounds that it had the structure and effect of a rule in the way it structured OSHA discretions (particularly in relation to the compliance program requirement for entry into the program). Therefore OSHA should have provided a public notice and comment period (see Sparrow 2000: 252–4).

The problem here was that OSHA attempted to rely on administrative discretion to change in a fundamental way how law and regulatory strategy applied to companies. In effect OSHA was attempting to condition a significant part of its regulatory program on the implementation of an effective self-regulation program. Parts of industry felt that OSHA could not simply set out guidelines for an effective self-regulation program as a matter of administrative discretion, if so much was to ride on it. The ruling against OSHA is not merely a 'temporary set back' (Sparrow 2000: 254). It also shows a fundamental need for change in the way the formal law sets out the powers that regulators should have in relation to corporate self-regulation programs. It also illustrates the accountability problem when regulators move ahead of the formal law's setting out of principles for self-regulation. In Australia the ACCC and other regulators have run into similar problems when they have tried to make agreements to implement broad-ranging preventive compliance programs part of settlement agreements. Again courts have seen this as going beyond the narrow confines of legislation that was not written with a company's capacity to self-regulate in mind (Voon 1998).

Regulatory powers and discretions set out in law must now be predicated on corporate capacity to self-regulate. Law should set out some basic principles for effective self-regulation, as proposed in Chapter 8 and in the discussion of prompting commitment above. This would mean that regulators' policies in relation to corporate self-regulation would be squarely within basic principles set out in the law, and regulators' discretions to be more flexible in the way they applied the law would be partially conditioned on principles of effective self-regulation clearly set out in the law. Regulators will need both more flexibility and more accountability than they currently have to use tiered strategies to build self-regulation capacity.

Similarly the formal terms of the law should change to explicitly recognize the range of appropriate regulatory responses to corporate attempts to institutionalize responsibility. I will also argue in the conclusion to this chapter that regulators should be held accountable for their choice of regulatory tools (both on a general industry/regulatory regime level or company by company level). They should be required to report on empirical evidence of state of industry compliance, knowledge and implementation of compliance systems, and impact of regulatory activity on those levels.

PHASE THREE: INSTITUTIONALIZATION OF PURPOSE

Ultimately communities and stakeholders need to know that corporate self-regulation policies and procedures do make a difference to day-to-day operating procedures, management practices and employee conduct – that the policy of self-regulation is robustly institutionalized throughout the company and has the desired effect. As we have seen, commitment is likely to peter out and institutionalization to become difficult in time. In the new regulatory state, corporate self-regulation should not be an easy way out for either government or industry. It is the state's role to evaluate corporate self-regulation, both to hold industry accountable and to make itself accountable to its own stakeholders (citizens who need to know whether government policy is accomplishing its objectives).

There are two traditional ways for law and regulators to hold companies accountable for how well they institutionalize the goals of regulation:

- *Outcome standards:* Here the company is liable in relation to its outcomes (e.g. pollution levels, worker injuries and deaths). It does not matter what self-regulation process is in place – the outcomes are what matters. Taxation and other economic incentives (e.g. emissions trading regimes) can be a more indirect way of attempting to regulate outcomes. Similarly, regulation of disclosure of information can be an indirect form of outcome regulation by requiring companies to disclose outcome information that is then used by third parties to hold the company accountable in various ways (in the market for finance or reputation).

• *Process regulation:* Secondly, the regulator can attempt to regulate the corporation's self-regulation processes (as discussed above) – for example, by requiring an affirmative action program with certain features, or affixing detailed standards for a program to a licensing regime. Here liability is attached to whether the process is in place rather than to its outcomes. The rationale is that by adopting the process the outcomes will generally improve. It also means that the regulator can be directly involved in supervising the standard of self-regulation implemented. I suggested above that process regulation is best suited to situations where industry compliance in an area is young. Disclosure regulation can also be aimed at processes rather than outcomes, such as Australia's affirmative action regime (discussed above) or the London Stock Exchange requirement that companies report on their implementation of the Cadbury Code for governance.

The *outcome regulation* approach does not explicitly recognize that law and regulatory action ought to recognize, foster and hold accountable the capacity for corporate self-regulation. It ignores internal self-regulation processes. This may be appropriate once effective permeable self-regulation processes are already well developed in an industry or a sector of an industry, and government interference is not necessary. But these situations are rare. Outcome regulation alone is not appropriate where there is little business knowledge and skills for self-regulation processes, or little diffusion of self-regulation skills and practices throughout industry. Furthermore, it does not accomplish the objectives set out in Chapter 8 in relation to the reporting and transparency of corporate self-regulation processes. This is necessary to facilitate stakeholder accountability and consultation, even for leading companies.

The *self-regulation process regulation* approach appears to overcome these problems. But the trouble is that regulators are not necessarily well equipped to evaluate corporate processes for compliance and self-regulation. The process regulation approach is only appropriate where the regulator can lead industry (or segments of it) in knowledge and skills for self-regulation. Often, however, regulatory agencies will be acquiring self-regulation system skills and knowledge at the same time as industry leaders, or even after them.

Many regulatory regimes combine process- and outcome-style regulation to cover each other's disadvantages. But combination approaches multiply regulation and standards. This is an approach to regulating self-regulation that does not leave any space for the integrity of the corporation's own internal self-governance, and therefore little space for *self*-regulation at all. How can regulation check that companies really do internally institutionalize legal and social responsibility, without destroying the integrity of self-regulation?

It is at this phase of corporate institutionalization of social and legal responsibility that the unique features of 'meta-regulation' are most important – regulation at one remove to preserve the integrity of corporate self-regulation while ensuring its 'permeability'.

Meta-evaluation

Effective corporate self-regulation depends on the company obtaining adequate information about its responsibilities in the context of its social and legal environment, relating that information to decision-making processes and operating norms, detecting significant deviations and taking corrective action. Self-regulation is not self-regulation at all if it does not include regular self-evaluation to determine whether the organization is accomplishing the objectives it set out to achieve in a changing set of internal and external contexts – 'double-loop learning'. As we saw in Chapter 8, self-evaluation is probably the point at which existing corporate self-regulation is weakest.

Ensuring that corporate self-evaluation of self-regulation occurs is also a weak part of regulators' performance. Most regulatory programs that seek to foster corporate compliance systems are content with implementation of a compliance program. They do not also require companies to disclose breaches discovered, and other results of self-regulation performance evaluations. Citizens require double-loop learning at the corporate level and a triple loop of regulatory learning: meta-evaluation. Regulators should revise their regulatory objectives (including their strategies for fostering and holding accountable self-regulation) in the light of corporate double-loop learning (see Figure 9.2).

Some scholars of corporate self-regulation and compliance propose strategies of meta-regulation in which regulators rely on independent

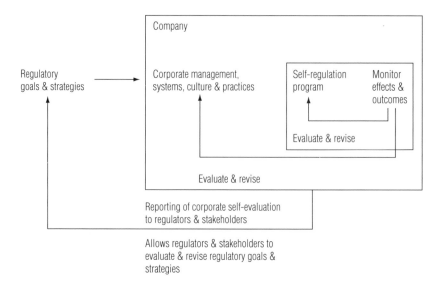

FIGURE 9.2 'Triple-loop' evaluation of self-regulation

audits of corporate self-regulation. For example, Coleman (1985: 84) has suggested that companies could hire private, independent professionals to perform functional audits of their compliance and ethics to uncover irregularities and report the results to regulators (see also Fisse and Braithwaite 1993; Grabosky 1995). The ACCC's enforceable undertakings (mentioned at the beginning of this chapter) rely on this strategy. A condition of the undertaking is that the company have an independent professional approved by the ACCC report on their implementation of the undertaking to management and to the ACCC at certain intervals.

The key to meta-evaluation is to enforce requirements for companies to go through their *own* processes of audit, review and continuous improvement, and to report those processes and their outcomes. Independent auditors should only need to conduct the primary evaluation where the company is 'on probation'. In general, corporate management should first evaluate their own self-regulation performance, since it is they who must learn from and act on the evaluation. Of course they will often choose to use independent professionals to help them in that process, and should also involve community representatives through initiatives such as the Canadian version of audits of Responsible Care implementation in the chemical industry (see Chapter 8). But evaluation should be seen firstly as a part of the self-regulation process itself, not as an external check. The role of the state is then to provide mechanisms for the meta-evaluation of these evaluations through standards and reporting requirements.

There are at least three ways in which regulation can meta-evaluate self-evaluation:

- reporting and verification requirements;
- self-evaluation as a regulatory requirement; and
- immunities for self-disclosure and self-correction.

Reporting and verification requirements

The first is to encourage self-evaluation by requiring companies to report on their implementation of self-regulation processes, what standards they meet, and their own evaluations of how well they are working. This facilitates broad diffusion of accountability – any stakeholder can evaluate their performance. Reporting requirements force corporate management to go through at least the level of self-evaluation that is necessary to make disclosure. In Chapter 8 I proposed that they should be required to report on:

- the implementation of *Justice Plans* (i.e. policies for contestation by stakeholders);
- the implementation and evaluation of 'systems' aspects of their self-regulation programs (i.e. their implementation of the *Self-Regulation Principles* suggested in Chapter 8); and
- the *outcomes or performance* of these systems.

More detailed reporting could be required by particular regulatory regimes in relation to specific issues of concern – for example, exact amounts of emissions of certain pollutants by environmental regulation, job by gender statistics by anti-discrimination regulators – or as a result of particular agreements between stakeholders and particular companies.

Regulatory reporting requirements (either in law, or stock exchange requirements) could be made subject to audit and verification requirements in order to improve the quality of the information disclosed. The problem is that traditional audit and verification methodologies are not well suited to checking what stakeholders really need to know about corporate institutionalization of self-regulation.

Firstly, there is a 'general tendency for audit processes to gravitate towards formal systems elements'. Regulators rely on auditors to provide 'cold comfort' certificates verifying companies' compliance process reviews, but generating no useful information concerning the substance of companies' self-regulation performance (Power 1997: 56, 126). Even if they do produce some useful information, there are no guarantees that the information has actually been used to improve the company's performance.

Secondly, self-regulation audits are frequently 'not designed to support public debate or to connect the audit process to wider representative organs or to further machinery of regulatory escalation ... the audit process ... is not a basis for rational public deliberation. It is a dead end in the chain of accountability' (Power 1997: 127). The idea of a 'social audit', a critical evaluation conducted by or with the participation of external stakeholders, became popular in the early 1970s but was never implemented sufficiently to live up to expectations (Ackerman and Bauer 1976: 225; Power 1997: 62–3).

Companies with leading self-regulation programs have developed a variety of *process* measures of systems and implementation, including:[18]

- reviews to determine whether hotlines are operating effectively, whether employees have been trained, whether environmental monitoring devices are properly installed and operating;
- keeping records of seminar attendance, requests for extra training, use of hotline, requests for assistance, use of guides/computerized compliance systems, functioning of compliance meetings;
- tests of staff understanding of compliance procedures and issues through surveys, computer-based training;
- keeping track of potential costs saved or value added through greater efficiency, and so on;
- setting management plans (both for systems and for staff) with objectives, targets and programs/tasks and keeping a record of whether those objectives have been achieved; and
- building compliance into the job profiles of management and operational staff and measuring for performance on the basis of supervisors' observations and reviews undertaken by compliance department, internal audit, and so on.

Leading companies use benchmarking as a measure of relative performance in process implementation. One company's compliance processes or outcomes are measured against other 'best-in-class' companies with similar operations. Two companies can choose to benchmark against one another, or one company can benchmark itself against industry or best-in-class averages obtained from survey data on ethics and self-regulation programs (now readily available from some of the large consulting firms). There is little if any publicly available data on which to benchmark (the consulting firms keep most of their data for paying clients, and regulators are only slowly collecting data on companies' self-regulation performance). This means that external stakeholders, including regulators and courts, have little data on which to judge relative performance or to discriminate between companies on the basis of their self-regulation systems. Furthermore, since benchmarking achieves only measures of relative performance, it will generally not give the objective assurance that regulators, courts and some external stakeholders would like. If industry performance is generally low in some area, even a good score in benchmarking may still indicate an unacceptable level of non-compliance or non-compliance risk.

A number of companies review their performance against voluntary management standards (a number of which have already been discussed). The most apposite is the Australian Standard on Compliance Programs: AS 3806–1998. This standard divides the requirements for a compliance program into 'structural, operational and maintenance elements'. The *structural* elements include a written statement of the organization's compliance policy and how it will be carried out, commitment to effective compliance from the board and senior management down through all levels of the organization, and adequate compliance staff. The *operational* elements set out how to implement a compliance program by firstly identifying the compliance issues likely to be raised by a particular company's organization and operation; secondly, creating ways for integrating compliance into day-to-day operating procedures; and then training staff to implement it, ensuring that managers supervise it, enforcing its implementation at every level, and putting in place systems for handling complaints, identifying compliance failures and rectifying them.

The standard also provides that the company should ensure the compliance program is appropriately *maintained* through practical education and training for staff at induction and on an ongoing basis, through regularly publicizing and communicating the organization's commitment to compliance and relevant compliance issues to staff, and liaising regularly with regulatory authorities and community groups to keep up to date with compliance issues. Most significantly, the program must also be monitored, assessed and reviewed to ensure its effectiveness. The organization should be made accountable for the effectiveness of the program by reporting on the operation of the compliance program against performance standards (which could include the AS 3806 itself). A number of consultants and auditors in Australia are now offering to help companies to achieve compliance with the AS 3806.

Accreditation or compliance to a management system standard such as the AS 3806 is mainly a measure that the *design* of the self-regulation system meets set criteria, and that the design has been implemented in corporate management processes. There is no assurance that managers and employees are actually behaving in compliance with corporate legal and social responsibilities (compliance outcomes), or that the system is adequate to improve the general outputs of the company (e.g. product safety, environmental health in the local area, perceptions of human rights abuses). However, most management system standards will require companies to have in place systems that attempt to make these judgments, so that they are not completely forgotten.

The AS 3806 also has some other problems. It is a confusing document which contains a multitude of detail for elements of compliance system processes, but no clear over-riding substantive principles and objectives. The three main organizing principles – structure, operation and mainte-nance – are purely process-oriented. It provides little guidance to compa-nies as to the substantive principles that make compliance work. This means that a company that self-reports or is independently accredited as AS 3806-compliant is not telling regulators and stakeholders information that they really need to know about how well it is performing in self-reg-ulation. The seven steps for effective compliance programs set out in the USSC's sentencing guidelines (set out above in this chapter) are more ele-gant (and therefore easier to use and understand) and more oriented towards the substance of what makes a difference in self-regulation.

Ultimately regulators and external stakeholders need to know from a company's evaluation of its own self-regulation program that:

- *basic self-regulation principles are in place*, as described in Chapter 8 (i.e. connection with employee values, stakeholder engage-ment, and management systems that include discipline, Justice Plans, appropriate governance arrangements, and self-evalua-tion; see Table 8.1);
- *breaches of the law and other social responsibilities (voluntarily adopted by the company) have been identified and corrected*. Regula-tors and stakeholders do not want merely the 'cold comfort' of seeing that self-regulation systems are in place. They need to

know that the systems are actually working to identify problems and to improve them. The assumption behind traditional audits is that they will simply verify the accounts of most companies (see Power 1997: 126). The assumption here, by contrast, is that if evaluations do not find breaches and problems (and lead to their correction and improvement), then there is something wrong with the evaluation process.

- there are *substantive outcomes* from the program. In order to judge a company's self-regulation, regulators and stakeholders need to know what impact, if any, it has on the values or goals it is supposed to promote, for example the environmental quality of the local area, total emissions, number of regulatory incidents and their outcomes, number of worker injuries, worker health, customer complaints and satisfaction.

It is to these standards that reporting and verification should be aimed. By requiring companies to publicly report this information in their annual reports, on their websites or to a public database kept by the regulator, this information can stimulate public debate and accountability. When all three categories of information are reported, stakeholders are in a position to turn 'cold comfort' audits into the 'heated discomfort' for corporate management that might prompt improvement.

Corporate self-evaluation
The second possibility moves beyond mere general reporting to building self-evaluation into substantive regulatory requirements. Companies could be required to engage in self-evaluation of their own self-regulation processes as an integral part of their broader regulatory requirements. This gives regulators more opportunity to check that business actually does something about the results of its self-evaluations. A self-evaluation requirement could be included in many substantive regulatory requirements. Licensing requirements, process regulation, discretionary exemption from the law, outcome standards, probation, and liability can all be predicated partly on adequate self-evaluation of self-regulation as judged by the regulator.

For example, it is particularly appropriate to include a self-evaluation requirement in corporate probation orders. Thus, recent s. 87B undertakings entered into by the ACCC require the companies to report their own progress or to have their progress audited and reported to the ACCC at certain intervals. This makes the compliance program self-executing and gives the regulator the roles of enforcing the audit process and of meta-evaluating the evaluation process conducted by the company itself. If the company does not report any self-evaluation process, or if its self-evaluation is inadequate, the regulator escalates up the pyramid to enforce the process or, in more serious cases, abandons the use of compliance strategies for that particular company or industry altogether. This leaves the regulator free to encourage and enforce processes of deep learning in those companies that are committed to compliance (Argyris 1994). It flags as risky those that are not committed.

Immunities for self-disclosure and self-correction

The final supporting regulatory strategy to promote corporate self-evaluation is an immunity policy for self-disclosure and correction of compliance breaches and problems. There are currently significant disincentives on companies to evaluate their own self-regulation performance because of the fear that liability for any problems will be increased by discovering them (see Conway 1995: 657–60). This occurs either because the self-evaluation process has created a documentary record of the problems that might be available to regulators or civil litigators in discovery (or indeed might be leaked to the media or a public interest organization), or because if it is discovered that corporate management knew about the problem but did nothing about it, the misconduct would be seen as more serious.

Some commentators and industry advocates have argued that a privilege, like legal professional privilege, ought to be provided to protect the products of any corporate self-evaluation of self-regulation from disclosure in litigation. Currently the application of legal professional privilege to self-regulation programs and evaluations is likely to be very limited in all common law countries where such a privilege is recognized (see Conway 1995: 631–4). If the compliance or self-regulation professional who directs that the document be produced or the evaluation conducted is not a legal professional, the privilege will not apply. Also, privilege is lost as soon as any matter on which privilege might have been claimed is voluntarily disclosed, or if material is not gathered for the dominant purpose of legal advice. For example, if matters are disclosed to a regulator to take advantage of a policy of leniency, or even if they are discussed broadly within the organization as part of an educational program, a prosecutor or civil opponent may be able to take advantage of them in a court case against the company. This seems unfair when the company has tried to 'do the right thing' by gathering or producing written material to help it proactively solve a compliance problem.

In the USA some federal cases have recognized the existence of a 'self-evaluative' privilege to protect the reports and records of internal self-critical discussions and investigations where there is a public interest in preserving the free flow of information within those internal processes, for example hospital staff meetings where staff critically evaluated the quality of care they provided (see Brown and Kandel 1995: para 9.06; Conway 1995: 634–41). More than 20 US states have passed legislation recognizing an environmental compliance audit privilege (Kaisersatt 1996: 414; Kubasek et al. 1998: 269–70). For example, Illinois legislation (passed in January 1998) in relation to insurance company compliance audits applies to a 'voluntary, internal evaluation, review, assessment or audit … of a company or an activity … or of management systems related to the company or activity, that is designed to identify and prevent non-compliance and to improve compliance with those statutes, rules or orders' (Kaplan 1998). The court may, however, require disclosure of otherwise protected material if the privilege is asserted for a fraudulent purpose or if the company failed to undertake reasonable corrective action or to eliminate non-compliance within a reasonable time. Also, in certain circumstances, material containing evidence relevant to the commission of a criminal offence is not protected.

US state legislation providing for environmental audit privileges tends to follow a similar pattern to this more general compliance self-evaluative privilege (see Kaisersatt 1996: 414–19; Kubasek et al. 1998: 270–3).[19] The evidentiary privilege usually applies to all information collected, generated and developed during the course of a voluntary self-audit designed to identify non-compliance or to improve efficiency or pollution prevention, unless information is discovered that demonstrates a clear, imminent and substantial danger to public health or the environment, or the information was compiled in bad faith. In some states the privilege does not apply if a violation was found and not promptly corrected. Immunities are generally provided from administrative and civil penalties for violations that are discovered through an environmental audit and are voluntarily disclosed (i.e. the disclosure is not required by law, they are disclosed promptly and the breach is diligently corrected).

However, Weinberg (1997: 651) concludes from his review of the evidence that state environmental audit privileges are not necessary to protect US companies from EPA prosecutions, and do not make any difference to how willing companies are to conduct environmental audits. He cites evidence that most environmental audits (90 per cent) are already performed to correct breaches before enforcement proceedings anyway, and that the number of audits continues to expand rapidly both in states with a privilege and those without. This suggests that a privilege is not needed to encourage audits.

These privileges provide a good signal to companies in the sense that they shift the focus of inquiry to what the company did to correct problems, rather than whether problems occurred. But they also increase secrecy and distrust between company and regulators or stakeholders (see Lewis 1998). They do not improve transparency and permeability. Instead they make the incentive to self-evaluate and self-correct the opportunity to keep the problem and its correction a secret. As Weinberg (1997: 651) argues, 'Privileges foster secrecy and undermine the fundamental principle that the courts are entitled to all evidence that will help the search for the truth'.

It would be much better to provide an incentive to report problems and their correction so that regulators and stakeholders can be involved in the solution, leaders can model their self-evaluation processes to other companies, and governments can keep track of patterns of problems arising in self-regulation. An immunity from enforcement action predicated on disclosure and correction immunity would increase rather than decrease the flow of information to regulators (and potentially to stakeholders) about self-evaluation measures, and also escape the ratcheting up of adversarialism inherent in a traditional privilege. This shifts the focus from causal fault to reactive fault. It focuses on whether the company takes active responsibility for doing justice, rather than merely identifying past injustices, and therefore fits the restorative justice approach to corporate liability discussed above.

Some regulators do already successfully use voluntary disclosure and leniency policies to support and reward self-regulation, self-disclosure and correction. These guidelines usually provide that if an entity discovers any violations of the law through the operation of its own internal compliance or self-regulatory system, and reports those violations and the corrective action taken to the regulator, they will not be liable for fines and penalties. For example, the US EPA's policy on 'Incentives for Self-Policing: Discovery, Disclosures, Correction and Prevention of Violations'[20] states that the EPA will refrain from recommending criminal prosecutions and forgo 'gravity-based' (punitive) civil fines if a company voluntarily has reported and corrected environmental violations found either through an audit program (as defined in the policy) or through a satisfactory 'due diligence' program to prevent, detect and correct violations. The EPA has, however, retained the discretion to seek economic-benefit penalties (i.e. to recover the entity's economic gain from the violation). Violations repeated within three years or as part of a pattern within five years, or that result in serious harm or danger to public health or the environment, do not qualify for leniency at all. A 1999 EPA evaluation found that use of the policy had been relatively widespread, with 455 entities disclosing violations at approximately 1850 sites between December 1995 and March 1999. Eighty-eight per cent of respondents who had used the policy said they would use it again, and 84 per cent said they would recommend it to clients or counterparts (Weinberg 1997: 649; see also the US Department of Justice, Antitrust Division's 'Corporate Leniency Statement').

However, simply leaving it to regulators to develop voluntary disclosure policies one by one is not enough. It is a recipe for differing standards for self-disclosure and correction measures, introduced at different times and with potentially conflicting coverage. Again, it leaves too much to the discretion of the regulator and creates an accountability deficit (the public cannot be sure that regulators' policies are fair and reasonable) and a lack of security for companies that might want to take advantage of the policies (they cannot be sure the regulator will not renege on its stated policy). Finally, it does not address the problem that information disclosed to a regulator may then become available to third parties to use in civil action against the company (since information about breaches discovered and corrected that were not commercial in confidence should be available to the public in order to hold accountable both the regulator and the companies).

Firstly, it would be desirable to give such immunities the force of law.[21] This means that both regulated companies and the public can hold the regulator to clear legal standards in the use of such immunities rather than leaving it to discretion. The law should be upfront in recognizing and rewarding companies that engage in rigorous self-evaluations of their own institutionalization of social and legal responsibility. Companies that report any problems they discover to relevant public authorities and correct them should not suffer punishment beyond that involved in correcting and reporting the wrongdoing.

Secondly, it would be helpful to provide that information disclosed under an immunity policy can only be used in civil actions to enforce the condition that the company has adequately corrected the wrong (which will often involve compensation to anyone who was harmed by the conduct). The rationale for this is that the regulator's granting of the immunity should have been predicated on appropriate corrective measures in the first place. Therefore there should be no further need for litigation to establish a right to compensation, and there is no need for punitive or deterrence-oriented private enforcement action, since the company has voluntarily discovered and corrected the wrong.

However, stakeholders ought to have a right to join the circle that helps to decide on appropriate response to wrongs discovered in any particular case, and to contest whether the corrective measures taken are adequate. Relevant stakeholders should therefore be included in consultations about granting the immunity in the first place. Indeed, in the best self-evaluation programs, management will have resolved issues with affected stakeholders (through the company's Justice Plan), even before the company comes to the regulator to take advantage of the policy. The standards for immunity-granting self-disclosure should recognize this, and the law should give third parties a right to enforce or contest appropriate corrective measures (similar to the proposals in Chapter 8 in relation to Justice Plans).

EVALUATING REGULATORS' PERFORMANCE

Regulators should generally have available to them a range of options to account for companies at different phases of the institutionalization of responsibility. Regulatory strategies for each phase are designed to provide (a) incentives and signals that will move corporate implementation of self-regulation along to the next phase, and/or (b) accountability mechanisms that will flip them back to re-working the previous phase if they do not perform adequately (see Table 9.1).

Some strategies rely more on formal legal action while others rely more on facilitating action by stakeholders, industry organizations and markets. There is a smorgasbord of options available. The crucial thing is to choose a menu of strategies that will work together to cover all three phases of corporate institutionalization of responsibility (see Gunningham and Grabosky 1998: 422–47 on which regulatory tools tend to work together well). Existing laws and regulatory programs have often experimented with one or two of these regulatory strategies. Internal corporate self-regulation programs are only likely to be effective if they have successfully moved through all three of the phases, and indeed continue to improve and learn through the self-evaluation inherent in the third phase. Meta-evaluation in Phase Three enables meta-learning – corporations that learn to improve their self-regulation, and regulators that learn to improve their regulatory strategies to reinforce leaders and move along laggards.

Corporate management must be made permeable to public justice (law and stakeholders) at each phase, not just at one or two. This means that in general a whole regulatory program must include integrated strategies that aim at each of the three phases. If there is good evidence to suggest that industry as a whole is at a particular phase of institutionalization, then the regulatory scheme can be angled towards moving industry along to the next phase. However, regulation aimed at any one phase is unlikely to be successful unless the other two phases are eventually covered.

It is the central task of the new regulatory state to connect the private capacity and practice of corporate self-regulation to public dialogue and justice. Regulators need to learn to evaluate how regulated entities contribute to their own social responsibility. They need to keep track of all those disputes resolved internally within companies' self-regulatory systems, with an eye to patterns and issues. They need to communicate this intelligence to industry and to stakeholders. They need to keep track of what issues suggest the need for legislative change, regulatory enforcement action, legal aid funding for test case litigation, and so on. They need to look for patterns of injustice that arise from reliance on self-regulation in order to determine where extra rights need to be given to protect or promote the bargaining power of stakeholders, or where regulation needs to be amended to promote better self-regulation management. In other words we need to build institutional capacity for regulators and legislators to learn about the regulatory space in which they act, and to change law and regulatory strategy in response to that. This means that a fundamental strategy of the new regulatory state should be to require companies to gather and disclose information, to report it to stakeholders, and to ensure that it is adequately verified/audited so that it is reliable. This provides a basis of information on which corporate self-regulation and its impacts can be judged (by regulators and stakeholders). It leaves the role for the state of meta-regulating the quality of the information disclosed, and means that the meta-regulation of the third phase of corporate self-regulation is in many ways the most important.

This requires significant regulatory flexibility. Ultimately the only way that regulators can be held accountable for their role in regulating self-regulation is via a third loop of regulatory self-evaluation and reporting. Regulators (and policy makers) themselves must: (a) collect information on the problems they are supposed to solve, and evaluate their own performance by reference to impacts on those problems; (b) report that data to governments, to stakeholders and to industry; and (c) use that information and feedback on it to adjust regulatory strategies and objectives.

This will mean some basic changes in the way regulatory performance is measured and judged. Few governments and regulators have consistently collected compliance rates or assessed the effects of regulatory interventions on social phenomena over time (e.g. environmental results, health effects, decline in injury rates). It is even more difficult to collect and analyse information about internal corporate self-regulation programs. As Malcolm Sparrow (2000: 119) has shown, the performance of regulatory agencies can be evaluated by reference to at least four different categories of factor:

1   *Effects/impacts/outcomes:* For example, environmental condition, health effects, decline in injury rates.
2   *Behavioural outcomes:* Compliance rates, and other outcomes (e.g. adoption of best practice, other risk reduction activities, 'beyond compliance' activities, voluntary actions).
3   *Agency activities/outputs:* For example, enforcement actions; inspections (number, nature, findings); education/outreach; collaborative partnerships; administration of voluntary programs.
4   *Resource efficiency:* With respect to use of agency resources; regulated enterprises' resources; state authority.

Traditionally performance measures for regulatory agencies have clustered around measures of agency activity, and, in more recent times, resource efficiency. Neither of these measures allows governments and citizens to hold agencies accountable for whether their activities are actually having any impact. The new regulatory state should supplement traditional activity-based performance measures (Categories Three and Four) with outcome-based measures (Categories One and Two). This is likely to require a complete change in measurement methodology, databases and management practice. This is the only basis for sound regulatory action and accountability in the context of a new regulatory state that relies on regulatory pluralism (see Parker 1999d: 39–46; Sparrow 2000).

Measures like these create the information flows that citizens need to connect corporate self-regulation and state meta-regulation to public democracy. In a democracy stakeholders need access to corporate reports of their self-evaluation of their own self-regulation, including how they have identified, prevented and corrected problems. They need regulators (both state regulators and private/informal regulatory agencies such as securities exchanges, accreditation agencies, industry associations) to evaluate that information: to ensure it meets appropriate standards, to sift for patterns of injustice and to regulate its reliability. Finally they need regulators to report on the outcomes of their meta-evaluations: to make public user-friendly information about corporate self-regulation practices, about the impacts of regulatory activity on corporate self-regulation, and the impact of regulatory activity on important policy goals (e.g. a healthier environment, less discrimination). It is only when all these layers of information collection and learning are in place that both regulators and stakeholders can meaningfully dialogue with corporate managements about self-regulation practices and goals.

10 | Conclusion

SELF-REGULATION AND LEGAL REGULATION

Corporate self-regulation is necessary to democracy. It is neither naive optimism nor a concession to market power to advocate reliance on corporate self-regulation as a matter of policy. We have no choice but to inquire into the conditions in which corporate self-regulation will occur effectively, because there will be no legal or socially responsible action by corporations if there is no self-management of responsibility. It is corporate management that will ultimately determine corporate compliance or non-compliance with social and legal responsibilities.

As a matter of fact, the new regulatory state is increasingly experimenting with deregulation and regulatory reform to work more 'naturally' in partnership with markets, business and other private interests. Regulatory compliance programs and voluntary self-regulation systems are increasingly popular with management as a means to manage legal and social responsibilities. I have proposed an ideal type of 'permeable' self-regulation as an explanation for how self-regulation can work, and as a normative ideal for companies, regulators and stakeholders. But mine is an ideal of self-regulation that is not purely self-regulation at all. Rather, it is a marriage between law, corporate self-management and external stakeholders.

Corporate management should be open to a broad range of stakeholder deliberation about values; and legal regulation should facilitate (and enforce) their permeation. In the open corporation, management self-critically reflects on past and future actions in the light of legal responsibilities and impacts on stakeholders. They go on to institutionalize operating procedures, habits and cultures that constantly seek to do

better at ensuring that the whole company complies with legal responsibilities, accomplishes the underlying goals and values of regulation, and
does justice in its impacts on stakeholders (even where no law has yet
defined what that involves). The open corporation is the good corporate
citizen in deliberative democracy. It is internally responsible for its own
actions through self-management, yet externally accountable through the
requirements of disclosure, dialogue, exposure and enforcement.

I have evaluated the empirical reality of corporate self-regulation in
the light of its potential to reach normative ideals of deliberative democracy throughout this book. This Conclusion turns the spotlight the other
way: what does the empirical analysis in this book suggest for conceptual understandings of the connection between law, deliberative
democracy and corporate self-regulation?

It may seem odd to define self-regulation by reference to its permeability to law and stakeholders in deliberative democracies. More standard definitions focus on the extent of autonomy in decision-making as
the characteristic feature of self-regulation. Is it still self-regulation if it
is permeable? It may also seem that I have proposed an inconsistent or
ambiguous role for law. I have argued that the legal regulation of corporations should recognize and facilitate self-regulation, but simultaneously hold it accountable by connecting private management to
public justice. Do these ideals make sense? Or are legal regulation and
self-regulation mutually incompatible?

Sceptics often raise the question of whether social responsibility is
compatible with the logic of business. Incompatibility would destroy any
potential for socially responsible self-regulation. The flipside of this issue
is that simultaneous self-regulation and legal accountability may also be
incompatible. In both cases, the potential problem is that business and
law (or democracy or society) might be disconnected systems with different rationalities and goals, and that connections are either impossible
or dangerous. Law will destroy self-regulation; social responsibility will
destroy business.

A leading theoretical argument for the significance of corporate self-
regulation as a means of control of corporate power is Teubner's (1985,
1987) version of '*systems theory*'. Teubner's work is based on Luhmann's
(1982, 1985) social theory of 'autopoiesis' (see Dunsire 1996 for a useful
summary). An autopoietic system continuously reproduces its own internal structure, without reference to any outside source. In an increasingly
differentiated society, each societal sub-system (economy, law, politics,
family, science, religion) is increasingly dependent on the others, but also

increasingly under pressure 'to ignore all features of its environment except those crucially salient to its ability to maintain its own integrity and identity' (Dunsire 1996: 301). The central insight is that each sub-system becomes locked into its own self-referential way of understanding the world. Therefore full knowledge of the internal relations within the system can never pass outwards, and no instruction from outside can penetrate inwards. The autonomous sub-systems bump up against each other, causing unpredictable reverberations inside. But they fail to connect, communicate or intervene in each other's functioning. This degree of differentiation in a complex society makes the effects of traditional government intervention and legal regulation ineffective, unpredictable and incomplete. Systems theory suggests that the economic rationality of business and the social responsibility of regulation/stakeholder deliberation may be so separate from each other that they inhabit different systems, with different languages that cannot even 'talk' to each other.

In contrast I have argued that pessimism about the possibility of substantive integrity between social responsibility, self-regulation, law and deliberative democracy is unwarranted for two main reasons. Firstly, the integrity of individuals, including top management and self-regulation professionals, is a resource for communication and connection between law, social values and business. Secondly, law/democracy and self-regulation can and must work in partnership to constitute each other.

INDIVIDUAL INTEGRITY

In Chapter 2 I argued that one of the fundamental problems of ethics in business organizations is the lack of opportunity for employees and management to act with integrity. In large organizations it is often difficult for people to connect the social groups, values and concerns that have formed them as people with the one-dimensional role morality associated with their job. The rest of the book provided a framework for organizational integrity through management that discovers and addresses salient corporate social and legal responsibilities. The empirical evidence gathered in this book suggests that individuals are a resource for integrity between business and social values at the organizational and societal level. Individual managers, employees, self-regulation professionals and stakeholders do not live their whole lives in isolation in separate 'systems'. The same people straddle them, and build communities within and among them. Their rationalities cannot be completely separate. The customer of one firm is the employee of another. The CEO of a chemical factory has family and friends who are concerned about factory pollution.

Responsible, or permeable, management is built on the foundations of:

- the individual and professional integrity of the members of the organization, starting with some commitment from top management (Chapters 3 and 4), spreading to the appointment of self-regulation professionals (Chapters 5 and 7), and, ultimately, connecting with all employees and their values (Chapter 8); and
- the societal integrity of a deliberative democracy (Chapter 2) where stakeholders' concerns permeate the corporate shell (Chapter 6), sustained by external legal regulation and internal self-regulation functions that ensure private management is connected to public justice (Chapter 9).

As we have seen, the integrity of individual self-regulation professionals, in particular, is a critical point of leverage for corporate responsibility and therefore the broader democracy. Their passion and commitment are the linchpin of permeability.

THE PARTNERSHIP OF LAW AND SELF-REGULATION

Different rationalities and orderings can and do interact with one another in society. Business and law are not confined to watching the reverberations when they bump against each other. They can connect and communicate. I have therefore proposed an ideal of the 'open' or 'permeable' corporation, rather than the 'transparent' corporation. Law and social pressures on the one hand, and internal management and cultures on the other, are mutually constitutive of corporate self-regulation. This does not make self-regulation meaningless.

An internal capacity for rationality and self-management is a resource for law and other regulatory orderings. No self-regulation means no rational or consistent response to law at all. Law and social pressure are impotent without self-regulation. As Selznick (1992: 471) puts it:

> ... some internal moralities are more effective than others. Most families can be relied on to care for their children without external interference or goading. An internal morality is sustained by parental love and by feelings of solidarity among close relatives. The internal morality of business arises from the demands of rationality, including the

utility of good relations among employees, customers, and suppliers. However, impoverished families and marginal firms are likely to have very weak internal moralities. These variations point to the limits of legal pluralism. The ideal depends on an underlying reality. Deference is unjustified if the institution in question has little or no potential for self-regulation.

The appropriate response to 'marginal' firms is liquidation or the removal of licences to operate, because no-one (internal or external to them) can trust them at all.

Selznick's insight recognizes that for corporate self-regulation the demands of internal morality relate, partly at least, to the 'utility of good relations' with a variety of stakeholders. I argued in Chapter 8 that corporate self-regulation is most robust when it makes the corporation an 'open system' engaged in a continuous dialogue (or feedback loop) with its environment (Morgan 1997: 40). The most secure basis for the concept of organizational morality is the idea that organizations must take into account 'limiting operating conditions' in decision-making (Ladd 1970). These conditions set the upper limits to an organization's operation. In Chapter 6 (and in Chapter 2) I argued that the new corporate risk management through self-regulation systems is making companies more and more aware of their legal and social responsibilities as 'limiting operating conditions'. There is no doubt that leading companies do respond to external values. In that sense, law, stakeholder concerns and informal/private regulation all partially constitute corporate self-regulation. There would be no need for self-regulation if corporations did not feel the strategic pressures of regulators and stakeholders.

The issue is not *whether* companies respond to social and legal values. It is *how* do companies respond to these limiting operating conditions through self-regulation? How will regulators and stakeholders put pressure on corporate management? Will they allow shallow public relations answers to the concerns of social stakeholders while financial stakeholders (such as bankers, insurers, and institutional investors) conduct change-inducing dialogue with corporate management? Or will regulation infuse corporate management with incentives to comply with the law and debate its values with a wider range of stakeholders? Chapter 8 set out the three strategies by which corporate management ought to make themselves permeable to stakeholder concerns and regulatory responsibilities. Chapter 9 set out how law and regulation ought to facilitate and hold accountable the permeation of stakeholder and regulatory values across the three corporate phases of institutionalization of responsibility.

Law and democracy 'make' corporate self-regulation: self-regulation only makes sense as a way in which a company sets and maintains objectives in response to the pressures it faces in the wider world. At the same time self-regulation 'makes' law and democracy: law and democracy are meaningless outside of their impacts on everyday life, including corporate behaviour. Self-regulation (personal or corporate) is the substratum upon which democracy rests. Permeable corporations are good corporate citizens: that is, they respond to (comply with) the obligations of democracy and law; and they participate in making the law and democratic institutions.

RESPONSIVE LAW AND PROCEDURAL REGULATION

Teubner (1987) proposes that only corporate 'reflexion' can integrate autonomous business organizations with other social sub-systems. Reflexion internalizes the corporation's external effects and puts the responsibility on the corporation to integrate itself with other sub-systems and the society as a whole. The corporation itself 'precariously' balances its 'function' in the wider society (e.g. to contribute to wealth for future needs satisfaction) with its 'performance', as it bumps against other social sub-systems (e.g. the relationship of the enterprise to consumers, employees, the natural environment). Law can only hope to regulate the processes of an 'organizational conscience' as it weighs different interests. For example, in company law this would mean that 'fiduciary duties should be transformed into duties of disclosure, audit, justification, consultation, and organization of internal control processes' (Teubner 1985: 167; see also Heyvaert 1999b: 36).

Like Teubner, I have argued that it is impossible to write laws and regulatory strategies that can lead, or even track, the counterpoint of corporate deliberation with stakeholders in detail. It is better to get companies themselves to be reflexive about their relations with law and stakeholders, rather than to impose social responsibility solutions on them. Does this have to mean that the role of the law and state in 'stimulating' reflexive corporate action be purely procedural?

Much of the role of law in permeable self-regulation will be procedural. Yet procedure is not enough. Companies will sometimes want guidance on which stakeholder values to take seriously. Stakeholders will also want law to decisively resolve some conflicts of value. We do not want every company to have to develop every aspect of its own foreign policy, environmental protection standards, health and safety minima, and so on. There are many basic principles, values and standards that can continue to be imposed upon companies by democratic governments. There is also still much room for debate about the proper extent of corporate social responsibilities. How do we balance the desirability of substantive regulation with the need to step back and let the procedures of self-regulation take their course? Different regulatory stances and strategies vis-a-vis substantive regulation and procedural self-regulation will be appropriate at different times and for different companies.

Firstly, law and government should 'responsively' set out substantive basic values and principles for corporate social responsibility, including the identification of relevant categories of stakeholder (see Selznick 1992: 463–75; see also Ayres and Braithwaite 1992 on 'responsive regulation').·Law should move from setting out rules to setting out the values, goals and outcomes that corporations should meet through self-regulation. This does not mean that we should have no rules in law. Chapter 9 suggested a number of ways in which law and regulation can be made more responsive to the differing self-regulation capacities and commitments of different companies. These responses utilize both rules and principles. The ultimate ideal is to build values into law and leave it to companies to innovate and self-regulate to acquire the skills and practices necessary to institutionalize those values. The move from rules to values recognizes that rules can never do a perfect job at articulating what justice would require (see Black 1997: 6). The statement of values, and principles in the law, allow us to connect rules to justice goals. As Selznick (1992: 473) argues, 'Instead of taking each rule as unproblematic, to be changed only by legislation, courts and other agencies look to the reasons behind the rule, that is, to the purposes, policies, and values it is supposed to achieve or fulfill'.

This means that 'legal institutions must be instruments of inquiry as well as of authority', that is 'they must be prepared to consider how far rules, procedures, and doctrines meet the needs they were meant to serve' (Selznick 1992: 472). Law and government should continuously assess how legal rules and self-regulation are doing at meeting those values. Law should have a built-in capacity to recognize and learn from its own failures to interact effectively, to keep up with changing environments, to work with and utilize pre-existing regulatory orderings – an ideal that I have summed up in the concept of 'triple-loop' learning. Responsive law makes legal and regulatory institutions less passive, and it also allows an opportunity for citizenship to be less passive. Companies and stakeholders take more responsibility for good democracy.

Secondly, leading companies should take responsibility for deliberation with stakeholders about emerging values and responsibilities that are not yet the subject of law and regulation. These companies will formulate their own self-regulatory responses to those emerging responsibilities. Stakeholders, non-government organizations, industry and professional associations, and institutional investors will all have a responsibility for sustaining democracy by engaging in the dialogue about corporate social responsibility and forcing companies to take new responsibilities into account. Eventually many of the issues identified will become the subject of formal legal regulation.

Thirdly, in some situations consensus may be growing that there is an issue of corporate responsibility to be addressed. Yet there may be no effective possibility for legal or government regulation – it may be an issue of transnational corporate practice that no national government can regulate, or sufficient consensus may not yet exist for government to act. Here informal regulators (such as industry associations, accreditation agencies, voluntary standard-setting bodies), non-government organizations and the partial governance institutions of international law can set out standards and monitor their implementation through self-regulation. In these circumstances the deliberative democracy of 'law' is accomplished through the partial institutions of informal, private or incomplete global regulation. These institutions are partial and fallible (just as state legal regulation is), and should be subject to the same processes of continuous self-assessment and triple-loop learning as state regulators.

Thus, permeable self-regulation will require more deliberation the earlier in the process of the emergence of social values/corporate responsibility issues the corporation chooses to respond. Companies that take a strategic approach to identifying and responding to emerging issues of values and responsibility for their corporation will need to invest more time and resources in stakeholder consultation, internal deliberation about appropriate responses, and development of relevant management systems. They will run the risk of getting it wrong, of responding too soon, of not correctly identifying the democratic movement. But they will also reap the reputational rewards of leadership and innovation, and the political rewards of the influence that active citizenship can bring.

Companies that implement 'best practice' once a regulator or well-formed social movement has already clearly identified corporate failures (their own or others) will have less choice, less expense, less confusion and less bother in tailoring compliance management to their organization. But they will run the risk of having to continuously react to, rather than lead, new and higher standards and expectations. Those who respond only once industry practice has already defined the taken-for-granted parameters of appropriate self-regulation management will spend little time or money on deliberation about their responses to social and legal responsibilities. They will simply follow what everybody else does. They will have no assurance that the systems they put in place will actually meet the risks of irresponsibility they face now and in the future.

Regulation should always be based on a justice that is grounded in a process of deliberation. But this does not mean that regulatory technique should limit itself to regulating deliberative and decision-making procedures within organizations. I have argued that a primary aim of regulation ought indeed to be to prompt internal procedures to engage in 'reflexion' in relation to their stakeholders. This will often be achieved through *procedural regulation*, especially via mandatory *disclosure* of procedures and their performance. However, secondly, deliberation within corporations must always be made subject to those principles decided through (what should be) the broadest, most inclusive deliberative procedures of society – those that are institutionalized and implemented in the law and administrative regulation. It is not within the scope of this book to set out a theory for how deliberative law-making and regulatory action can occur (see Habermas 1996; Pettit 1997). The focus here is to assume (or advocate) that law/regulation sets out some basic principles of justice, including some substantive regulatory standards (e.g. limits on pollution, responsibility for employee deaths in certain situations, product safety standards) and stakeholder rights (to information or remedies) on a deliberative democratic basis. Corporate self-regulation must be subject to the democracy of these standards.

If corporate self-regulation systems have a tendency to privatize, individualize and deflect conflict in remedying injustice, *then* the role of regulation ought to be to connect individual corporate self-regulation initiatives back up to the quest for social justice by gathering intelligence on patterns of injustice in corporate self-regulation, and using its problem-solving and enforcement capacities to restore justice.

If it is problematic to rely on the deliberative politics of social activism (e.g. media, social movements, stakeholder activism) to make it strategic for companies to comply with their responsibilities because stakeholder activism is partial, piecemeal and often not based on adequate information and access, *then* the role of law is to identify legitimate stakeholders for particular issues, guarantee them adequate access and information, broker opportunities for stakeholder engagement and contestation, and provide sanctions and enforcement that back up the informal regulatory tools available to stakeholders.

If corporate self-regulation management systems frequently lack the capacity or commitment to improve on past performance, to learn from individual mistakes and consumer complaints, and to engage in the discipline of self-evaluation, *then* the role of regulation is to meta-evaluate corporate self-evaluation and organizational learning and to hold companies responsible for how they react to and resolve injustices that they cause.

Permeable self-regulation is about corporate citizenship – the marriage between management, democracy and law. The potential of self-regulation to build up trust, integrity and social capital in some of our most economically powerful organizations is great. It can help reconnect our human desire to live and work in societies that strive to fulfil social goals (such as healthy and safe environments, equal opportunity for all, safe products, and well-informed consumers) with the powerful drivers of our global economy (that we hope will securely meet our material needs). The emerging self-regulation professionals have the capacity to act as midwives in the birth of open corporations.

The challenge for law and regulators is to provide the motive force that will make permeability happen at each of the three phases of corporate self-regulation:

- to catalyse commitment through liability and restorative justice;
- to nurture the acquisition of expertise; and
- to hold the ongoing systems of self-regulation accountable through standards and exposure to public debate and dialogues.

Regulators and rule-makers (national and international) must ensure that corporate self-management becomes part of a triple loop – of self-regulation, self-evaluation that is publicly disclosed, and democratic deliberation about appropriate regulatory strategies – that holds both regulators and management accountable as to whether the substantive goals of the good society are actually being met.

Appendix: Methodology

The primary empirical research conducted for this book was via unstructured, in-depth interviews with regulators and self-regulation professionals in four regulatory areas in which corporate compliance systems are common: sexual harassment, consumer protection and antitrust, financial services, and environment. Interviews were conducted with Equal Employment Opportunity (EEO) officers, compliance professionals and regulators in relation to *sexual harassment* and *trade practices*, in Australia only. Interviews were conducted with *environmental* managers and *financial services* compliance managers and regulators in Australia, England, Germany, Switzerland and the USA. The primary research is also based on extensive participation in and observation of the activities of the Association for Compliance Professionals of Australia (ACPA) over a period of four years and secondary materials on self-regulation practice, including other scholars' research and written materials produced by self-regulation professionals in Australia, Europe and the USA.

Sampling for interviews

In each case the self-regulation practitioners were chosen by asking regulators for their opinions on the leading self-regulation practitioners and 'best practice' self-regulation programs in their area. I also used scholarly and popular literature to identify examples of companies that were likely to exhibit best practice in their compliance or self-regulation system in each particular regulatory area. Self-regulation practitioners were also asked to suggest potential interviewees who would fit the best practice criteria. The sample was therefore based upon both an objective choice from the broad sweep of literature and regulators' data, and a purposive snowball methodology in which interviewees were asked to suggest others (Minichiello et al. 1990: 198). Sampling methods differed slightly from regulatory arena to regulatory arena and are described separately below.

The interview sampling methodology used was not random but deliberately sought to elicit best corporate self-regulation practice. The primary purpose was not to draw conclusions about the prevalence of the practices studied. The original research design did incorporate a proposal for a survey of compliance practitioners in Australia that would have generated data on the prevalence and success of various compliance practices. However, after long discussions, access to the most appropriate mailing list (of self-regulation practitioners) was denied. At that stage, the qualitative interviews were well advanced. Therefore I decided to abandon the quantitative part of the proposed research since there was no other appropriate mailing list likely to become available, and an alternative sampling strategy would have been considerably more time-consuming and expensive. I continued with the qualitative interviews, and used corporate reports, other quantitative data provided in interviews, and other research and surveys to put the interviews in context. I have attempted to evaluate the effectiveness of the self-regulation systems studied, wherever this was possible, using corporate reports and external information. I have also placed the qualitative interview data within the context of quantitative data on the prevalence of self-regulation practices, where such data are available.

The main purpose of the interviews was to inquire into what the best tools and role models currently available to officers responsible for corporate self-regulation policies are, and then to test those empirical findings against normative theory and evaluative research to define the potential for corporate self-regulation systems to contribute to good corporate citizenship. There is plenty of evidence that responsibility failures and regulatory compliance breaches are common in large corporations (although further research inside companies is surely necessary to describe and analyse the conditions in which failures occur). The normative challenge for those interested in good corporate citizenship and good regulatory policy is to move beyond cataloguing failures, to identifying the conditions in which good corporate citizenship might be possible and what can be done to encourage those conditions to flourish. Therefore this study begins with what regulators and industry currently see as the best self-regulation systems and professionals.

Most regulators and self-regulation professionals were very willing to help with the research, and there was no shortage of willing respondents to interview. Surprisingly few refusals for interviews were received. This was probably partly because the research framework was not threatening to business (as it focused on best practice organizations), and respondents probably believed they too could learn something through the process of dialogue with a researcher with connections to other self-regulation professionals and regulators. Indeed, many were anxious for my opinion on how their programs matched other programs I had heard about, whether theirs was better and whether others had solved problems they had not been able to solve. Clearly, however, one must be cautious about generalizing from such a small sample of interviewees, which was intended to represent only best practice self-regulation professionals. My interview findings therefore cannot be taken to imply anything about self-regulation professionals more generally, except where backed up by more representative research.

Since the 'compliance' community is still relatively small in Australia, there was a high degree of agreement on the Australian practitioners interviewed as those who represented best practice. The high degree of congruence in views and practices among this best practice Australian sample suggests that the interview data do reliably identify the conception of best practice compliance policy implementation currently dominant in Australian companies. There was also a high degree of congruence among the stories told by financial services compliance officers in Australia, the USA and England, suggesting that these interviews also identified a common picture of best practice. As can be seen in my analysis of the data throughout the book, there is also a great deal of agreement on ideas of best practice self-regulation across regulatory regimes and across continents in general.

The names of the interviewees' companies are coded throughout the book in order to preserve confidentiality (except where the interviewee explicitly consented to identification). Some companies provided more than one interviewee at different times and from different regulatory arenas, or in different countries. Below I provide a comprehensive listing of the coded names of the companies where interviews were conducted and how many were interviewed at each company. Where the same company appears under more than one category, different people were interviewed in relation to the different substantive areas of self-regulation.

Sexual harassment interviews

Interviews with regulators and practitioners about anti-sexual harassment systems took place in Australia only. State and federal sex discrimination regulators were contacted and asked for their opinion on best practice in the implementation of sexual harassment policies. Opinion converged on the finance industry as the sector in which such policies were most advanced. It was suggested by some of the lawyers and regulators that the relatively high proportion of women employed in the industry and the fact that it had had serious anti-discrimination problems in the past may have led to development of better practice.[1]

The preliminary conversations with anti-discrimination agency members and leading lawyers pointed to eight financial institutions that were reputed to be of best practice. In each case a letter was written to the chief executive officer asking for an appointment with the relevant officer. In every case the letter was passed on to the responsible officer who rang me to arrange an appointment, and in all but one case an interview was carried out. Twelve people in seven firms were interviewed in corporate head offices in Sydney and Melbourne. Seven were female human resources staff in central human resources departments. Two were male lawyers, one in a legal department and one in central human resources, and three were male central human resources staff. In some companies two or three persons were interviewed because the original contact set up a meeting with all those responsible for the sexual harassment policy. A further female EEO officer in a medium sized pharmaceuticals manufacturer (coded Pets & Health) was also interviewed because she was particularly recommended as responsible for one of the most innovative programs in Sydney. The total sample size was therefore thirteen.

The companies where interviews took place were coded as:

- Banksafe Australasia (two interviewees)
- Big Bucks Australia (one interviewee)
- Credit4Oz (two interviewees)
- Good as Gold Australia (one interviewee)
- Aussie Dollars (three interviewees)
- Trustus (Australia) (one interviewee)
- AssurOz (one interviewee)
- Pets & Health (one interviewee)
- Adviser Five (one early interview conducted with a leading sexual harassment lawyer).
- Two anti-discrimination regulators were interviewed over the phone. (These are not coded.)

Consumer protection and antitrust interviews

Interviews were conducted with five former and/or current senior officers of the Australian Competition and Consumer Commission (ACCC) with significant involvement in compliance issues, and seven trade practices compliance advisers working in private practice as lawyers, consultants or inhouse compliance advisers in Sydney. They were chosen by asking members of the ACCC for their opinions about leading practitioners, and then asking those who were interviewed for further suggestions of people to interview. Since the trade practices compliance community is still fairly small, there was general agreement that the seven practitioners who were interviewed represented best practice. Australian financial services compliance managers also have trade practices compliance as a major concern. So interviews with those compliance managers (described below) also uncovered trade practices issues. Many of those who are involved in the ACPA work primarily in the area of trade practices or financial services compliance, and a number of trade practices regulators also attend meetings. Therefore my participant observation work focused greatly on consumer protection and antitrust compliance. Since much of the discussion at these meetings focused on description of trade practices compliance systems, and the politics of implementing them, it was judged unnecessary to conduct further interviews of individual compliance professionals in this area.

The companies in which interviews in this category took place were coded as follows:

- GarbageRUs (one interviewee)
- Aussie Products (one interviewee)
- Connexions (one interviewee)
- Chemical Kings (Australia) (one interviewee)
- Rainy Days (Australia) (one interviewee)

Five private trade practices compliance consultants or advisers were also interviewed (coded Advisers One, Two, Three, Four and Seven). Numerous corporate trade practices compliance managers and private consultants also gave their views during formal sessions and informal conversations at the ACPA meetings that I attended over a four-year period. Five former and/or current senior officers of the ACCC were interviewed. (These are identified by name or by general category throughout the book and are therefore not coded.)

Financial services interviews

In this area, interviews were conducted in Australia, New York and London, with supplementary interviews in Germany and France. Since compliance practice is most innovative in the USA (New York), and London is also a centre of best practice compliance in financial services regulation, interviews had to be conducted in these two cities in order to approach best practice.

During a first trip to London, interviews were conducted with three regulators in the financial services area and with office bearers of the Compliance Institute (a professional association in the financial services area). These interviewees were asked for contacts of best practice compliance practitioners, and these suggestions were pursued on a later visit when compliance managers in four firms were interviewed. Best practice compliance managers were identified in New York via two contacts who had worked in the area, resulting in two interviews at firms. Compliance managers in five financial institutions in Australia were identified by members of the ACCC and other practitioners as representing best practice, and one Australian financial regulator was also interviewed on compliance issues. A further two interviews with financial services compliance managers in Europe took place. Other interviews in Europe were requested, but were not agreed to. From the two interviews that did take place, it seemed that continental compliance systems were behind and following the best practice lead of America and, to a lesser extent, London. Two further financial services regulators in Europe were also interviewed. Interviews in Australia, London and New York identified a high degree of confluence in elements of compliance systems and role and approach of compliance managers. Saturation in new information in interviews was reached very quickly.

The firms in which these interviews took place are coded as follows. All include an indication of their country:

- Convict Cash Australia (one interviewee)
- Trustus (Australia) (two interviewees)
- Big Bucks Australia (two interviewees)
- Alpine Insurance (Australia) (two interviewees)
- Eurostock (UK) (one interviewee)
- GloboBucks (UK) (one interviewee)
- Trustus (UK) (one interviewee)
- Silver Lining (UK) (one interviewee)
- Trustus (US) (one interviewee)
- Money Machine (US) (one interviewee)
- Loads'o'Dough (France)
- Marks Bank (Germany)

Five regulators in London and continental Europe were also interviewed.

Environment interviews

The interviews in this area occurred in three parts. The first was a few preliminary interviews in Australia on environmental management systems with compliance practitioners and regulators: Chemical Kings (Australia); GarbageRUs; and Industry Association Two.

The second was a narrowing of this focus to Australian companies that had voluntarily joined the Greenhouse Challenge program. This narrowing was necessary because the area of environmental regulation and compliance was too broad to identify best practice organizations. The Greenhouse Challenge is a purely voluntary program to enter into an agreement with the government to reduce greenhouse gas emissions. Companies who had joined the program early and been conscientious in fulfilling their reporting requirements under the scheme were chosen for interview. These companies were thought to represent best practice in this area, and possibly in environmental management more generally. Certainly the interviews often covered general elements of their environmental management system as well as greenhouse issues, and the fact that this was a purely voluntary program provided a useful counterpoint to the other interviews which concentrated more on self-regulation systems in areas where mandatory regulation applied.

Eleven corporate Greenhouse Challenge coordinators were interviewed in Sydney and Melbourne. Three industry association members of the Greenhouse Challenge were also interviewed. The interviewees were chosen from a list of participants who entered the program early and had been diligent in meeting their annual reporting requirement. Five staff of the Australian Greenhouse Office were also interviewed at different times over a two-year period. Interviews were conducted at twelve companies (out of forty who had submitted at least one annual report, as required by the scheme). Two did not reply to interview requests. The others either could not be contacted or were located outside of Sydney, Melbourne or Canberra and were therefore inaccessible for interviews.

Companies where interviews were conducted were coded as:

- Holes in the Ground Australia (one interviewee)
- Mine of Riches (one interviewee)
- Chemical Kings (Australia) (one interviewee)
- Big Bucks Australia (one interviewee)
- Chemola Australia (one interviewee)
- Fuel for the Fire (Australia) (one interviewee)
- Power To Go (one interviewee)
- Credit4Oz (one interviewee)
- Industry Association One
- Industry Association Two
- Industry Association Three
- Industry Association Four

Thirdly, interviews were conducted with environmental managers of international companies based in Europe (and one in the USA). These companies were chosen because it was judged by the literature that European companies tended to lead in innovation in environmental management systems. A list of the top 200 companies was obtained and European companies with a major chemical, pharmaceutical, mining or manufacturing interest in London, Germany and Switzerland were targeted for interviews, as these were judged to be most likely to present best practice:

- Fuel for the Fire (Group HQ, UK)
- Chemical Kings (Group HQ, UK)
- Pharmarama (Switzerland)
- Wonderchem (Switzerland)
- Chemcloud (Germany)
- Hot Rods (Germany)
- SustainAbility (UK, consultants; this is their real name)
- Pro-Chem (USA)

Other interviews

Three general compliance advisers in the USA (Advisers Five, Eight and Nine) were interviewed. Several interviews were conducted with the secretary of the ACPA in Australia and I had much contact with several of its senior office bearers. Officers at the United States Sentencing Commission, responsible for the corporate sentencing guidelines (which encourage corporate compliance systems), were interviewed.

CONDUCT OF INTERVIEWS

Interviews usually lasted between one hour and two hours. Over half of the interviews were conducted with only one self-regulation professional or regulatory official, but up to three interviewees were sometimes present in the same interview. Interviews were conducted at the office of the person being interviewed. Copious notes were taken during each interview, including much verbatim material, and written up immediately afterwards. Tape recorders were not used, because of the sensitive information being discussed. In the researcher's experience, interviewees (especially lawyers) speak more freely without a tape running. Confidentiality and anonymity were promised to each interviewee, but some expressly indicated that this was not necessary.

Interviews with *regulators* were aimed at discovering how they encourage the use of self-regulation programs, and how well they believe companies implement them. Issues discussed varied greatly, and usually focused on description and assessment of particular innovative programs to encourage the implementation of high-quality self-regulation systems. Regulators were also asked for their opinions on companies with best practice self-regulation systems, an assessment that most were happy to provide.

The purpose of the interviews with *self-regulation professionals* was to identify best practice self-regulation systems in terms of the strategies applied by the officers responsible, the structural elements of the organization that made it possible, and the external (regulatory) conditions in which the system existed. Therefore I began each interview by telling the self-regulation professional that I was interested in the following:[2]

1 Why their company had implemented a self-regulation system in the particular area (i.e. sexual harassment, consumer protection and antitrust, environment or financial services) in the first place. During discussion of this issue I attempted to gauge the level and motivations for top-management commitment to the self-regulation system.
2 A briefing on the main elements of their self-regulation system and how it was implemented in practice. I usually asked them how they made it 'come alive' in their organization. During the discussion of this section of the interview, I would ask many detailed questions aimed at making sure I understood how the system worked as a structure, what it included and did not include, how it was received by middle management and workers, and what the interviewee believed were its strengths and weaknesses. I also asked questions about whether they thought they were doing things similarly or differently to industry peers.

3 How they attempted to evaluate the performance of their compliance system. This was usually a very short discussion in all but the interviews on environmental management systems, since many self-regulation systems lack effective (or any) evaluation measures.

4 What characteristics and commitments they believed someone in their position needed in order to be an effective self-regulation manager. Here I would ask clarification questions aimed at understanding how they saw their professional role and ethics.

The questions asked in the interviews varied according to the particular characteristics of the interviewee and the data already collected from other interviewees. The interview schedules did not need to be exactly the same for each interviewee since the aim was to thoroughly explore specific and particular models of best practice self-regulation programs. The secondary materials provided the broader context in which interviewees' responses could be compared and correlated.

Opportunities were taken to cross-check the claims of corporate self-regulation professionals for the effectiveness of their programs against regulators' perceptions and also against publicly available information from regulators and community groups. However, since confidentiality was promised to most interviewees, it has been generally impossible to footnote corroborating information in relation to their claims in the text of this book without breaching anonymity.

Analysis of interview data

The interview data were analysed using an 'iterated adjustment' method (see Parker 1999b). They were divided into bites and sorted into categories, constantly comparing each new piece of information with all the previous bites in each category, until all the information in the interviews had been accounted for and nothing new was being discovered, following a simplified version of Glaser and Strauss' (1967) 'constant comparative method'. The categories derived directly from the data were then compared again with theoretical concepts applied to the study of compliance and regulation and adjusted again. Throughout the book, the analytical categories developed from the interviewees' descriptions of their practices are intertwined with scholarly descriptive and normative analyses relating to corporate regulation and compliance. Thus, the analysis shuttles between micro and macro levels of description and between normative and explanatory theory, adjusting each against the other in order to produce descriptive results with salience at the level of the individual compliance manager, as well as policy-oriented conclusions pragmatically grounded in well-elaborated explanation.

OTHER CONSIDERATIONS

Firstly, my data from interviews with compliance managers may be considered less relevant to gauging and understanding many issues of compliance and corporate citizenship, such as top-management commitment (see Chapters 3 and 4) or stakeholder dialogue, than interviews with top executives might have been. It is true that there are disadvantages in relying solely on the self-regulation professionals to give a picture of the company's whole self-regulation practice. Nevertheless, self-regulation managers are the best, accessible, one source of information about an organization and its self-regulation history and commitment that is available to a researcher. They are likely to have experienced the different commitments and opinions of different top managers over time within the same organization or between different organizations. They are also the ones who, because of their position, most frequently have to practically test the extent of management commitment and institutionalization of the goals of the compliance system. They are therefore excellent judges of management opinion and commitment, and this is something they frequently conveyed consciously or unconsciously in their interviews with me. On this issue, as with other issues, throughout the book, I have placed the interview data against quantitative studies of top-management motivations and opinions wherever possible to try to enhance the reliability of my analysis.

Secondly, my sample of companies where interviews were conducted seemed biased towards those where something new was happening in the compliance system. For example, particularly among the sexual harassment interviewees, many were fairly new to their posts and involved in major revisions to their company's sexual harassment and EEO policies. It is not surprising that the sample should be biased in this way, since the companies most well known for best practice compliance at any particular time are likely to be those where some movement is happening. Since the purpose of the sample was to seek out leading-edge practice, this bias was judged not to be a problem.

Notes

Preface

1 The details of the Mitsubishi case are all based on the following newspaper articles: J. Cradden, 'Mitsubishi recalls cars as defects cover-up admitted', *Irish Times*, 24 August 2000; A. Harney, 'Mitsubishi orders pay cuts', *Financial Times*, 28 September 2000; A. Harney and G. Impey, 'Mitsubishi shares hit by scandal', *Financial Times*, 22 August 2000; D. Ibison and B. Rahman, 'Cover-up takes toll on Mitsubishi', *Financial Times*, 2 October 2000; 'Ministry suspects Mitsubishi Motors hid complaints', *Yomiuri Shimbun/Daily Yomiuri*, 19 July 2000.

1 Introduction

1 He maps this empirically by reference to the proportions of natural and corporate actors on the front page of the *New York Times*, and in court cases in the New York State Court of Appeals.

2 Throughout this book I use the terms 'self-regulation system' and '(regulatory) compliance program/system' largely interchangeably to refer to the programs that companies actually implement. I will argue below, however, that it is the concept of 'self-regulation' rather than 'compliance' that is important in understanding what makes these programs effective.

3 See Donaldson and Dunfee (1999; Dunfee 1999) for a reworking of similar ideas into 'Integrative Social Contracts Theory' that sees corporate power as subject to accepted community norms. This conception does not rely on the grant of incorporation from the state as the basis for 'ethical' organizational behaviour.

4 This approach is sympathetic with another strand of theories that take seriously the institutional features of companies – that is, those theories that see transaction costs and bounded rationality as creating the need for organization (e.g. Williamson 1985; see also Langlois and Robertson 1995).

5   Critics often state that it is difficult to identify (and balance the interests of) legitimate stakeholders. This is not a reason not to do it. It is a reason to make the process of stakeholder identification itself the subject of deliberative democracy in the most inclusive possible forums, that is state and international regulatory rule-making (see Chapters 8 and 9).

6   However, Hood et al. (1999) argue that 'meta-regulation' is not a strength of British public sector regulation – that is, ironically the regulators of government have not themselves been subject to regulation.

7   Available at <www.unglobalcompact.org>.

8   In a survey of the US Ethics Officer Association, 85 per cent reported that their position had been created in their organization in 1992 or later, and only 4 per cent before 1986 (Petry 2001).

9   Interview at Office of Fair Trading, July 1998. The new antitrust laws introduced in 1998 have given the OFT a new interest in working with companies to develop compliance systems.

10 Interviews with staff at the United States Sentencing Commission, November 1998. The idea essentially came from Win Swenson who then worked for the Commission, but staff believe that influential businesses supported it because of their experience with the Defense Industry Initiative. Overall the guidelines for organizations were a very small part of the Commission's work and not seen as highly significant at the time. See Clark (1998) for a detailed history of the drafting of the Guidelines.

11 This was true of all the international companies where I conducted interviews.

12 The federal program started with eleven participants in 1982 and had expanded to 369 by 1998. See <http://www.osha.gov/oshprogs/vpp/fedgrow.html> (accessed December 1998). (State programs have additional participants.)

13 These surveys show a self-selection type bias. For example in the 1996 Price Waterhouse study (Ward 1997), only 262 companies responded to a survey sent out to 5000. The other surveys reported also have low response rates. Those that self-selected to respond to the survey are probably more likely than non-respondents to have a compliance system, so percentages having in place certain elements of compliance systems should not be generalized. Nevertheless, the absolute numbers themselves give some indication of a small but influential movement towards implementation of such systems. For example, the Price Waterhouse study shows that at least 225 (86 per cent of 262 respondents) large US companies have implemented formal compliance systems.

14 This was a common account of the history of compliance practice by interviewees.

2 The potential for self-regulation

1   There are a few more studies that look at self-regulatory schemes at an industry or association level. Two of these (Rees 1988, 1994) have been

included in Table 2.1 because they also show a concern with compliance at the level of the individual organization.

2 Chaganti and Phatak (1983) analyse the evolution of corporate environmental affairs functions in four US companies according to this model.

3 This pattern is confirmed by other empirical researchers in this area such as Hoffman (1997), and, as we will see in Chapter 3, also fits comfortably with a neo-institutionalist perspective on organizational responses to normative issues.

3 Motivating top-management commitment

1 See the Appendix for a description of the methodology used for the primary research reported throughout this chapter and the remainder of the book.

2 The 'business case' is a term that is used in the USA, UK, Europe, Canada and Australia, and is used by compliance managers in every regulatory area in which I interviewed (see, for example, Parry 2000).

3 Calkins (1997: 145) concludes from his interviews with CEOs that in the USA a criminal fine is more likely to accomplish this result than a civil fine.

4 However, as we shall see in Chapter 6, top-management commitment to ethics (as distinct from environmental factors) explained better how the formal elements of the program were actually implemented (Weaver et al. 1999b: 54).

5 'No regrets' because participants need only reduce emissions to the extent it is efficient to do so, that is to manage energy efficiently.

4 Cultivating self-regulation leadership

1 All interviewees were chosen because of a reputation for having better than average self-regulation systems in some area (this is not necessarily the same as having an excellent record of actual compliance), and this provides some corroboration for their claims about their high level of commitment. The fact that not all best practice compliance managers interviewed did claim to have a leading system or high management compliance commitment provides some confidence that interviewees were prepared to give an honest assessment of the strengths of their self-regulation programs. While we cannot expect the compliance managers to have listed all the negatives of their work during my interviews, an absence of success stories in many interviews suggests we can have some confidence that they have not completely fabricated positive stories.

2 There may be a sampling bias effect here, as I was more likely to hear about the compliance programs of people who had recently had a public experience of compliance problems and responses.

3 I did not find contract requirements in my interviews as a reason for implementing a compliance system, but this is probably because the interviews focused on the very large organizations that were doing the influencing rather than the smaller ones who were following.

4   Cone Communications & Roper Starch Worldwide, 'Polls & Surveys', <http://www.goodmoney.com/survey~.htm> (accessed 15 February 2000).
5   <http://www.epa.gov/enviro/html/tris/tris_overview.html> (accessed 22 March 2000).
6   See <www.unep.ch> for further information on financial and insurance industry initiatives on environmentalism.
7   See <http://www.socialinvest.org>.
8   The figure of $100 billion was reported in Cowe (1999).
9   Linda Descano, vice-president of environmental affairs at Solomon, Smith, Barney, and chair of the United Nations Financial Institutions Initiative on the Environment, interviewed by Alexandra De Blas for Australian Radio National's EarthBeat program, 12 June 1999.
10 Reports available at <http://www.bsr.org/resourcecenter> report on Shareholder Engagement under Governance topic (accessed 27 January 2000).
11 This highlights the difficulties in defining socially responsible investing. Some 'ethical funds' simply screen out one or two categories of company, for example tobacco companies, while others use a variety of screens or look for more positive indicia of social responsibility.

5 Self-regulation methodology

1   In the USA the number of inhouse lawyers showed massive growth between 1950 and 1980, with a doubling between 1970 and 1980 (Mackie 1989: 22; see also Daly 1997: 1059–62; Liggio 1997; Spangler 1986: 70). In the UK, while private solicitors with practising certificates grew in number two and half times between 1956 and 1984, the number of inhouse counsel increased at least fivefold in the same period (Mackie 1989: 20). (All these statistics under-estimate the number of inhouse counsel since they rely on measures of lawyers with practising certificates and not all inhouse lawyers require such certificates.)
2   This information is from an interview with a compliance manager in a major bank/broker-dealer based in New York.
3   Interview with Martin Hankey, secretary of the Institute, July 1998.
4   Interviews with Peter Cardinali (IMRO) and Mike Parker (SFA), July 1998.
5   Interview with a compliance manager at a major bank headquartered in Frankfurt.
6   *EOA News*, October 2000, vol. 2(3), available at <http://www.eoa.org> (accessed 19 December 2000).
7   Lisa Cotton, 1998, 'Compliance theory and the "real world"', presentation to Second Annual Conference of the Association for Compliance Professionals of Australia, Melbourne. (Notes of presentation on file with the author.)
8   See Newton (1998: 105) for a completely independent use of the term 'changing hearts and minds' to explain one of the aims of compliance programs in British financial institutions.
9   See Novartis (1998), *Health, Safety and Environment Report: Innovation and Accountability*, p. 22.

10   These systems vary in comprehensiveness and in the extent to which the centre sets specific goals or the business units are given more autonomy.
11   *Economist* 2 October 1999, pp. 79–80.
12   B. Dee, 1997, 'Compliance: Where it's been, where it is now, where it is heading?' after-dinner speech, ACPA annual conference dinner.
13   Cotterrell sees Durkheim's theory about law as more helpful as a normative vision of how moral cohesion and social solidarity are sociologically possible through different ideal-type forms of law, rather than as a descriptive analysis of the nature of law in any existing society: 'Since his treatment of law serves this purpose and *not* that of a full account of the political reality, his lack of attention to that wider political reality, including especially the elements of power and conflict fundamental to law, is less surprising than it otherwise seems' (Cotterrell 1995: 201–2).

6 The pathologies of self-regulation

1   Reported in Martinson (1998). The Australian Managed Investments Act 1998 (Commonwealth) imposes some similar reporting obligations on auditors of compliance programs and members of compliance committees.
2   'At will' employment is the norm in the USA and employees, including compliance professionals, rarely have written contracts spelling out what their role within their organization is and what protections they are entitled to. By contrast, in Australia and Europe most full-time employees, including compliance staff, are likely to have contracts and to be protected by industrial awards.
3   See also Office of Fair Trading (1998) for a UK proposal to use third party monitored standards to regulate consumer protection.
4   According to Braithwaite and Drahos (2000: 281), in the USA it is construed as requiring system improvements only and in Europe and Australia it is outcomes that must improve.
5   However, as I shall argue, it is an empirical question to what extent public demands require substantive change. And it is a normative challenge to ensure that substantive change is demanded.
6   This can occur individually, or collectively through industry associations, including compliance professional associations.
7   Another survey found evidence of these two orientations and another two: 'programs that are oriented toward satisfying the expectations of external stakeholders, and programs oriented toward protecting top management from blame in the event of any legal or ethical improprieties' (Weaver and Trevino 1999: 316).
8   See Cave (1999) and Hills (1999).
9   Joe Rooney in a panel discussion at ACPA's 1998 seminar on the Managed Investment Act. Consider the title of an article in the *Business Review Weekly* (22 February 1999, p. 91) on the same topic: 'New law opens a niche for professional scapegoats'. The article comments that 'Larbalestier warns that compliance committee members can't resign at will and leave a vacancy.

They must find a replacement. He suggests that before filling a vacancy, candidates should understand why old committee members left and "what may blow up in their faces".'

10 SustainAbility uses its business consultancy activities to fund and inform social action, including research and the publication of reports that promote best practice in corporate sustainability management and that shame worst practice corporate offenders, such as *The 1997 Benchmark Survey*, *The Non-Reporting Report* (1998), *The Social Reporting Report* (1999).

11 All information and quotations on SustainAbility's relationship with Monsanto is from a report by Vernon Jennings, director of SustainAbility, on SustainAbility's website: <http://www.sustainability.co.uk> (accessed 23 June 1999).

12 Information in this paragraph is based on a report in the *Guardian Weekly*, 14–20 October 1999, p. 12.

13 *Guardian Weekly*, Thursday 7 October 1999, p. 1.

14 *Guardian Weekly*, 14–20 October 1999, p. 12.

15 *Guardian Weekly*, 14–20 October 1999, pp. 1, 12; and 7 October 1999, p.1.

16 Shell is not the only oil company subject to these concerns in Nigeria; Chevron has been similarly implicated and targeted by campaigners (see Karliner 1997: 58–97).

17 Obi (1997) makes the point that in deciding their strategy the Ogoni resistance leaders over-estimated the extent to which global civil society could hold Shell and the Nigerian state accountable.

18 For example, see John Vidal, 'Strife flares in oil-rich delta', *Guardian Weekly* 29 September 1999, p. 3.

19 This policy was set at corporate level and then the chair of the committee of the managing directors of each business in the group 'invited' the boards of operating units to adopt it and tell him when they had done so. This made adoption more or less mandatory. The outputs of the external verification and certification processes and internal management processes go to the group board each year for assurance. However, these targets were to be met in a further ten years and Shell, like other large multinationals, still says that the environment can 'absorb' more pollution in some countries than others.

20 Linda Morris and Greg Bearup, 'Shell goes well with slick public relations blitz', *Sydney Morning Herald*, 5 August 1999.

21 See <http://www.corpwatch.org> (accessed 10 September 1999). Independent assessments of corporate self-regulation performance are rare, and this is one of the few comparative indices available.

22 See 'Bank rules in disarray', *Economist*, 27 November 1999, pp. 79–80.

7 Model corporate citizens

1 Randal Dennings, 'Ensuring compliance', Managed Investments Seminar, ACPA, Sydney, 16 April 1998.

2 No doubt there are many more not revealed by my research strategy which focused on best practice compliance practitioners.

3   Grant Snowden, 'Liaison with the regulator', Second Annual Compliance Conference, ACPA, Melbourne, September 1998.

4   From a presentation by Anne Gardiner, associate director, Rothschild Australia Asset Management Limited: 'What should the regulator look for – The regulatee's view', Business Law Education Centre First Annual Compliance Conference, 1998. See also Snowden quoted above and McMurray (1997).

5   The Health Care Compliance Association in the USA and the UK Compliance Institute (financial services compliance). These initiatives were discussed in Chapter 5.

6   The US Ethics Officer Association is now considering working on a similar international standard on 'business conduct' (Essrig 2001).

7   Anne Gardiner (see Note 4).

8   This interviewee also made the point that formal structures supported his personal skills and commitment (he had a direct reporting line to head office in New York).

9   In relation to this aspect of the fieldwork, I found that interviewees were not so forthcoming on the political battles they had had to fight. Although they did not deny the politics of their work if I asked, on the whole they were unwilling to volunteer concrete information on their experience. This was partly because of obvious sensitivities around confidentiality. But I also suspect that many of them were not very successful at winning such battles and therefore did not have a lot to say that would positively reflect on themselves.

10 Code of Ethics for Health Care Compliance Professionals, supplied by Joseph E. Murphy, September 1999.

8 The three strategies of 'permeability'

1   However, in Weaver and Trevino's studies, a 'value' orientation alone was not sufficient. There are times when the interaction between compliance and values-oriented elements of the same organizational ethics management system are crucial to its success. One of those issues is whistle-blowing. They found that a perception of a combined values and compliance orientation was more strongly associated with employees' willingness to report ethical violations to management than either orientation alone (1999: 324).

2   Obviously this needs to be balanced with the need for accountability. See Chapter 9 for further discussion of these issues.

3   I was not able to verify whether this system had indeed been implemented, utilized effectively or taken seriously by management.

4   Those interviewed were specifically asked about stakeholder engagement and all but one or two reported little, if any, activity in that area. It seems that stakeholder consultation that does occur in the organization does not usually do so under the direct control of the compliance or self-regulation function.

5   Pluralistic theories have their origins in Berle and Mean's (1968) theory of the separation of ownership and control in the modern corporation

(Graham 1989: 203–4). Corporate social responsibility was only secured by the professionalization of benevolent, 'soulful' top management. See Company Law Review Steering Committee (1999: 37–49) for one explanation of what stakeholder pluralism might mean for corporate law reform.

6   I am particularly indebted to Angus Corbett for helping me to clarify this point.

7   Study by EthicScan for the Canadian Auditor-General, reported at <http://www.bsr.org/bsr> (accessed 23 July 1999) under the 'Social Audits and Accountability' heading.

8   The 'opportunistic reporting hypothesis' (Blair and Ramsay 1998) holds sway strongly here, since frequently if the company does not volunteer social responsibility information itself, there is little probability that stakeholders will find out independently.

9   These two initiatives are reported under 'Social Audits and Accountability' on the Business and Social Responsibility website, <http://www.bsr.org/bsr > (accessed 23 July 1999).

10   According to White and Zinkl (1998: 34), these guidelines are used by more than fifty firms, primarily in the USA.

11   'Ethical investment: Morality plays', *Economist*, 8 July 2000, p. 82; P. Kelso, 'Charities face ethical dimension over pensions', *Guardian Weekly*, 8–14 June 2000, p. 10.

12   See under 'Social Audits and Accountability' at <http://www.bsr.org/bsr>.

13   Another new industry attempt at a self-regulation program with stakeholder involvement is the Pension, Protection and Investment Accreditation Board. In December 1999, a group of CEOs in the British pensions, savings and protection industries worked together in the Savings and Long-Term Risk Project under the auspices of the Association of British Insurers and in consultation with government, regulators and consumer groups to develop standards to guarantee consumers high standards of advice and product quality covering clarity of information, appropriateness of product bought and quality of service provided for pension protection and investment products. They have formed an independent body, the Pension, Protection and Investment Accreditation Board, run by people outside the industry to ensure that brands that apply for accreditation measure up to specific standards and to run periodic checks to ensure performance is maintained. See 'After mis-selling, the clean-up: Pension and insurance providers are creating tough quality standards to restore consumer confidence', *Financial Times*, 9 December 1999.

14   However, the monitors will not publicly disclose violations. Avon was the first company to receive accreditation (see Liubicic 1998: 127).

15   EIPs generally operate within a voluntary framework, so there is no remedy if it goes wrong. However, the aura of the regulator's involvement and encouragement surrounds it (i.e. the same regulator who decides licensing requests and deals with community complaints). The legislation does give the EPA power to order a site to implement an EIP in certain circumstances. As of mid-1999, there were thirty-five EIPs agreed by local

consultative groups already in effect and more than a dozen more in the process of consultation and agreement (EPA 1999b: 3). The EIPs have resulted in significant improvements in environmental outcomes for particular sites, including a halving in emissions of volatile organic compounds at Altona between 1989 and 1998.

16   Indeed, it is consistent with the OECD Principles of Corporate Governance (OECD Ad Hoc Taskforce on Corporate Governance 1999) which already recommend that 'Where stakeholder interests are protected by law, stakeholders should have the opportunity to obtain effective redress for violation of their rights' (Principle IIIA).

17   Information at AAMI website, <http://www.aami.com.au> (accessed 27 August 2000).

18   This summary is taken from Morgan's (1997: 86) discussion of 'organizations as brains'. He argues that these principles are essential for any organization to 'self-regulate' a steady state.

19   Note that there was only a 32 per cent response rate for this survey.

20   See Webb and Morrison (1999) for an analysis of mechanisms by which law directly or indirectly enforces environmental standards.

21   That is, the principles and strategies I have set out in this chapter.

9 Meta-regulation

1   The ACCC was called the Trade Practices Commission before 1995. This section is based on interviews with five past and present senior officials of the ACCC (see Methodology Appendix), and unfootnoted assertions are from the history and perceptions reported in those interviews. See Parker (1999a) for further analysis of this data.

2   In 1988 the ACCC published a major overview of self-regulation in Australia, which also set out the principles that characterized good codes of practice (Trade Practices Commission 1988). It was followed by a series of studies of self-regulation in specific industries and professions (e.g. Trade Practices Commission 1992, 1994).

3   The Compliance Education Unit was disbanded in 1997, partially because of potential conflicts of interest. In 1997 the Law Council of Australia (the peak body for the Australian legal profession) complained to the federal Attorney-General that the Compliance Education Unit was effectively forcing s. 87B companies to buy its services and that the ACCC as regulator should not be involved in selling consulting services to companies.

4   Trade Practices Commission, *Guide to Codes of Conduct* (1991). Commonwealth, State and Territory Consumer Affairs Agencies, *Fair Trading Codes of Conduct: Why Have Them, How to Prepare Them* (1996). See also Department of Industry, Science and Tourism, *Benchmarks for Customer Dispute Resolution Schemes* (1997).

5   No data are available on the extent to which Australian companies have implemented trade practices compliance programs, although submissions to the Australian Law Reform Commission and anecdotal evidence from

lawyers suggests that the high profile of the ACCC's activities has led most large companies to implement programs (Australian Law Reform Commission 1994: 15–16).

6 A number of researchers have found Ayres and Braithwaite's (1992) pyramid of regulatory strategies useful as a descriptive tool to explain where regulation is successful in accomplishing compliance, and as a normative theory for how compliance could be improved: for example, Rees (1988, 1994) on occupational health and safety regulation and nuclear power industry self-regulation, Gunningham (1994) on environmental regulation, Parker (1997a, 1999a, 1999b) on regulation of the legal profession, competition and consumer protection law, and anti-discrimination law, Hopkins (1995; see, generally, Hopkins 1994:432) on occupational health and safety, Burby and Paterson (1993) on environmental regulation in the USA, and Haines (1997) on safety in the construction industry. Gunningham and Grabosky (1998; see also Sinclair 1997) have further developed Braithwaite's pyramid of regulatory strategies and explicitly addressed which regulatory policy instruments can be used together most successfully.

7 *Daniels & Ors v AWA* (1995) 13 ACLC 614.

8 AWA decided to hedge against foreign currency fluctuations by forward purchases of foreign currency against contracts for imported goods. The company lost over A\$49 million, although the accounts appeared to show they had made a substantial profit. The company's management had relied on one person to control the dealing, and on the external auditors to check what went on. The management failed to set up an adequate system of internal control and record-keeping, and did not act upon the failures in internal controls that were brought to its attention by the auditors.

9 However, Parker and Atkins (1999) found no significant increase in penalty levels.

10 US Department of Health and Human Services, Office of Inspector General, *Publication of the OIG's Provider Self-Disclosure Protocol, Federal Register*, vol. 63, no. 210, Friday 30 October 1998.

11 US Environment Protection Agency, *Incentives for Self-Policing: Discovery, Disclosure, Correction and Prevention of Violations*, January 1996 (reprinted in Kaplan et al. 2000: Appendix 3).

12 Department of Defense Inspector, *General Voluntary Disclosure Policy* (reprinted in Kaplan et al. 2000: Appendix 16C).

13 US Department of Justice, Antitrust Division, *Corporate Leniency Statement*; US Department of Justice, *Factors in Decision on Criminal Prosecutions for Environmental Violations in the Context of Significant Voluntary Compliance or Disclosure Efforts by the Violator* (reprinted in Kaplan et al. 2000: Appendix 2); *Federal Prosecution of Corporations*, June 1999, Washington DC (see Kaplan 2000).

14 However, under the current law anti-discrimination agencies usually do not have any power to enforce a conciliated settlement that includes a requirement to introduce a sexual harassment policy nor to require it to accord with standards and guidelines issued.

15 This model was explicitly supported by the Australian chemical industry association in an interview.

16   The program was adopted by OSHA in 1982 and now covers about 214 000 employees at 370 sites throughout the USA.

17   All Maine employers experienced a drop of 27 per cent over the same period. However, there has not yet been sufficient reporting and monitoring to determine the program's impact in terms of real reduction in injuries and illnesses.

18   This list is based on my fieldwork interviews.

19   This approach has also been partially adopted in Australia where voluntary audits are protected from inspection by the regulator and from discovery in court where they have been carried out by an approved auditor: Protection of the Environment Operations Act 1997 (NSW) ss 181–183. See Gunningham and Sinclair (1999).

20   See <http://es.epa.gov/oeca/oppa/evalu.html> (accessed 22 June 1999).

21   The US Ethics Resource Center, an organization to support and educate ethics and compliance officers, has proposed model legislation to 'recognize privileges for the good faith use of effective compliance programs to discover and report suspected misconduct and potential illegalities' (Desio 1999). See Model Four: Good Faith Compliance Immunity Act.

Appendix

1   Still's (1997) analysis of the affirmative action reports of the top seventy-five Australian financial institutions also showed that their affirmative action performance on personnel policies was strongest in relation to sexual harassment. Eighty-seven per cent self-reported that management actively promoted a work environment free of harassment, and 81 per cent reported that formal procedures were in place to deal with complaints of sexual harassment in their firms. That study also suggested that paper policies had translated into some real change in corporate culture, as judged by women employees: an attitudinal questionnaire found that only 26 per cent of women employees in three major banks thought that 'sexual harassment occurs at pre-executive and executive level' in their firm, while 71 per cent agreed that 'managers promote an harassment free workplace' (Still 1997: 41–2, 44). See Parker and Wolff (2000).

2   In some cases, not all of the following issues were covered.

References

Aalders, M. 1993, Regulation and in-company environmental management in the Netherlands, *Law & Policy* 15: 75–94.

Aalders, M. and Wilthagen, T. 1997, Moving beyond command-and-control: Reflexivity in the regulation of occupational health and safety and the environment, *Law & Policy* 19: 415–43.

Abbott, A. 1988, *The System of Professions*, University of Chicago Press.

Abel, R. 1988, *The Legal Profession in England and Wales*, Oxford, Basil Blackwell.

—— 1989, *American Lawyers*, New York, Oxford University Press.

Ackerman, R. and Bauer, R. 1976, *Corporate Social Responsiveness: The Modern Dilemma*, Virginia, Reston Publishing Company.

ACT Consumer Affairs Bureau 1996, New international business charter, *ACT Alert* June: 8.

Adams, S. 1984, *Roche Versus Adams*, London, Jonathan Cape.

Affirmative Action Agency 1997, *Annual Report 1996–1997*, Canberra, Department of Workplace Relations and Small Business.

Allen, W. 1992, Our schizophrenic conception of the business corporation, *Cardozo Law Review* 14: 262–81.

Andersen, O. 1996, The Norwegian internal control system: A tool in corporate environmental management?, *Eco-Management and Auditing* 3: 26–9.

Anti-Discrimination Board of New South Wales 1997, *Anti-Discrimination and Equal Employment Opportunity Guidelines*, Sydney.

Apel, A. 1995, A national study of compliance practices, in United States Sentencing Commission, *Corporate Crime in America: Strengthening the Good Citizen Corporation*, Washington DC, pp. 125–8.

Argyris, C. 1994, Litigation mentality and organizational learning, in Sitkin, S. and Bies, R. (eds) *The Legalistic Organization*, California, Sage Publications, pp. 347–58.

Arlen, J. and Kraakman, R. 1997, Controlling corporate misconduct: An analysis of corporate liability regimes, *New York University Law Review* 72: 687–779.

Arthurs, H. and Kreklewich, R. 1996, Law, legal institutions, and the legal profession in the new economy, *Osgoode Hall Law Journal* 34: 1–60.

Ashby, S. and Diacon, S. 1996, Motives for occupational risk management in large UK companies, *Safety Science* 22: 229–43.

Australian Law Reform Commission 1994, *Report No 68: Compliance with the Trade Practices Act 1974*, Sydney.

Ayres, I. and Braithwaite, J. 1992, *Responsive Regulation: Transcending the Deregulation Debate*, New York, Oxford University Press.

Bacchi, C. and Jose, J. 1994, Dealing with sexual harassment: Persuade, discipline, or punish?, *Australian Journal of Law & Society* 10: 1–13.

Baldwin, R. 1997, Regulation after command and control, in Hawkins, K. (ed.) *The Human Face of Law*, Oxford, Clarendon Press, pp. 65–84.

Baldwin, R. and Cave, M. 1999, *Understanding Regulation: Theory, Strategy & Practice*, Oxford University Press.

Baldwin, R., Scott, C. and Hood, C. 1998, *A Reader on Regulation*, Oxford University Press.

Barber, B. 1984, *Strong Democracy: Participatory Politics for a New Age*, Berkeley, University of California Press.

Bardach, E. and Kagan, R. 1982, *Going by the Book: The Problem of Regulatory Unreasonableness*, Philadelphia, Temple University Press.

Barnard, J. 1999, Reintegrative shaming in corporate sentencing, *Southern California Review* 72: 959–1007.

Beck, U. 1992, *Risk Society: Towards a New Modernity*, London, Sage Publications.

Beckenstein, A. and Gabel, H. 1983, Antitrust compliance: Results of a survey of legal opinion, *Antitrust Law Journal* 51: 459–516.

Becker, G. 1968, Crime and punishment: An economic approach, *Journal of Political Economy* 76: 169–217.

Beder, S. 1997, *Global Spin: The Corporate Assault on Environmentalism*, Melbourne, Scribe Books.

Belcher, A. 1995, Regulation by the market: The case of the Cadbury Code and compliance statement, *Journal of Business Law*, pp. 321–42.

Berenbeim, R. 2000, *Company Programs for Resisting Corrupt Practices: A Global Study*, New York, Conference Board.

Berle, A. and Means, G. 1968, *The Modern Corporation and Private Property*, New York, Harcourt Brace World.

Better Regulation Task Force (n.d.), *Principles of Good Regulation*, London, Horse Guards Road.

Bird, F. 1996, *The Muted Conscience: Moral Silence and the Practice of Ethics in Business*, Connecticut, Quorum Books.

Black, J. 1996, Constitutionalising self-regulation, *Modern Law Review* 59: 24–55.

—— 1997, *Rules and Regulators*, Oxford, Clarendon Press.

—— 1999, Using rules effectively, in McCrudden, C. (ed.) *Regulation and Deregulation*, Oxford University Press, pp. 94–121.

—— 2000, Proceduralising regulation: Part 1, *Oxford Journal of Legal Studies* 20: 597–614.

—— 2001, Proceduralising regulation: Part 2, *Oxford Journal of Legal Studies* 21: 33–58.

Blair, M. and Ramsay, I. 1998, Mandatory corporate disclosure rules and securities regulation, in Walker, G., Fisse, B. and Ramsay, I. (eds) *Securities Regu-*

lation in Australia and New Zealand, Sydney, LBC Information Services, pp. 55–87.

Blair, M. and Stout, L. 1999, A team production theory of corporate law, *Journal of Corporation Law* Summer: 751–805.

Blair, T. 1998, *The Third Way: New Politics for a New Society*, Fabian Pamphlet 588, London, Fabian Society.

Bohman, J. 1994, Complexity, pluralism, and the constitutional state: On Habermas's *Faktizitat und Geltung, Law & Society Review* 28: 897–930.

Boisjoly, R., Curtis, E. Foster and Mellican, E. 1989, The *Challenger* disaster: Organisational demands and personal ethics, reprinted in Ermann, D. and Lundman, R. (eds) 1996, *Corporate and Governmental Deviance: Problems of Organizational Behavior in Contemporary Society*, New York, Oxford University Press, pp. 207–31.

Bottomley, S. 1997, From contractualism to constitutionalism: A framework for corporate governance, *Sydney Law Review* 19: 277–313.

Boucher, D. and Vincent, A. 1993, *A Radical Hegelian: The Political and Social Philosophy of Henry Jones*, Cardiff, University of Wales Press.

Bovens, M. 1998, *The Quest for Responsibility: Accountability and Citizenship in Complex Organisations*, Cambridge University Press.

Boxall, L. 1998, The business case for compliance, in Business Law Education Centre, *First Annual Compliance Conference: Volume One*, Sydney, BLEC Books, pp. 1–22.

Boyd, J. 1998, *Searching for the Profit in Pollution Prevention: Case Studies in the Corporate Evaluation of Environmental Opportunities*, Discussion Paper 98–30, Washington DC, Resources for the Future.

Braithwaite, J. 1984, *Corporate Crime in the Pharmaceutical Industry*, London, Routledge & Kegan Paul.

—— 1985, *To Punish or Persuade: Enforcement of Coal Mine Safety*, Albany, State University of New York Press.

—— 1989, *Crime, Shame and Reintegration*, Cambridge University Press.

—— 1993, *Improving Regulatory Compliance: Strategies and Practical Applications in OECD Countries*, Paris, OECD.

—— 1997, On speaking softly and carrying sticks: Neglected dimensions of a republican separation of powers, *University of Toronto Law Journal* 47: 305–61.

—— 1999, Restorative justice: Assessing optimistic and pessimistic accounts, in Tonry, M. (ed.) *Crime and Justice: A Review of Research*, University of Chicago Press, pp. 241–364.

—— 2000, The new regulatory state and the transformation of criminology, *British Journal of Criminology* 40: 222–38.

Braithwaite, J. and Drahos, P. 2000, *Global Business Regulation*, Cambridge University Press.

Braithwaite, J. and Makkai, T. 1991, Testing an expected utility model of corporate deterrence, *Law & Society Review* 25: 7–40.

—— 1994, Trust and compliance, *Policing & Society* 4: 1–12.

Braithwaite, J. and Murphy, J. 1993, Clout and internal compliance systems, *Corporate Conduct Quarterly* Spring: 52–3.

Braithwaite, J. and Pettit, P. 1990, *Not Just Deserts: A Republican Theory of Criminal Justice*, Oxford University Press.

Braithwaite, J. and Roche, D. 2001, Responsibility and restorative justice, in Schiff, M. and Bazemore, G. (eds) *Restorative Community Justice: Repairing Harm and Restoring Communities*, Cincinnati, Anderson Publishing.

Braithwaite, V. 1992, *First Steps: Business Reactions to Implementing the Affirmative Action Act*, Report to the Affirmative Action Agency, Canberra, Australian National University.

—— 1993, The Australian government's affirmative action legislation: Achieving social change through human resource management, *Law & Policy* 15: 327–54.

—— 1995, Games of engagement: Postures within the regulatory community, *Law & Policy* 17: 225–55.

Brown, L. and Kandel, A. 1995, *The Legal Audit: Corporate Internal Investigation* (looseleaf service), Illinois, Clark Boardman Callaghan.

Brown, P. 1998, Shell re-uses Brent Spar platform, *Guardian Weekly*, 8 February: 7.

Burby, R. and Paterson, R. 1993, Improving compliance with state environmental regulations, *Journal of Policy Analysis and Management* 12: 753–72.

Burchell, G., Gordon, C. and Miller, P. (eds) 1991, *The Foucault Effect: Studies in Governmentality*, University of Chicago Press.

Bureau of International Labor Affairs 1996, *The Apparel Industry and Codes of Conduct: A Solution to the International Child Labor Problem?*, Washington DC, US Department of Labor.

Cain, M. 1994, The symbol traders, in Cain, M. and Harrington, C. (eds) *Lawyers in a Postmodern World: Translation and Transgression*, New York University Press, pp. 15–48.

Cairncross, F. 1995, *Green, Inc.: A Guide to Business and the Environment*, London, Earthscan Publications.

Calkins, S. 1997, Corporate compliance and antitrust agencies' bi-modal penalties, *Law & Contemporary Problems* 60(3): 127–67.

Casey, C. 1995, *Work, Self and Society after Industrialism*, London, Routledge.

Cave, M. 1999, Longford leaves ugly scars at Esso, *Australian Financial Review*, 22 September: 16.

Center for Business Ethics 1992, Instilling ethical values in large corporations, *Journal of Business Ethics* 11: 863–7.

Centre for Corporate Public Affairs 2000, *Corporate Community Involvement: Establishing a Business Case*, Canberra, Australian Capital Territory Department of Family and Community Services.

Chaganti, R. and Phatak, A. 1983, Evolution and role of the corporate environmental affairs function, *Research in Corporate Social Performance and Policy* 5: 183–203.

Chambliss, E. 1996, Title VII as a displacement of conflict, *Temple Political and Civil Rights Law Review* 6: 1–54.

Chayes, A. 1960, The modern corporation and the rule of law, in Mason, E. (ed.) *The Corporation in Modern Society*, Cambridge, Harvard University Press, pp. 25–45.

Clark, N. 1998, Chapter Two: Corporate sentencing guidelines: Drafting history, in Kaplan, J., Murphy, J. and Swenson, W. *Compliance Programs and the Corporate Sentencing Guidelines* (looseleaf service), Eagan, Michigan, West Group.

Cleek, M. and Leonard, S. 1998, Can corporate codes of ethics influence behavior?, *Journal of Business Ethics* 17: 619–30.

Clinard, M. 1983, *Corporate Ethics and Crime: The Role of Middle Management*, Beverly Hills, Sage Publications.

Coffee, J. 1981, No soul to damn, no body to kick: An unscandalised inquiry into the problem of corporate punishment, *Michigan Law Review* 79: 386–459.

Coffee, J., Gruner, R. and Stone, C. 1988, Standards for organizational probation: A proposal to the United States Sentencing Commission, *Whittier Law Review* 10: 77–102.

Coleman, J. 1982, *The Asymmetric Society*, Syracuse, NY, Syracuse University Press.

—— 1985, Responsibility in corporate action: A sociologist's view, in Hopt, K. and Teubner, G. (eds) *Corporate Governance and Directors Liabilities: Legal, Economic and Sociological Analyses on Corporate Social Responsibility*, Berlin, Walter de Gruyter, pp. 69–91.

Collins, J. and Porras, J. 1998, *Built To Last: Successful Habits of Visionary Companies*, London, Century Business.

Combs, N. 1994, Understanding Kaye Scholer: The autonomous citizen, the managed subject and the role of the lawyer, *California Law Review*, pp. 663–716.

Company Law Review Steering Group 1999, *Modern Company Law for a Competitive Economy: The Strategic Framework*, UK, Department of Trade and Industry.

—— 2000a, *Modern Company Law for a Competitive Economy: Developing the Framework*, UK, Department of Trade and Industry.

—— 2000b, *Modern Company Law for a Competitive Economy: Completing the Structure*, UK, Department of Trade and Industry.

Compliance News 2001, ACPA survey results, *Compliance News* 18: 5–6.

Conway, J. 1995, Self-evaluative privilege and corporate compliance audits, *Southern California Law Review* 68: 621–61.

Cotterrell, R. 1995, *Law's Community: Legal Theory in Sociological Perspective*, Oxford University Press.

Cowe, R. 1999, Corporate America faces GM onslaught, *Guardian*, 20 December: 20.

Cragg, W. 1992, *The Practice of Punishment: Towards a Theory of Restorative Justice*, London, Routledge.

Cronin, V. 1992, *The Flowering of the Renaissance*, London, Pimlico.

Cruickshanks-Boyd, D. and Mantle, J. 1996, Best practice in health, safety and environment regulation, *Environment Law, Policy and Public Opinion*, pp. 100–2.

Dahl, R. 1972, A prelude to corporate reform, *Business & Society Review* 1: 17–23.

Daly, M. 1997, The cultural, ethical and legal challenges in lawyering for a global organization: The role of the general counsel, *Emory Law Journal* 46: 1057–111.

Dan-Cohen, M. 1986, *Rights, Persons and Organisations: A Legal Theory for Bureaucratic Society*, Berkeley and Los Angeles, University of California Press.

D'Antonio, L., Johnsen, T. and Hutton, B. 1997, Expanding socially screened portfolios: An attribution analysis of bond performance, *Journal of Investing* 16(4): 79–87.

d'Arville, G. and Duffy, C. 2000, The behaviourist manifesto: Questions for the compliance industry, *Compliance News* 14: 10–22.

Davidson, W., Worrell, D. and Cheng, L. 1995, Are OSHA penalties effective?, *Business & Society Review* 92: 25–8.

Day, P. and Klein, R. 1987, The regulation of nursing homes: A comparative perspective, *Milbank Quarterly* 65: 303–47.

Deal, T. and Kennedy, A. 1999, *The New Corporate Cultures*, Cambridge, Mass., Perseus Publishing.

Dee, B. 1998, Characterising conduct as behavioural or procedural: A new paradigm for more effective compliance and a new corporate compliance ethos, *Compliance News* 5: 5.

Deegan, C. 1996, Environmental reporting for Australian corporations: An analysis of contemporary Australian and overseas reporting practices, *Environmental & Planning Law Journal* 13: 120–32.

—— 1999, Mandatory public environmental reporting in Australia: Here today, gone tomorrow?, *Environmental & Planning Law Journal* 16: 473–81.

Deegan, C. and Gordon, B. 1996, A study of the environmental disclosure policies of Australian corporations, *Accounting & Business Research* 26: 187–99.

Deegan, C. and Rankin, M. 1996, Do Australian companies report environmental news objectively? An analysis of environmental disclosures by firms prosecuted successfully by the Environment Protection Authority, *Accounting, Auditing & Accountability Journal* 9: 52–69.

DeMott, D. 1997, Organizational incentives to care about the law, *Law & Contemporary Problems* 60: 39–66.

Derber, C. 1998, *Corporation Nation: How Corporations Are Taking Over Our Lives and What We Can Do about It*, New York, St Martins Press.

Desio, P. 1998, Powerful or powerless: Does your compliance officer make the grade?, *Ethikos* 12(1): 11–12.

—— (ed.) 1999, *Employee Confidentiality and Non-Retributory Reporting Systems*, Ethics Resource Center Fellows Program, available at <http://www.ethics.org/fellows/confirpt.html> (accessed 20 December 2000).

Devereux, A. 1996, Human rights by agreement? A case study of the Human Rights and Equal Opportunity Commission's use of conciliation, *Australian Dispute Resolution Journal* 7: 280–301.

Dezalay, Y. 1996, Between the state, law and the market: The social and professional stakes in the construction and definition of a regulatory arena, in McCahery, J., Bratton, W., Picciotto, S. and Scott, C. (eds) *International Regulatory Competition and Coordination*, Oxford, Clarendon Press, pp. 59–87.

Dezalay, Y. and Garth, B. 1996, *Dealing in Virtue: International Commercial Arbitration and the Construction of a Transnational Legal Order*, University of Chicago Press.

Dhrymes, P. 1998, Socially responsible investment: Is it profitable?, in *The Investment Research Guide to Socially Responsible Investing*, Washington DC, Colloquium on Socially Responsible Investing.

Didier, M. and Swenson, W. 1995, Thou shall not improperly delegate authority: Thoughts on the US Sentencing Commission's Step Three, *Preventive Law Reporter* 14(4): 9–14.

Dierkes. M. 1985, Corporate social reporting and auditing: Theory and practice, in Hopt, K. and Teubner, G. (eds) *Corporate Governance and Directors Liabilities: Legal, Economic and Sociological Analyses on Corporate Social Responsibility*, Berlin, Walter de Gruyter, pp. 354–79.

DiMaggio, P. and Powell, W. 1991, The iron cage revisited: Institutional isomorphism and collective rationality in organizational fields, in Powell, W. and DiMaggio, P. (eds) *The New Institutionalism in Organizational Analysis*, University of Chicago Press, pp. 63–82.

Dimento, J. 1986, *Environmental Law and American Business: Dilemmas of Compliance*, New York, Plenum Press.

Ditz, D. 1998, Be pro-active, or be forced to react, *Environmental Forum*, November/December: 53–4.

Dobbin, F., Edelman, L., Meyer, J., Scott, W. R. and Swidler, A. 1988, The expansion of due process in organizations, in Zucker, L. (ed.) *Institutional Patterns and Organizations: Culture and Environment*, Cambridge, Mass., Ballinger Publishing Co., pp. 71–98.

Donaldson, L. 1990, The ethereal hand: Organizational economics and management theory, *Academy of Management Review* 15: 369–81.

Donaldson, L. and Davis, J. 1991, Stewardship theory or agency theory: CEO governance and shareholder returns, *Australian Journal of Management* 16: 49–53.

Donaldson, T. and Dunfee, T. 1999, *Ties That Bind: A Social Contracts Approach to Business Ethics*, Boston, Harvard Business School Press.

Downs, A. 1972, Up and down with ecology: The issue-attention cycle, *Public Interest* 28: 38–50.

Driscoll, D., Hoffman, W. and Murphy, J. 1998, Business ethics and compliance: What management is doing and why, *Business & Society Review* 99: 35–51.

Driscoll, D., Hoffman, W. and Petry, E. 1995, *The Ethical Edge: Tales of Organizations that Have Faced Moral Crises*, New York, Mastermedia.

Dryzek, J. 1990, *Discursive Democracy: Politics, Policy and Political Science*, Cambridge University Press.

—— 2000, *Deliberative Democracy and Beyond: Liberals, Critics, Contestations*, Oxford University Press.

Ducret, A. 1993, The sale of insurance at Aboriginal communities, *Criminology Australia* 14(3): 6–8.

Dunfee, T. 1999, Corporate governance in a market with morality, *Law & Contemporary Problems* 62(3): 129–57.

Dunsire, A. 1996, Tipping the balance: Autopoiesis and governance, *Administration & Society* 28: 299–334.

Durkheim, E. 1964 (trs. Simpson), *The Division of Labor in Society*, New York, Free Press.

—— 1992, *Professional Ethics and Civic Morals*, London, Routledge (new edn).

Edelman, L. 1990, Legal environments and organisational governance: The expansion of due process in the American workplace, *American Journal of Sociology* 95: 1401–40.

Edelman, L., Erlanger, H. and Lande, J. 1993, Internal dispute resolution: The transformation of civil rights in the workplace, *Law & Society Review* 27: 497–534.

Edelman, L., Petterson, S., Chambliss, E. and Erlanger, H. 1991, Legal ambiguity and the politics of compliance: Affirmative action officers' dilemma, *Law & Policy* 13: 73–97.

Eisenstein, H. 1996, *Inside Agitators: Australian Femocrats and the State*, Sydney, Allen & Unwin.

Elkington, J. 1998, *Cannibals with Forks: The Triple Bottom Line of 21st Century*, Gabrida Island BC, Canada, New Society Publishers.

Elkington, J. and Trisoglio, A. 1996, Developing realistic scenarios for the environment: Lessons from Brent Spar, *Long Range Planning* 29: 762–9.

Environment Protection Authority (Victoria) (EPA) 1993a, *Information Bulletin: Environment Improvement Plans*, Melbourne.

—— 1993b, *A Question of Trust: Accredited Licensee Concept. A Discussion Paper*, Melbourne.

—— 1996, *25 Years of Making a Difference*, Melbourne.

—— 1999a, *Environment Improvement Plan Guidelines*, Melbourne.

—— 1999b, *Annual Report 1999*, Melbourne.

Essrig, C. 2001, An international management system standard for business conduct, *Ethikos* 15(3): 7–9, 13.

Ethics Officer Association 1999, *General Information*, <http://www.eoa.org/general.htm> (23/07/99).

Ethics Resource Center 1995, The Ethics Resource Center's survey of ethics practices and employee perceptions, in United States Sentencing Commission, *Corporate Crime in America: Strengthening the Good Citizen Corporation*, Washington, DC, USSC, pp. 136–9.

Ethikos 2000, Chronikos, *Ethikos* 14(2): 10–11.

Eyring, A. and Stead, B. 1998, Shattering the glass ceiling: Some successful corporate practices, *Journal of Business Ethics* 17: 245–51.

Fabian, T. 1998, *Social Accountability 8000 (SA 8000) The First Auditable, Global, Standard for Ethical Sourcing Driven by CEPAA*, at <http://www.citinv.it/org/CNMS/archivio/lavoro/Presentazione SA8000.html> (accessed 3 April 1999).

Fama, E. 1980, Agency problems and the theory of the firm, *Journal of Political Economy* 88: 288–317.

Farr, T., Patterson, C., Witheriff, J. and Wilks, J. 1994, An occupational analysis of Queensland workplace health and safety practitioners, *Journal of Occupational Health and Safety Australia and New Zealand* 10(1): 17–25.

Feitshans, O. with Oliver, C. 1997, More than just a pretty program: OSHA Voluntary Protection Programs improve compliance by facing problems head on, *Corporate Conduct Quarterly* 5: 69–73, 79.

Fels, A. 2000, The Trade Practices Act: The past, the present and the future, Trade Practices and Consumer Law Conference, 27 May 2000, Sydney, available at <http://www.accc.gov.au/speeches/2000/tpa_past_present future.htm> (accessed 20 January 2001).

Fiorelli, P. 1993, Fine reductions through effective ethics programs, *Albany Law Review* 56: 403–40.

Fischer, K. and Schot, J. (eds) 1993, *Environmental Strategies for Industry: International Perspectives on Research Needs and Policy Implications*, Washington DC, Island Press.

Fisse, B. 1989, Corporate compliance programmes: The Trade Practices Act and beyond, *Australian Business Law Review* 17: 356–99.

Fisse, B. and Braithwaite, J. 1983, *The Impact of Publicity on Corporate Offenders*, Albany, State University of New York Press.

—— 1993, *Corporations, Crime and Accountability*, Cambridge University Press.

Fogg, R. 1994, *Nursing Home Regulations: Survey, Certification and Enforcement Manual*, New York, Thompson Publishing Group.

Forcese, C. 1997, *Commerce with Conscience? Human Rights and Corporate Codes of Conduct*, Montreal, International Centre for Human Rights and Democratic Development.

Fort, T. and Noone, J. 1999, Banded contracts, mediating institutions, and corporate governance: A naturalist analysis of contractual theories of the firm, *Law & Contemporary Problems* 62(3): 163–213.

Foster, C., Poe, S. and Braswell, M. 1998, Compliance programs: An alternative to punitive damages for corporate defendants, *South Carolina Law Review* 49: 247–72.

Foucault, M. (tr. A. Sheridan) 1977, *Discipline and Punish*, London, Penguin Books.

Fraser, A. 1998, *Reinventing Aristocracy: The Constitutional Reformation of Corporate Governance*, Aldershot, Dartmouth Press.

Freyer, D. 1996, Corporate compliance programs for FDA-regulated companies: Incentives for their development and the impact of the Federal Sentencing Guidelines for Organizations, *Food & Drug Law Journal* 51: 225–42.

Friedman, M. 1972, The social responsibility of business is to make profits, *New York Times Magazine*, 13 September: 32–3, 122–6.

Friedrichs, D. 1996, *Trusted Criminals: White Collar Crime in Contemporary Society*, Belmont, CA, Wadsworth Publishing.

Frye, R. 1998, The role of private banks in promoting sustainable development, from outside counsel's perspective, *Law & Policy in International Business* 29: 481–99.

Futrell, J. 1994, Environmental ethics, legal ethics, and codes of professional responsibility, *Loyola of Los Angeles Law Review* 27: 825–40.

Galaway, B. and Hudson, J. 1990, *Criminal Justice, Restitution and Reconciliation*, New York, Criminal Justice Press.

Garland, D. 1997, Governmentality and the problem of crime: Foucault, criminology, sociology, *Theoretical Criminology* 1: 173–214.

Geltman, E. and Skroback, A. 1998, Reinventing the EPA to conform with the new American environmentality, *Columbia Journal of Environmental Law* 23: 1–56.

GEMI 1998, *Measuring Environmental Performance: A Primer and Survey of Metrics in Use*, Washington DC, Global Environmental Management Initiative.

Genn, H. 1993, Business responses to the regulation of health and safety in England, *Law & Policy* 15: 219–33.

Giesel, G. 1992, The ethics or employment dilemma of in-house counsel, *Georgetown Journal of Legal Ethics* 5: 535–96.

Gilbert, D. 1996, *Ethics through Corporate Strategy*, New York, Oxford University Press.

Gilboy, J. 1998, Compelled third-party participation in the regulatory process: Legal duties, culture and noncompliance, *Law & Policy* 20: 135–55.

Gioia, D. 1992, Why I didn't recognise Pinto fire hazards: How organisational scripts channel managers' thoughts and actions, reprinted in Ermann, D. and Lundman, R. (eds) 1996, *Corporate and Governmental Deviance: Problems of Organizational Behavior in Contemporary Society*, New York, Oxford University Press, pp. 139–57.

Glaser, B. and Strauss, A. 1967, *The Discovery of Grounded Theory: Strategies for Qualitative Research*, Chicago, Aldine.

Goodpaster, K. 1991, Business ethics and stakeholder analysis, *Business Ethics Quarterly* 1: 53–73, reprinted in Beauchamp, T. and Bowie, N. (eds) 1993, *Ethical Theory and Business*, New Jersey, Prentice Hall, pp. 85–93.

Gordon, C. 1991, Governmental rationality: An introduction, in Burchell, G., Gordon, C. and Miller, P. (eds) *The Foucault Effect: Studies in Governmentality*, University of Chicago Press, pp. 1–52.

Gordon, R. and Simon, W. 1992, The redemption of professionalism?, in Nelson, R., Trubek, D. and Solomon, R. (eds) *Lawyers Ideals/Lawyers Practices: Transformations in the American Legal Profession*, New York, Cornell University Press, pp. 230–57.

Grabosky, P. 1990, Professional advisers and white collar illegality: Towards explaining and excusing professional failure, *University of New South Wales Law Journal* 13: 73–96.

—— 1994, Green markets: Environmental regulation by the private sector, *Law & Policy* 16: 419–48.

—— 1995, Using non-governmental resources to foster regulatory compliance, *Governance: An International Journal of Policy and Administration* 8: 527–50.

Grabosky, P. and Braithwaite, J. 1986, *Of Manners Gentle: Enforcement Strategies of Australian Business Regulatory Agencies*, Melbourne, Oxford University Press.

Graham, C. 1989, Regulating the company, in Hancher, L. and Moran, M. (eds) *Capitalism, Culture and Economic Regulation*, Oxford, Clarendon Press, pp. 199–223.

Gray, J. 1998, How regulation finds its way through the corporate veil, in Rider, B. (ed.) *The Corporate Dimension*, Bristol, Jordans, pp. 255–71.

Gray, R., Owen, D. and Adams, C. 1996, *Accounting and Accountability: Changes and Challenges in Social and Environmental Reporting*, London, Prentice Hall.

Gray, W. and Scholz, J. 1991, Analysing the equity and efficiency of OSHA enforcement, *Law & Policy* 13: 185–214.

Gruner, R. 1994, *Corporate Crime and Sentencing*, Virginia, Michie Company.

—— 1997, General counsel in an era of compliance programs and corporate self-policing, *Emory Law Journal* 46: 1113–99.

Gunningham, N. 1994, Beyond compliance: Management of environmental risk, in Boer, B., Fowler, R. and Gunningham, N. (eds) *Environmental Outlook: Law and Policy*, Sydney, Federation Press, pp. 254–81.

—— 1995, Environment, self-regulation, and the chemical industry: Assessing responsible care, *Law & Policy* 17: 57–109.

—— 1998, Environmental management systems and community participation: Rethinking chemical industry regulation, mimeo, Canberra, Australian Centre for Environmental Law, Australian National University.

Gunningham, N. and Grabosky, P. 1998, *Smart Regulation: Designing Environmental Policy*, Oxford University Press.

Gunningham, N. and Johnstone, R. 1999, *Regulating Workplace Safety: Systems and Sanctions*, Oxford University Press.

Gunningham, N. and Sinclair, D. 1999, Environment management systems, regulation and the pulp and paper industry: ISO 14001 in practice, *Environmental & Planning Law Journal* 16: 5–24.

Habermas, J. (tr. T. McCarthy) 1987, *The Theory of Communicative Action. Volume Two: Lifeworld and System: A Critique of Functionalist Reason*, Cambridge, Polity Press.

—— (tr. W. Rehg) 1996, *Between Facts and Norms: Contributions to a Discourse Theory of Law and Democracy*, Cambridge, Mass., MIT Press.

Haines, F. 1997, *Corporate Regulation: Beyond Punish or Persuade*, Oxford University Press.

Halliday, T. and Carruthers, B. 1996, The moral regulation of markets: Professions, privatization and the English Insolvency Act 1986, *Accounting, Organizations & Society* 21: 371–413.

Hancher, L. and Moran, M. 1989, Organising regulatory space, in Hancher, L. and Moran, M. (eds) *Capitalism, Culture and Economic Regulation*, Oxford University Press, pp. 271–99.

Hancock, J. 1998, *The Ethical Investor*, London, Financial Times and Prentice Hall Publishing.

Handy, C. 1992, Balancing corporate power: A new federalist paper, *Harvard Business Review*, November/December: 59–72.

Harr, J. 1997, *A Civil Action*, London, Arrow.

Harvard Law Review 1996, Growing the carrot: Encouraging effective corporate compliance, *Harvard Law Review* 109: 1783–800.

Hawkins, K. 1984, *Environment and Enforcement: Regulation and the Social Definition of Pollution*, Oxford University Press.

Hawkins, K. and Hutter, B. 1993, The response of business to social regulation in England and Wales: An enforcement perspective, *Law & Policy* 15: 199–217.

Hayek, F. 1948, *Individualism and Economic Order*, University of Chicago Press.

Heimer, C. 1996, Explaining variation in the impact of law: Organizations, institutions and professions, *Studies in Law, Politics & Society* 15: 29–59.

—— 1997, Legislating responsibility, *American Bar Foundation Working Paper #9711*, Chicago.

Heller, J. and Guetter, J. 1999, Is compliance officer a tough job, or what?, *Journal of Health Care Compliance* 1(3): 45–50.

Heller, J., Murphy, J. and Meaney, M. (eds) 2001, *Guide to Professional Development in Compliance*, Gaithersberg, Maryland, Aspen Publications.

Henry, S. 1983, *Private Justice: Towards Integrated Theorising in the Sociology of Law*, London, Routledge & Kegan Paul.

Hess, D. 1999, Social reporting: A reflexive law approach to corporate social responsiveness, *Journal of Corporation Law* Fall: 41–84.

Hessen, R. 1979, *In Defense of the Corporation*, Stanford, Hoover Institution Press.

Heyvaert, V. 1999a, Reconceptualizing risk assessment, *Review of European Community and International Environmental Law* 8: 135–43.

—— 1999b, Coping with Uncertainty: The Regulation of Chemicals in the European Union, PhD thesis submitted at European University Institute, Florence, April 1999.

Hill, J. 1998, Public beginnings, private ends: Should corporate law privilege the interests of shareholders?, *Australian Journal of Corporate Law* 9: 21–38.

—— 1999, Deconstructing Sunbeam: Contemporary issues in corporate governance, *Company & Securities Law Journal* 17: 288–306.

Hills, B. 1999, Oil giants strategy to cover up disasters, *Sydney Morning Herald*, 24 March: 1, 16–17.

Hoffman, A. 1997, *From Heresy to Dogma: An Institutional History of Corporate Environmentalism*, San Francisco, New Lexington Press.

Hood, C., James, O., Jones, G. and Scott, C. 1999, *Regulation inside Government: Waste-Watchers, Quality Police, and Sleazebusters*, Oxford University Press.

Hopkins, A. 1994, Compliance with what? The fundamental regulatory question, *British Journal of Criminology* 34: 431–43.

—— 1995, *Making Safety Work*, Sydney, Allen & Unwin.

—— 2000, *Lessons from Longford: The Esso Gas Plant Explosion*, Sydney, CCH Australia.

Howard, P. 1994, *The Death of Common Sense: How Law is Suffocating America*, New York, Random House.

Hutter, B. 1997, *Compliance: Regulation and Environment*, Oxford University Press.

—— 2001, *Regulation and Risk: Occupational Health and Safety on the Railways*, Oxford University Press.

Hutton, W. 1996, *The State We're In*, London, Vintage Press.

ICEM 1997, *Rio Tinto: Tainted Titan. The Stakeholders Report*, Brussels.

—— 1998, *Rio Tinto: Behind the Façade. 1998 Stakeholders Report*, Brussels.

International Auditing Practices Committee 1995, *The Audit Profession and the Environment*, Melbourne, International Federation of Accountants and Auditing Standards Board of Australian Accounting Research Foundation.

International Council of Chemical Associations 1998, *Responsible Care Status Report 1998*, Brussels.

Investment Management Regulatory Organisation 1997, *Compliance Arrangements Scorecard*, London.

Jackall, R. 1988, *Moral Mazes: The World of Corporate Managers*, New York, Oxford University Press.

Jay, A. 1987, *Management and Machiavelli: Power and Authority in Business Life*, London, Hutchinson.

Jeffcott, B. and Yanz, L. 1998, Code-breaking, *New Internationalist* 302: 23–4.

Joly, C. c. 1997, Climate change, insurance and investment management in OECD, *Climate Change: Mobilising Global Effort*, Paris, pp. 51–60.

Jutsen, J. 1995, Voluntary agreements with industry for reducing greenhouse gas emissions, in *Towards a Sustainable Future: Challenges and Responses, National Conference on Environmental Engineering*, Canberra, Institution of Engineers, pp. 25–9.

Kagan, R. and Scholz, J. 1984, The criminology of the corporation and regulatory enforcement strategies, in Hawkins, K. and Thomas, J. (eds) *Enforcing Regulation*, Boston, Kluwer Nijhoff Publishing, pp. 67–95.

Kaisersatt, J. 1996, Criminal enforcement as a disincentive to environmental compliance: Is a federal environmental audit privilege the right answer?, *American Journal of Criminal Law* 23: 405–30.

Kaplan, J. 1991, The corporate sentencing guidelines: Making compliance programs effective, *Corporate Conduct Quarterly* 1(1): 1–3.

—— 1998, In Illinois only: Insurers compliance audits are privileged, *Ethikos* 11(5): 1–3.

—— 2000, Justices guidance on prosecuting corporations: A booster shot for ethics officers, *Ethikos* 14(1): 1–3, 11.

—— 2001, The Sentencing Guidelines: The first ten years, *Ethikos* 15(3): 1–3, 10.

Kaplan, J., Murphy, J. and Swenson, W. (eds) 1998 (with annual supplement), *Compliance Programs and the Corporate Sentencing Guidelines*, Eagan, MI, West Group.

—— 2000, *Compliance Programs and the Corporate Sentencing Guidelines*, Eagan, MI, West Group.

Karliner, J. 1997, *The Corporate Planet: Ecology and Politics in the Age of Globalization*, San Francisco, Sierra Club Books.

Keffer, C. and Lehni, M. 1999, *Eco-Efficiency Indicators and Reporting: Report on the Status of the Projects Work in Progress and Guideline for Pilot Application*, Geneva, World Business Council for Sustainable Development.

Kihnley, J. 2000, Unraveling the ivory fabric: Institutional obstacles to the handling of sexual harassment complaints, *Law & Social Inquiry* 25: 69–90.

King, G. 1999, The implications of an organization's structure on whistle-blowing, *Journal of Business Ethics* 20: 315–26.

Klein, N. 2000, *No Logo*, London, HarperCollins.

Kohn, A. 1993, *Punished by Rewards: The Trouble with Gold Stars, Incentive Plans, A's, Praise and Other Bribes*, Boston, Houghton Mifflin.

Korten, D. 1995, *When Corporations Rule the World*, West Hartford, Conn. and San Francisco, Kumarian Press and Berrett-Koehler Publishers.

KPMG 1997, *1997 Business Ethics Survey*, Toronto.

—— 1998, *1998 KPMG Business Ethics Survey: Ethical Risk for Canadian Corporations*, Toronto.

Krut, R. and Gleckman, H. 1998, *ISO 14001: A Missed Opportunity for Global Industrial Development*, London, Earthscan Publications.

Kubasek, N., Browne, M., Jennings, K. and Williamson, C. 1998, Mandatory environmental auditing: A better way to secure environmental protection in the United States and Canada, *Journal of Land, Resources & Environmental Law* 18: 261–91.

Kurtz, L. 1997, The impact of social screening on growth-oriented investment strategies, *Journal of Performance Measurement* Spring: 43–6.

Ladd, J. 1970, Morality and the ideal of rationality in formal organizations, *Monist* 54: 488–516.

Langlois, R. and Robertson, P. 1995, *Firms, Markets and Economic Change: A Dynamic Theory of Business Organisations*, London, Routledge.

Larson, M. 1977, *The Rise of Professionalism*, Berkeley, University of California Press.

Laufer, W. 1995, A study of small business compliance practices, in United States Sentencing Commission, *Corporate Crime in America: Strengthening the Good Citizen Corporation*, Washington, DC, USSC, pp. 129–31.

—— 1999, Corporate liability, risk shifting and the paradox of compliance, *Vanderbilt Law Review* 52: 1341–420.

Laufer, W. and Robertson, D. 1997, Corporate ethics initiatives as social control, *Journal of Business Ethics* 16: 1029–48.

LeClair, D. Thorne, Ferrell, O. and Fraedrich, J. 1998, *Integrity Management: A Guide to Managing Legal and Ethical Issues in the Workplace*, Florida, University of Tampa Press.

Ledgerwood, G. 1997, The Global 500, big oil and corporate environmental governance: How Shell became transparent in the 1990s, in Ledgerwood, G. (ed.) *Greening the Boardroom: Corporate Governance and Business Sustainability*, Sheffield, Greenleaf Publishing, pp. 189–205.

Levi, M. 1987, *Regulating Fraud: White Collar Crime and the Criminal Process*, London and New York, Tavistock Publications.

—— 1988, *Of Rule and Revenue*, Berkeley, University of California Press.

Lewis, S. 1998, The corporate right to cover up, *Multinational Monitor* May: 9–11.

Liggio, C. 1997, The changing role of corporate counsel, *Emory Law Journal* 46: 1201–22.

Lister, R. 1995, Dilemmas in engendering citizenship, *Economy & Society* 24: 1–40.

Liubicic, R. 1998, Corporate codes of conduct and product labeling schemes: The limits and possibilities of promoting international labor rights through private initiatives, *Law & Policy in International Business* 30: 111–58.

Luhmann, N. 1982, *The Differentiation of Society*, New York, Columbia University Press.

—— 1985, The self-reproduction of law and its limits, in Teubner, G. (ed.) *Dilemmas of Law in the Welfare State*, Berlin, Walter de Gruyter, pp. 111–27.

Lytton, W. and Denton, M. 1998, Chapter 14: Employee discipline, in Kaplan et al., *Compliance Programs and the Corporate Sentencing Guidelines*.

McBarnet, D. 1994, Legal creativity: Law, capital and legal avoidance, in Cain, M. and Harrington, C. (eds) *Lawyers in a Postmodern World: Translation and Transgression*, New York University Press, pp. 73–84.

McBarnet, D. and Whelan, C. 1997, Creative compliance and the defeat of legal control: The magic of the orphan subsidiary, in Hawkins, K. (ed.) *The Human Face of Law*, Oxford University Press, pp. 177–98.

—— 1999, *Creative Accounting and the Cross-Eyed Javelin Thrower*, Chichester, John Wiley & Sons.

McCaffrey, D. and Hart, D. 1998, *Wall Street Polices Itself: How Securities Firms Manage the Legal Hazards of Competitive Pressures*, New York, Oxford University Press.

McMurray, G. 1997, Managing the firm–regulator relationship, *Journal of Financial Regulation & Compliance* 5: 327–30.

Mackie, K. 1989, *Lawyers in Business: And the Law Business*, Basingstoke, Hampshire, Macmillan Press.

Majone, G. 1994, The rise of the regulatory state in Europe, *West European Politics* 17: 77–101.

—— 1996, *Regulating Europe*, London, Routledge.

Makkai, T. and Braithwaite, J. 1993, Praise, pride and corporate compliance, *International Journal of the Sociology of Law* 21: 73–91.

—— 1994, Reintegrative shaming and regulatory compliance, *Criminology* 32: 361–85.

—— 1995, In and out of the revolving door: Making sense of regulatory capture, *Journal of Public Policy* 1: 61–78.

Makkai, T. and Braithwaite, V. 1993, Professionalism, organizations and compliance, *Law & Social Inquiry*, 33–59.

Manning, P. 1987, Ironies of compliance, in Shearing, C. and Stenning, P. (eds) *Private Policing*, California, Sage Publications.

March, J. and Simon, H. 1958, *Organizations*, New York, Wiley.

Marshall, T. 1985, *Alternatives to Criminal Courts*, Aldershot, Gower.

Martinson, J. 1998, Tough penalties for ex-MGAM men, *Financial Times*, Thursday 21 May.

—— 1999, Monsanto pays GM price, *Guardian Weekly*, 21 December: 19.

Mathews, J. 1997, More innovative workplaces = safer workplaces: Organisational innovation and the protection of workers health and safety, *Journal of Occupational Health and Safety Australia and New Zealand* 13: 319–29.

May, L. 1996, *The Socially Responsive Self: Social Theory and Professional Ethics*, University of Chicago Press.

Meaney, M. 2001, Thinking like a compliance professional: The HCCA Code of Ethics for health care compliance professionals, in Heller, Murphy and Meaney (eds), pp. 77–91.

Meidinger, E. 1987, Regulatory culture: A theoretical outline, *Law & Policy* 9: 355–86.

Messmer, H. and Otto, H. 1992, Restorative justice: Steps on the way toward a good idea, in Messmer, H. and Otto, H. (eds) *Restorative Justice on Trial*, Dordrecht, Kluwer, pp. 1–12.

Metzger, M. 1987, Organisations and the law, *American Business Law Journal* 25: 407–41.

Miller, A. 1991, *Socially Responsible Investing: How To Invest with Your Conscience*, New York, Simon & Schuster.

Millon, D. 1995, Communitarianism in corporate law: Foundations and law reform strategies, in Mitchell, L. (ed.) *Progressive Corporate Law*, Colorado, Westview Press, pp. 1–33.

Minichiello, V., Aroni, R., Timewell, E. and Alexander, R. 1990, *In-Depth Interviewing: Researching People*, Melbourne, Longman Cheshire.

Mitchell, T., Daniels, D., Hopper, H., George-Falvy, J. and Ferris, G. 1996, Perceived correlates of illegal behaviour in organizations, *Journal of Business Ethics* 15: 439–55.

Mokhiber, R. and Weissman, R. 1997, Beat the devil: The 10 worst corporations of 1997, *Multinational Monitor*, December: 9–18.

—— 2001, New century, same as the old century: The ten worst corporations of 2000, *Focus on the Corporation*, available at <http://www.corporatepredators. org> (accessed 27 December 2000).

Morf, D., Schumacher, M. and Vitell, S. 1999, A survey of ethics officers in large organizations, *Journal of Business Ethics* 20: 265–71.

Morgan, G. 1997, *Images of Organization*, California, Sage Publications.

Morris, L. 1998, Department of Health and Human Services Office of Inspector General: Voluntary Disclosure Program, in Basri, C., Murphy, J. and Wallance, G. (eds) *Corporate Compliance: Caremark and the Globalization of Good Corporate Conduct*, New York, Practising Law Institute, pp. 933–46.

Moses, L. N. and Savage, I. 1994, The effect of firm characteristics on truck accidents, *Accident Analysis and Prevention* 26: 173–9.

Murphy, J. 1994, Evaluations, incentives and rewards in compliance programs: Bringing the carrot indoors, *Corporate Conduct Quarterly* 3(3): 40–3.

—— 1998, Enhancing the compliance officers authority: Preparing an employment contract, *Ethikos* 11(6): 5–7, 16.

Nader, L. 1979, Disputing without the force of law, *Yale Law Journal* 88: 998–1021.

Nader, R., Green, M. and Seligman, J. 1976, *Taming the Giant Corporation*, New York, Norton.

Nelson, R. and Nielsen, L. 2000, Cops, counsel, and entrepreneurs: Constructing the role of inside counsel in large corporations, *Law & Society Review* 34: 457–93.

Nesterczuk, G. 1996, Reviewing the national performance review, *Regulation* 3: 31–9.

Newton, A. 1998, *Compliance: Making Ethics Work in Financial Services*, London, Financial Times and Pitman Publishing.

Nielsen, R. 1996, *The Politics of Ethics: Methods for Acting, Learning, and Sometimes Fighting with Others in Addressing Ethics Problems in Organizational Life*, New York, Oxford University Press.

—— 2000, Do internal due process systems permit adequate political and moral space for ethics voice, praxis, and community?, *Journal of Business Ethics* 24: 1–27.

Novartis 1998, *Health, Safety and Environment Report: Innovation and Accountability*, Basel, Novartis International AG.

Obi, C. 1997, Globalisation and local resistance: The case of the Ogoni versus Shell, *New Political Economy* 2(1): 137–48.

OECD 1997a, *The OECD Report on Regulatory Reform Volume II: Thematic Studies*, Paris.
—— 1997b, *Regulatory Impact Analysis: Best Practices in OECD Countries*, Paris.
—— 1997c, *Small Business, Job Creation and Growth, Facts, Obstacles and Best Practices*, Paris.
—— 1997d, *The OECD Declaration and Decisions on International Investment and Multinational Enterprises: Basic Texts*, Paris.
—— 1997e, *Public Management Occasional Papers No. 18 Co-operative Approaches to Regulation*, Paris.
OECD Ad Hoc Taskforce on Corporate Governance 1999, *OECD Principles of Corporate Governance*, OECD, Paris.
Office of Fair Trading 1998, *Raising Standards of Consumer Care: Progressing beyond Codes of Practice*, UK, Her Majesty's Stationery Office.
Ogus, A. 1994, *Regulation: Legal Form and Economic Theory*, Oxford University Press.
Oldfield, A. 1990, *Citizenship and Community: Civic Republicanism and the Modern World*, London, Routledge.
Osaghae, E. 1995, The Ogoni uprising: Oil politics, minority agitation and the future of the Nigerian state, *African Affairs* 94: 325–44.
Osborne, D. and Gaebler, T. 1992, *Reinventing Government: How the Entrepreneurial Spirit is Transforming the Public Sector*, Reading, Mass., Addison-Wesley.
Oxenburgh, M. 1991, *Increasing Productivity and Profit through Health and Safety*, Sydney, CCH International.
Paine, L. 1994, Managing for organizational integrity, *Harvard Business Review* 15: 106–17.
Painter, R. 1994, The moral interdependence of corporate lawyers and their clients, *Southern California Law Review* 67: 507–84.
Parker, C. 1997a, Converting the lawyers: The dynamics of competition and accountability reform, *Australian and New Zealand Journal of Sociology* 33: 39–55.
—— 1997b, Competing images of the legal profession: Competing regulatory strategies, *International Journal of the Sociology of Law* 25: 385–409.
—— 1999a, Compliance professionalism and regulatory community: The Australian trade practices regime, *Journal of Law & Society* 26: 215–39.
—— 1999b, *Just Lawyers*, Oxford Socio-Legal Studies Series, Oxford University Press.
—— 1999c, How to win hearts and minds: Corporate compliance policies for sexual harassment, *Law & Policy* 21: 21–48.
—— 1999d, *The State of Regulatory Compliance: Issues, Trends and Challenges*, PUMA/REG(99)3, Paris, OECD.
—— 2000a, Reinventing regulation within the corporation: Compliance-oriented regulatory innovation, *Administration & Society* 32: 529–65.
—— 2000b, The ethics of advising on regulatory compliance: Autonomy or interdependence?, *Journal of Business Ethics* 28: 339–51.
—— 2001, Conflicts of interest and conflicts of loyalty, in Heller, Murphy and Meaney (eds), pp. 93–114.

Parker, C. and Connolly, O. (forthcoming), Is there a duty to implement a compliance system in Australian law?, *Australian Business Law Review*.

Parker, C. and Wolff, L. 2000, Sexual harassment and the corporation in Australia and Japan: The potential for corporate governance of human rights, *Federal Law Review* 28(3): 509–48.

Parker, J. and Atkins, R. 1999, Did the corporate criminal sentencing guidelines matter? Some preliminary empirical observations, *Journal of Law & Economics* XLII: 423–53.

Parkinson, J. 1993, *Corporate Power and Responsibility: Issues in the Theory of Company Law*, Oxford University Press.

Parry, P. 2000, *The Bottom Line: How To Build a Business Case for ISO 14001*, Boca Raton, Florida, St Lucie Press.

Parsons, T. 1954, A sociologist looks at the legal profession, in Parsons, T., *Essays in Sociological Theory*, Illinois, Free Press, pp. 370–85.

Partlett, D. and Szweda, E. 1991, An embattled profession: The role of lawyers in the regulatory state, *University of New South Wales Law Journal* 14: 8–45.

Pastin, M. and Brecto, C. 1995, The impact of corporate ethics and compliance practices: A survey, *Corporate Conduct Quarterly* 3(4): 51–4.

Paternoster, R. and Simpson, S. 1996, Sanction threats and appeals to morality: Testing a rational choice model of corporate crime, *Law & Society Review* 30: 549–83.

Pava, M. and Krausz, J. 1995, *Corporate Responsibility and Financial Performance: The Paradox of Social Cost*, Westport, Conn., Quorum Books.

Pearce, F. and Tombs, S. 1990, Ideology, hegemony, and empiricism: Compliance theories of regulation, *British Journal of Criminology* 30: 423–43.

—— 1997, Hazards, law and class: Contextualising the regulation of corporate crime, *Social & Legal Studies* 6: 79–107.

—— 1998, *Toxic Capitalism: Corporate Crime and the Chemical Industry*, Aldershot, Ashgate.

Petry, E. 1995, A study of compliance practices in compliance aware companies, in United States Sentencing Commission, *Corporate Crime in America: Strengthening the Good Citizen Corporation*, Washington DC, pp. 132–5.

—— 2001, EOA Survey: Companies seeking to integrate ethics through the whole organization, *Ethikos* 15(1): 1–3, 16.

Petry, E., Mujica, A. and Vickery, D. 1998, Sources and consequences of workplace pressure: Increasing the risk of unethical and illegal business practices, *Business & Society Review* 99: 25–30.

Pettet, B. 1998, The combined code: A firm place for self-regulation in corporate governance, *Journal of International Business Law* 12: 394–400.

Pettit, P. 1997, *Republicanism: A Theory of Freedom and Government*, Oxford University Press.

Phillips, A. 1991, *Engendering Democracy*, Cambridge, Polity Press.

Pinchot, G. and Pinchot, E. 1994, *The Intelligent Organization: Engaging the Talent and Initiative of Everyone in the Workplace*, San Francisco, Berrett-Koehler Publishers.

Plender, J. 1999, Stakeholder power, *Financial Times* 15 July.

Porter, M. and van der Linde, C. 1995, Green and competitive: Ending the stalemate, *Harvard Business Review*, September/October: 120–34.

Power, M. 1997, *The Audit Society: Rituals of Verification*, Oxford University Press.
—— 2000, The new risk management, *European Business Forum* 1: 60–1.
Price Waterhouse LLP, 1997, *1996 Survey of Corporate Compliance Practices*, New York.
Pusey, M. 1991, *Economic Rationalism in Canberra: A Nation Building State Changes Its Mind*, Cambridge University Press.
Quinlan, M. and Bohle, P. 1991, *Managing Occupational Health and Safety in Australia: A Multi-Disciplinary Approach*, South Melbourne, Macmillan Education.
Rees, J. 1988, *Reforming the Workplace: A Study of Self-Regulation in Occupational Safety*, Philadelphia, University of Pennsylvania Press.
—— 1994, *Hostages of Each Other: The Transformation of Nuclear Safety since Three Mile Island*, University of Chicago Press.
—— 1997, Development of communitarian regulation in the chemical industry, *Law & Policy* 19: 477–528.
Reichman, N. 1992, Moving backstage: Uncovering the role of compliance practices in shaping regulatory policy, in Schlegel, K. and Weisburd, C. (eds) *White Collar Crime Reconsidered*, Boston, Northeastern University Press, pp. 245–67.
Reiss, A. J. 1984, Selecting strategies of social control over organisational life, in Hawkins, K. and Thomas, J. (eds) *Enforcing Regulation*, Boston, Kluwer-Nijhoff, pp. 23–35.
Rhodes, R. 1996, The new governance: Governing without government, *Political Studies* XLIV: 652–67.
—— 1997, *Understanding Governance: Policy Networks, Governance, Reflexivity and Accountability*, Buckingham, Open University Press.
Roberts, B., Chaset, A., Haac, L. and O'Neill, H. 1995, Preventive medicine for corporate crime, *Business & Society Review* 94: 34–9.
Rosen, R. 1989, The inside counsel movement, professional judgment and organizational representation, *Indiana Law Journal* 64: 479–553.
Ruimschotel, D., van Reenen, P. and Klaasen, H. 1999, The table of eleven: A conceptual framework and an instrument of law enforcement issues (mimeo).
Sauer, D. 1997, The impact of social-responsibility screens on investment performance: Evidence from the Domini 400 Social Index and Domini Equity Mutual Fund, *Review of Financial Economics* 6: 137–50.
Schlegel, K. 1990, *Just Deserts for Corporate Criminals*, Boston, Northeastern University Press.
Schmidheiny, S. and Zorraquin, F. 1996, *Financing Change: The Financial Community, Eco-Efficiency and Sustainable Development*, Cambridge, Mass., MIT Press.
Schmitt, R. 1994, The Amoco/EPA Yorktown experience and regulating the right thing, *Natural Resources and Environment* 9: 11–13, 51.
Scholz, J. 1997, Enforcement policy and corporate misconduct: The changing perspective of deterrence theory, *Law & Contemporary Problems* 60: 253–68.
Scholz, J. and Gray, W. 1990, OSHA enforcement and workplace injuries: A behavioural approach to risk assessment, *Journal of Risk and Uncertainty* 3: 283–303.
Schwartz, M. 1998, Compliance and business ethics are coming of age in Canada, *Ethikos & Corporate Conduct Quarterly* 12(1): 7–9. 12.

Scott, C. 1995, Criminalising the trader to protect the consumer: The fragmentation and consolidation of trading standards regulation, in Loveland, I. (ed.) *Frontiers of Criminality*, London, Sweet & Maxwell, pp. 149–72.

—— 2001, Analysing regulatory space: Fragmented resources and institutional design, *Public Law*, pp. 329–53.

Scott, W. 1995, *Institutions and Organizations*, Thousand Oaks, Calif., Sage Publications.

Scutt, J. 1988, The privatisation of justice: Power differentials, inequality, and the palliative of counselling and mediation, *Womens Studies International Forum* 11: 503–20.

Seidenfeld, M. 2000, Empowering stakeholders: Limits on collaboration as the basis for flexible regulation, *William & Mary Law Review* 41: 411–501.

Selznick, P. 1969, *Law, Society and Industrial Justice*, New York, Russell Sage Foundation.

—— 1992, *The Moral Commonwealth*, Berkeley, University of California Press.

Senge, P. 1992, *The Fifth Discipline: The Art and Practice of the Learning Organization*, Sydney, Random House.

Sharpe, B. 1996, *Making Legal Compliance Work*, Sydney, CCH.

Shaw, A. and Blewett, V. 1996, Telling tales: OHS and organisational culture, *Journal of Occupational Health and Safety Australia and New Zealand* 12: 185–91.

Shearing, C. 1993, A constitutive conception of regulation, in Grabosky, P. and Braithwaite, J. (eds) *Business Regulation and Australia's Future*, Canberra, Australian Institute of Criminology, pp. 67–79.

Shearing, C. and Stenning, P. 1987, Say cheese!: The Disney order that is not so Mickey Mouse, in Shearing, C. and Stenning, P. (eds) *Private Policing*, Newbury Park, Calif., Sage Publications, pp. 309–23.

Sheikh, S. 1996, *Corporate Social Responsibilities: Law and Practice*, London, Cavendish Publishing.

Shell 1998, *Report on Health, Safety and Environmental Performance 1998*, London.

—— 1999, *The Shell Report 1999: People, Planet and Profits: An Act of Commitment*, London.

Shelton, R. and Shopley, J. 1997, Beyond the green wall: Rethinking the environment for business advantage, in Ledgerwood, G. (ed.) *Greening the Boardroom: Corporate Governance and Business Sustainability*, Sheffield, Greenleaf Publishing.

Shils, E. and Rheinstein, M. (eds and trs) 1954, *Max Weber on Law in Economy and Society*, Cambridge, Mass., Harvard University Press.

Sigler, J. and Murphy, J. 1988, *Interactive Corporate Compliance: An Alternative to Regulatory Compulsion*, New York, Quorum Books.

Silverstein, D. 1987, Managing corporate social responsibility in a changing legal environment, *American Business Law Journal* 25: 524–66.

Simon, H. 1952, A behavioral model of rational choice, *Quarterly Journal of Economics* 59: 99–118.

Simpson, A. 1991, *The Greening of Global Investment: How the Environment, Ethics and Politics are Reshaping Strategies*, London, Economist Publications.

Sims, R. 1994, *Ethics and Organizational Decision Making: A Call for Renewal*, Westport, Conn., Quorum Books.

Sinclair, D. 1997, Self-regulation versus command and control? Beyond false dichotomies, *Law & Policy* 19: 529–59.

Singer, A. 1998, Coming soon: Certification for compliance officers, *Ethikos* 12: 12–13.

—— 2000, Regulations spur a new organization: The Privacy Officers Association, *Ethikos* 14(3): 12–13.

Sitkin, S. and Bies, R. 1994, The legalization of organizations: A multi-theoretical perspective, in Sitkin, S. and Bies, R. (eds) *The Legalistic Organization*, Thousand Oaks, Calif., Sage Publications, pp. 19–49.

Slovak, J. 1981, The ethics of corporate lawyers: A sociological approach, *American Bar Foundation Research Journal*, pp. 753–80.

Smith, I., Goddard, C. and Randall, N. 1993, *Health and Safety: The New Legal Framework*, London, Butterworths.

Smith, M. 1990, *Morality and the Market: Consumer Pressure for Corporate Accountability*, London, Routledge.

Smith, S. 1997, Consumer charters: The next dimension in consumer protection?, *Alternative Law Journal* 22: 138–40.

Smith, T. 1998, *The Myth of Green Marketing: Tending Our Goats at the Edge of Apocalypse*, University of Toronto Press.

Social Investment Forum 1997, *1997 Report on Responsible Investing Trends in the United States*, Washington DC.

—— 1999, *1999 Report on Responsible Investing Trends in the United States*, Washington DC.

Spangler, E. 1986, *Lawyers for Hire: Salaried Professionals at Work*, New Haven, Yale University Press.

Sparrow, M. 1994, *Imposing Duties: Governments Changing Approach to Compliance*, Westport, Conn., Praeger Publishers.

—— 2000, *The Regulatory Craft: Controlling Risks, Solving Problems, and Managing Compliance*, Washington DC, Brookings Institution.

Standards Australia 1998, *AS3806–Compliance Programs*.

Stigler, G. 1970, The optimum enforcement of laws, *Journal of Political Economy* 78: 526–36.

Still, L. 1997, *Glass Floors and Sticky Ceilings: Barriers to the Careers of Women in the Australian Finance Industry*, Sydney, Human Rights and Equal Opportunity Commission.

Stoker, G. 1998, Governance: Five propositions, *International Social Science Journal*, March: 17–28.

Stone, C. 1975, *Where the Law Ends: The Social Control of Corporate Behaviour*, New York, Harper & Row.

Streets, S. 1998, Prosecuting directors and managers in Australia: A brave new response to old problem, *Melbourne University Law Review* 22: 693–718.

Suchman, M. and Edelman, L. 1997, Legal rational myths: The new institutionalism and the law and society tradition, *Law & Social Inquiry* 21: 903–41.

Sunstein, C. 1988, Beyond the republican revival, *Yale Law Journal* 97: 1539–90.

—— 1993, *Democracy and the Problem of Free Speech*, New York, Free Press.

Tamblyn, J. 1993, Progress towards a more responsive trade practices strategy, in Grabosky, P. and Braithwaite, J. (eds) *Business Regulation and Australia's Future*, Canberra, Australian Institute of Criminology, pp. 151–67.

TARP 1995a, *American Express SOCAP Study of Complaint Handling in Australia: Report One: Consumer Complaint Behaviour in Australia*, Geelong, Society of Consumer Affairs Professionals in Business Australia.

—— 1995b, *American Express SOCAP Study of Complaint Handling in Australia: Report Two: A Profile of Enquiry and Complaint Handling by Australian Business*, Geelong, Society of Consumer Affairs Professionals in Business Australia.

Taylor, S. 1984, *Making Bureaucracies Think: The Environmental Impact Statement Strategy of Administrative Reform*, Stanford University Press.

Terrell, T. 1997, Professionalism as trust: The unique internal role of the corporate general counsel, *Emory Law Journal* 46: 1005–10.

Teubner, G. 1985, Corporate fiduciary duties and their beneficiaries: A functional approach to the legal institutionalization of corporate responsibility, in Hopt, K. and Teubner, G. (eds) *Corporate Governance and Directors Liabilities: Legal, Economic and Sociological Analyses of Corporate Social Responsibility*, Berlin, Walter de Gruyter, pp. 149–77.

—— 1987, Juridification: Concepts, aspects, limits, solutions, in Teubner, G. (ed.) *Juridification of Social Spheres: A Comparative Analysis of the Areas of Labor, Corporate, Antitrust and Social Welfare Law*, Berlin, Walter de Gruyter, pp. 3–48.

Thornton, M. 1989, Equivocations of conciliation: The resolution of discrimination complaints in Australia, *Modern Law Review* 52: 7–33.

—— 1991, The public/private dichotomy: Gendered and discriminatory, *Journal of Law & Society* 18: 4–48.

Tombs, S. 1992, Stemming the flow of blood? The illusion of self-regulation, *Journal of Human Justice* 3: 75–92.

Trade Practices Commission 1988, *Self-Regulation in Australian Industry and the Professions: Report by the Trade Practices Commission*, Canberra, Australian Government Publishing Service.

—— 1992, *Final Report by the Trade Practices Commission on the Self-Regulation of Promotion and Advertising of Therapeutic Goods*, Canberra.

—— 1994, *Study of the Professions: Legal: Final Report*, Canberra.

—— 1995, *Section 87B of the Trade Practices Act: A Guideline on the Trade Practices Commission's Use of Enforceable Undertakings*, Canberra, Australian Government Publishing Service.

Trevino, L., Weaver, G., Gibson, D. and Toffler, B. 1999, Managing ethics and legal compliance: What works and what hurts, *California Management Review* 41(2): 131–51.

Tucker, E. 1995, And defeat goes on: An assessment of third-wave health and safety regulation, in Pearce, F. and Snider, L. (eds) *Corporate Crime: Contemporary Debates*, University of Toronto Press, pp. 245–67.

Tyler, T. 1996, Trust and democratic governance, paper presented to Workshop on Trust and Democratic Governance, Research School of Social Sciences, Australian National University, Canberra.

Tyler, T. and Dawes, R. 1993, Fairness in groups: Comparing the self-interest and social identity perspectives, in Mellers, B. and Baron, J. (eds) *Psychological Perspectives on Justice: Theory and Applications*, Cambridge University Press, pp. 87–108.

United States Sentencing Commission (USSC) 1992, *United States Sentencing Commission Guidelines Manual*, Washington DC.

—— 1998, *1997 Annual Report*, Washington DC.

University of Tampa Center for Ethics 1997, *Ethics and Compliance Officer Survey*, Florida.

Vandivier, K. 1972, Why should my conscience bother me? Hiding aircraft brake hazards, reprinted in Ermann, D. and Lundman, R. (eds) 1996, *Corporate and Governmental Deviance: Problems of Organizational Behavior in Contemporary Society*, New York, Oxford University Press, pp. 118–38.

Van Ness, D. 1986, *Crime and Its Victims*, Downers Grove, Ill., Intervarsity Press.

Varley, P. (ed.) 1998, *The Sweatshop Quandary: Corporate Responsibility on the Global Frontier*, Washington DC, Investor Responsibility Research Center.

Vidal, J. 1999, First among equals, *Guardian Weekly*, 14 March: 21.

Voon, T. 1998, Overstated undertakings: Recent developments for compliance programs, *Trade Practices Law Journal* 6: 196–202.

Waddock, S., Graves, S. and Gorski, R. 1998, Social and traditional investment: Stakeholder and performance characteristics, in *Investment Guide to Socially Responsible Investing*, Washington DC, Colloquium on Socially Responsible Investing.

Ward, A. 1997, Compliance surveys: Companies say better safe than sorry, *Corporate Legal Times* 62(7): 1–3.

Warin, F. and Schwartz, J. 1998, Corporate compliance programs as a component of plea agreements and civil and administrative settlements, *Journal of Corporation Law*, Fall: 71–87.

Weait, M. 1994, The role of the compliance officer in firms carrying on investment business, *Butterworths Journal of International Banking and Financial Law*, September: 381–4.

Weaver, G. and Trevino, L. 1999, Compliance and values oriented ethics programs: Influences on employees' attitudes and behavior, *Business Ethics Quarterly* 9: 315–35.

Weaver, G., Trevino, L. and Cochran, P. 1999a, Corporate ethics practices in the mid-1990s: An empirical study of the Fortune 1000, *Journal of Business Ethics* 18: 283–94.

—— 1999b, Corporate ethics programs as control systems: Influences of executive commitment and environmental factors, *Academy of Management Journal* 42: 41–57.

Webb, K. and Morrison, A. 1999, Voluntary approaches, the environment and the law: A Canadian perspective, in Carraro, C. and Leveque, F. (eds) *Voluntary Approaches in Environmental Policy*, Dordrecht, Kluwer, pp. 229–59.

Weil, D. 1996, If OSHA is so bad, why is compliance so good?, *RAND Journal of Economics* 27: 618–40.

Weinberg, J. 1996, OSHA consultation: A voluntary approach to workplace safety and health compliance, *Corporate Conduct Quarterly* 5(2): 21–4.

Weinberg, P. 1997, If it ain't broke…: We don't need another privileges and immunities clause for environmental audits, *Journal of Corporation Law*, pp. 643–59.

Weinberger, A. 1990, Preventing insider trading violations: A survey of corporate compliance programs, *Securities Law Regulation Journal* 18: 180–93.

Weiss, E. 1981, Social regulation of business activity: Reforming the corporate governance system to resolve an institutional impasse, *UCLA Law Review* 28: 343–437.

Wells, C. 1998, Corporate responsibility, in Chadwick, R. (ed.-in-chief) *Encyclopedia of Applied Ethics*, San Diego, Academic Press, pp. 653–60.

Wetherell, V. 1998, Counting results, *Environmental Forum* January/February: 21–6.

Wheeler, D. and Sillanpaa M. 1997, *The Stakeholder Corporation: A Blueprint for Maximising Stakeholder Value*, London, Pitman Publishing.

Wheeler, S. 1998, Inclusive communities and dialogical stakeholders: A methodology for an authentic corporate citizenship, *Australian Journal of Corporate Law* 9: 1–20.

Wheeler, S. and Wilson, G. 1998, Corporate law firms and the spirit of community, *Northern Ireland Legal Quarterly* 49: 239–66.

White, A. and Zinkl, D. 1998, Raising standardization, *Environmental Forum*, January/February: 28–37.

Williamson, O. 1985, *The Economic Institutions of Capitalism*, New York, Free Press.

Worden, S. 1998, The Case against Carbon Tax: The Industry Greenhouse Networks 1994/1995 Campaign, unpublished thesis submitted for degree of M.Bus. (Communication Management), Queensland University of Technology.

World Business Council for Sustainable Development 1999, *Corporate Social Responsibility: Meeting Changing Expectations*, Geneva, World Business Council for Sustainable Development.

Wren, J. 1995, A survey of New Zealand occupational safety and health practitioners, *Journal of Occupational Health and Safety Australia and New Zealand* 11: 373–9.

Wright, U. 1998, The new breed of managers will be leaders, *Environmental Forum*, November/December: 57–8.

Young, I. 1990, *Justice and the Politics of Difference*, Princeton University Press.

—— 1993, Justice and communicative democracy, in Gottlieb, R. (ed.) *Radical Philosophy: Tradition, Counter-Tradition, Politics*, Philadelphia, Temple University Press, pp. 123–43.

Yuspeh, A. 1998, Chapter 16: Industry practice: The defense industry experience, in Kaplan, J., Murphy, J. and Swenson, W. (eds) *Compliance Programs and the Corporate Sentencing Guidelines*, Eagan, Mich., West Group.

Zinn, H. 1999, Some organizations call it compliance officer, some call it designated felon: Considerations in designating, empowering and supporting your organization's compliance leader, in *Corporate Compliance 1999 Volume One*, New York, Practising Law Institute, pp. 533–47.

Index